P9-ARM-133

ALASKA

PROMYSHLENNIK AND SOURDOUGH

ALASKA

PROMYSHLENNIK AND SOURDOUGH

By Stuart Ramsay Tompkins

NORMAN
UNIVERSITY OF OKLAHOMA PRESS
1945

By

STUART RAMSAY TOMPKINS

Russia Through the Ages

New York, 1940

PUBLISHING DIVISION OF THE UNIVERSITY
COMPOSED AND PRINTED AT NORMAN, OKLAHOMA, U.S.A.
BY THE UNIVERSITY OF OKLAHOMA PRESS
FIRST EDITION

To

JIM *and* MORA WILSON
and all the goodly fellowship
of sourdoughs

Preface

IT IS A MISTAKE TO ASSUME THAT ALASKA'S HISTORY BEGAN WITH THE gold rush of 1898. On the contrary, long before that sensational event it had passed through stirring times and had been for one hundred and fifty years the prize for which four nations contended in a long and bitter struggle. Indeed its very position gives it international significance. In this latitude the surrounding ocean shrinks to the dimensions of a strait and allows the two opposed land masses to approach each other within hailing distance. But it holds them sufficiently apart to provide a passage north into the Arctic. At the same time, as a paradoxical result of the earth's curvature, the southern limit of this strait and the island chain that marks it all but coincide with the shortest of the seaways that span the North Pacific. In modern air travel both Alaska and the islands assume even greater importance since they provide indispensable stepping stones from continent to continent.

It was the proximity of America to Asia that drew the first explorers eastward. In their wake followed traders and adventurers attracted by the fur trade. Other countries sent their quota and for over one hundred years continued to jostle one another until the purchase of Alaska in 1867 rang down the curtain on this act.

While it is essential to secure the proper focus that we cast the eye backward over the storied past, if we wish to forecast the future, it is no less needful to contemplate the present. To achieve a true perspective it is necessary to correct misconceptions of the country and of the men who have made it and will shape its future destiny.

The people of the North have yet to obtain full justice at the hands of the literary world. The generation of writers that included Rex Beach and Jack London have written picturesque, perhaps overdrawn accounts of the gold rush. This trend towards the unusual has continued unabated. Hollywood lends its aid to crown with a halo of romance northern prospectors, miners, Eskimos, and mounted policemen. It is time that a note of realism should be struck to redress the balance and to enable us to understand the peculiar problems of the sourdough. To the bane of Alaska, the conditions under which "outsiders" see the country have served to perpetuate this unfortunate tradition. Travelers visiting the territory do so during the brief summer; they make a whirlwind tour along the few lines of communication that traverse its vast spaces. They carry with them a book of Service's poems, look into the old dance halls, hastily survey the creeks that are now worked out or the newer ones where dredges or hydraulic monitors are operating; they see a few Indians or, perhaps, even some Eskimos; they thrill to see a herd of caribou swim the Yukon across their steamer's track; they marvel at the unending twilight of a northern summer; and they buy articles of personal adornment, carved from walrus or mastodon ivory. The officials of the railways and the steamers help to foster these nostalgic illusions of a bygone age. The people of the North themselves are not above gratifying this yearning for the bizarre for profit or amusement. Most tourists return with their prejudice confirmed that Alaska is a sort of topsy-turvy wonderland where ordinary values are reversed. Whatever the cause of this situation, the net result is a great gulf of misunderstanding between the sourdough and the "outside world."

This unhealthy situation makes difficult the relations between the federal government and the northern community. This want of sympathy leads to friction, which at times has broken out into open conflict. Such clashes have been fairly frequent in the past, and the immediate future seems likely to be no less fruitful in misunderstandings. Under the surface pin-pricks, two fundamental issues divide both sides. First is the fact that little of the wealth produced accrues to the benefit of the permanent population. According to the view of sourdoughs, they are being robbed of their birthright for the profit of other than local interests. Their own labor and enterprise goes largely unrewarded. The second factor is that the people wring a precarious livelihood in a struggle against the greatest odds, in transportation, living conditions, and community life. Nature is a severe and sometimes cruel taskmaster. Adversity is likely to be a frequent caller; danger is a constant attendant. The slightest mischance or illness may, for want of prompt medical care, prove fatal. The vigilance called for is to many an echo faintly heard from our pioneer past but in Alaska is the price demanded for survival. This ever-present reality must be borne in mind when we endeavor to assess the attitude of people of the North on any vital issue. It goes far to explain what at first sight may seem impatient or unreasonable.

A story was current some years ago that a former president had sourly remarked that out of the white population of the territory, half were on the federal payroll and the other half trying to get on. It was a gross slander, but was probably apocryphal. It was undoubtedly an echo of official impatience with insistent demands for patronage and perquisites. This in turn is in part the result of denial to the territory of full control over its own destiny—an end that still seems fairly remote. Whether Alaska with its sparse population and poor communications is ready for admission to the Union as a state is a question to which an offhand answer cannot be given. But so long as a considerable part of its administrative services are subject to remote control and its industries are in the hands of outside interests, it will be hard to persuade Alaskans that they are masters in their own house. Meantime some measure of mutual understanding can perhaps be attained by a wider dissemination of a knowledge of the past history and present problems of the country.

The writing of this book was greatly facilitated by assistance on which I have drawn heavily. First and foremost, a generous grant from the Rockefeller Foundation of New York made provision for travel to gather material and gave the necessary leisure to write. In this way the book was brought to completion much earlier than would otherwise have been the case. The University of Oklahoma also bought materials and paid for translation of importance sources.

It is impossible to make acknowledgement of all help received from individuals. The authorities in Washington and Ottawa courteously placed their resources at the disposal of the writer. At Ottawa, the Department of Mines and Resources in their library have most of the published and some unpublished works on early days in the Yukon. The librarian, Miss Jean Matheson, was extremely helpful in locating material. Dr. H. S. Bostock of the Geological Survey of Canada supplemented this with his very considerable knowledge of the geology of Yukon Territory and recent mining developments there. The author particularly wishes to record his debt to Dr. Lawrence Burpee of the International Joint Commission for assistance generously proffered from time to time. Commissioner S. T. Wood, C. M. G., of the Royal Canadian Mounted Police allowed access to police reports and the papers of the late Major Walsh, in addition to donating copies of old reports where duplicates were available.

In Washington, also, every facility was provided for securing information. Dr. Philip Smith of the Alaska Branch of the United States Geological Survey is one of the distinguished company of men who have made the Survey justly famous for a record of high achievement, and it is a pleasure to acknowledge the help and encouragement given by him. Dr. F. H. Moffit also was generous with time and trouble in imparting useful information on the Copper River Country. The Public Roads Administration of the Federal Works Agency furnished data on, and donated photographs of, the Alaska Highway. I am also indebted to the Wildlife Service of the Department of the Interior for pictures of wild life generously lent.

Hon. Anthony Dimond, former delegate for Alaska in the House of Representatives was instrumental in securing copies of two reports on the status of the Tlingit (Kolosh) Indians under the Russians, prepared by Mr. Vladimir Gsovski of the Library of Congress. To both of these I wish to express my gratitude.

Mr. Ira Eppler of Seattle was zealous in securing advance information and arranging interviews with old-timers in that city, which went far to make the trip to the West Coast a great success.

The transliteration of Russian names and words follows in the main the system used by the Library of Congress with certain modifications and exceptions. Where translations are not credited to a specific source, the author accepts responsibility.

Chapter XI appeared in another form in the *Canadian Historical Review* for March, 1945.

Norman, Oklahoma
August 23, 1945

STUART RAMSAY TOMPKINS

Contents

Illustrations

Maps

ALASKA

PROMYSHLENNIK AND SOURDOUGH

I

The Land

TO THE NORTHWEST AMERICA YEARNS TOWARDS ASIA AS IF MINDFUL of an ancient unity when man and other mammals passed over a waterway that is more a link than a break between the two continents. Here the great backbone of the Cordillera bending around to the west prolongs the framework of the continent to the Bering Sea. Nature has failed to add much to the framework. This remote region has been left much as it came from the hand of a titan, its peaks raising giant heads to the skies, its ice fields piled deep on the bleak and wind-swept uplands and sending long tongues of ice grinding down the valleys or scouring out the coastal plains on their way to the sea, its rivers sawing through the barriers flung in their path by volcanic action. There is nothing of quiet, sylvan beauty or the subdued peace of a settled countryside. Here man confronts Nature in her grimmest aspects.

While this extension thus carries into far northern latitudes the general features of the continental Cordillera region—the intermontane plateaus of the United States and British Columbia—the approach has until now been by sea. Alaska and the Yukon politically are not continental, but insular. From the deck of a steamer that threads the inside passage, the traveler as he goes north sees merely the beautiful tree-clad but modest heights of the Coast Range almost imperceptibly assume more massive and forbidding proportions. The fresh salt air of the south gives way to chilling winds that sweep down from the snow fields; intermittently glaciers break the unending panorama of forest and mountain. The very azure of the sky gives way to a steel blue. The people, even the very ships, take on a sturdiness that befits the surroundings; both going their several ways with an easy confidence but with a sternness that speaks of continual war with Nature. One has crossed the frontier of Alaska, and, though no man-made monument marks it, one feels that he has entered a very different world. The maze of islands and channels that border and mingle with the shore stretch on endlessly to the north—Clarence Strait, Sumner Pass, Gastineau Channel, Chatham Strait, and Lynn Canal, where the inside passage ends; through Cross Strait one slips out into the open sea. The coast, which hitherto has in the main trended northwest, now turns to the west past Yakutat Bay, Malaspina Glacier, Icy Bay, and Bering Glacier to the great indentation of Prince William Sound; turning then southwest past Kenai Peninsula to the entrance of Cook Inlet, through Shelikof Strait between Kodiak Island and the mainland, along the southern shore of the Alaska Peninsula to False Pass (Isanotski Strait), where begins the Aleutian chain; then for another eight hundred miles these islands are spaced like a giant's causeway thrust out towards Kamchatka. This seaward front of Alaska forms a great arc, extending a full fifteen hundred miles, of scenery sublime and grim by turns. For the most part but a narrow strip of shoreward mountain slopes or forested peninsulas and islands, it maintains a precarious foothold confined between the towering ranges on the one hand and the surging waters on the other. This is a land of abundant moisture, as the lush growth testifies. In the south the rainfall may be as great as one hundred inches a year; westward the climate is drier, the peninsula of Alaska by comparison almost a parched country of grass-covered slopes interspersed with trees. To the west the Aleutians, though shrouded with continuous fog and swept with frequent showers, still are drier than the islands of Alexander Archipelago and the mainland beyond. But it is from here as from a veritable cave of Aeolus that issue the great storms that sweep across Alaska and south along the mountains to the Great Plains and the Gulf of Mexico. What the meteorologist calls a "seasonal low" here broods over the northwestern and western part of the North American continent.

The Aleutian Islands are subject to visits of the "williwaw," a dreaded wind of hurricane velocity that sweeps across the naked ridges of the hills and swoops down with devastating ferocity on the unprotected harbors and coastal waters. These icy winds, even when attended with no precipitation, leave destruction in their wake. Snow, sleet, and driving rain make them a scourge to be feared. Shelter must be obtained if one clings to life.

This coastal region is the historic Alaska. However primitive man crossed the intervening waters, it was along this part of the North Pacific coast that the Russian mariners, Bering and Chirikov, made their momentous landfalls in 1741. Following their course, the unskilled *promyshlenniki* (fur traders) in their crazy, homemade craft used these same islands as steppingstones in their eastward progress and built their settlements along these selfsame coasts. They were drawn by the lure of the sea otter. Indeed, the sea was not only the source of their profit but also their sole reliance for food and clothing—salmon for food, sea otter for gain, seals for body covering. But the stormy waters from which they wrung their living were a heartless foster mother. For long stretches the rugged, shoal-studded coast offers few harbors, and, driven ashore by the buffeting of storms, their craft were frequently dashed to destruction on the rocks. The inland channels, while offering shelter from storms, might become death traps as the inrushing or outrushing tide sought to escape. In fact, few coasts were so treacherous.

Three distinct movements of the waters offshore are to be reckoned with: the Japan current—the Kuroshiwo—at some distance from the coast is a steady drift of the ocean eastward across the Pacific in the region south of the Aleutian Islands, the Alaska Peninsula, and Kodiak, across the Gulf of Alaska towards the Alexander Archipelago, turning southward and running parallel to the coast of Alaska and British Columbia; closer inshore is found a countercurrent setting westwards; and then there are the tides, almost unpredictable in the maze of islands and passages, rising and falling twice daily in the eastern portion but recurring at gradually greater intervals of time until they become merely diurnal. Together these three make up a labyrinth of eddies, crosscurrents, and tide rips that try the boldest mariners' courage and skill. An added menace to navigation is that the floor of the ocean, uneven as the land it washes, throws up unseen pinnacle rocks which rear their jagged heads hundreds of feet high, sometimes reaching to within a few feet of the surface of the water. Many a ship has plowed her way across the hidden reef, tearing the keel from the bottom, and freed herself finally only to be swallowed up in the deep water beyond. Careful mapping of these coastal waters with drag lines is gradually reducing this risk, but in the more distant regions much remains to be done.

The coastal area of Alaska in the panhandle narrows to a mere fringe. As it turns west along peninsular Alaska, it widens to embrace Prince William Sound and Cook Inlet with innumerable peninsulas and bays. Indeed, valleys that penetrate some distance into the mountain barrier prolong the distinctive character of the coast into the interior. At its widest, it extends more than one hundred miles inland. Westward again, it narrows to a mere knife edge formed by the Alaska Peninsula and the Aleutian Islands. At its greatest extent, it traverses fifty-five degrees of longitude.

Sharply setting off the coastal region from the interior, the mountain barrier sweeps around the Gulf of Alaska roughly parallel to the shore line. In the south the summits of the Coast Range look down directly on tidewater a bare twenty miles away. North of Lynn Canal, this range turns inland and dies away to the west of Whitehorse, Yukon Territory. Westward there now begins the St. Elias Range which culminates in the peaks of Mounts St. Elias and Logan and their vast snow fields. Beyond the one hundred and forty-first meridian this dominating range broadens and divides into three ranges: the Chugach Mountains that follow the coast and terminate in the Kenai Peninsula (between Prince William Sound and Cook Inlet); the Wrangell Mountains, a volcanic range stretching northwestward to the Copper River; and, to the north, the Nutzotin Mountains that extend far to the northwest and link with the great Alaska Range, whose culminating point is Mount McKinley, the highest peak in North America. At this point the mountain region achieves its greatest breadth, about two hundred miles from the nearest tidewater at the head of Cook Inlet. From here the range trends southwest; to the west of Cook Inlet the Aleutian Mountains form the backbone of the Alaska Peninsula and are prolonged westward across the Pacific in the Aleutian Islands themselves.

Few rivers traverse this mountain barrier. In the south the Stikine and the Taku find their way to the sea across the Alaska panhandle; beyond the Lynn Canal the Alsek, rising west of Whitehorse, flows into the sea at Icy Bay; the Copper and its tributary, the Chitina, drain the south slopes of Mount Wrangell and the Alaska Range and chisel a pathway through the Chugach Range; the Matanuska and the Susitna drain the western part of the Copper

River Plateau, but the headwaters of the latter reach the Alaska Range, which sharply severs the waters flowing to the Pacific from those flowing into Bering Sea. This tangle of mountain ridges, elevated plateaus, gorges, or broad valleys set deep amid regions of perpetual snow presents varied aspects. On the seaward side where elevation and rainfall are suitable, especially about Cook Inlet and Prince William Sound, abundant forest-covered soil surrounds the heads of the inlets with broad, flat expanses of cultivable lands; to the west less abundant rainfall and more rigorous climate leave the Alaska Peninsula and the Aleutian Islands almost bare of timber. Some of the valleys, such as the Matanuska, afford suitable soil and climate for a limited agriculture. The great ranges that shoulder the clouds are much too high for any but the scantiest growth, and their valleys are mostly alpine meadows.

North of this great rampart lies what many would call the "real" Alaska. A broad basin which is an extension of the interior plateau of British Columbia, from which it is set off by low passes near the northern boundary of that province, widens northward, flanked on the one side by the Mackenzie Mountains—the northern prongs of the Rocky Mountain system—and on the other by the Coast and the St. Elias and Alaska ranges. The former bend westward near the sixty-eighth parallel of north latitude and are continued through Alaska by the Brooks and its subordinate ranges, the Endicott, the Baird, and the DeLong mountains. Buttressed by these ranges on the north and the Alaska and allied ranges on the south, the valley of the Yukon stretches over a total length of two thousand miles from the lakes that cradle it in the southern part of Yukon Territory to its final home in Bering Sea. It is roughly five hundred miles in width. At first sight the term "basin" seems a misnomer for this region. However, the traveler, if he proceeds by river or rail, will see country from stream level, so that his horizon is always bounded by lofty hills close at hand or distant ranges—hence a basin. If he travels by air, he will view a different scene. The summits are frequently broad ridges undulating gently to the skyline, and, when the intervening valleys are not visible, present the appearance of a rolling plain, in the distance beyond which may tower the real mountains. Only the valleys and the sides of the mountains in favored spots are timbered.

This vast region declines from a height of five thousand feet in the southeast to sea level in the west, and through it the Yukon River and its tributaries have carved well-defined paths to the sea. Their principal source lies in the cluster of lakes near the northern boundary of British Columbia—Atlin, indescribably beautiful, and Tagish and Bennett—all glacier fed. The river that issues from them goes by various local names, but is officially the Lewes. Joined by the Teslin (locally the Hootalinqua), the Big Salmon, the Little Salmon, and the Nordenskiold, at Fort Selkirk it receives the waters of the Pelly, draining the distant Mackenzie Mountains to the east. This river now becomes officially the Yukon, and flowing northwestward is joined by the White, coming from the lofty St. Elias Range, the Stewart from the east, and a host of lesser tributaries. Between Fortymile and Eagle it crosses the international boundary, and at Circle City it enters the Yukon Flats, which it traverses to Fort Yukon, at which point it touches the Arctic Circle.

The Yukon Flats are a great alluvial depression in the plateau, approximately two hundred miles in length and from ten to twenty miles wide. Through this area the river meanders in a maze of islands, gravel bars, riffles, and channels that make up a waste of water and land—a landscape ever shifting, dissolving and reforming with startling suddenness. No landmarks guide the traveler. He must read the signs in the water ahead and decide whether he is entering a blind slough or a channel that will bear him safely through. The dreariness is enhanced by the gloomy spruce that clothes the islands with a monotonous growth. The loon floats along the waters; the wild goose nests in the remoter inlets. Here the beaver builds his house. Through the pervading stillness is heard at intervals a noise like artillery fire, as the stream, having undercut a forest-clad bank, brings down a vast mass of earth, roots, and trees, snapping off the giant trunks and sweeping them away in its currents.

Below Fort Yukon, the river receives the waters of one of its largest tributaries, the Porcupine, from Canadian territory. Turning now to the southwest, it emerges from the Flats at Stevens and shortly afterward enters the Ramparts. Below them it is joined by the Tanana River from the south, draining the northern slopes of the Alaska and Nutzotin ranges. Two hundred miles to the west it is joined by the Koyukuk River from the north. Here it turns to the south, a course it pursues as far as Holy Cross, where it bends to the west past Russian Mission to Andreafsky. Then it comes to the delta and through it makes its way northward into Norton Sound. In its lower course the river has odd vagaries. At Unalakleet it is a bare fifty miles from the head of Norton Sound, yet turns shyly away and reaches its destined haven only after a circuitous route of three hundred miles. At Paimiut, the Kuskokwim River is only fifteen miles away, yet does not join the Yukon but diverges to enter Bering Sea at a point two hundred miles to the south of the Yukon Delta. It seems that the slightest of barriers prevented the Kuskokwim from being a tributary of the Yukon. The delta regions are dreary, swampy wastes; indeed, severe climatic conditions turn the whole coast of Bering Sea into Arctic tundra.

The vast interior of Alaska was all but unknown to the Russians, who do not seem to have penetrated the Yukon far above its junction with the Koyukuk, though Russian goods ascended the river as far as Fort Yukon. It was the Anglo-Americans, not the Russians, who tamed these regions. This part of Alaska was preeminently the land of the gold seeker, of the dog train, and of the river steamboat. Yet in the past century man has made slight impression on the wilderness. His settlements are tiny posts strung out along the rivers, fifty miles or more apart. Great herds of caribou pursue their age-old seasonal migrations oblivious to man's presence in this wilderness. The moose still browse undisturbed on the margins of a thousand lakes, or slake their thirst at eventide in the shadow-splashed sloughs or swift-rushing streams. In spring king salmon swarm up the inland waters, their gleaming sides turning the river blood red. The howl of the wolf, the bark of the fox, and the cry of the loon are the only sounds breaking the solitude. Man is still the outsider here.

North from the valley of the Yukon one enters the true polar region. The drainage runs partly northward into the Arctic, partly westward into Bering Sea. A broad, lowland plain rims the Arctic Ocean; here the rigorous climate, with a brief, cool summer and a long and stormy winter, has fixed this as the abode of the Eskimo. Since he wrings his livelihood from the sea, the severity of the climate and the sterility of the soil are to him a handicap perhaps, but not a deterrent. Save for the infrequent whaling vessel or trader bound for the Mackenzie Delta, sea travel is all but unknown. A radio post and weather observation post are maintained at Point Barrow. It is mainly here in the north and west that the reindeer have been introduced which have enabled the Eskimo to attain a somewhat higher standard of life. There is little to attract the white man.

Geographically the whole of Alaska and the neighboring Yukon Territory in Canada is set off from the rest of the continent. But while the very isolation of this land gives it a distinct unity, it just as naturally falls into separate divisions, because of climate, terrain, and other factors: the coastal area, the interior plateau, and the Arctic lowland. In many respects the coast of Bering Sea and Seward Peninsula, more nearly resembling the polar regions, are a world apart from the rest of the Yukon Valley. But since geographical divisions, like logical classifications, are more nearly conveniences to aid thought than absolutes, these three divisions seem sufficient for the present purpose.

The Alaska climate is as varied as its scenery. The coastal region of the south enjoys abundant rainfall (somewhat less bountiful in the west), winters that are cold but not severe, summers that are moderate with only occasional heat. The dank vegetation of the lower valleys and the coastal regions bears ample testimony to this: garden truck and many kinds of flowers are raised, small fruits are grown where there is sufficient sunlight, but cereals requiring sunshine and dry, hot weather do not mature. Yet even here agriculture is not without its possibilities. The mean winter temperature of the panhandle and the islands is about the same as the climate of the Middle Atlantic states, though less variable and with more fog. At the head of Prince William Sound and particularly at Cook Inlet, the climate is more severe, and the upper end of Cook Inlet freezes in winter. The Alaska Peninsula and the Aleutian Islands are shrouded in fogs or clouds the greater part of the time.

Once the coastal barrier is crossed, one is in a land of sunshine save at certain seasons, and rain is moderate and seldom accompanied by severe storms. But the climate is continental and knows the greatest extremes. Summer temperatures as high as one hundred degrees in the shade are not unknown in the Yukon Valley, while in winter the thermometer may drop to sixty and go down, it is said, even to eighty degrees (Fahrenheit) below zero. Considerable local variations occur because of differences in altitude or exposure, but the seasonal variations are fairly uniform over the whole valley. Snow is heavy at times, but not excessive. Only where moisture-laden winds from the Pacific encounter mountain ranges and are forced to high altitudes does one get extreme precipitation. Despite its reputation for severity of climate, this country belongs to the North Temperate Zone. In many places there are at least one hundred days free from frost, and at reasonable altitudes all ordinary crops mature that can be grown on the northern plains—cereals (including wheat), potatoes, hay, cabbage, and most garden truck. Much of the subsoil is frozen; though once its surface is broken, the heat penetrates, and thawing takes place. Stock can be raised, but the long winter makes feeding of cattle for beef profitless. Farming has, therefore, plenty of obstacles to overcome, though it can continue to develop to provide for the needs of the local population. However much the weather may vary from coastal region to mountains and from mountains to river valleys of the interior, there is a remarkable uniformity in the summer temperatures. Where other conditions are favorable, long hours of sunlight and the relatively high temperatures encourage an astonishing growth of vegetation.

The Europeans who reached the northwest coast of America were not the first discoverers of an untenanted wilderness. Proximity of Seward Peninsula to the Asiatic mainland early suggested that America derived its first inhabitants from there. To visit Bering Strait and to view the narrow water gap that parts the opposing ends of the two continents is almost to be convinced that it is the route traversed by man in his early migrations from Asia to America. The Russians, however, approached Alaska along the chain of the Aleutians, a fact which suggests that there may have been an alternative route. But the comings and goings of the natives of both continents in these days and the feat of traversing the straits in winter on foot, which has been performed by more than one white man, gives reasonable support to the earlier conjecture. Man certainly arrived in America from the west, even if we cannot be entirely sure of the exact route he followed.

Four main races peopled what is now Alaska and the northwest portion of the continent at the coming of the white man. The Arctic coast from Labrador to Bering Strait was occupied by the Eskimos (Innuit), who also lived along the shores of Bering Strait, the Asiatic coast west of Chukotskii Nos', and Bering Sea, as far south as the Alaska Peninsula. This they shared with Aleuts, who lived mostly on the north side (facing Bering Sea) and on the southwestern tip of the peninsula; from here westward along the Aleutian Islands were also found the Aleuts (closely akin to the Eskimos). Small groups of Aleuts were found, too, on Kodiak Island and on the tip of Kenai Peninsula. The coast of Cook Inlet and Prince William Sound, as well as the vast interior, was peopled by Indians of Athapascan stock. The Eskimos were restricted to the more or less treeless tundra; they occupied the lower courses of the rivers flowing into Bering Sea, and, of course, dominated all the Arctic slope, leaving the remainder of the interior to the Indians. The Tlingit Indians were found east of Prince William Sound and along the coast as far south as Dixon Entrance, beyond which were the Haida, Tsimshian, Salishan, Kwakiutl, and Nootka Indians. In the vast interior, in northern British Columbia, as well as in Yukon Territory and Alaska, lived various groups of the Athapascan family.

The culture of these groups of aborigines varies with their environment. The Eskimo lives from the sea, from which he gets food—seal, walrus, fish, and whale. His ordinary mode of locomotion formerly was the kayak, the one-man, water-tight skin canoe. He was also skilled in the use of dogs and sleds for crossing the tundra where he hunted caribou and other animals. To the country's original resources of wild life he has added the raising of domestic reindeer, a vocation introduced in the last part of the nineteenth century and now providing him with food and transportation in abundance.

To the Aleut, as to the Eskimo, the sea is his storehouse—a larder constantly replenished. He formerly traveled with ease and security in his graceful, one-man *baidar* (much like the Eskimo kayak) or in the larger *baidarka,* in which he never hesitated to cross wide stretches of open water. In these craft he hunted the sea otter, the seal, and the sea lion and caught the fish that made up most of his diet. He lacked the Eskimo's method of winter travel, for his native islands did not require it.

The coast Indians are largely a fish-eating folk. The seas in-shore swarm with fish, and each year the salmon migrate up the rivers that flow into the Pacific. The Indians hunt and trap fur-bearing animals, which they likewise use for food. Transportation for them is principally by water, and they use a large and rather awkward-looking war canoe. Of all the native races, perhaps these west-coast Indians are the most formidable. The Russians lived long in fear of the Kolosh (Tlingit) Indians, and within our own time the Haida Indians farther to the south, despite the supremacy of the white man, have shown themselves intractable. The Tlingit attacked and burned the Russian settlement at Sitka in 1801; indeed the post seldom enjoyed security. In 1852 the Chilkat Indians crossed the Coast Range, traveled down the Lewes River, and burned the Hudson's Bay post, Fort Selkirk, at the mouth of the Pelly River. The Hudson's Bay post at Wrangell was later attacked with some loss of life.

The Indians of the interior lived by hunting and fishing. Once a year the swarms of salmon struggling up the Yukon and its tributaries furnished them with winter food for both man and dog. The dominating feature of the Alaska native village today is the fish racks hung with salmon drying in the sun. To vary the diet, the natives hunt the herds of caribou wandering across the country in their seasonal migrations. Moose are found in abundance, and in the mountains are sheep and goats; and trapping the fur-bearing species now gives the natives ready cash for their needs.

Outside of the unique sea-going craft of the inhabitants living along the Pacific Ocean and Bering Sea, certain articles of dress are common to all. Such is the parka, the knee-length smock of fur or heavy cotton with a hood, the cold weather garb of everyone. Its merit lies not in its weight, but in its imperviousness to wind. Cotton, being lighter in weight, is more desirable than fur, warmth being provided by woolens underneath. On the other hand, on the coast only is found the *ḳamlei* or *ḳamleiḳa,* a water-proof garment somewhat similar to the parka but made from the intestines of seal. Footgear in the interior is invariably moccasins, made usually from moosehide, more rarely from caribou. For the coast of the

Arctic or Bering Sea *mukluks* are preferred—waterproof footwear usually knee length or higher and made from sealskin.

The dog is the beast of burden and the power for transportation. He is used either as a pack animal in summer or for pulling sleds in winter. He has a very thick coat, and his feet are well adapted for working in snow. There are two methods of harnessing the sled dogs. They may be hitched one behind the other or driven in pairs abreast with a single lead dog. The latter method is preferred in the lower Yukon. These means of transportation the Alaskans have in common with the natives of the adjacent parts of Siberia, from which the Eskimos doubtless originally acquired them.

As the greater part of Alaska and the Yukon Territory lies within the timbered parts of North America, log houses are the rule. On the coast the houses are built perhaps more elaborately and are very substantial and profusely decorated. In the interior, the teepee has given way to the house borrowed from the white man. On the tundra coasts the Eskimo can still, if he lacks other building material, erect his snow igloo. In summer a simple shelter can be built of driftwood.

To a traveler from the more settled parts of continental United States, Alaska seems a land apart. Its landscapes are seldom merely pleasing. They either entrance or overawe. The northern summer, with its long hours of amber sunlight and its night a brief interlude of twilight between sunset and sunrise; the all too short autumn, then the swift onset of winter, with its almost overpowering cold; the winter landscape, lonely, yet with a sparkling beauty of its own; the sublime loveliness of the northern lights of early winter; the gladness of the advent of spring; the mad rush of waters that heralds the break-up of the winter ice and the approach once more of summer—everything tempts the cheechako to hyperbole and even the sourdough to the grudging admission that the "country gets you." But she is a hard foster mother. In a few short weeks of summer men must wring from their farms the sustenance they, their families, and their livestock will need through eight winter months. The brief runoff of the winter snows in spring must be used at once for the spring clean-up of gold; and Nature's niggardly store of water throughout the short summer must be carefully husbanded for the season's mining operations. The natives must labor long hours during the salmon run to gather stores of food for themselves and their dogs. Everywhere is abundance followed by a long period of scarcity. After the haste and activity of summer come the long silence and sloth of winter. It is feast or famine, for there Nature knows no golden mean.

Since the settlement of the great international rivalries of the nineteenth century, Alaska has been remote from world affairs. But events have moved to make the North Pacific a stage for a new drama. Its presence on the flank of the Great Circle transpacific route which passes just south of the Aleutians makes both the main Alaska coast and the Aleutian Islands at once an outpost for attack and a bulwark of defense in war in the Pacific. The development of air transport and the great reduction in distances made possible by either transpolar routes or the Great Circle routes between the continents will tend to transform Alaska into a well-traveled crossroad in the future. The new highway will provide the United States with a land connection with its peninsular outpost. Naval bases, air fields, and military depots now spinkled generously over its vast extent attest its importance. What until yesterday was an empty wilderness has become a bastion to dominate the North Pacific.

II

Asia and America: One Continent or Two

THE WAVE OF DISCOVERY THAT ATTENDED THE RENAISSANCE HAD stopped short of the North Pacific. Magellan and Drake had rounded South America and traversed the vast reaches of the Pacific. The Englishman may even have ventured into the seas that wash the rock-bound, foggy coasts of the Oregon country. The Spaniards discovered and annexed the Philippines, and the Manila galley established what may be called regular connection with Acapulco. Dutch and English vied for the possession of the Spice Islands, and the boldest of the Netherlanders were soon to push north along the China coast to Japan. But with the outbreak of the fanatical wars of religion, the great work was left half done. The whole of both polar seas was quite unknown, while much even of the Pacific, both north and south of the equator, was still wrapped in mystery. The more venturesome or the most plausible tale-bearers brought back word of shadowy continents in the midst of this great ocean. Straits that penetrated the continents were said to link the vast ocean with the familiar Atlantic and to offer countries that could broach them profitable short cuts to the riches of the Indies.

Lack of exact knowledge served but to stimulate the imagination, and it was easy to people these unknown islands and continents with folk whose appearance and endowments were of no ordinary kind. When the wars of religion had at last spent themselves and a new, if troubled, peace had come, man turned from bloodshed and devastation to the more constructive tasks of knowing the universe he lived in and piercing the mist of uncertainty and superstition with which his world was still enshrouded. A great upsurge carried him on in the field of knowledge, and no small part of his achievement was to roll back the map of the earth until its last secret would stand revealed.

In this new geographical interest it was certain that the regions where the New World approached the Old would occupy the center of the picture. There were many reasons for this. Already the Muscovite state had begun to reach out for the farthest limits of Asia. By the sixteenth century the empire of Jenghis Khan had crumbled into a score of fragments. From these the old vigor of the Mongol conqueror had gone. The power of the Golden Horde was broken, and the Horde in its weakness had submitted as a faithful vassal to the Ottoman Porte. The empire of Tamerlane had sunk into sloth and stagnation; the Tartars of Kazan had yielded to Ivan the Terrible; and the last obstacle that barred the way to the Urals was down. The merchant family of Strogonov had already pushed up the Vychegda and over to the Kama Valley where they had received grants of extensive privileges. Hither in 1584 came Yermak Timofeyevich, a former Don Cossack, fleeing from the wrath of the tsar's soldiers for brigandage on the lower Volga. With little to lose, he induced Maxim and Semyon Strogonov to equip a sort of filibustering expedition across the mountains to retaliate for raids by subjects of the Tartar Khan Kuchum and to open these frontier regions to exploitation, if that should prove feasible. Yermak succeeded beyond his hopes and, seizing the Tartar stronghold Sibir, or Isker, drove Kuchum into the steppes. Yermak was later ambushed and killed, but the tsar's government took over the struggle, and the Tartars never succeeded in breaking the hold of Moscow. One after another of the primitive, *yassak*-paying folk of the grass steppe and the *taiga* submitted to their new master. Within less than fifty years Russian rule was firmly planted at Okhotsk on the Pacific Ocean and at Yakutsk on the Lena River.

Hearing of a favored land to the south through which a great river flowed eastward to the sea, the *voyevode* of Yakutsk dispatched a band under Poyarkov to reconnoiter. Poyarkov's expedition, 1643–45, and that of Khabarov, 1650–52, opened the Amur Valley to Russian exploitation; and for the next thirty-five years the Russians continued to plant posts along the course of this river in order to hold the natives in awe. But they were now threatening the home of the Manchu princes, only recently installed at Peking as lords of China; and the Manchus, determined to keep their homeland inviolate, marshaled sufficient military force to check and turn back the Russians. In 1689, at Nerchinsk, peace was arranged between the two countries and a frontier drawn that entirely excluded the Muscovite from the Amur Valley for nearly two hundred years.

On the heels of this military advance had come a spiritual one. Jesuits intent on the propagation of the faith had pressed eastward into China, some traveling through Muscovite territory. The western sciences and arts they brought with them soon recommended them to the service of the Manchu emperor, and they were commissioned to explore and map his dominions. Indeed their help in this connection had proved invaluable to China when the treaty of Nerchinsk was negotiated. A rich store of knowledge of this new world found its way back to Europe, and towards the close of the seventeenth century books and maps began to appear that revealed for the first time the Far East to Western readers.

Commercial exploitation had brought its offerings to this new extension of geographic knowledge. England and Holland had been rivals for the trade of the East. The resources of each were poured into a struggle that went on by sea and land. Both had turned to Russia as a field for their commercial enterprise and as a route to the East. For decades both also had sought a passage by sea to the north of Europe and Asia. In this field the Dutch had considerable success. In 1664 an embassy under Jakob Borel appeared at Moscow to promote Dutch trade. One of the members of this group, Nicolaes Witsen, availed himself of the opportunity to gather information on Russia's Asiatic possessions, which he afterwards embodied in a famous book, *Noord en Oost Tartarye,* published first at Amsterdam in 1692. But our chief interest in Witsen is that he later became the friend and confidant of Peter the Great during the latter's first tour of Europe in 1697, for it was Peter who gathered together into one concerted movement the diverse factors leading to exploration.

Peter had become heir to the Romanov empire somewhat prematurely, at a critical period in Moscow's fortunes. During his adolescent years his precocious genius had eagerly sought outlet in activities that were a strange foretaste of his man's estate. He had sailed his crude playboats on the ponds at Preobrazhenskoe, as taught him by old ships' carpenters, and later had marshaled his

Courtesy National Park Service

MT. MCKINLEY

Courtesy The National Geographic Society

LOOKING ACROSS BERING STRAIT

servitors and playmates in regiments that he loved to exercise in the fashion of Western Europe, as taught by the old soldiers he met in the German quarter of Moscow. We can well believe that he had listened enthralled to the tales of voyages of the English sea dogs in the Spanish main and the stories of the sea fights of the Dutch sea beggars, and fought again the battles of Gustavus Adolphus or Condé or Turenne. He envisaged the Russian navy he was to create; already he saw the army with which he would defeat Charles XII at Poltava some twenty years later.

But it was Peter's journey abroad in 1697–98 that set his Eastern ventures in motion. At Amsterdam he was entertained by Witsen, now burgomaster of Amsterdam, and he listened eagerly to what that distinguished writer had to tell. However, Peter was soon absorbed with a more pressing task—that of driving the Swedes from the Baltic Sea. The Northern War consumed his energies for many years, and only in the comparative leisure of the years after Poltava could he turn to other more congenial labors. He had for some time been in communication with Leibniz (probably through Witsen), and in 1713 he brought Leibniz into the Russian service. Later, in 1716, Peter again traveled abroad. He became a member of the Royal Academy of France and in passing through Germany met Leibniz, with whom he discussed the problem of founding an academy in Russia. The result of these contacts with learned men was that Peter was seized with a new enthusiasm for the exploration of his vast lands beyond the Ural Mountains. To the intellectual world it was even more vital that the unexplored regions of the East should be penetrated, and to that special task Peter now addressed himself.

Man's early migration from Asia to America seems to have faded from race memory by this time. When the Russians first reached the northeastern tip of Asia, they found there the Chukchi, a primitive folk who had vague ideas about their own neighborhood and extremely meager information on what lay beyond it. Russian travelers brought back stories of a "great land" that lay somewhere over the horizon. The natives had only a hazy conception of the geography of their own coasts. That the mainland came to an end here seems never to have dawned on them. They passed from the Arctic coast to the borders of Bering Sea seemingly oblivious to the fact that they had rounded the tip of the continent. Perhaps they failed to notice this feature because they usually made the journey by land; or because during winter, when all was white, land and sea merged; or because for months the sun was below the horizon, confounding all sense of direction. Any incentive to curiosity was lacking, so that not only the natives but even the Russians had no knowledge of the most rudimentary facts regarding their surroundings. The state viewed these regions primarily as a source of tribute in rich peltries from the indigenous peoples. A few adventurous merchants grew fat in the traffic in the skins of sable, marten, and ermine, while the local *voyevode* was concerned to "make hay while the sun shone," to enrich himself by illicit traffic against the day of his return. In the existing state of Muscovite society of the late seventeenth century the acquiring of geographical knowledge made slight appeal, and what little information had been secured gathered dust in the official archives.

Thus, at the end of the seventeenth century an exact understanding of the North Pacific and the shores of the neighboring continents was lacking. Drake had sailed probably farthest to the north of any of the European explorers. The voyages of Juan de Fuca, as far as contributions to science went, might very well be apocryphal. Indeed, no progress had been made by the Spaniards in exploring the western coast of America since the voyages of Cabrillo in 1543. The pilot of the Spanish galleon bound from Manila to Acapulco was concerned only with locating with some degree of accuracy Cabo San Lucas at the southern tip of Lower California as a convenient landfall. On the Asiatic side, the Portuguese had reached China and southern Japan, while the Dutch, penetrating somewhat further north, had located the Japanese Islands with reasonable certitude; but knowledge of everything else to the north and east was largely conjectural. Indeed, what lay north of the thirtieth parallel of latitude was the subject of a queer mélange of geography, legend, myth, and surmise. Yezo, Gama Land, and Company Land were names of islands or parts of continents that either existed only in name or had been lifted by cartographers from their true positions and transplanted bodily in the midst of the wide Pacific.

Continental Siberia had by now been embraced within the

area of reasonably accurate geographical knowledge. To extend this information further by sea involved unprecedented difficulties. To pursue explorations from a Siberian base, travelers had to make shift with such craft as could be put together from local material by men unskilled in shipbuilding; and not being proficient in navigation, these amateur mariners had to hug the coast, hardly daring to risk the buffeting of the open sea. Hence, it was natural that the peninsula of Kamchatka should first be reached by land through the country of the warlike Koriaks. Not until after the establishment of the *Ostrog* of Anadyrsk on the Anadyr River for the collection of *yassak* do we hear of Russians pushing on to Kamchatka. The early history of the peninsula is obscure, but it appears that the Cossacks or officers of the army were dispatched there from Yakutsk to levy tribute. The unchecked brutality and the misgovernment of these officials invited reprisals on the part of the natives; excesses on both sides led to anarchy. Nothing was done to check this condition until 1697, when Atlasov, a Cossack, was sent to bring order. Atlasov, despite the confidence of his government as attested by the grant of extensive powers, was little better than his predecessors; and on his return from Kamchatka in 1700, he was thrown into prison on charges of corruption and brutality. Released in 1706, he again went to Kamchatka, where he showed great energy in reasserting Muscovite authority but eventually was killed. Nevertheless, order was gradually restored, and the Kamchadals recalled to their allegiance.

Russian power in the Far East was beginning to feel the impact of Peter's astonishing energy. In the midst of his duel with Charles XII of Sweden he had found time to give some stimulus to exploration in the East. Native Russians were encouraged to build ships and to venture out to sea to reconnoiter the near-by islands and to search for the mysterious lands laid down in maps of the time on the basis of earlier discoveries imperfectly reported. One adventurer, Sokolov, is said to have pioneered in crossing by sea from Okhotsk to Kamchatka in 1715.

In 1719 Peter had authorized Ivan Yevreinov and Fedor Luzhin, "geodesists," as they were called, to take a government ship to:

proceed to Kamchatka and further, whither their instructions directed them to explore these regions; to ascertain whether America and Asia were united, which they were to do very carefully, not only to the south and north, but also to the east and west and to mark it all on a map.

Secret instructions, whose nature is unknown, were also given them. The travelers reached Irkutsk in May, 1720, and sailed from Okhotsk in September. After wintering at Nizhnii Kamchatsk, they left the mouth of the Bolshaya Reka the following spring for the Kurile Islands. The farthest point south was the sixth island. On their return, they put in to Paramushiru (the second island) after considerable buffeting by storms and after running out of supplies. They returned in October to Okhotsk with little to show for their voyage, not even having reconnoitered the silver mines the Japanese were supposed to have in the Kurile Islands.

There was no adequate incentive for private individuals to take on themselves the onerous work of discovery. Moreover, Peter's subjects also lacked the technical knowledge needed to prosecute such undertakings. Peter's mind was now toying with the idea of enrolling foreigners for this work. Some of his Swedish prisoners dispatched to distant posts were encouraged to seek an escape from the monotony of confinement by devoting themselves to the gathering and recording of information about "Tartarye." One of these, Strahlenburg, afterwards published a book containing the facts he had assembled. Then in 1721 Peter concluded peace with Sweden at Nystadt, and this left him free for the more vigorous prosecution of his ambitious designs. By 1725 he had succeeded in attracting into the Russian service a formidable roster of scientists and scholars, and arrangements were made for organizing them into an academy modeled after the French Royal Academy. Untimely death removed Peter, and it fell to his successor to launch this institution on its way. However, the restless, forceful Peter had not waited for ripening plans, and thus, before his death, a project had been set in motion for the solution of the great geographical problem of the time, whether or not Asia and America were one. In January, 1725, Vitus Bering had left St. Petersburg on the first of his momentous expeditions to the unknown wastes of the North Pacific Ocean.

Bering was one of the many mariners whom Peter had drawn

from abroad into his newly created navy. His record in the service was undistinguished; all we know is that Bering became dissatisfied with his treatment and retired in 1724. The following year he was recalled and induced to accept command of an expedition projected across the waters off northeastern Siberia. The instructions drawn up for him by Peter were comprehensive and direct.

1. You are to construct at Kamchatka one or two boats with decks.

2. You are to proceed in these along the coast which extends to the north and which seems, in all probability (since we do not know where it ends), to be a part of America.

3. With this in view you are to try to find where it is joined to America, and to reach some city in European possession, and to enquire what it is called, and to make a note of it, and to secure exact information and to mark this on a map and then to return home.

The directive was as simple as that. There was no mention of the five thousand miles of forest, steppe, and mountain over which the necessary tools, cordage, and tackle had to be dragged; of the rigor of the climate that the carpenters, ship's company, and army of workers would have to endure; or of the perils to which they would be exposed en route. Months, even years, must elapse before even the preliminaries to the task were completed and the company arrived with their equipment on the shores of the Pacific. Supposing they were able to surmount the obstacles of this stage and build their ships, the labors and perils of the next step would be a thousandfold greater; and to fear-inspiring reality was added vague terror of the unknown. Imagination pictured raging seas and forbidding and treacherous coasts, peopled by savages or by no less hostile and potentially menacing Europeans.

This action was typical of Peter. He seldom counted the cost. He delighted in giving his subordinates impossible assignments. This was the way he had built St. Petersburg. No thought had been given to the immense labors of driving piles into the marshes of the Neva River on which his city was to rest, or to the bodies of the uncounted peasants, drafted for this dreadful work, who would be swallowed up in the ooze—a living sacrifice demanded before the Palmyra of the North could rear its towers and battlements over the dreary landscape. In the case of Bering, however, Peter's trust was not ill placed. The formidable difficulties and the incredible hardships which would have daunted less determined men were overcome. Within a reasonable time Bering had moved his men and supplies across Siberia, and on the shores of the Pacific on a bleak sandspit at the mouth of the Okhota River he had put together the first seagoing vessel to be constructed in these distant regions, as far as we know.

Thus the problem posed by the scientific world of the day—"Is America joined to Asia?"—was now in a fair way of being solved. Witsen had first raised the question in Peter's mind, the French Academy had urged Peter to seek an answer, and finally Leibniz, who entered the Russian service in 1713, had added the weight of his authority to the counsel that Peter should earn the gratitude of posterity by finally unveiling the mystery of both the northeast and the northwest passages.

III

Vitus Bering

ACCOMPANIED BY A PACK TRAIN BEARING EQUIPMENT AND SUPPLIES, Bering reached Okhotsk in the latter part of October, 1726, after almost literally blazing a trail over the height of land, through forest, across tundra and mountains. His company and his freight kept straggling in for nine months; Spangberg, who brought the greater part of the supplies by boat up the Aldan and the Maya rivers, had been caught by the freeze-up at the mouth of the Yudoma, where he had left the cargo while he pushed on over the summit at Yudoma Cross. He secured men and sledges with which to make two trips back to the boats for the stores left behind. The last man in was Chirikov, who reached Okhotsk from Yakutsk in midsummer, 1727.

Bering, with the help of his ship's carpenters, now set about putting together a *shitik*, a not too seaworthy craft, constructed out of local timber with the equipment he had brought overland. Most of the horses with which the journey from Yakutsk had begun had died of starvation, and the timber felled in the forest had to be hauled out by hand before the building of the vessel began. When it was completed, Bering used it to ferry his company across to Bolsheretsk at the mouth of the Bolshaya River in Kamchatka, and from there the goods were freighted across the peninsula of Kamchatka, ascending the Bystraya River to its source and descending the Kamchatka River to Nizhnii Kamchatskii *Ostrog* at its mouth. Moving these supplies across the peninsula, a distance of five hundred miles from Bolsheretsk to Nizhnii Kamchatsk, was accomplished only after surmounting incredible hardships and by driving the native Kamchadals to the limit of endurance. Most of the dogs had perished on this trip, and the men were left without means of transport. Many of Bering's own men also had lost their lives. On their arrival here they began the construction of a thor-

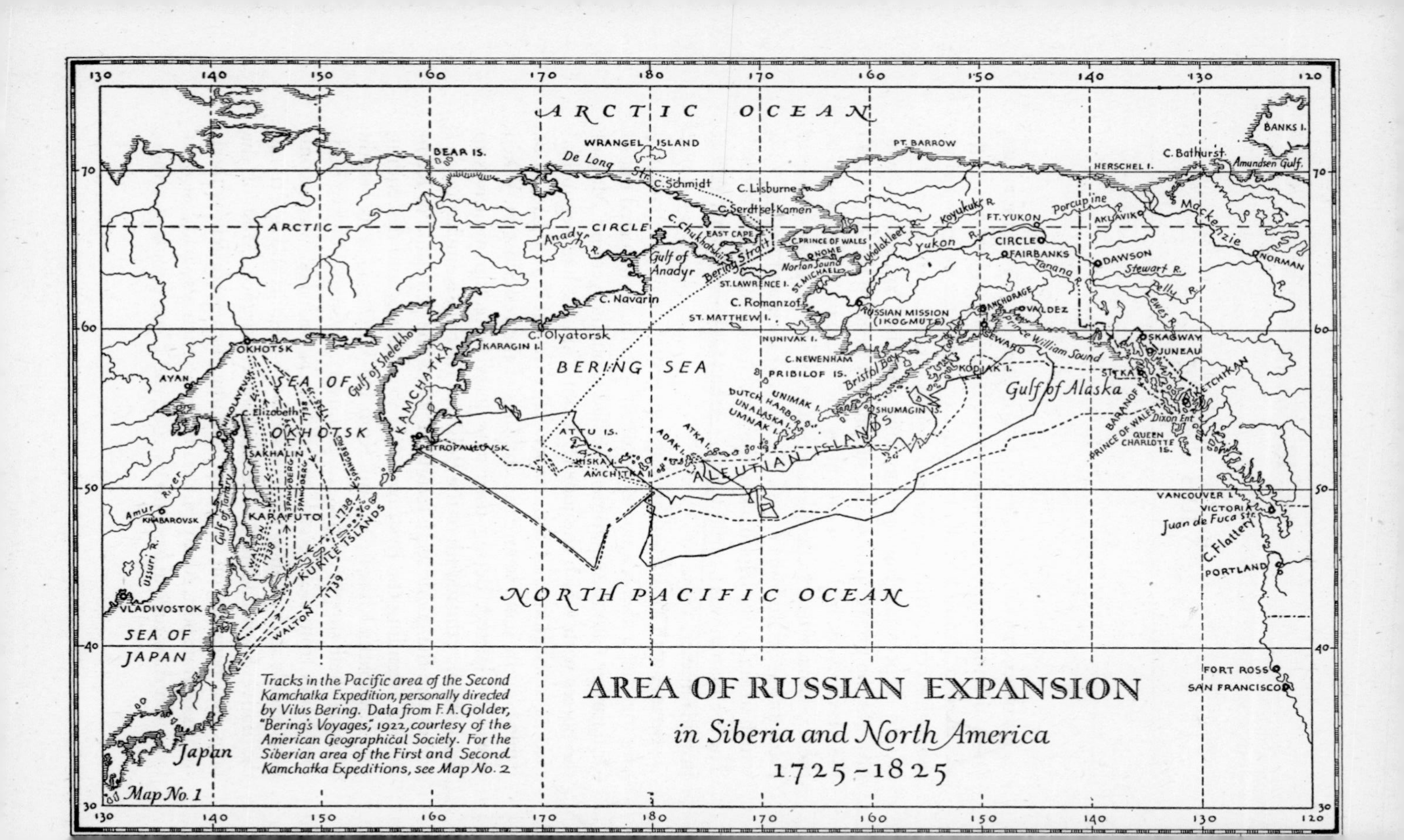
ARCTIC OCEAN
WRANGEL ISLAND
De Long Str.
C. Schmidt
BEAR IS.
PT. BARROW
C. Lisburne
C. Serdtse Kamen
EAST CAPE
C. Chukhotski
Bering Strait
ARCTIC CIRCLE
Anadyr R.
Gulf of Anadyr
C. Navarin
C. Olyatorsk
KARAGIN I.
BERING SEA
ST. LAWRENCE I.
ST. MATTHEW I.
C. Romanzof
NUNIVAK I.
C. NEWENHAM
PRIBILOF IS.
Bristol Bay
UNIMAK I.
DUTCH HARBOR
UNALASKA I.
UMNAK I.
SHUMAGIN IS.
ATKA I.
ADAK I.
KISKA I.
AMCHITKA I.
ATTU IS.
ALEUTIAN ISLANDS
KODIAK I.
SEWARD
ANCHORAGE
VALDEZ
Prince William Sound
Gulf of Alaska
RUSSIAN MISSION (IKOGMUTE)
ST. MICHAEL
Norton Sound
NOME
C. PRINCE OF WALES
Unalakleet
Yukon R.
Koyukuk R.
FT. YUKON
CIRCLE
FAIRBANKS
Tanana R.
Porcupine R.
DAWSON
Stewart R.
Pelly R.
Lewes R.
AKLAVIK
HERSCHEL I.
C. Bathurst
Amundsen Gulf
BANKS I.
Mackenzie
NORMAN
SKAGWAY
JUNEAU
SITKA
KETCHIKAN
BARANOF
PRINCE OF WALES I.
Dixon Ent.
QUEEN CHARLOTTE IS.
VANCOUVER I.
VICTORIA
Juan de Fuca Str.
C. Flattery
PORTLAND
FORT ROSS
SAN FRANCISCO
NORTH PACIFIC OCEAN
OKHOTSK
AYAN
SEA OF OKHOTSK
Gulf of Shelekhov
KAMCHATKA
PETROPAVLOVSK
NIKOLAEVSK
C. Elizabeth
SAKHALIN
Gulf of Tartary
KARAFUTO
KURILE ISLANDS
SPANGBERG
WALTON
1738
1739
Amur River
KHABAROVSK
Ussuri R.
VLADIVOSTOK
SEA OF JAPAN
Japan
Map No. 1
Tracks in the Pacific area of the Second Kamchatka Expedition, personally directed by Vitus Bering. Data from F. A. Golder, "Bering's Voyages," 1922, courtesy of the American Geographical Society. For the Siberian area of the First and Second Kamchatka Expeditions, see Map No. 2
AREA OF RUSSIAN EXPANSION
in Siberia and North America
1725-1825

oughly seaworthy vessel suitable for the voyage of exploration. By the summer of 1728 the new ship being completed was launched and named the *Gabriel*. Early in July stores were taken on board, the crew embarked, and the *Gabriel* dropped down to the mouth of the river where the turbulent Pacific bore her off on a momentous voyage.

Bering charted his course to the north, keeping close inshore, and after rounding Cape Thaddeus on July 27, entered the Gulf of Anadyr, where on July 31 he saw land extending along the northern horizon. Turning to the east, the company rounded Chukotskii Nos on August 9, sighted the island of St. Lawrence on August 11, passed (without knowing it) through Bering Strait, and continued for four more days on their course to the north. At three o'clock on August 15, having reached latitude 67° 18′ north and longitude 193° 7′ east of Greenwich, Bering turned back on the same course he had followed north, this time keeping well out from the coast until near his destination. On August 2, 1728, he arrived at the mouth of the Kamchatka River.

Bering was vaguely dissatisfied with the results of his expedition. Therefore, in order to test a hypothesis already forming in his mind that land existed to the east of Kamchatka, he put to sea the following spring. Setting his course to the east, he encountered a storm somewhere off Kamchatka, was driven southward from his course, and passed between the southern tip of Kamchatka (Cape Lopatka) and the northern Kurile Islands. As the ship had suffered from its buffeting in the Sea of Okhotsk, he put into the nearest harbor, which proved to be Bolsheretskii *Ostrog*. He thus unexpectedly discovered the southern limits of Kamchatka and the sea route from Bolsheretsk to Nizhnii Kamchatsk. From Bolsheretsk he turned westward and late in July, 1729, reached Okhotsk, when he proceeded overland to St. Petersburg, arriving there on March 1, 1730.

By the time Bering reached the Russian capital, his fame had preceded him. Critics at home and abroad were beginning to carp at his achievements and to point to the inconclusiveness of his findings. Thus, as an act of self-exculpation, Bering felt bound to recommend to the government the further prosecution of these explorations, to link them with discoveries already made in connection with the American mainland. He drew up a series of recommendations to submit to the Administrative Senate:

> 1. According to my observations, the waves of eastern Kamchatka are smaller than in other seas, and I found on Karaginskii Island large fir trees that do not grow on Kamchatka. These signs indicate that America, or some other land on this side of it, is not far from Kamchatka—perhaps from 150 to 200 miles. This could easily be ascertained by building a vessel of about fifty tons and sending it to investigate. If this is so, a trade might be established between the empire and the inhabitants of these regions.
>
> 2. Such a ship could be built at Kamchatka because the necessary timber could be obtained more easily. The same holds true in the matter of food—fish and game are especially cheap there. Then, again, more help may be had from the natives of Kamchatka than from those of Okhotsk. One other reason should not be overlooked—the mouth of the Kamchatka River is deeper and offers a better shelter for boats.
>
> 3. It would not be without advantage to find a sea route from the Kamchatka or Okhota Rivers to the Amur River or Japan since it is known that these regions are inhabited. It would be very profitable to open trade relations with these people, particularly the Japanese. And as we have no ships there, we might arrange with the Japanese that they meet us half way in their boats, for such an expedition a ship about the size of the one mentioned would be needed or one somewhat smaller might serve the purpose.
>
> 4. The cost of such an expedition—not including salaries, provisions and materials taken from here or Siberia—would be from 10,000 to 12,000 roubles.
>
> 5. If it should be considered wise to map the northern regions of the coast of Siberia from the Ob' to the Yenisei and from there to the Lena—this could be done by boats or by land since these regions are under Russian jurisdiction.

Conditions had changed greatly since Bering had left the capital in 1725. Three different sovereigns had occupied the throne left vacant by Peter's death. Moreover the turbulent nobility were struggling to recover some of the power they had exercised in the old days of the *Boyarskaya Duma*. This attempted recovery, which would have annulled the Petrine reforms, was blocked by the new

Empress Anne. Anne's every instinct as a true Muscovite impelled her to disown the semiconstitutional regime which had been forced upon her at her accession by the Golitsyns and Dolgorukiis. She reverted gladly to the role of autocrat and might conceivably have headed a reaction but for the fact that she had married a German prince, Friedrich Wilhelm, Duke of Courland, and had lived at Mitau in a German atmosphere. Somewhat predisposed to favor Germans, she found several installed at court—Heinrich Johann Friedrich Ostermann, already vice-chancellor, and Burckhard Christoph von Münnich (both of whom had been brought to Russia by Peter and given preferment), the latter a Balt (Baltic German). These men were inclined to regard Russia as a fief for themselves and their Teutonic countrymen to exploit, and they readily rallied to the support of reforms along European lines.

The Academy of Sciences also was preponderantly staffed with foreigners, the majority of them Germans. Its personnel had been assembled by Peter in the last year of his life, though it was left to his consort actually to launch it on its career. It had taken over the direction of the scientific exploration already begun by Peter, the first results being an expedition under Louis Delisle de la Croyère in 1727 to Archangel and the Kola Peninsula (hence the first Kamchatka expedition was not of its making). Along with all other things foreign, the Academy suffered eclipse under the second Peter, but with the accession of Anne and the coming to power of the German element, fortune once more was with it. It was Bering's good luck that his return to St. Petersburg coincided with this happy circumstance.

The state's experience with native Russian talent for exploration in its eastern Asiatic possessions had not been fruitful. In 1719 Yevreinov and Luzhin had received instructions from Peter to:

> Proceed to Kamchatka and beyond, wherever you are instructed to explore the region, there to determine whether America is joined to Asia, which you are to do very carefully not only to the north and south, but also to the east and west and to mark everything accurately on a map.

The expenses of the expedition were to be borne by the provincial government of Siberia. There is no definite record that the state ever received any adequate returns from this outlay of funds. Yevreinov and Luzhin seem to have made the journey, however, for the geographical information they secured is said to have been used in the official atlas of 1745. In 1727 the Senate, while awaiting the successful completion by Bering of his first voyage, turned to the practical task of subjugating the Chukchi and other natives and reducing them to the status of tribute payers. A Cossack leader, Afanasii Shestakov, was, on March 21 of this year, authorized to undertake this task. An attack by land and sea failed to reduce the Chukchi. In 1731, his successor, Dmitrii Pavlutskii, securing Bering's vessel, the *Gabriel* (Bering by now having returned to St. Petersburg), directed a subordinate, Melnikov, to load supplies and come northward to reconnoiter for land which had been descried opposite East Cape, Bering Sea. The vessel was taken by an officer, Michael Gvozdev, into Bering Sea, and he seems to have discovered the Diomede Islands and probably the American mainland. But the navigators had little nautical training, and the crews were mutinous. Haphazard explorations such as these could scarcely yield important results, and the Russian government had to admit that the tasks demanded qualities and training possessed by few of its countrymen.

Bering's reports came to the Senate at a time when it was considering a project of prosecuting the search for America by an expedition dispatched from the west by sea. But a purely scientific expedition, however much it might impress London or Paris, had perhaps little appeal to native Russians or to those who promoted it. The Academy, whose fortune was now in the ascendant, had a score of highly paid foreigners in its employ. They naturally turned to von Münnich and Ostermann as allies to aid their ambitions, and Bering's recommendations contained a suggestion that was eagerly seized as an added bait to attract public favor: namely, a land exploration of the Asiatic coast. Somehow, probably on the initiative of Ivan Kirilovich Kirilov, chief secretary of the Administrative Senate, this project, hitherto barely mentioned, crept into the scheme; i.e., to use the staff to study the fauna, flora, human, and other resources of Siberia. To appeal to the Empress, who was always financially embarrassed, it was provided that prospecting should take place for metals, especially the precious ones.

So, like a snowball, the scheme grew. The original modest suggestions of Bering began to assume ever greater proportions, contemplating nothing less than the mapping and the exploration of the resources of the vast solitudes of Siberia. When Bering left the capital in 1732, he was charged with full responsibility for three distinct tasks, each of them prodigious in scope.

1. The exploration and mapping of the whole of the Arctic coast from Archangel to the mouth of the Kolyma River in eastern Siberia, and, if possible, as far as the eastern extremity of the continent and along its eastern coast to Kamchatka.

2. A voyage eastward to America (to be carried out by Bering and Chirikov) and southeast to Japan (to be performed by Spangberg and Walton).

3. Thoroughgoing reconnaissance of Siberia, its geography, fauna, flora, its natural resources, its inhabitants, their language, customs, folklore; to be under the direction of Gerhard Friedrich Müller and Johann Georg Gmelin and their assistants.

The project was to be undertaken jointly by the Admiralty College and the Academy of Sciences, the whole to be under the supreme direction of Bering. It was expressly provided in the instructions that in all that concerned their special scientific fields, the scientists were to be subject to no control. In other matters it was specifically enjoined on Bering that he was to consult his subordinates. Thus the principle by which authority and responsibility are closely linked was violated at the start, and Bering was charged with a great undertaking without being given the requisite authority.

In February of 1733 Bering's expedition began to get under way, the various units leaving successively. The order of their departure was determined in the main by the objectives of each section, the shipbuilders for the Pacific coast and the Arctic going first, followed at appropriate intervals by the men who were to assemble supplies in Siberia, the personnel of the expedition, and, lastly, the scientists. The intention was that Bering should leave after all the others to insure that, as he traveled east, the several projects would be well in hand before he began his own special task. At Tobolsk on May 2, 1734, the shallop *Tobol* was launched and on May 14 began the descent of the Irtysh and the Ob' rivers under the com-

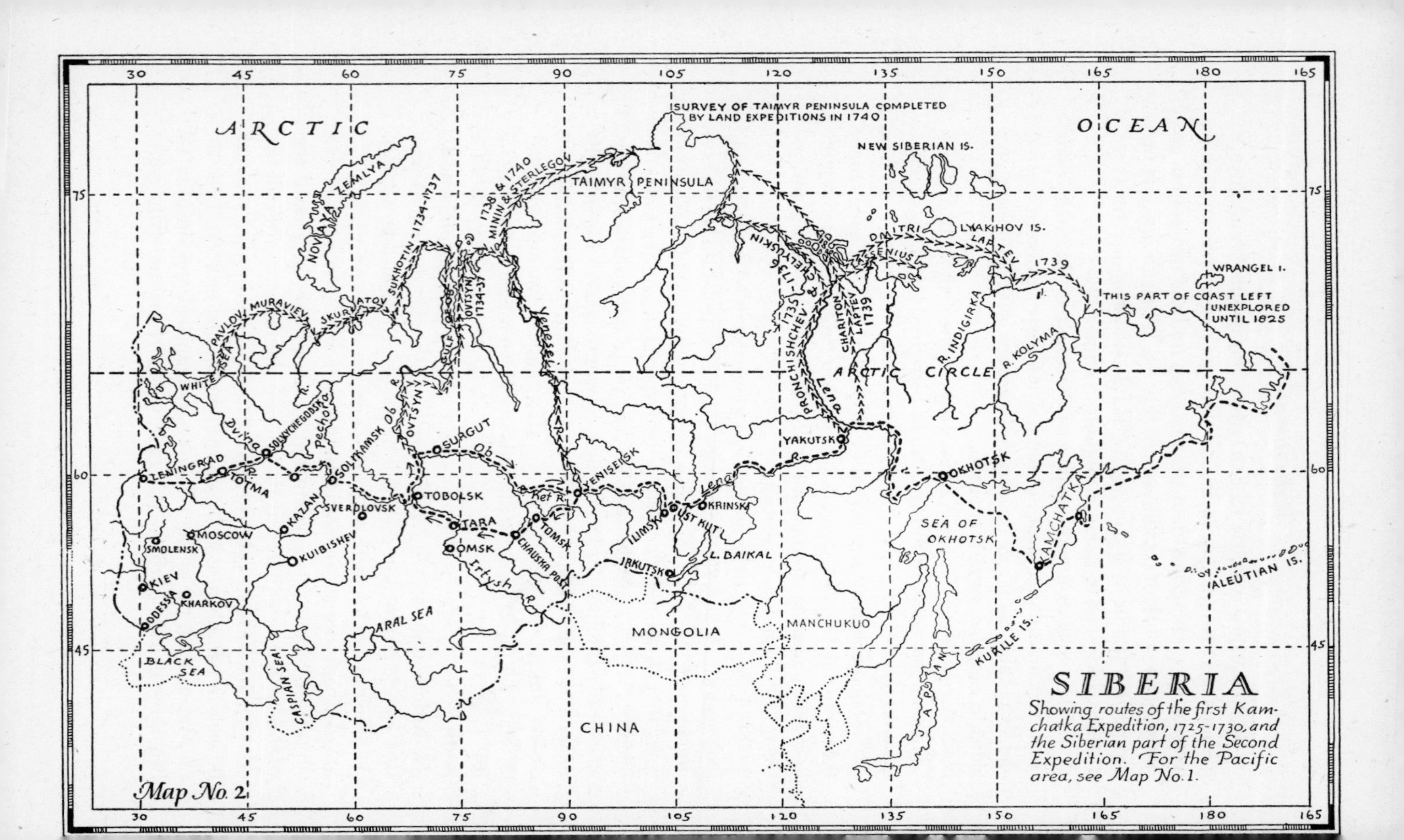

SIBERIA

Showing routes of the first Kamchatka Expedition, 1725-1730, and the Siberian part of the Second Expedition. For the Pacific area, see Map No. 1.

Map No. 2

mand of Lieutenant Dmitrii Leont'evich Ovtsyn to begin her part of the great venture—the mapping of the Arctic coast from the Ob' eastward. In October of this year Bering reached Yakutsk on the Lena River, where he began the construction of two boats designed for use along the northern coast of Siberia, eastward and westward of the mouth of the Lena. The sloop *Yakutsk,* under Lieutenant Vasilii Pronchishchev, was to cruise along the coast westward around the Taimyr Peninsula to the mouth of the Yenisei; and the decked boat *Irkutsk,* under Lieutenant Peter Lassenius, was to proceed eastward to ascertain the relation of Asia to North America and, if possible, to enter Bering Sea and proceed to Kamchatka.

These various expeditions set off in 1734. The first, from Archangel to the mouth of the Ob', proceeded in two vessels, the *Ob'* and the *Expedition,* commanded respectively by Lieutenants Pavlov and Muraviev, and left Archangel on July 4, 1734. The first season they made only slight progress across the Kara Sea and along the coast of Yalmal to latitude 72° 35′. They were compelled to return to the Pechora and winter at Pustoozersk. The following year, 1735, they made no better progress, being forced back by ice from the neighborhood of latitude 73° north. The Admiralty College thereupon ordered the construction of two new and more suitable vessels to be put under Skuratov and Suchotin, the old vessels to be commanded by Stepan Gavrilovich Malygin. In 1736 the new vessels made a rendezvous with Malygin, one of the boats under Suchotin returning to Archangel. The others turned eastward to the Kara River, where they wintered. The late start occasioned by ice in the summer of 1737 did not prevent their rounding Cape Yalmal for the first time in history and entering the estuary of the Ob', finally reaching Sosva, where the vessels were laid up and the crews proceeded to Beresov. Malygin returned overland, while Skuratov took the ships back in 1739.

Meanwhile, Lieutenant Ovtsyn had sailed from Tobolsk (on the Ob' River) in the *Tobol* on May 15, 1734, proceeding downriver and passing out to sea through the easternmost arm of the river. His party erected a storehouse on the coast in latitude 66° 36′, then pushed north and east to 70° 4′, where they were stopped by ice. They decided to return to Obdorsk for the winter and to resume their voyage the following year. This they did on July 20, 1735, but they were held up by ice in latitude 68° 40′, and the crew were taken sick with scurvy. Ovtsyn had to return to Tobolsk.

Ovtsyn then secured permission of the Admiralty to construct a new ship, which was not ready until August. Ice in latitude 72° 40′ turned the expedition back in 1736; meantime, a second ship was built to be ready in the spring of 1737; and with the two vessels Ovtsyn sailed downriver and renewed the attempt at that time. This effort was successful. He rounded Cape Mattesal and reached the mouth of the Yenisei River in latitude 71° 33′ on September 1, 1737. Ovtsyn had done yeoman service in mapping the Gulf of Ob' and the Bays of Tas and Gyda, but fell into disgrace for visiting Prince Dolgorukii in Beresov in defiance of the law which forbade any official to have personal relations with a convict. He was later taken by Bering as a common sailor on his voyage to America.

The task of penetrating from the Yenisei eastward, which should have been entrusted to Ovtsyn, was, in consequence of his disgrace, assigned to Minin and Sterlegov. They made two attempts in 1738, but got no further than the *Zimovies* at the mouth of the Yenisei, where Minin was stopped by ice. Sterlegov reached latitude 73° 14′ before being turned back. The expedition of 1739 was still less successful. In 1740 Minin reached the western coast of the Taimyr, along which he proceeded northward to latitude 75° 26′, where a stone cairn was erected. No further effort was made to complete this part of the exploration.

On June 30, 1735, two double sloops left Yakutsk (on the Lena River) under command respectively of Lieutenants Pronchishchev and Peter Lassenius to put the final touches on the exploration of the Arctic coast; Pronchishchev to proceed westward and round the Taimyr Peninsula; Lassenius to set his course eastward and go, if possible, as far as Bering Sea and Kamchatka. Pronchishchev made his way westward to the mouth of the Onelek, where he prepared winter quarters. The next year, 1736, he left these waters on August 3 and pushed northeast to the Chatango River in latitude 74° 9′. Some distance north of the mouth of this river, in latitude 77° 29′, his vessel was suddenly beset by ice. When he turned back, both vessel and ice were driven by a strong north wind to the south, the ice breaking up and freeing the vessel. The party reached the mouth of the Olenek River on August 25, but experienced great difficulty in getting past this point. During the tedious delay, Pronchishchev, who had been ill for some time, died, his death being followed a few days later by that of his young wife who had accompanied him. Chelyuskin took command, and the crew went into winter quarters here.

Late in the year Chelyuskin returned to Yakutsk to report to Bering, who referred the matter to St. Petersburg. The Admiralty ordered a new expedition and put it under command of Lieutenant Chariton Laptev. The latter, who set out on June 9, 1739, was able to reach only as far as Cape Thaddeus in latitude 76° 47′ before he was compelled to turn back to the mouth of the Chatanga River, where he wintered.

The following spring progress was made in mapping the coast by two land expeditions. The first, led by Chekin, traveled from west to east; and the other, under Medvyedev, journeyed in the opposite direction, between the Ryasin and the Taimyr rivers. Laptev dropped down the river, the weather turned cold, and the ship was unexpectedly caught in the ice which forms quickly in the very low temperature. The crew went ashore dragging their stores with them. But on August 20 a strong wind suddenly sprang up and swept the vessel out to sea. It was only with the greatest exertions and after enduring the most extreme hardships that Laptev and his men made their way to safety overland, and some of the men perished. In the following year, 1740, it was decided to complete the survey of the Taimyr Peninsula by land. The work was divided among three parties, led by Laptev, Chekin, and Chelyuskin, and the country from the Chatanga River to the Taimyr River was mapped. In 1741 a special expedition under Chelyuskin was authorized to make a circuit of the peninsula, and thus the northernmost point of Asia was reached and located accurately by Chelyuskin, whose name it perpetuates.

The expedition eastward from the Lena in the decked boat *Irkutsk* in 1735 was even more unfortunate than the others. The party proceeded eastward until August 21, when they were beset with ice in the Gulf of Borkhaya just east of the Lena Delta and forced to spend the winter there. Scurvy broke out, and Lassenius and most of his crew died. A relief expedition sent out under

Lieutenant Charbinin found the survivors and took them back to civilization.

Dmitrii Laptev was put in charge of the new expedition for 1736, but he had no better success. His party was frozen in just east of the Lena and suffered from scurvy, and he reported personally to the Admiralty in 1737 that it was impossible to round Cape Borkhaya and Svyatoi Nos, which lay between the Lena and the Indigirka rivers. Nevertheless, the Admiralty was obdurate and insisted that the effort be made to round the northeast extremity of Asia. Explorations for 1738 were confined to expeditions by land, but in 1739 Laptev, going by sea, had the good luck to round these capes and make his way to the mouth of the Indigirka, where he wintered. During the following year, 1740, the attempt was renewed in the vessel which had been reconditioned. Laptev passed the Bear Islands and reached the Kolyma River, but, when he attempted to push on further, he was held up and forced back to the Kolyma. During the warm weather ensuing, he renewed the attempt; but ice stopped him at Cape Baranov, and once more he returned to the Kolyma for the winter. He now ceased his efforts to penetrate to Bering Sea by water and devoted the years 1741 and 1742 to reaching the Anadyr overland and surveying that river. Thus the attempt to map the whole of the Arctic Ocean and to extend the survey to the Pacific Ocean and Bering Sea stopped just short of being complete.

After seeing the various Arctic expeditions off, Bering, in 1736, was free to assemble at Yakutsk the supplies for his own expedition and to transport them over the Stanovoi Mountains to Okhotsk. But it was not until 1737 that he moved his headquarters to Okhotsk, where he found that Spangberg had built and equipped two new seagoing vessels, the *Archangel Gabriel* and the *Hope,* in addition to repairing Bering's two old ships, the *Fortuna* and the *Gabriel.* Lack of provisions was holding up Spangberg's expedition to Japan. These began arriving slowly in 1738, but only after incredible difficulties had been overcome in transporting them. They were moved down the Lena, up the Aldan, the Maya, and the Yudoma rivers, then across the mountain portage to the Uda River to the sea.

By the spring of 1738 Spangberg was ready for his great enterprise with his colleagues Walton and Schelting; Spangberg in command of the *Archangel Michael,* a three-masted brig, Lieutenant Walton in command of the three-masted double sloop, *Hope,* and Schelting in charge of Bering's old vessel, the *Gabriel.* Spangberg succeeded in charting a considerable part of the Kurile Archipelago, reaching the island of Urup (the Kompaniland of the Dutch), whence he was compelled by lack of provisions to turn back. Lieutenant Walton, who had parted company with his chief, pushed southward as far as the island of Yezo (Hokkaido) before he also returned. The expedition was repeated in 1739, both navigators independently reaching the main Japanese island of Honshu. From here Spangberg turned northward to complete the exploration and charting of the Kurile Islands. He found a suitable anchorage in latitude 38° 25′, where he received visits from the Japanese, who brought supplies and articles to barter. But although the bearing of the visitors was cordial, the Russian commander feared to linger; therefore, after getting his full complement of stores and satisfying his curiosity, he withdrew and returned home. Walton appears to have reached a point on the coast somewhat farther south. Here he sent a party ashore in a harbor to secure food and water. Their relations with the Japanese were amicable, but the captain's nervousness for his safety moved him to a speedy departure. Returning to Okhotsk, Spangberg submitted a report to the Senate by courier, later proceeding in person to St. Petersburg in accordance with previous instructions. The Senate, on reading his report, concluded that his expedition had been a failure and stopped him on his way to the capital with orders to turn back and repeat his effort. This third expedition, launched in haste and without adequate preparation, resulted in complete failure; and Spangberg returned to Siberia without having succeeded in completely lifting the veil of mystery that hung over these northern islands.

Nor was Bering spared friction with the authorities in St. Petersburg. In his report of 1732 he had made an estimate of 10,000 to 12,000 rubles as the probable cost of the expedition, apart from salaries, supplies, and maintenance. The time required for completing the expedition had been set originally at six years; yet, engrossed as Bering had been with the subsidiary expeditions, he had not left Yakutsk for Okhotsk until 1737. Even then the various

Arctic voyages were far from complete. Spangberg had yet to undertake his expedition to Japan, and the voyage to America seemed as far off as ever. In addition to supplying and sending off the various Arctic voyages, Bering had been burdened with the care of the many scientific parties of Müller, Gmelin, and la Croyère, encumbered with stores of equipment which had to be moved across Siberia in large caravans. The problem of feeding this great army was in itself a formidable task. Provisions had to be brought, for the most part, from western Siberia. Bering had just begun to think of his own special task when he encountered official displeasure.

As early as 1736 the Senate had begun to listen to the tittle-tattle that drifted back from the explorers, much of which was due to the strain which hardships and toil had put upon the personal relations of the various leaders. As some of these were men of distinction, they tended to chafe under discipline; and as they could not get a hearing from Bering, they directed their complaints to the capital. Moreover, the long delay aggravated the situation. Bering's estimate of the probable cost had been exceeded in the first months: 300,000 rubles had been sucked in, and the end was not yet. Those who had backed the original project for the political advantages that its success would bring had seen that hope deferred time after time. They began to lose faith in the venture and to lay the blame for failure at Bering's door. Under pressure from the Senate, the Admiralty showered Bering with querulous dispatches upbraiding him for slackness in the discharge of his duties. The charges were vague and merely echoed the inevitable dissatisfaction and disappointment of members of the party. There were complaints that Bering refused to take the advice of his subordinates, as required by the original instructions. The Senate finally stopped his supplementary pay and threatened that stronger action would follow if he could not show results, or, as an alternative, make a satisfactory explanation.

To help remove these misunderstandings and delays, special officials were sent to Siberia to take charge of the assembling and forwarding of supplies. Bering was thus happily relieved of these onerous and irksome responsibilities. Gmelin's and Müller's querulous complaints about their health, which seem to have been motivated in part by their dread of the hardships and privations involved in a journey to Kamchatka, resulted in their being relieved of this duty. Steller and Krasheninnikov took over the scientific work connected with the Kamchatka expedition, leaving the others to pursue their studies at leisure in the comparative comfort of central and western Siberia.

The mystery is how Bering could endure this perpetual backbiting and intrigue in addition to the enormous hardships he had to undergo. The difficulties he had to surmount placed on him responsibilities that would have crushed a lesser man. It speaks well for his tenacity, patience, and administrative ability that he rose above his tribulations and carried through his task to a successful conclusion, though the accumulated burdens broke his health.

The second Kamchatka expedition set sail in 1741 from Okhotsk in five vessels—two large vessels, the *St. Peter* and the *St. Paul,* two smaller transports, and a still smaller one to carry the scientists. The first objective was Avacha Bay on the eastern coast of Kamchatka, where Bering's mate, Yelagin, had been sent in 1739 to prepare winter quarters in a harbor on the north side of the bay and where Bering now found reasonably commodious accommodation ready for occupation. Unfortunately for Bering, one of the vessels loaded with stores went aground on the bar of the Okhota River, and its cargo was lost. The cargo of the other was discharged at Bolsheretsk and had to be hauled across the peninsula by natives. The mutinous disorders among these natives, occasioned in carrying out this work, led to serious delays. This accumulation of mishaps caused Bering to postpone his departure, and when he did finally leave, he had but five months' rations instead of the two years' supplies originally planned. This lack was to have momentous effects on the expedition.

The final departure was from the newly named port of Petropavlovsk on Avacha Bay on June 4, 1741, with Bering in command of the *St. Peter,* with a crew of seventy-five, and Chirikov in command of the *St. Paul,* with a complement of seventy-six men. The route to be followed had been a matter of some concern to Bering. According to the instructions of the Senate he was bound:

to prosecute his search with the greatest energy and zeal and with the utmost fidelity to follow his instructions which have been drafted in accordance with the latest nautical information, and to further this end, to take counsel with the professor [de l'Isle de la Croyère] sent out by the Academy of Sciences as has been shown in the instructions to the Academy of Sciences with reference to the different routes to America which are to be communicated to Bering and Chirikov.

La Croyère, like his brother, believed that Gamaland was a westerly extension of the American continent. A course to the southeast would reach it in the shortest time. They held such a course until June 12, and latitude 46° 30′ north and longitude 14° 30′ east of Avacha Bay was reached on the twentieth. Here the two boats became separated. Bering remained in the vicinity until the twenty-second, when he turned south to the forty-sixth parallel, along which he proceeded eastward. Turning then to the northeast, he continued in this direction until July 13, when, alarmed by the distance he had traversed from west to east without discovering land, he decided to turn due north. At noon on July 16 in latitude computed as 58° 14′ and longitude 49° 30′ east of Avacha, the clouds parted and the party saw to the north a rugged landscape, fringed on the seaward side with islands and culminating inland in a great snow-capped mountain peak. Thus Bering had at last found America. As the day was St. Elias Day, the mountain was named in honor of the saint, and the same name was also given to the point of land off which the vessel lay. The island probably is that now known as Kayak.

Khitrov and fifteen men were dispatched to sail around the island in search of a harbor, while Steller, who discharged the duties of naturalist, was put ashore to reconnoiter the island's wild life as well as its human inhabitants. But Bering was not disposed to linger off these inhospitable coasts. Recalling Steller from the land and refusing permission for the further prosecution of his studies, Bering somewhat arbitrarily announced his decision to proceed on the voyage.

Anxiety for the future, occasioned by the inadequate stores as well as by lack of confidence in the seaworthiness of his ship, was apparently the determining factor. The seas through which these explorers passed are today, even with charts, extremely difficult to navigate, and through these unfamiliar waters Bering had to make his way. Fog beset him constantly; whenever it lifted, the mountainous mainland of the Kenai Peninsula lowered threateningly to the north; reefs and rocks appeared in his course, menacing his frail craft, while incalculable tidal currents swept him continually from his course. He managed to elude destruction, rounded Kodiak Island, and sighted Chirikof Island and Semidi Islands to the north. Scurvy was now rampant among the crew, and after the ship had been buffeted by headwinds for several days, it was decided to abandon further efforts at discovery and to return forthwith. Because water was running low, the crew took advantage of their proximity to the Shumagin group to put in to land. Here Steller secured antiscorbutic plants, with which he was able to relieve Bering's condition. But time was consumed by Khitrov in reconnoitering the island, and the longboat was lost in this venture. Leaving Shumagin Islands finally, the *St. Peter* proceeded westward, but was driven by storms southward, far from its course. Working their way along the forty-eighth parallel, the party managed to make some progress, but the low water supply induced them to turn north to the fifty-second parallel, and here on October 25 they suddenly saw land again in latitude 50° 50′ (50° 35′ is the correct position according to Sarychev)—Amchitka Island, possibly. Beating back to the southeast, they resumed their westward course. On October 28 Kiska was sighted (St. Stephen) and later the Semichi Islands (St. Abraham). Apparently Attu was left on the port side as they proceeded north. Again taking a westward direction, on November 4 they saw high land to the west, which was assumed to be Kamchatka. Care had to be exercised to prevent the ship's being driven on a lee shore by the east wind. But the crew were in the last extremity of weakness and could not work the ship. After lying offshore for two days in the hope of getting a chance to maneuver into a favorable position to land, the vessel was eventually swept by the ebb tide towards a reef. The anchors thrown out failed to hold, and to the terror of all on board the ship struck the reef, dragged her length grinding and lunging forward, seemingly to destruction, but finally with a great effort cleared the reef and rode into comparatively calm water beyond.

When the *St. Peter* thus drove into the cove on the eastern side of what came to be known as Bering Island, almost all of the ship's company, including the commander, were prostrate with scurvy. Indeed, the partial shipwreck was due primarily to the weakness of the men. On the sixth of November Steller and Pleniser went ashore to reconnoiter, but it was not until the following day that those who were still sound began to disembark, taking the sick and the stores with them. Owing to the debility of the men, progress was slow and laborious in the extreme and the landing was not completed until the tenth. The increasing severity of the weather made it imperative that some sort of shelter from the elements be provided. As no wood was available, the men immediately improvised dwellings by scooping dugouts in the sandbanks that rose from the bed of the small stream at whose mouth they had landed. These dugouts were roofed with driftwood and chinked with anything that lay at hand, even the carcasses of the Arctic foxes they killed. But the sides of these makeshift dwellings, being sand, kept sloughing off and running down into the burrows, burying the occupants. Bering was housed in one of these shelters, but he was now far gone, and all that could be done was to ease his suffering. He continued to sink until December 8, when he died.

The plight of the crew was grave, if not desperate. They soon had reason to suspect that, contrary to their first belief, they had been cast ashore on an island, not on the mainland of Kamchatka. Most of their remaining food had been spoiled when the ship had finally been driven ashore at the end of November and had broken up. The majority of the crew were unable to shift for themselves, and the few who were still healthy were overburdened with the work of providing shelter and caring for their sick comrades. Death and suffering were present on every hand. The only relief in the black outlook was the abundance of game and fresh water. Arctic foxes moved freely and fearlessly among the men, the shores and the neighboring waters swarmed with sea otter, fur seals, and sea cows, and even a stranded whale was found. These animals, supplemented with sea fowl, provided an abundance of fresh meat. But scurvy had made too heavy inroads on the health of the crew, and death continued to reduce their number. By January 5 thirty-one of the company of seventy-seven had been carried off by the disease.

The remainder of the crew gradually recovered health and

strength, despite the severe conditions under which they passed the winter. As strength returned, they began to carry out reconnaissances and were able finally to confirm their suspicion that they had landed on an uninhabited island just off the coast of Kamchatka. When the vessel had broken up, they had managed to salvage the timber, and out of this they constructed a smaller vessel to essay the voyage back to Avacha Bay, which they reached at last in the summer of 1742.

After becoming separated from Bering on June 20, Chirikov had remained in the vicinity until June 23, when he gave up the search for his commander and set a course east-north-east half east. By July 11 signs of land appeared, and on July 15 in latitude 55° 21′ and longitude 61° 55′ from Avacha, the crew sighted it. On the next day, July 16, a party was sent ashore in latitude 56° 15′, longitude 60° 57′ 2″, but as there was no suitable anchorage, they were unable to land. After their return, the ship proceeded on its course, apparently towards the north. On July 17 in latitude 57° 39′, longitude 58° 54′, the navigator, Dementiev, with a crew of ten men, landed to reconnoiter. As the party neither signalled nor returned, the commander on the twenty-third put ashore another party under the boatswain, Sevelyev. This time elaborate arrangements were made for the men to maintain contact by signals—to send word of their arrival and to summon aid if it should be needed. Despite the precautions this boat and its crew also vanished as mysteriously as the first. In constant danger of being carried on to a lee shore, Chirikov concluded that, since he had no more small boats, he could do nothing. Hence, albeit reluctantly, he sailed away. It was decided to set course for Kamchatka. Sighting a threatening coast off Kenai Peninsula on August 1, he bore away to the southwest. There being no chance of replenishing the water supply, the crew were put on an allowance. On September 4 they were within sight of Umnak, the next island west of Unalaska. On September 8, when the fog lifted, they found themselves suddenly surrounded by a rugged, rocky coast, evidently the islands of the Four Mountains, or else Adak, one of the Andreanof Islands. They were visited by natives, with whom they bartered various articles, receiving arrows and edible roots in exchange. The wind rising, they stood out to sea and continued their voyage. They eked out their slender store of water by distilling sea water. The results were far from satisfactory, but this water kept the majority of the men alive, though a number of the crew suffered from scurvy. Some deaths occurred, and Chirikov was prostrated. On September 25 in latitude 52° 36′, they descried through the mist what was apparently the last of the Aleutians, the island of Attu, which, like the other islands he had seen, Chirikov believed to be a continuation of the American mainland. They reached Avacha Bay on October 8, where they learned to their concern that Bering had not turned up. Louis de l'Isle de la Croyère died as he was being taken ashore.

The following spring Chirikov, now recovered, set out in search of Bering, but was forced by unfavorable weather to turn back. The survivors of Bering's company reached Petropavlovsk on August 27, thus removing the need for continuing the search; and Chirikov then returned to Yakutsk.

Bering has been much criticized for his precipitate return, which allowed the members of the expedition (especially Steller) no time or opportunity for explorations. The commander's caution is attested by his favorite motto:

Tu, nisi ventis
Debes ludibrium, cave.[1]

Considering what he achieved, the ordeals he suffered, and the immense responsibilities he bore for the safety of the expedition, posterity can well afford to withhold adverse judgment.

[1] "Unless thou wouldst see thy craft the sport of winds, beware."—Horace, *Odes,* I, 14.

IV

Buccaneers of the Pacific

THE INSPIRATION OF THE SECOND KAMCHATKA EXPEDITION WAS lost when Bering died on a hitherto unknown island in the Pacific. La Croyère lived only to catch sight of Petropavlovsk, Steller died on the return journey across Siberia, while Walton lay in an unmarked grave. The general gloom which surrounded the closing days of the explorations obscured the brilliant results that had been attained. Chirikov reached the capital to submit his report, but lived only a short time afterwards. Moreover, death had removed the sovereign under whose orders the expedition had been undertaken. The Empress Elizabeth, while intelligent and devoted to the interests of her land, had come to power by invoking native patriotism, largely against the foreigners in government circles. The inevitable reaction against foreigners involved the Academy of Sciences, and for twenty years that institution was inactive. The scientists, Gmelin, Müller, and their helpers, returned from Siberia and began the compilation of the results of their researches, but no steps were taken to publish them. Eventually two of the members of the academy, Gmelin and Delisle, published their findings abroad in violation of regulations. This forced the hand of the government, which gradually allowed some of the vast collection of material assembled by the expedition to appear in print. But nothing was done to carry on the work of Bering and his associates, and less than justice was done to their memory. It remained for the nineteenth century to bring their deeds before the world.

The next phase in the exploration of the North Pacific was to be the work neither of the government nor of its servants, but of private individuals recruited from the motley class of adventurers who made up the population of Siberia at this time. The initiative came largely from merchants. Russian literature contains many references to the Siberian merchants, hard and perhaps none too scrupulous bargainers, given at times to sharp practice, but also open-handed adventurers whose Gargantuan revels were legendary, who appeared unannounced at intervals at the great fairs and commercial marts of European Russia, Arctic Siberia, and the Chinese border, and as unceremoniously disappeared. Second only in importance to these were the *promyshlenniki,* the Russian counterpart of the *coureurs de bois* of North America—the hard-living, hard-drinking but robust sons of the forest, whose calling was the pursuit of the peltries of sable, marten, ermine, and beaver and otter for the markets of China and Europe. Accustomed to the rugged life of their trade in Siberia, the *promyshlenniki* cheerfully exchanged the dog sled and the river boat for means of transport suited to the sea. They built and manned the ships that put forth to the new islands that beckoned. Unaccustomed as they were to reefing a sail or piloting a ship, they made but indifferent mariners. But they were not wanting in courage or hardihood. They dared these uncharted and unknown waters; they learned the treacherous currents and tide rips and reefs that lie in wait for the unwary mariner. They plotted by trial and error. Ignorant and unskillful, yet they succeeded where even the most experienced and cautious might well have failed.

The survivors of Bering's crew had brought back a cargo of pelts which included the hitherto unknown sea otter, and the news of the unusually high prices these commanded at Kiakhta when offered to the Chinese at once spread throughout Siberia. Immediately a group was formed to send a ship and crew for more. This vessel, under Emilian Bassov, merely reconnoitered Bering's Island and other islands of the Kommandorskii group, returning in July, 1746.

Following the first attempt, a company formed by Afanasii Tsebaevskii, Yakob Tsyuprov, and others raised the money needed for a ship, which was built at the mouth of the Kamchatka River. It was what was known as a *shitik,* a simple craft, flat bottomed, with a deck and a sail, which called for minimum skill on the part of ships' carpenters. Michael Nevodchikov, a native of Tobolsk, was put in command; his crew was composed of *promyshlenniki.* These men found the most westerly of the Aleutians, those which came to be known as the Near Islands. They landed first on Agattu, then put in to Attu, where they passed the winter in search of skins. However, they became too intimate with the natives, and trouble over women led to a shocking crime—the slaughter by a party of Russians of all the males of one settlement.[1] Their vessel was wrecked, and the crew had to return across the wide stretches of ocean in *baidars,* which some natives showed them how to build and navigate. Rumors of the misconduct reached officials of the company, and a strict inquiry was ordered. Apparently no action was taken to punish individuals who had taken part in the massacre, perhaps because of doubtful jurisdiction. The government, however, eventually made rules under which permission to conduct these expeditions had to be sought. After 1749 steps were taken to impose on the islanders *yassak,* the tribute in furs which had been levied on the Siberian natives, and for the purpose of collection, it was customary to send along some representative of the state, usually a Cossack. Even with this system it was difficult to prevent abuses, and the continued excesses practiced by the various expeditions finally led to its discontinuance.

For the first twenty years, aside from the imposts collected on each cargo by the port authorities and the *yassak* levied by the government on the natives of the Aleutian and Kurile Islands, there was little regulation of these expeditions. The constant recurrence of names indicates that a more or less restricted group of persons organized and controlled them. The names of Yugov, Trapeznikov, Tolstykh, Serebrennikov, and Novikov appear again and again. The ventures seem to have been joint-stock companies, in which the original partners owned the larger shares, but the *promyshlenniki* who took part in the expeditions also got shares, from which they received the "pay-off" on their return. The motive invariably was gain, and while many of the expeditions were failures, the successes were striking enough to encourage those who failed to make just one more attempt.

Gradually the secrets hidden by the northern mists were revealed, and the various groups of islands came to be named—the

[1] Hence the name "Massacre Bay," given to an anchorage on the southern shore of the island. Here one of the forces of United States troops landed on May 11, 1943, to launch the operations that led to the recapture of the island from the Japanese.

Near Islands, the Andreanof Islands, and the Rat and Fox Islands. The crudest notes were kept, but as the government levied a tax on the cargo besides enforcing the collection of *yassak,* some records had to be preserved. There was little interest in geographical discovery or historical records, and it is not possible to reconstruct a clear picture of these ventures or the exact order of events. Many years later a curious English scholar, Coxe by name, visited the Russian court and by order of Catherine was given access to the scanty archives. He put together all that was known of these spacious times. Coxe's *Account of Russian Discoveries* told the world something of the epic story, and that his book filled a long-felt want is evidenced by the fact that it ran through four editions. Towards the middle of the nineteenth century a native Russian visited Russian America and there gleaned what was known of these early voyages. He consulted local and family tradition, interviewed the descendants of men who had taken part, and opened the meager archives dealing with events in which the government took little interest, and all these facts enabled him to piece out the story. Berkh's book on Bering's first voyage, which he followed with his *Khronologicheskaya Istoriya Otkrytiya Aleutskikh Ostrovov ili podvigi Rossiiskago Kupechestva,*[2] supplements Coxe to give us practically all that is known of these stirring years.

While the voyages overlap and there is much confusion in the story, we can pick out certain salient facts. Apparently the second group of islands—the Rat Islands—were visited by Serebrennikov in 1753. Trapeznikov, Krasil'nikov, and Andrean Tolstykh followed this up by reaching Amlia and Adak Islands of the Andreanof group. Glotov is supposed to have discovered the Fox Islands—the most easterly of the Aleutians—while the mainland of Alaska was seen for the first time by Gavrilo Pushkarev in 1761. Here the Russians were indiscreet enough to antagonize the natives by carrying off a number of their women as hostages, some of whom committed suicide rather than remain in durance. This outrage reached the ears of the authorities, and a strict warning was issued against its repetition. But the harm had already been done for which the Russians were to pay heavily.

[2] *Chronological History of the Discovery of the Aleutian Islands, or the Exploits of Russian Merchants.*

A turning point in the history of the Aleutian Islands came in the year 1764. All the repressed fury and resentment of the islanders, that had been smoldering since the first landing of the Russians, burst forth in savage warfare between natives and Russians, in which no quarter was given.

The greater part of the blame must be laid at the door of the government of Elizabeth, which was too preoccupied with events in Europe to concern itself with matters in this out-of-the-way corner of the empire. The country was administered by a governor-general living at Tobolsk, a vice-governor at Irkutsk, and a *voyevode* at Yakutsk, while Okhotsk and Bolsheretsk appear to have had merely commandants who represented the Colleges of Admiralty, War, Commerce, and Police Administration. But the authority of the central government in these regions was feeble. The chief concern of the state was the revenue derived from the fur tribute levied on natives (that part of the catch which evidently exiles, and even free trappers, were required to pay the state) and on the catch obtained by each vessel sailing to the Aleutian Islands (one-tenth of the catch), as well as the tribute taken from the islanders themselves. From time to time this revenue might be augmented by the Muscovite practice of granting an exclusive short-term monopoly of the fur catch of an island or a group of islands, in which case the share of the state might be as much as one-third. These exorbitant demands were merely the beginning. They were further increased by the cupidity of officials whose palms had to be greased at every turn to secure the barest justice. The men chosen as officers were not of the highest type, most of them regarding service as equivalent to banishment, whose only compensation was graft. The enforcement of law was fitful and capricious. There was no distinction between enforcing law and dispensing justice, which functions were entrusted invariably to the same official. Moreover, the whole tone of public and private life was low in the extreme. Drunkenness and lewdness were the rule, and lawlessness was prevalent everywhere. It had been bad enough in the time of Bering, but nothing had been done to improve matters. The stream of political exiles whom the last reign had directed hither (Elizabeth would not hear of capital punishment, which was abolished in her reign, but she did not object to banishment to these desolate regions for life) did not tend to improve the moral atmosphere. Thorough demoralization had set in. It culminated in the incident of 1771 when Benyowski, a Hungarian exile, and his accomplices overpowered the garrison of Bolsheretsk, killed the governor, and seized a ship, in which they escaped to China and eventually to Europe. If this was possible on the mainland under the very nose of the government, what about the regions over the sea? Obviously the tsar's authority stopped at the shore. Once they were on the high seas, nothing could hold in check *promyshlenniki,* Cossacks, and merchants but fear of the rather remote chances of punishment should they commit outrages on the natives, crimes that even on the mainland went unpunished.

From the beginning the Russians had been guilty of excesses. Fifteen natives had been massacred by Byelaev on Attu in 1745. As one after another of the Near Islands, with their rich hunting grounds, was discovered, it became the practice of the Russians to supply the natives with traps and nets to catch foxes and sea otters while they remained behind in the shelters in dalliance with the native women.

As the Russians pushed farther east, they encountered ever increasing hostility and opposition from the natives. A certain trader from Archangel, Bashmakov by name, came into sharp conflict with the inhabitants of the Andreanof Islands in 1752, first on the occasion of his party's landing on Adak, when the Russians had one man killed and one wounded, and the second in 1757 upon disembarking on Kanaga. In the absence of the commander and a part of the crew who had gone in search of timber which they needed, the natives fell on those men left behind at the harbor. The rest of the story is furnished by a Russian writer:

The Russians under the protection of their ship opened fire from their guns and turned the Aleut to flight. At the battle site there remained two skin boats with two seriously wounded Aleuts in them, and in one of the skin boats was also found an Aleut boy. He was taken to Kamchatka, baptized, and later became a Cossack under the name of Ivan Cherepanov. Three days after the skirmish the father of the boy, accompanied by relatives, came to propose a ransom for the boy. The Aleut refused to come aboard, fearing vengeance. But by some ruse the

GREGORII SHELEKHOV

elder Aleut and another man were lured to the Russian ship. There they were put on deck and with their arms and legs stretched out by thongs, subjected to tortures; scalding hot tar was poured on their bodies. After that the elder was beheaded. Some time later Bashmakov sent to the village his laborers, who committed an awful butchery and then plundered and burned the village.

Incidents such as these may not have been altogether typical of the relations of the Russians with the Aleuts, but they go far to explain the savagery of the Aleut rising of 1764.

The discovery and occupation of the Andreanof Islands by Andrean Tolstykh (after whom they were named) appear to have been accomplished without a clash with the natives; but the expedition financed by Bechevin and commanded by Gavrilo Pushkarev—which in the same year (1761) reached Fox Islands, the most easterly in the Aleutians, and the neighboring mainland (called the peninsula Alaksu or Alakshak[3])—was distinguished by the truculent behavior of its members. Attempts to violate girls on Unga led to bloodshed, and on their return home the Russians carried off by force some of the men of Umnak and their wives. Rumors of their inhumanity to the natives had preceded them to Siberia, and an inquiry was instituted. But the harm was already done. It was one thing to abuse the helpless natives of the western islands, few in numbers and isolated, but it was a different matter to take such liberties with the inhabitants of the more populous islands of the Fox group or of the mainland, who could render one another mutual support and thus could confront the Russians with overwhelming numbers.; According to Coxe:

> The *toigons* [chiefs] of Umnak, Akutan, and Toshko with their relations of Unalashka had formed a confederacy; they agreed not to disturb the Russians on their first landing, but to attack them at the same time in their different hunting excursions.

In the year 1762 four ships sailed from Okhotsk for the Fox Islands. Three of these were ventures of the same company, in which appear the well-known names of Trapeznikov, Popov, Protasov, Ivan Lapin, and others. The first ship was the *Zakharii*

[3] This included Unimak, since the Russians did not know then of the existence of False Pass, which makes Unimak an island.

i Elizaveta, commanded by Druzhinin, the second the *Trinity,* commanded by Ivan Korovin, and the third, name unknown, commanded by Denis Medvyedev. Druzhinin wintered in Petropavlovsk and proceeded in July, 1763, to Umnak, where he found Glotov in command of a fourth expedition, and where the other ships of Korovin and Medvyedev were waiting. From here Druzhinin sailed to the north shore of Unalaska, where he hunted. For this purpose he split his crew into three parties, two of which were dispatched in different directions, the third remaining near the harbor. Each of these groups was attacked separately, and two of the parties were wiped out. The third fought the natives off, struggled along the coast, and managed to rejoin the ship commanded by Korovin.

Korovin had reached Unalaska on August 15, 1763, in company with Medvyedev, with whom he had joined forces. Korovin selected winter quarters for the trapping parties being sent out on various missions from time to time and for exchanging messages with other Russian groups on the islands, while Medvyedev returned to Umnak. Finally, during the course of the winter, survivors from Druzhinin's ship apprised Korovin of the capture of their ship and the loss of most of the crew. Korovin's camp was also attacked by large numbers of natives. The Russians fought them off during the winter, though the vessel, which had to be left in an exposed anchorage, became a total wreck. Eventually the company, reduced considerably in numbers, escaped in July, 1764, in *baidars* to the island of Umnak. Here on the beach they discovered the burnt remains of Medvyedev's vessel, with ship's tackle and stores spread around in confusion. In a hut near by they found the bodies of all the crew, including the commander. Only an unexpected turn of fortune saved the situation for the Korovin group.

Stepan Glotov had been dispatched by Terentii Tsebaevskii in 1764 in command of the *Andrean* and the *Natalia.* Glotov had sailed to Umnak where he had met Druzhinin, but he had gone on almost immediately to the island of Kodiak. From the first he had been threatened by the natives, whose hostility had compelled him to put his ship and the camp he had established in a state of constant readiness. Since this had prevented his crew from engaging in taking fur, he resolved to return in May. Passing along the coast of Alaksu, he reached Umnak, where he found traces of the tragedy that had taken place on the island. On July 5 he discovered the remains of Medvyedev's vessel and his murdered crew. On August 2 he met Korovin and the survivors of his party, and together they decided to look for a good, defensible position to lay up the ship.

Ivan Solov'ev, who commanded a ship, *The Holy Apostles Peter and Paul,* owned by Yakob Ulednikov, which had left the mouth of the Kamchatka River on August 25, 1764, avenged the dead Russians. He reached Umnak; then crossed the strait that separates Umnak from Unalaska and dropped anchor off the north shore of that island. Finding the remains of Russian camps, Solov'ev drew from a native who had acted as interpreter for one of the unlucky crews the whole mournful story of the destruction of the three vessels and the massacre of their crews. He also heard of the arrival of Glotov. Solov'ev at once doubled his watch and prepared to take stern measures. He was joined at length by Korovin and the other survivors, and they finally went into winter quarters. He had already been unsuccessfully attacked by the natives, had killed a number, and had taken some as prisoners, whom he kept closely guarded as surety for the conduct of the rest. He required the natives to give up the goods they had plundered and the tackle they had stripped from the vessel of Korovin. But he could not bring the natives to amicable terms and was kept constantly on the alert. Finally, on November 10, the natives made a concerted assault. This was beaten off only after savage fighting, in which nineteen of the natives were killed. All that winter the state of alarm prevailed. Crossing over to Umnak, Solov'ev sought to recover some of Korovin's stores; but his parties on Unalaska continued to be waylaid and attacked, though one group under Korenov managed to kill fifteen of their assailants. These victories and the severe punishment dealt out by Solov'ev had the hoped for effect, and the cowed islanders never again found the courage to resist the Russians. Solov'ev finally returned from his expedition in 1766, and Glotov likewise found his way back about this time.

A change of sovereigns inaugurated a new era in the affairs of Russia's new Pacific possessions. Empress Catherine, an ardent admirer of Peter the Great, felt called on to finish the work of exploration he had begun. The aim was doubtless laudable, but the instruments she laid hold of were mediocre and her methods ineffective. The first of her measures was the sending of Lieutenant Synd in 1764 on a voyage of discovery from Okhotsk northeast towards what was supposed to be the coast of the mainland of North America. The Russians had done little exploring in Bering Sea. On August 24, 1748, Simeon Novikov of Yakutsk and Ivan Bakkov of Ustyug (agents for Ivan Shilkin), after having built a vessel at Anadyrsk, the construction of which took two years, had dropped down the Anadyr River and on out to sea. The findings of their voyage were inconclusive, but they had arrived at last at Kamchatka. Lieutenant Synd put to sea from Okhotsk in 1764, but did not clear the southern point of Kamchatka before 1766. He set his course to the northeast into Bering Sea. He seems to have discovered some islands between latitudes 61° and 62°, and farther north he apparently saw the mainland on the American side of the strait between latitudes 64° and 66°. He landed, but he remained a short time only and returned to Okhotsk in 1768. Ismailov, who accompanied Synd, gave Cook to understand in 1778 that Synd had made no discoveries.

During that year a second and more pretentious expedition was sent out under Captain Krenitsyn in the galliot *St. Catherine* and Lieutenant Levashev in the hooker *St. Paul*. This voyage was to complete the work begun by Bering, and the voyagers were supplied with the records of Bering's expedition. They shaped their course eastward, passing to the north of the Aleutian Islands until they reached the Alaksu (Alaska) Peninsula, where they seem to have wintered in False Pass, which separates the Alaska Peninsula from the island of Unimak. At any rate, they reported very shoal water, a circumstance which strongly suggests that this is where they were. The next year they wintered at Unalaska. Beyond observing the habits and characteristics of the natives and their relations with the Russian *promyshlenniki,* Krenitsyn and Levashev apparently did not exert themselves to carry out explorations. Even their maps were defective.

The Empress did not confine her efforts in this direction solely to official expeditions. She encouraged in merchants the zealous prosecution of both exploration and trade, lending support to their efforts by the distribution of rewards and some exemptions. In return, the recipients of these favors redoubled their efforts and saw that the best skins were placed at the disposal of the Empress' agents. How far imperial patronage such as this went to expand Russian influence in these waters we do not know. It is likely that other factors weighed more than imperial condescension. For one thing, the merchants and *promyshlenniki* had now extended their operations throughout the Aleutians. Unaided by the government, they had made Russia a power to be respected in these regions. However much we condemn their excesses—for which in many cases they paid dearly—they had finally cowed the natives and made traveling and the taking of fur safe. The Aleutian Islands were now ripe for exploitation. The town of Okhotsk was a flourishing place of some nine hundred souls, most of whom engaged in trade with the islands. Merchants and traders had flocked to the country from all over the empire to take advantage of the opportunity. Small wonder, then, that the period from 1770 to 1790 was the heyday of the fur trade in the Aleutians; and in this trade the individual merchant was the chief participant.

The pioneering period was over, and an entirely new phase of operations was about to begin. Some of the older men had dropped out of the race; others had lost their lives in the waters of the North Pacific and in fighting the natives. New faces were appearing at Okhotsk, those of men with keener ambitions and perhaps greater resources. The expeditions that left now were larger and better equipped. With financial resources that had accrued from the profits of early exploits or were drawn from elsewhere, the new magnates engaged in bitter rivalry and sought every advantage in the struggle, including special privileges gained by official favor. Such favor was perhaps to be gained by flattering a luxury-loving empress with gifts of the finest products of the chase, or by proving superior skill in navigation, or by seeking authority for a voyage of exploration under semiofficial auspices. Moreover, with the increasing profits, better men were attracted. Catherine's pro-Hellenic policy had attracted to the Russian service many Greek merchants and seamen, and by the grant of citizenship and equality of rights with Russians they were lured to the East. Greek names now begin to appear on the roster.

Of these new organizations only a few of the most important need be mentioned. Potap Zaikov made expeditions in 1772 and 1778. Alexei Kholodilov fitted out the *Archangel Michael* and sent her off with a crew of sixty-three men under Dmitrii Polutov in 1772; and in 1774 he sent a second expedition to Unalaska and Kodiak, where Polutov found it impossible to do business with the natives. On that account he returned to Atka, and from there he came back to Okhotsk in 1777. Petr and Grigorii Panov conducted Totema's expedition in 1772. Fedor Burenin of Vologda sent out an expedition on the *Sv. Evyel* in 1773, which joined Zaikov in Umnak. Ivan Novikov made two trips, in 1773 and 1774, to the Aleutians. Protodiakanov and Okonishnikov sent out an expedition in 1774, which returned in 1776 with one of the first cargos of seal skins (39,500); their second cargo was valued at 93,840 rubles. Osokin, the Tobol merchant, sent out the *Sv. Pavel* (*St. Paul*) in 1774. In 1776 Grigorii and Petr Panov sent to the Aleutians the *Sv. Aleksandr,* which returned in 1779.

Towards the end of the seventies we begin to find the big operators—the giants of the fur business—first and foremost of whom are Grigorii Ivanovich Shelekhov of Rylsk, Oryekhov (one of the most successful operators, who usually teamed up with Lapin and Shilov), Ivan Larionovich Golikov of Kursk, Yakov Protasov (one of the old hands), Grigorii and Petr Panov (also old-timers), Lebedev Lastochkin (one of the buccaneers of the fur trade), and, of course, Zaikov. These men began to dominate the scene. They exploited the Aleutians thoroughly and efficiently, as their profits testify.

The government was now taking more interest in eastern affairs. When the first partition of Poland had been carried through (1772) and the war with Turkey had ended (Treaty of Kutchuk Kainardji, 1774), Catherine resumed with accustomed vigor the oversight of other affairs in her vast dominion. In the East the first fruits were the suppression in the Aleutian Islands of *yassak,* which the natives had never understood and which had led to frequent clashes.

But it seems that Catherine had far more ambitious aims than just the welfare of her islanders, who apparently had not yet been officially recognized as Russian subjects. For one thing, events in the Far East were now moving with a tempo hitherto unknown. In 1725 Peter had directed Bering to look for European settlements if the coast of America was reached; and when the second Kamchatka expedition was prepared in 1732, it had been thought advisable to provide secret instructions for the Russians in case they encountered representatives of Spain or other European powers. What had been a remote contingency in 1732 had by 1780 become a reality. That was the arrival in the North Pacific of competitors, England and Spain—ancient rivals also in the South Pacific and both now roused to supreme efforts by the news of Russia's advances in the north. In 1769 a royal order was signed by the King of Spain and dispatched to the Marquis de Croix, the viceroy of New Spain, instructing him to take the proper measures to meet Russian aggression in the New World. In fulfillment of these instructions the Viceroy and the visitor-general of the Franciscan missions of Old California dispatched an expedition to Alta California to establish garrisons and to plant under their protection missions to convert and civilize the Indians. The result was the establishment of the mission and presidio of San Diego. During the next year the presidio and mission of San Carlos in Monterey Bay was established, and reconnaissance made further north as far as San Francisco Bay with a view to founding a mission at that place.

Then in 1773 it was decided to send an expedition to explore the coast as far north as 60° north latitude. This expedition, under Pérez, got under way in 1774, sailed as far the Queen Charlotte Islands, trafficked with the Indians, and secured information about them. Pérez also took possession of the country in the name of the King of Spain. His party discovered Nootka Sound on the west coast of Vancouver Island and named it the Port of San Lorenzo. The following year a second expedition, commanded by Bucareli, was sent out under Don Bruno Heceta. It proceeded up the coast, discovering the mouth of the Columbia River, and went north past Vancouver Island, the Queen Charlotte Islands, and Sitka (Norfolk) Sound. The explorers entered and named Bucareli Bay and identified Mount Edgecumbe.

A third expedition was ordered, but the construction of a ship was delayed for several years. Finally in 1779 the *Princesa* and the *Favorita* sailed from San Blas for the north in command of Lieutenant Ignacio Arteaga, with Lieutenant Juan Francisco de Bodega y Quadra, who had accompanied the expedition of 1775 as commander of the *Felicidad,* second in command. The ships entered Bucareli Sound on May 2 and carried out a fairly extensive reconnaissance. Starting north on July 1, they sighted Mount St. Elias on the ninth, passed Kayak Island, and put into Nuchek Bay, where they took possession of the country in the name of the King of Spain. Turning southward, they sighted Iliamna Volcano on the far side of Cook Inlet and anchored off Cape Elizabeth. They decided on August 7 to return to Cape Mendocino from here. This exploring party had no contacts with the Russians, though there unquestionably were Russian vessels present somewhere in the waters explored.

V

England Takes a Hand

MEANWHILE ENGLAND HAD DECIDED TO TAKE A HAND IN THE exploration of the North Pacific. Her motives were somewhat different from those of the other participants. The British had displayed considerable interest in the search for new lands in the great reaches of the South Pacific and had sent out a number of expeditions under Byron, Wallis, and Carteret. The familiarity with the South Pacific thus acquired naturally served as a basis for the exploration of the North, but other considerations motivated the expedition of 1776. The project of seeking a northwest passage had agitated the minds of a number of prominent people interested in the Hudson Bay region. A series of expeditions had been sent, some by the Hudson's Bay Company and others by private individuals, to find this supposed passage. These had failed, but a party sent out by the company by land in 1770 under Samuel Hearne had succeeded in reaching the mouth of the Coppermine River on the northern coast of the continent. However, the finding of the northwest passage seemed as far off as ever. With the objective of locating the passage the commissioners for executing the office of Lord High Admiral for Great Britain and Ireland, on July 6, 1776, issued instructions to Captain James Cook to proceed with Captain Clerke in His Majesty's sloops *Resolution* and *Discovery* in an attempt to find a northern passage by sea from the Pacific Ocean to the Atlantic. He was to go by way of the Cape of Good Hope, New Zealand, and Tahiti (or the Society Islands) to the coast of New Albion, particular injunctions being given not to touch at any Spanish port. Having reached the coast of New Albion, he was to sail northward and

not to lose any time in exploring rivers or inlets, or upon any other account, until you get into the afore-mentioned latitude of 65°. . . . When you get that length, you are very carefully to search for, and to explore such rivers or inlets as may appear to be of a considerable extent, and pointing towards Hudson's or Baffin's Bay; and if, from your observations, or from information you may receive from the natives . . . there shall appear to be a certainty, or even a probability, of a water passage into the afore-mentioned bays, or either of them, you are, in such case, to use your utmost endeavour to pass through with one or both of the sloops, unless you shall be of the opinion that the passage may be effected with more certainty, or with greater probability, by smaller vessels; in which case, you are to set up the frames of one or both of the small vessels with which you are provided, and, when they are put together, and are properly fitted, stored and victualled, you are to dispatch one or both of them, under the care of proper officers, with a sufficient number of petty officers, men and boats, in order to attempt the said passage; with such instructions for their rejoining you, if they should fail, or for their farther proceedings, if they should succeed in the attempt, as you may judge most proper. . . . In case you shall be satisfied that there is no passage through to the above-mentioned bays, sufficient for the purposes of navigation, you are, at the proper season of the year to repair to the port of St. Peter and St. Paul in Kamchatka, or wherever else you shall judge more proper to refresh your people and pass the winter; and, in the spring of the ensuing year 1778 to proceed from thence to the Northward, as far as, in your prudence, you may think proper, in further search of a North East or North West passage from the Pacific Ocean into the Atlantic Ocean or the North Sea; and if, from your own observation, or information, you may receive, there shall appear to be a probability of such a passage, you are to proceed as above directed; and, having discovered such passage, or failed in the attempt, make the best of your way back to England by such route as you may think best for the improvement of geography and navigation; repairing to Spithead with both sloops where they are to remain till further order.

To supplement Cook's efforts, arrangements were also made for a similar attempt to find the north passage from the east. A vessel was sent in 1776 under Lieutenant Pickersgill to proceed into Baffin Bay on this quest. Pickersgill returned without success, and the attempt was renewed the next year by Lieutenant Young. As an added inducement to increase the zeal of the participants, the reward of twenty thousand pounds, which had been held out by an act of Parliament to ships of any of His Majesty's subjects not in His Majesty's service who might find such a passage, was extended by a new law to ships belonging to His Majesty.

Cook's voyage was to some extent, though less than later voyages, influenced by the erroneous ideas of geography that had become current in the eighteenth century. For while the western Pacific had its Gama Land, its Company Land, and its Yezo, exploration of the eastern Pacific was diverted from its proper purpose by the popularization of stories of a series of alleged discoveries at an earlier date. These included the voyages of Juan de Fuca and Maldonaldo in the sixteenth century and of Admiral de Fonte (or Fuente) in the seventeenth century. The tales all had in common the claim that they proved the existence of a passage of some sort that would facilitate navigation between the Atlantic and the Pacific through or around the northern part of the American continent. Accounts of these alleged voyages and the conclusions drawn from them about the geography of the North Pacific acquired wide currency during the eighteenth century. But they do not seem to have affected the earlier period. Bering knew nothing of them, and they are not mentioned in Cook's *Instructions* nor in the *Introduction* to his voyages. But Cook did know of them and regarded it as one of his duties, as far as it was in keeping with his instructions, to clear the matter up. He says in his *Voyages*:

> With such weather, and the wind between South South East and South West, I continued the same course till the 30th, at four in the morning, when I steered North by West, in order to make the land. I regretted very much indeed that I could not do it sooner, for this obvious reason, that we were now passing the place where geographers have placed the pretended strait of Admiral de Fonte. For my own part, I gave no credit to such vague and improbable stories, that carry their own confutation with them. Nevertheless, I was very desirous of keeping the American coast aboard, in order to clear up this point beyond dispute.

But the account of Cook's voyage was not published until 1785, and the wide publicity given these stories had created considerable

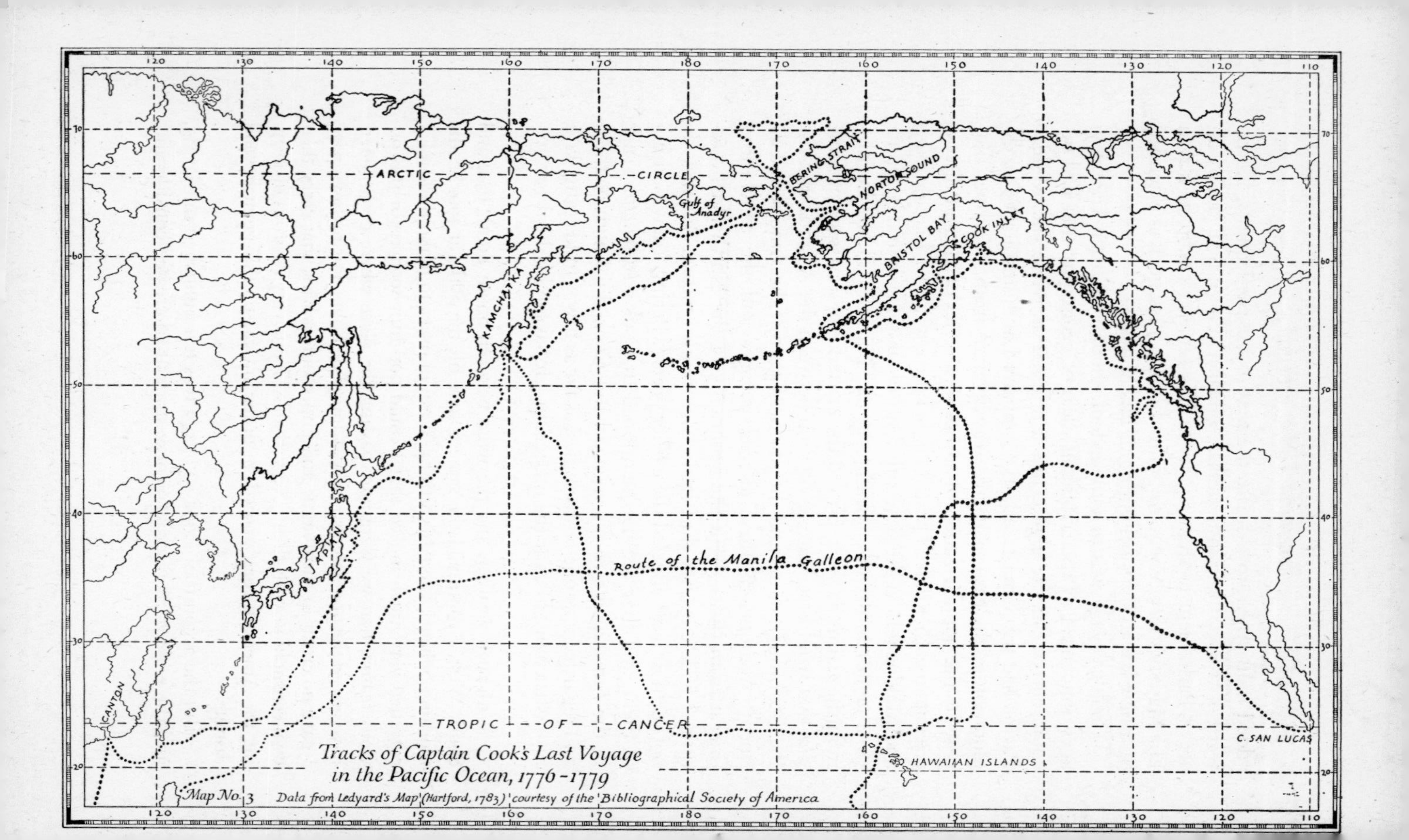

Tracks of Captain Cook's Last Voyage in the Pacific Ocean, 1776-1779

Map No. 3 Data from Ledyard's Map (Hartford, 1783) courtesy of the Bibliographical Society of America

sensation in geographical circles, so that travelers in the North Pacific continued to search for the mythical passage of de Fonte. Interest was so intense that the Spanish government commissioned D. Martín Fernández Navarrete to search for the original accounts of the voyages of Lorenzo Ferrer Maldonaldo and Admiral de Fonte. Navarrete not only discharged this task but also included the expedition of Juan de Fuca. He concluded that all of these voyages were "apocryphal," but as his work was not published until 1802, some time after his death, the refutation of the current popular geographers did not appear in time to prevent many of the later Spanish mariners from looking for this mythical passage.

Following his instructions, Cook sailed around the Cape of Good Hope, across the Indian Ocean, touched at Van Diemen's Land (Australia), and New Zealand; and then set his course across the Pacific, where he explored and visited the Friendly Islands, Tahiti, and the Society Islands. Leaving these on December 8, 1777, he crossed the equator, discovered the Hawaiian Islands, and on Sunday, March 29, 1778, made a landfall in latitude 44° 43′ north and longitude 235° 20′ east of Greenwich. Standing north, he passed a cape to which he gave the name Flattery. Cook remarked:

> It is in this very latitude where we now were that geographers have placed the pretended strait of Juan de Fuca. But we saw nothing like it; nor is there the least probability that ever any such thing existed.

Finally, in latitude 49° 33′ north and longitude 233° 12′ east of Greenwich, he entered a bay to which he gave the name King George's Sound, but which later was called by its original one, Nootka Sound. Here he became acquainted for the first time with the natives of the northwest coast, observed their customs, and prepared for his voyage to the north.

Leaving Nootka Sound on April 26, Cook proceeded north, but because of thick weather he did not see land again until he reached latitude 57°, when he sighted a mountain to which he gave the name Mount Edgecumbe. Mount Fairweather was his next important landmark, and then Cross Sound was passed and named. In latitude 59° 18′, he felt himself to be near landfall of the Bering expedition, for he remarks in his *Voyage,* "It is here where I suppose Commodore Beering to have anchored." To the north he descried a mountain, which "we supposed to be Beering's Mount St. Elias." Rounding Kayak Island, he entered Prince William Sound, as he named it. Proceeding along the coast, actually Kenai Peninsula, he rounded Cape Hermogenes and entered a bay which he assumed to be the estuary of a river. He persevered in penetrating the so-called river as far as was consistent with safety, remarking:

> It was a satisfaction to me however, to reflect, that if I had not examined this very considerable inlet, it would have been assumed, by speculative fabricators of geography, as a fact, that it communicated with the sea to the north, or with Baffin's or Hudson's Bay to the east, and have been marked, perhaps, on future maps of the world, with greater precision, and more certain signs of reality, than the invisible, because imaginary Straits of de Fuca and of de Fonte.

As Cook had left a blank for the name of the supposed river and then neglected to fill it in, Lord Sandwich directed that the name Cook be given to it. This is Cook Inlet.

Running out of the inlet with the ebb tide, Cook tried at first to go through Shelikof Strait, but since the wind was not favorable, he passed between Kodiak Island and Cape Elizabeth (the southwestern end of Kenai Peninsula) and proceeded southward, keeping to the east of Kodiak. Rounding the south end of Kodiak, he saw and named Trinity Islands; then turning westward, he sighted the Shumagin group, which he avoided by a wide sweep southward on account of the presence of reefs. For some reason he identified one of the westerly islands of this group as Kodiak Island. Finally sighting Pogromni Volcano, he steered for this landmark and so opened Unimak Pass, running northwestward between Unimak and Unalaska.

Though there were evidences of the proximity of Russians, from whom he might have learned much, a search for them would have meant delay; and Cook refused to be diverted from the major purpose of the expedition, the exploration of the coast northward of 65° of north latitude. Entering Bristol Bay, he was prevented from following the coast by thick weather; but as he felt his way northward, he came in sight of a cape which he named Newenham. He rounded it, entering the delta of the Kuskokwim River. Shoaling water here forced him to retire as he had come in; and, as even to the west there were shoals, he pushed well south before turning west. He proceeded cautiously northward in heavy fog, missing the island of Nunivak and the mouth of the Yukon River. The first prominent landmark he picked up was Sledge Island in the vicinity of Nome. An island was seen to the northwest, probably St. Lawrence. He then entered Bering Strait, the land trending off to the northwest, and soon was able to see that this land was a part of the American continent and that it was probably its most westerly point. Unable to make Cape Prince of Wales, he stood out into the strait to secure anchorage behind the Diomede Islands but changed his mind and decided instead to cross over to the Asiatic coast, where he made his first acquaintance of the Chukchi. From here he directed his course first to the east, then passed through the strait with both coasts in sight, and headed northeast. In latitude 70° 33′, he was turned back by ice. Sailing south again, he discovered and named Cape Lisburne in latitude 69° 5′, and after getting clear of the ice, directed his course to the west towards Asia, continuing in this direction until he was finally stopped by ice. He retreated, and then when his vessels were well clear of ice, turned towards the coast and continued as far as he could go in a westerly direction before again being held up by ice and the proximity of a dangerously low coast, which made it expedient to retire eastward. As he followed the coast back, he identified what he believed to be the Serdze Kamen of Müller and finally a point beyond, where the coast, which had hitherto been trending southeast, now turned south. Cook assumed that this point was the eastern tip of the continent, hence he gave to it the name East Cape. After he rounded this, the weather cleared, and he saw the whole of the Asiatic side of the strait and perhaps, though he fails to say so, the American side, too. The southern end of the coast that forms the Asiatic side of the strait he identified as Chukotskii Cape (Tschukotskoi Nos). From this point he crossed to the American side to clear up a further difficulty that still remained, namely, the possibility that the peninsula of which Cape Prince of Wales is the western extremity might be an island—the Island of Alaschka of

Staehlin. But the sound (Norton Sound) he entered proved to be really a bay. This discovery therefore ended his explorations. Because the search for wood and water, to which he then gave his attention, proved disappointing, he stood out to sea to clear the shoal water near the delta of the Yukon, which he again missed, and set his course for Unalaska. It was reached on October 3. Here in the old roadstead of Samganoodha, Captain Cook anchored.

On Unalaska he had his first meeting with Russians. Corporal Ledyard of the marines was sent out to scour the country in search of the Cook party, since there were signs of an expedition's being in the neighborhood. His search was successful, and Captain Cook was visited by a number of Russian *promyshlenniki*. Some days afterwards Gerasim Grigorievich Ismailov, who apparently was in charge of Russian interests, appeared and was entertained by Cook. Ismailov was a very interesting man. He was thoroughly familiar with the North Pacific, had served an apprenticeship as navigator, and had been sent by the Russian government on some of the early expeditions to the Aleutians. He had later accompanied Lieutenant Synd on his voyage into Bering Sea and, as Cook tells us, had accompanied the adventurer Benyowski on his wild dash for freedom down the China coast in 1771, and had made his way back to Europe.

Although neither of these men spoke the other's language, both managed to exchange information on geography. Ismailov was able to give Cook information on the number and location of the islands. Regarding Bering Sea and Bering Strait, he could do little more than retail for Cook's benefit what was generally known of Bering's first expedition, the first Kamchatka expedition. There is no doubt that Ismailov also received much useful information from Cook, particularly on Prince William Sound, which no Russian up to that time had seen.

From Unalaska the members of Cook's expedition proceeded to the Hawaiian Islands, where they proposed to spend the winter before resuming their explorations. However, during the winter Cook met his death at the hands of the natives. The command of the expedition then devolved on Captain Clerke, and Captain Gore took command of the *Discovery*. Sailing northward to make a second attempt to find a northwest passage in accordance with instruc-

Courtesy Fish and Wildlife Service

FUR SEALS ON ST. PAUL ISLAND

Courtesy Fish and Wildlife Service

CARIBOU

tions from the Admiralty, they found their way into Avacha Bay and anchored before Petropavlovsk on May 4. They presented the letters they had received from Ismailov and proceeded to secure what provisions they could in Kamchatka. Stores were procured with great difficulty, but on the morning of June 13 they dropped down the bay and with the ebb tide stood out to sea.

Running north, they endeavored to keep close inshore in order to get accurate observations of the latitude and longitude of the important landmarks. But fog enveloped them until they were well into Bering Strait, where they located St. Lawrence Island and Chukotskii Nos. Through the strait they were favored with exceptional weather, which enabled them to see both continents, as well as the Diomede Islands. After entering the Arctic Ocean, their experiences differed little from those of the previous year. Their northward progress was barred by ice near latitude 70°, and, turning south to get clear of the ice, they then steered westward to make what progress they could in that direction. But again they were forced back, and Captain Clerke resolved on one more attempt to pass through the ice on the American coast. His second effort had no more success than his first, and in latitude 70° it was decided to give up all further attempts to penetrate the ice here and to go back to essay further exploration on the Asiatic side. This decision resulted in their getting into ice and having the *Discovery* considerably damaged in addition to the serious risk they ran. Captain Gore appealed to Clerke to turn south to repair the damage and to abandon all attempts to find the long-sought passage.

It can now be seen that the expedition begun by Captain Cook and carried through by his subordinates described the general contours of the northeastern part of Asia and the northwestern part of America beyond all doubt. They had sailed twice through Bering Strait into a great ocean beyond, where their progress was stopped not by the presence of land but by floating ice. They had sailed along the coasts of both continents, in the one case to the northwest and in the other to the northeast, to the vicinity of latitude 70° north. The question of whether the two continents were joined together was for all practical purposes answered in the negative. But two circumstances still left the remotest possibility that Cook might have been mistaken. One was that the surveys of the Arctic coast of Siberia had never been joined together. Dmitrii Laptev had in 1739 succeeded in reaching slightly beyond the mouth of the Kolyma, while the farthest point reached by Cook was Cape North. The gap, therefore, would be three hundred and fifty miles or less, as the crow flies. In the words of Captain King:

> The continent, left undetermined in our chart, between Cape North and the mouth of the Kolyma, is, in longitudinal extent, one hundred and twenty-five leagues. One third, or about forty leagues, of this distance, from the Kolyma eastward, was explored in the year 1723, by a Sinbojarskoi of Jakutz, whose name was Feodor Amossoff; by whom Mr. Müller was informed, that its direction was to the Eastward. It is said to have been since accurately surveyed by Shalauroff, whose chart makes it trend to the North East by East, as far as Shelatskoi Noss, which he places about forty-three leagues to the Eastward of the Kolyma. The space between this Noss and Cape North, about eighty-two leagues, is therefore the only part of the Russian empire that now remains unascertained.
>
> But if the River Kolyma be erroneously situated with respect to its longitude, as well as in its latitude, a supposition for which probable grounds are not wanting, the extent of the unexplored coast will become proportionately diminished. . . . If this be so, it will follow, that, as we were probably not more than 1° to the southward of Shelatskoi Noss, only sixty miles of the Asiatic coast remained unascertained.

The other circumstance was the false deductions that had been drawn by Müller from experiences of early Russian travelers and incorporated in Russian maps, thus acquiring currency simply because the conclusions had never been contradicted. Captain King explained the situation in these words:

> Mr. Müller, in his map, published in the year 1754, supposes the country to extend towards the North East, to the 75° of latitude, and in longitude 190° East of Greenwich, and to terminate in a round cape, which he calls Tschukotskoi Noss. To the southward of this cape, he conceives the coast to form a bay to the westward, bounded in latitude 67° 18′ by Serdze Kamen, the Northernmost point seen by Beering in his expeditions in the year 1728. The map, published by the academy of St. Petersburg, in the year 1776, gives the whole peninsula entirely

a new form, placing its North easternmost extremity in the latitude 73°, longitude 178° 30′. All the other maps we saw, both printed and in manuscript, vary between these two, apparently more according to the fancy of the compiler, than on any grounds of more accurate information. The only point in which there is any general coincidence, without any considerable variation, is in the position of East Cape in latitude 66°. The form of the coast, both to the South and North of this Cape, in the map of the academy, is exceedingly erroneous, and may be totally disregarded. In that of Mr. Müller, the coast to the Northward bears a considerable resemblance to our survey, except that it does not trend sufficiently to the Westward; receding only about 5° of longitude, between the latitude of 66° and 69°; whereas in reality, it recedes near ten. Between the latitude 69° and 74° he makes the coast bend round to the North and North East, and to form a considerable promontory.

In other words, although only a relatively small part of the northern coast of Siberia had been left unexplored, geographers, following Müller's lead, had seen fit to place there a great promontory stretching out towards the north and northeast to latitude 75° and approaching, if not actually reaching, the northern coast of America. To this promontory the name of Chukotskoi Nos was given. King, undoubtedly following Captain Cook, claimed that this error was due entirely to false interpretation placed on early exploration, particularly that credited to Deshnev; that no such promontory existed and no recent geographical exploration gave the slightest confirmation of this fantastic idea; that it was reasonable to suppose that the extent of coast that had not been described merely trended in the same general direction observed both to the east and to the west of the area. Because this reasonable conjecture of Cook's has since been borne out, it does not seem improper to give him the credit for having proved the separation of the two continents and having correctly described the northern coasts of the continents on either side of Bering Strait.

The voyage of Captain James Cook made history even more than that of Vitus Bering. Cook's sailors on their arrival in Canton were able to dispose of their stock of sea-otter skins for two thousand pounds, though they had already allowed a number either to spoil or to be disposed of in barter. King records that the members of the crew were seized with a frantic desire to return to the northwest coast to engage in fur trade to make their fortunes. It was difficult for him to check this urge. He was somewhat carried away himself by the idea and proposed to organize, at some future time, an expedition to sail from India in quest of furs. This design of Cook's men fell to the lot of others to carry through.

As has been pointed out, Cook had, despite the lack of a common language, managed to acquire some information from Gerasim Ismailov at Unalaska, and Ismailov had doubtless also received valuable information from Cook. Likewise, after Cook's death when the expedition commanded by Clerke had visited Petropavlovsk and had entertained the local populace and been entertained by them, there was considerable exchange of information. During these meetings the Russians for the first time had heard of Prince William Sound, which had not yet been visited by Europeans, and had been told of the abundance and size of the sea-otter skins to be obtained from the natives. It was therefore inevitable that great efforts would be put forth to open these regions for exploitation.

VI

English Traders Clash with Spain

NEXT TO THE RUSSIANS, THE EARLIEST IN THE FIELD OF NORTH Pacific explorations were the English. Word of the profits to be won from the trade in sea otters passed around English circles at Canton, and thus it was from there that the first venture was made. In April, 1785, Captain James Hanna sailed from Macao in a small brig for the northwest coast. In spite of brushes with the Indians he secured a valuable cargo of five hundred sea-otter skins. His success prompted him to repeat the expedition the next year in the *Sea Otter,* with what results it is not known. Hanna was followed in 1787 by at least three expeditions, all English: the first that of Captain John Meares in the *Nootka* and Captain Tipping in the *Sea Otter* from Bengal; the second from Bombay in the *Captain Cook,* commanded by Captain Lowrie, and the *Experiment,* commanded by Captain Guise; the third equipped and dispatched by the King George's Sound Company from England in the *King George,* commanded by Captain Nathaniel Portlock, and the *Queen Charlotte,* under the command of Captain George Dixon. After calling at Nootka Sound both of these last vessels made their way north along the coast, at least one of them running into and exploring Prince William Sound before setting out on the return to China and Europe.

Captain Meares set his course northward from the Hawaiian Islands, ran far to the west, and as a result encountered the usual fog that hangs over the Aleutians. After the ship had barely escaped destruction, the fog lifted, and a Russian boat came out and piloted the party into Unalaska Bay. Since it was not possible to trade with the Russians, Meares weighed anchor, slipped out, and, coasting along the Alaska Peninsula, passed through Shelikof Strait and entered Cook Inlet. Here again he found the Russians active; therefore, he proceeded northeast along the coast into Prince William Sound. There he was caught by cold weather, and his decision to winter at that point proved disastrous. Scurvy attacked his men, and twenty-three of the crew died before the ship was released from the ice the following spring. When Captains Portlock and Dixon returned from wintering in the Hawaiian Islands, they entered Prince William Sound, where they found and succored Meares, despite the fact that he was infringing on the monopoly of the South Sea Company for which Dixon was trading. However, Dixon, in return for the assistance he had given, exacted a promise from Meares that he would immediately leave the coast without engaging further in trade. Thus began the bitter controversy and violent recrimination in which Dixon and Meares engaged for many years.

Portlock and Dixon continued their voyage separately, the *King George* under Portlock remaining on the Alaska coast while Dixon proceeded southward. He spent some time in the neighborhood of the Queen Charlotte Islands, which he named, and gave his own name to the strait between this archipelago and Prince of Wales Island. He finally headed for the Hawaiian Islands and made his way to China the following year, 1788. Other expeditions of the year 1787 were those of Captain Barkley of the *Imperial Eagle,* sailing under the Austrian flag from Ostend, and Captains Colnett and Duncan, commanding respectively the *Prince of Wales* and the *Princess Royal,* who had left England in September, 1786. The crews of these last two ships encountered Dixon in the vicinity of the Queen Charlotte Islands, where they appear to have traded.

Meares returned to China and then went on to India, where he proceeded to organize a company of merchants. Returning to Macao, he brought into the company a Portuguese, Cavalho by name, and through him obtained Portuguese papers and employed Portuguese captains. His purpose ostensibly was to avoid the heavy port dues levied on the English, but he probably also availed himself of Portuguese registry to make unnecessary the obtaining of licenses from the East Indian and the South Sea companies. Two vessels were equipped—the *Felice Adventurer,* commanded by Captain Meares, and the *Iphigenia Nubiana,* commanded by Captain William Douglas. Leaving Macao in January, 1788, the *Iphigenia* directed her course to the Alaska coast. Captain Meares landed at Nootka Sound on May 13. He put ashore stores and workmen, with instructions to build a house and to lay the keel of a vessel to be built for the coast trade. Meares himself left on a trip southward for the combined purposes of exploration and trade, from which he returned on July 26. On his way north he had taken possession of Juan de Fuca straits and the surrounding regions in the name of King George. Just outside Nootka Sound he met Captain Duncan in the *Princess Royal,* outward bound after a successful year on the coast. In the sound he found one of the two American ships which had reached the coast that spring, the first in these waters—the *Lady Washington* under Captain Gray. The cargoes of fur were put on board the *Felice,* which left for China on September 21. The next day Captain Gray's companion ship, the *Columbia* under Captain Kendrick, arrived from the Alaska coast where the commander had been trading. The *Iphigenia Nubiana* and the *Northwest Coast,* the snow that had been built by Meares' men here, left in October to spend the winter in Hawaii. Kendrick and Gray prepared to winter in Nootka Sound. In the spring of 1789 Gray made a trading trip to the north and returned in the latter half of June after some success.

Meanwhile the activity in the North Pacific roused Spain to resume her explorations, which had been suspended since 1780. The Spanish government had become alarmed over the voyage of La Perouse in 1786, the object of which was said to be the acquisition by France of trading posts on the northwest coast. Even more alarming were the rumors of the continued Russian advance and the fear that she was endeavoring to expand southward. A royal order was issued that an expedition consisting of two vessels should be dispatched northward in 1788 on a reconnaissance to attempt to find out what Muscovite intentions were in these regions. Don Estévan José Martínez, chosen to command the *Princesa* and to head the expedition, had accompanied Pérez on his voyage of 1774. López de Haro, to be second in command in the *San Carlos,* had recently been brought from the Caribbean Sea to the west coast. The viceroy, Flórez, issued precise orders to these leaders, defining the purpose of the expedition and stating the course they were to follow. Proceeding north to Prince William Sound, they tried to enter the sound by the north entrance, but were unable to do so and finally desisted in their attempt. They did, however, discover definite traces of the Russians in what seems to have been an abandoned post on one of the islands. On leaving the sound, they became separated. Martínez sailed past Kodiak to the Trinity Islands, where his ship was boarded by a Russian and some natives, from whom he gleaned meager information through the interpreter, Mendofia.[1] López de Haro was more fortunate. Indians, approaching his vessel in canoes, induced him to come ashore, where he found the settlement of Three Saints with Delarov in charge. In spite of the absence of the interpreter, the two men got on famously, and the Spaniard secured considerable information about the Russian posts in the North Pacific.

On July 3 Haro joined his commander off the Trinity Islands, and together they proceeded to Unalaska. They anchored in the bay and fired their guns when a *baidarka* was seen approaching them from shore. It proved to have on board the Russian commandant, Potap Kuzmich Zaikov, whom we have met before as one of the pioneers in Prince William Sound. The Spaniards remained from July 22 to August 18 and visited back and forth on land and on shipboard with the Russians. Martínez was able to satisfy to the full his curiosity concerning the nature and extent of the Russian establishment. The most sensational development, however, was the confirmation of the news already communicated to Haro by Delarov on Kodiak, that the Empress Catherine intended to send an expedition of four vessels (two, according to Delarov) to occupy Nootka Sound and so forestall the English.

This story does not carry much conviction. It was already of ancient vintage, since the Russian admitted that he had heard it in 1785 from an English captain who had visited these waters.[2] The most plausible explanation is that it was a rumor in garbled form of the Billings expedition, planned as early as 1785 and now carrying out its preliminary tasks on the northern Asiatic coast. At any rate Spanish nerves were jumpy, and the report received by the

[1] The natives astonished the Spaniards by insisting on calling the ship's dog "Towser," a fairly sure indication that they had been in contact with nationals of a third European power.

[2] There is no known voyage of an English vessel into the North Pacific in 1785, nor does the name of the Englishman, Grek (according to Delarov), sound very convincing.

viceroy was accepted by him as sufficient grounds for the dispatch of a further expedition in 1789 to occupy Nootka Sound. The same two commanders and the same vessels were chosen. They left San Blas on February 17, 1789. Their purpose was to head off the Russians. Actually it was the English whom they found at the sound, and it was a clash with them that precipitated the Nootka Sound affair.

On reaching the sound on May 6, Martínez found the *Iphigenia* under Captain Douglas in considerable distress, which the Spaniard did his best to relieve. Haro arrived on the thirteenth. On the fourteenth Martínez, after having a meeting with Kendrick, returned, summoned Douglas and Viana (the Portuguese captain) on board and declared them his prisoners and the *Iphigenia* prize of war. Later he apparently relented, released the ship and her captains, furnished them with supplies for Hawaii, receiving bills on Macao in exchange. In addition, Douglas agreed in writing that if the vessel were declared lawful prize of war, she would be restored to Spain. Under protest, but as a condition of release, he signed what purported to be written instructions to turn over the *Northwest America* to the Spanish on his return. Actually the document merely informed Funton of the Spaniard's demand and left it to his own discretion to conform to it or not. Leaving Nootka Sound, Douglas turned to the north and spent the rest of the season on the northwest coast.

Martínez took possession of the *Northwest America* on its return and sent it off on a trading cruise, the original crew being sent to China on the *Columbia*. Meanwhile, on June 14, the *Princess Royal,* commanded by Captain Hudson, arrived from Macao reporting the bankruptcy of Cavalho and Company. On July 3 Captain James Colnett arrived in the *Argonaut*, and fresh trouble started. Martínez was already exasperated by the now worthless bills he had accepted on Macao for the supplies he had let Douglas have. Therefore, when Colnett informed him in no uncertain terms that he had authority to take possession in the name of the English king, authority which he intended to use, a quarrel ensued between the two commanders on board the *Princesa*. Martínez promptly put Colnett under arrest, took possession of the *Argonaut* as prize, and made its crew prisoners. The *Princess Royal* under

Captain Hudson, which returned on July 14, was treated in the same way. Both vessels were dispatched to San Blas as prizes, with the captains and crews as prisoners. Thus began the famous Nootka Sound controversy between Great Britain and Spain.

The first word of the difficulties between Martínez and Colnett reached Spain on December 30, 1789, in a letter written by Viceroy Flórez from Mexico City; this was followed three days later by a packet of documents that had been forwarded from Mexico City on September 26. News of the contents of these papers began to leak out, and on the basis of the rumors Anthony Merry, the English chargé d'affaires at Madrid, gave his government a conjectural account of the proceedings. But it was not until February 11 that the secretary of state for foreign affairs, the Duke of Leeds, received from the Spanish ambassador the first official though very incomplete and distorted account of the incident. The British reply to this communication took an uncompromising tone:

> As yet no precise information has been received relative to the events mentioned in your excellency's letter, but while awaiting such I have His Majesty's orders to inform your excellency that the act of violence spoken of in your letters as having been committed by Mr. Martinez, in seizing a British vessel under the circumstances reported, makes it necessary henceforth to suspend all discussion of the pretensions set forth in that letter until a just and adequate satisfaction shall have been made for a proceeding so injurious to Great Britain.[3]

The English note was received in Spain with considerable indignation, and the Spanish government forthwith began immediate preparations for war, though without giving England cause for alarm. The reply of Spain on April 20 reasserted in typical manner the "incontestable right of Spain to exclusive sovereignty, navigation and commerce," but sought to disarm the English and calm resentment by announcing that the Viceroy had liberated the prisoners and the vessels.

[3] Letters from Leeds to Campo, Whitehall, February 26, 1790. MS documents copied from the *Archivo Histórico Nacional,* Madrid, Sec. *Estado* 4291. Cited by William Ray Manning in "The Nootka Sound Controversy," *Annual Report,* American Historical Association, 1904 (Fifty-eighth Congress, 3 sess., *House Doc.* 429, Ser. 4884), 369–70.

At this juncture Captain Meares arrived in London and at once submitted a memorial to the British government. As a result the British government confirmed its unyielding course towards Spain and pressed for the satisfaction that had been demanded. Efforts to put the British fleet on a war footing were immediately redoubled, and feelers were extended towards England's partners in the Triple Alliance, Prussia and Holland, for presentation of a united front.

Meanwhile Spain was far from idle in her military and diplomatic preparations. She had joined the Family Compact, which insured joint action with France. Indeed, the two had co-operated as early as the Seven Years' War, as well as in the war for American independence. It was therefore natural that Spain should now turn to France for diplomatic and military support; France, however, was in the throes of the revolution. In January, 1790, Floridablanca sent to the French minister of foreign affairs a dispatch couched in the most general terms but laying the ground for a future appeal. In April the Spanish ambassador at the French court was directed to ask for a conference with the French minister on the crisis which had arisen in Anglo-Spanish relations. The French government, in deference to Spain's request, put some of its naval forces on a war footing. The announcement of this move and the international tension which occasioned it precipitated a debate in the National Assembly as to whether the right to make peace and war rested with the king or the people. The armament was approved, but after a lengthy debate it was decreed that war could be declared only by the Assembly and then only after a formal proposal of the king, whose confirmation of its decision was also required.

The formal demand of Spain for French armed support on June 16 drew from Montmorin, the French minister of foreign affairs, the response that the matter must be submitted to the Assembly and determined by that body, but the request was not presented to the Assembly until August 3. It was decided then that, since the question involved a treaty to which France was a party and might lead to war, it should be referred to the diplomatic committee of the Assembly. Mirabeau, as spokesman for this committee, submitted its report on August 25. The committee recommended that the defensive and commercial terms of the treaty should be adhered to, but that negotiations should be opened for revising and renewing the treaty as a whole. This report was adopted in the Assembly on August 26.

Meanwhile, the dilatory actions of the French Assembly had convinced Floridablanca that he could not expect effective support from that quarter. He therefore agreed on July 22 to an exchange of declarations with the British government, by which Spain undertook to give the British complete satisfaction, restoring the vessels seized and indemnifying the persons interested for their losses. Spain however, maintained that this action did not prejudice Spanish claims to an exclusive establishment at Nootka; Britain, on the other hand, in the counterdeclaration, just as stoutly upheld British rights to make an establishment at Nootka. This exchange settled only the question of satisfaction for seizure, and left undetermined the respective rights of the two countries on the northwest coast. To back her demands that the matter must still be settled, Britain continued her warlike preparations. However, the British cabinet drew up a plan for a treaty and submitted it to Spain. Since it involved the question of a frontier between Spanish and British possessions about which little was known, Floridablanca preferred to negotiate a temporary or provisional settlement; and broad hints of a possible alliance with England were thrown out. The result of this friendly gesture was merely to convince England that Spain was yielding and should be pressed still harder. Accordingly, on September 10, the British government submitted peremptory demands that Spain should come to an immediate settlement. Two alternative projects for a treaty were forwarded, and the Spanish government was given ten days to return a definite reply.

On being received in Madrid, these demands were brought before an extraordinary session of the *Junta*. After considering the situation, it recommended their summary rejection. Despite this action and with a view to working out a compromise, Floridablanca continued to negotiate with Fitzherbert, the British minister. On October 24 Floridablanca was able to report to the British Minister that the King of Spain had agreed to the final draft of the treaty which the two had worked out. The exchange of full powers was carried out on October 26, and on October 28 the formal act of signing the treaty took place.

The treaty provided for restoration of buildings and lands of which any British subjects had been dispossessed since April, 1789, and for just reparation for acts of violence and hostility to which they had been subjected. Subjects of both England and Spain were to be free to navigate, fish, or trade throughout the Pacific, provided English subjects did not make such activity a pretext for carrying on illicit trade with Spanish subjects. As an additional measure to prevent such trade, it was decreed that British subjects were not to approach for this purpose closer than ten maritime leagues any part of the coast held by Spain. There was no definite pronouncement with regard to the territorial limits within which each of the powers was to exercise exclusive rights, and to that extent the treaty failed to delimit what each country was to possess. But it certainly put an end to Spanish pretensions to a monopoly of the northwest coast of America, as contemporaries recognized.

The ships and crews affected by the seizure of Martínez had already been released by Revillagigedo even before the receipt of definite instructions from Madrid to let them go. Damages were finally paid to the extent of $210,000. With regard to the buildings and property, Vancouver was instructed to meet Quadra, the Spanish captain, at Nootka in 1792 and receive them back. But Quadra, on inquiry, claimed not to be able to learn of any buildings and property that had been owned by Meares in Nootka Sound. The matter was referred to England, and on January 11, 1794, a further convention was concluded, according to which a British official was to receive from a Spanish official the buildings and lands of which British subjects were dispossessed. Then he was to unfurl the British flag as a sign of possession, both officials were to withdraw, and both governments agreed to make no further permanent establishment there, though both were to have access to the port. Thus the Nootka Sound case was finally closed.

This incident, which has been described at length, was of supreme importance in settling territorial claims to the northwest coast. Though occasioned by events that might be considered trivial, it was a critical point in diplomatic relations of the great powers. In some respects its issues seem to have little to do with the circumstances in which it originated. But it produced a profound change in the fortunes of at least two of the major states—Great Britain and Spain.

Whatever else the American Revolution may have been in English history, it was a great diplomatic defeat. George III's heart had been set on getting rid of the Whig party and on charting his own course in domestic affairs. But in accomplishing these objectives, he had made two major mistakes in foreign relations. He had alienated Frederick II of Prussia by cutting off the English subsidies, and he had allowed English sea power to be overtaken by France, thanks to the farsightedness of Vergennes. The result was that when the Revolutionary War broke out, Great Britain was isolated from the Continent; she was sure of France's enmity and the Family Compact insured that of Spain. Her attempt to stop commercial intercourse between the New World and Europe led to the League of Armed Neutrality. She was "ringed about with enemies," and nothing but a miracle could prevent her from being despoiled—and the miracle was not forthcoming. A series of ghastly mistakes cost her her colonies, and she suffered one of the bitterest humiliations in her long history. When Pitt took over the direction of England's affairs, it fell to his lot to repair Britain's fences, a job which he did with consummate skill. The commercial treaty of 1785 with France, negotiated under the treaty of Versailles "on terms of reciprocity and mutual convenience," while a wise measure, was felt to have been imposed on England as a result of military defeat and grudgingly granted as little as possible. Nevertheless, by 1788 Pitt had welded together the Triple Alliance with the Netherlands and Prussia. This gave Pitt new confidence in facing Spain. The weakening of the Family Compact as a result of the revolution in France held before him the prospect of inflicting humiliation on Spain and destroying once and for all her claims to a monopoly on the coast. England's whole career as a colonizing power on the eastern coast of North America was a challenge to that claim, however Spain might cling to her shadowy rights to all the rest of the new continent, rights which she hoped to assert with the aid of France. Queen Elizabeth's reply, given in 1580 to the Spanish ambassador who complained of the plunder of one of his sovereign's vessels by the English, admirably expressed the English point of view at this later date:

That the Spaniards had drawn these inconveniences upon themselves by their severe and unjust dealings in their American commerce; for she did not understand why either her subjects, or those of any other European prince, should be debarred from traffic with the Indies; that, as she did not acknowledge the Spaniards to have any title, by donation of the Bishop of Rome, so she knew no right they had to any places other than those they were in actual possession of; for their having touched only here and there upon the coast, and given names to a few rivers or capes, were such insignificant things as could in no way entitle them to a propriety farther than in the parts where they actually settled, and continued to inhabit.

Moreover, a second weak joint in the Spanish armor was the grave unrest in the Spanish colonies. Stimulated by the success of the English colonies in throwing off the control of England, it was in great part the result of centuries of bad colonial government by Spain. The arrival in England at this time of Miranda, the South American revolutionist, and his talks with Pitt suggested to Pitt the chance of doing Spain a mortal injury and perhaps ultimately securing for England some compensation for her colonial losses. Pitt certainly played with the idea of an English expedition to the New World to rouse the Spanish colonists against the mother country—a proposal that later, when England went to war with Spain in 1796, assumed concrete form. But his firmest hopes seemed to rest on splitting the Family Compact. He unquestionably had secret dealings with the elements that controlled the National Assembly, and, while there seems to be no proof of money changing hands, it is certainly a fact that the attitude of Mirabeau, Lameth, Robespierre and others coincided exactly with the interests of England.

VII

Catherine Concerns Herself with America

IT SEEMS THAT THE ACTIONS OF RUSSIA HAD AN EVEN DEEPER SIGNIFIcance than those of England. On her assumption of power in 1762 the Empress Catherine had been too preoccupied to concern herself with affairs in her distant dominions or in far commercial enterprises. She had, however, interested herself from time to time, as leisure allowed or fancy dictated, in her remote Asiatic possessions. Of course, even under Elizabeth, the authorities had to concern themselves with commercial voyages across the North Pacific. As has been related, it was customary on these expeditions to levy *yassak* in furs and for this purpose to send along a Cossack to represent the government, who saw that the tax was levied and collected in the proper way. But it was not until Catherine's time that we find vital interest on the part of the sovereign. A rescript of Catherine's, dated March 2, 1766, which enjoined the *promyshlenniki* to treat kindly their new brothers, implies that official action had been taken to annex the Aleutians. But the fact that gifts of the finest skins were frequently sent to St. Petersburg and that the fur traders often secured a remission of the regular levy of 10 per cent, suggests that the merchants were not overlooking the possibility of obtaining imperial protection and perhaps a monopoly of the fur trade. Catherine was, however, soon preoccupied with the first Turkish War, the Pugachev Revolt, and the Partition of Poland, and these activities effectively prevented her from showing more than casual interest in other matters. She did manage to send out two voyages of discovery, the voyage of Lieutenant Synd into Bering Sea in 1764 and the expedition of Lieutenants Krenitsyn and Levashev to the Aleutian Islands in 1768–69. For the rest the Empress contented herself with bestowing medals on the men who returned, explorers especially, if they had laid claim to land in the name of the Russian crown.

ALEXANDER BARANOV

Catherine Concerns Herself with America

It was not until after 1780 that Catherine was able to pick up the thread of Eastern matters. Her foreign policy now took a new turn. She had humbled the Ottoman Porte and all but acquired the so long desired littoral of the Black Sea. Her League of Armed Neutrality had greatly strengthened Russia in foreign affairs, while England, France, and Spain had become involved in expensive and exhausting wars. Thus Catherine felt free to resume the expansion of her empire in the East. A new expedition rivaling that of Bering was now, under the impulse of P. S. Pallas, the scientist, in the making; and Joseph Billings, an English mariner who had served under Cook, had been chosen for the task of completing the work begun by Bering.

This expedition left St. Petersburg late in 1785 and arrived at Yakutsk at the beginning of 1786. From Yakutsk the party crossed the mountains to Okhotsk; and, after leaving crews to construct seagoing vessels, the expedition set out northwards to the headwaters of the Kolyma. Here the men constructed boats and descended the Kolyma to its mouth during the early part of 1787. In June they made a series of unsuccessful attempts to push north and east towards Bering Strait. Billings finally gave up the attempt and returned to Yakutsk and thence to Okhotsk. By the end of 1789 the seagoing vessels had been constructed and the stores assembled for the sea voyage to America. When the vessels were launched, one of them came to grief on the bar at the mouth of the Okhota River; but with the other Billings sailed for Petropavlovsk. Here he built a second small seagoing craft to replace the one lost at Okhotsk. In the spring of the year 1790 he sailed for America. He passed south of the Aleutians towards Kodiak. He had been authorized to assume the title of fleet captain of the first rank when he reached Cape St. Elias (on Kayak Island) at the entrance to Prince William Sound. This he now proceeded to do, and then returned to Kamchatka for the winter. The following year he proceeded along the north side of the Aleutians to Unalaska, turned north into Bering Sea, then into Bering Strait, and so into the Arctic. Unable to penetrate westward to the Kolyma River, he returned to the mouth of the Anadyr River and made a land journey across to the Kolyma River, which he ascended to its headwaters, arriving at Yakutsk in 1792.

The results of the Billings' explorations were of slight consequence. He had utterly failed to fill in the gaps on the map of the Arctic coast of Siberia. Catherine, who could usually rely on her own judgment to select the right man for the task, in this case had taken the advice of others, and Billings accomplished little more than Synd or Krenitsyn and Levashev.

One strange incident strongly suggests that behind the Billings expedition a major political move by Russia was afoot in the North Pacific. During 1786 there had appeared at Paris one John Ledyard (Lediard), an American corporal of marines on Captain Cook's last voyage. On his return from this voyage, Ledyard had visited his home in New England, but soon had become restive and decided to go to Europe, where he was variously engaged. In 1786 he had met Thomas Jefferson in Paris and through Jefferson had made the acquaintance of Lafayette. He seems to have accepted a proposal made by Jefferson that he proceed to Russia, make his way across Siberia to Kamchatka, and from there secure passage on a vessel to America. Since Russia at that time had not recognized the United States, it must have been through Lafayette's good services that he had been able to get permission to go to Russia; and his welfare seems to have been looked after by the French embassy. In St. Petersburg he had met Pallas, with whom he had dined, doubtless imparting information and in return receiving certain confidences which he had passed on to Jefferson. These perhaps concerned a secret expedition of four vessels which the Empress was proposing to send to America—not the Billings expedition (which did not have four vessels and which was a matter of public knowledge). What was this secret expedition? Below are related the facts, insofar as they are now ascertainable, that throw light on the proposed voyage.

In the late summer of 1786 there had appeared at Constantinople the celebrated South American revolutionist, Francisco Miranda, who had already been hailed by English newspapers as the future emancipator of Spanish America. From the Russian ambassador to the Sublime Porte, Y. I. Bulgakov, Miranda had received warm recommendations to the governor of Kherson, A. I. Vyasemskii. Armed with these, Miranda arrived at Kherson at the end of September. Through Vyasemskii a meeting with Potemkin was arranged, and through Potemkin Miranda secured an audience with the Empress Catherine at Kiev, when she reached there on her grand tour of the recently acquired provinces of New Russia.

Catherine late in 1786 had received an account of Shelekhov's voyage in 1783–85 to Kodiak Island. It had made a profound impression on her mind, and she had decided to dispatch in the spring of 1787 an expedition of four Russian vessels to the Pacific Ocean under command of G. I. Mulovskii. Later she issued orders for additional keels to be laid. It turned out that a whole new squadron under the English captain, James Trevenin, was to be made up in the spring of 1787 to assert Russian power in the Pacific. It was at this moment that Miranda appeared at the Russian capital. Making use of his services on this expedition to prepare the ground for Russian intervention in the Spanish colonies, the Empress took him under her protection and apparently bestowed a pension on him. When the French and Spanish ambassadors protested against her extension of protection to a traitor Catherine replied: 'Since Madrid and St. Petersburg are a considerable distance apart, her Imperial Majesty can hardly see how Count Miranda can be a menace to the Spanish King." That closed the matter, and Catherine later addressed letters to the various Russian embassies in Europe recommending Miranda to their protection. Miranda found it expedient, however, to cease to wear his uniform as colonel in the Spanish army and to put on that of the Russian army.

The Ottoman Porte in August, 1787, made war on Russia and her new-found Austrian ally. The schemes for an attack on the Spanish possessions in the Pacific area were dropped, but not in time to save Ledyard from an unpleasant experience. He had secured permission to make his way across Siberia on foot. Provided with funds secured by drawing on Sir Joseph Banks in London, he set out in the early summer of 1787 in company with a Scottish physician, William Brown, for Siberia. They reached Irkutsk without mishap, and Ledyard secured the consent of the governor-general to proceed to Yakutsk in company with Lieutenant Laxman. On reaching Yakutsk, he found the commandant rather cold towards his intention of continuing his journey across the Stanovoi Mountains to Okhotsk. The commandant affected great solicitude for the American traveler's welfare, but there is little doubt that he was acting under orders to prevent Ledyard from proceeding further. Meanwhile, Billings reached Yakutsk on his return from the Kolyma; and since he and Ledyard had been shipmates on Cook's last expedition, invited him to accompany him back to Irkutsk. They arrived in the eastern Siberia capital on January 14. On February 24 Ledyard was placed under arrest on explicit instructions from the Empress and was charged with being a spy in French pay. He was hurried off to Moscow under guard. Whether or not he was subjected to an examination there it is difficult to say, but he was eventually conducted to the frontier between Poland and Prussia, which he reached at the beginning of May. Here he was released, with a warning not to return to Russia under pain of death.

It seems obvious that Ledyard, having reached Russia in the absence of the Empress, was at the instance of Count Segur, the French ambassador, given permission to make the journey, but that on her return from her Crimean voyage, Catherine decided to recall him, allegedly for his own protection. It is probable that Catherine's action was not unconnected with her plans for a secret expedition. How much Ledyard knew was uncertain, but she could ill afford to risk an indiscretion on his part. Spain was already becoming nervous about her possessions in the New World now threatened by Russian *promyshlenniki*. It would be little short of disastrous if Catherine's plan leaked out, for Spain was in a position to embarrass Russia by withholding use of her ports from Russian naval forces operating in the Mediterranean.

VIII

Free Trading Gives Way to Monopoly

THE FURS WHICH CAPTAIN COOK'S CREW BROUGHT WITH THEM TO Canton from America made no little stir among the English traders there. Furs that had reached China hitherto had for the most part come over the land frontier through Kiakhta and had not been of the first quality. Chinese merchants, to their great delight, now beheld prime sea-otter skins, and so keen was the bidding, that they offered what seemed to the simple sailors fantastic figures. The low-quality skins bought by the sailors for their own personal use were produced and found ready sale. Even worn and soiled skins fetched unbelievable prices. The profits so astounded the English that more than one member of the crew vowed to return, when the present voyage was over, to seek their fortunes on the American coast. News of their good luck found its way back to Bengal on the returning East Indiamen, passed from mouth to mouth along the waterfronts, and spread among the young and venturesome the yearning to seek their share of the riches.

Cook's expedition also fanned to fresh life the ardor of the Siberian traders. Fur trade in the Aleutians was declining, and new sources of furs must now be sought. The chance words dropped by Cook on his visit to Unalaska fell on ears attuned to catch the slightest hint when profits were at stake. The maps showing Cook Inlet and Prince William Sound which he displayed to Zaikov disclosed to the trained *promyshlennik* fresh, inviting fields of endeavor. Zaikov shared the information thus gained with his fellows and communicated his enthusiasm to others. The colony of merchants at Okhotsk, always ready to gamble the profits of one voyage on fitting out another, raised among themselves the necessary funds; and in 1783 three ships sailed under Zaikov to trade in Prince William Sound. One of these ships was placed in charge of Delarov, a Greek; another was commanded by Mukhlopev. The venture came to grief because of the irreconcilable hostility of the natives. The Russians had constantly to be on guard, and this arduous duty left no time to press the trade in furs. The company decided, therefore, to give up any attempt to trade and to go back to the Aleutians.

But Zaikov's failure did not deter others. The Siberian *promyshlennik* may have been a mediocre seaman; individually he was sometimes cruel to the natives; he lived on a primitive moral plane and frequently amid the most squalid surroundings; but courage and enterprise he did not want. His reckless bravado might expose him at times to incredible hardships. His indifference to danger and his neglect of ordinary precautions might involve him in perilous situations, but in tenacity and endurance he had few equals anywhere. The older generation of traders was also, for the most part, made up of men of this type. Some of them had been lost with the ships they sailed. Others had died a pauper's death ashore. Andrean Tolstykh, Glotov, Solov'ev, Ocheredin, and the Panovs had done the pioneering. The new generation now coming to the fore included men who were perhaps more skillful mariners and more experienced traders, but who were of lesser stature, like Samoilov, Izmailov, and Bocharov, competent in their own way, but fitted rather to play subordinate roles. Greeks—like Pelopinisov, Delarov, and Lenzhi—from the Aegean and the Black seas brought to this adventurous world the sea-faring tradition of the Mediterranean and the shrewd trading instinct of the Levantine traders. The new era which now opened demanded a different type —men who had perhaps all these virtues and, in addition, other talents. Originality of conception, breadth of view, knowledge of the world, and the skill of the promoter were needed as conditions for success. No longer were precedents adequate guides, nor were mere endurance and courage sufficient. One had to meet the new, exacting tests of resourcefulness and courage to enter into the new inheritance.

For succeeding in the changed circumstances Grigorii Ivanovich Shelekhov was endowed with unique talents. Born in the city of Rylsk of a merchant family, he migrated to Siberia, where at Okhotsk in 1776 he formed a partnership with Lebedev-Lastochkin of Yakutsk for a trading voyage to the Aleutians. At the same time he shared in another expedition to the Aleutians, from which he and his fellows realized a profit of 74,240 rubles. In 1778 he organized a further venture along with Ivan Solov'ev and Grigorii and Petr Panov for a still more ambitious scheme. The ship they fitted out—the *Barfolomei i Varnava* (*Bartholomew and Barnabas*)—sailed under command of Afanasii Ocheredin to the island of Kodiak in 1779. For taking fur animals they had brought with them Aleuts recruited in their native islands—the first time we hear of this practice of making use of the islanders to trap, a system later adopted by the Russian-American Company. Not content to wait for the return of these ships, Shelekhov managed to send out still another vessel the following year, the *Sv. Ioann Predtechy* (*St. John the Forerunner*), which sailed to the Near Islands and brought back a substantial cargo of peltries to Okhotsk in 1784.

In 1781 Shelekhov had taken a decisive step by entering into formal partnership with Ivan Larionovich Golikov, a merchant of Kursk. Golikov has enjoyed a modest reputation with posterity for having written a pretentious but wretched biography of Peter the Great. In his own day his claim to distinction was that he had been chosen mayor of his native city. He had unhappily been involved in some shady transactions in the collection of taxes, which compromised him with the government. But in eighteenth century Russia this was no bar to advancement, and Golikov had lived down his disgrace and been restored to favor. Of this favor his partner took full advantage. No less momentous for Shelekhov was his marriage with Natalia Alexeyevna, a woman of the gentry. Her wealth and her spirit were to be great assets to her husband in after years. Shelekhov had now realized a modest ambition. His ships had almost invariably come back with rich cargoes. If a ship was lost, he nearly always saved the cargoes, while other merchants lost their fortunes in one shipwreck. More than one of the great figures of this adventurous age died a pauper, but Shelekhov seemed to have the Midas touch. His profits grew. He was able to secure easy loans from the Demidovs, the iron founders of the Urals, and with these resources he resolved to stake all on a still bolder and more ambitious project—the opening of a new fur country along the coast of the mainland of America.

Shelekhov's plan involved nothing less than the fitting out of an expedition of three ships, which were, in the clumsy Russian fashion of the time called *Trekh Sviatitelei* (*Three Saints*), *Sv. Semen i Predskazatel'nitsa Anna* (*St. Simeon and the Prophetess Anna*), and the *Sv. Mikhail* (*St. Michael*). Shelekhov took personal charge of the expedition, and his wife sailed with him. What must have been the feelings of Natalia Alexeyevna, the first European woman to embark onto these stormy wastes, as the shore of Siberia was lost to her view? Desolate as that was, it meant home. Ahead the staunch little vessel breasted the long swell of the ocean as the party made their way into the mists and gloom of the perilous North Pacific.

They left Okhotsk at the opening of summer, crossed the Sea of Okhotsk, and passed through the strait between two of the Kurile Islands, setting a course northward for Bering Island, where two of the vessels arrived late in the season, the other having become separated from them in a storm. Here it was decided to winter. The next spring, although the *St. Michael* had not turned up, Shelekhov went on with the other two ships, cruised along south of the Rat and Andreanof islands, keeping within sight of them, past the islands of the Four Mountains and the Fox Islands, finally dropping anchor in Captain Bay on Unalaska Island. Impatient to proceed, Shelekhov paused here only long enough to leave word for Delarov to follow and to overtake him, if possible, and then pushed on to Kodiak. The party landed on the northeast coast of Kodiak in a bay to which they gave the name Three Saints.

At first the natives showed friendliness, but later became sullen and distrustful. Finally this ill will broke into open hostilities, but Shelekhov was not to be deterred by menaces. The Russians under his command showed themselves capable of looking after themselves, and attacks were repelled. When the natives gathered threateningly on a distant promontory, the Russians attacked them and inflicted severe losses. Shelekhov's firmness and diplomacy finally won the natives over to some degree of amity, and the Russians were not molested when they built living quarters for the winter. Under Shelekhov's leadership the crews were very active and built in addition three fortresses (probably posts)—one on Afognak Island, one on Cook Inlet, and one at Cape St. Elias. The winter was spent in a thorough exploration of the surrounding seas and a survey of the neighboring coast, the country, and its resources. On his return in the *Three Saints* Shelekhov had already formed a clear and far-seeing plan for the new fur empire he was to establish in these hitherto unexploited lands.

After thus occupying Kodiak and part of the neighboring mainland, Shelekhov now made plans for maintaining this hold. He had intended that Delarov should take charge of the post at the harbor of Three Saints as well as assume general supervision of all the company's interests in Cook Inlet and Prince William Sound. But Delarov had not arrived when Shelekhov left in the spring of 1786. Stress of weather and repeated mishaps had forced him to put back to Unalaska, and Shelekhov had to leave Samoilov as manager of the post, while Izmailov was under orders to continue the explorations begun by Shelekhov himself. According to the account afterwards published by Shelekhov, Lituya Bay was the extreme limit of the voyage of Izmailov in 1787. Wherever the crew visited, there seemed to be signs of recent visits by European traders. The grenadier caps and copper medals the natives so proudly displayed were doubtless brought by an English ship which had made its first appearance here in 1786. An anchor bought from the natives of Lituya Bay was one lost by La Perouse on his unfortunate visit in 1786.

The following year rumors reached the colony of the presence of vessels, and at Nuchek Island the Russians all but met a three-masted schooner, which had left only two days before. It was probably one of the ships of the Martínez expedition of 1788; Haro later reported that he had sent the longboat ashore in the harbor of Three Saints on June 30 or July 1. It had returned with four Russians, one of whom identified himself as Del Haro, a Greek born at Constantinople. This was Delarov, who had by this time arrived from Unalaska. At any rate the courtly Delarov treated the Spaniards with every polite consideration and was at great pains to point out on the map which he had the various Russian establishments and the extent of Russian claims. These claims must have been rather inspired by Shelekhov's ambitious designs than based on actual occupation. The expedition sent to the east had not yet returned from Yakutat and Lituya bays, and some of the posts indicated must have existed only in the imagination of the Greek. Moreover, he added some touches to the picture calculated to alarm the Spanish guests. He mentioned casually the yearly trips of a Russian galliot along the coast as far south as Nootka Sound and incidentally disclosed the intention of the Russian government to occupy that place the following summer in order to put a stop to the trade the English were carrying on with the natives.

Was Delarov's remark merely a bow drawn at a venture? Both he and Haro undoubtedly knew of the Billings expedition, which had now returned from the Arctic Coast and was probably at this time at Okhotsk preparing for its voyage to the American coast. He may have known of the project advanced at St. Petersburg for sending a squadron of four vessels, under Mulovskii, around the world from Kronstadt to the Pacific. Oddly enough the information furnished by Delarov to Haro agreed with what Zaikov told Martínez at Unalaska, though Zaikov had proceeded to muddy the waters by saying that he had this information from an Englishman named Grec who had put in to Unalaska in 1785 on his way back from the coast of America to Canton with a cargo of furs. There is no evidence of an English ship being in the Aleutian Islands in 1785, and it is extremely unlikely that such secret information had been relayed by so circuitous a route as from Russia to England to India to China instead of directly from St. Petersburg. One suspects that the interpreter Mendofia misunderstood Zaikov. The outbreak of the Second War with Turkey in 1787 and the war with Sweden in the same year left but little of those grandiose schemes, whatever they were, but the Spaniards saw in these chance remarks a threatened assault on their whole position in America; and forthwith His Catholic Majesty was compelled to vindicate his claims by the occupation of a hitherto unknown Indian encampment along the coast. This step created an incident whose repercussions were felt throughout the civilized world.

Shelekhov had reached Bolsheretsk in Kamchatka on August 7, 1786. Gossip concerning the arrival of an English ship and the chance of striking a profitable bargain with its captain, William Peters, sent him off posthaste to Petropavlovsk. This trip across the peninsula and the slow voyage back around the south end of Kamchatka to Bolsheretsk delayed him so much that it was autumn before he was able at last to leave for Okhotsk. His ship having already left Bolsheretsk, he had to make the journey by land. Winter overtook Shelekhov and his wife, who had accompanied him, en route, and they were forced to complete the journey by dog sled, arriving at Okhotsk only after the first of the year, 1787. They pushed on across the Stanovoi Mountains to Yakutsk and up the Lena to Irkutsk. Cold weather set in, and they experienced the full rigor of the Siberian winter. Heavy snow and extreme cold were their constant traveling companions. The dreaded *purga* descended upon them and tried them to the extreme limit of endurance. Shelekov himself, though inured to hardship, comments on their sufferings. It was an experience that must have been trying for a woman. They won through, however, reaching Irkutsk towards the end of the winter. From Irkutsk they pursued their journey in relative comfort along the Siberian post road, where roadhouses were spaced at convenient intervals, and arrived in St. Petersburg in the autumn of 1787.

Shelekhov's return all but coincided with the conclusion of Catherine's tour of her new Crimean possessions. To Shelekhov the time seemed propitious for approaching the throne with a petition for extensive privileges for his company in the east. Shelekhov had staked out a claim to the new fur-trapping country along the south coast of Alaska, but the cost of operating in these remote regions would be prohibitive unless the company were assured of a monopoly. He foresaw further that the competition of rival companies would eventually exhaust the supply of fur. Moreover, the appearance of English ships in the North Pacific was an indication that he would have even more formidable rivals than his compatriots, with the certainty that such competition would be backed by English sea power. Spain, too, after a slumber of centuries was now in the field, demanding that her exclusive claims be respected. Shelekhov's prescience of international complications stirred him to try to secure, in advance, the protection of his government for his venture.

From now on both he and Golikov gave their energies to realizing this dream of an exclusive control over the area just opened up on the northwestern coast of America. Since the Aleutian Islands had become for all practical purposes Russian possessions, they had, with the express approval of the state, extended Russia's occupation to the mainland and the islands lying offshore (southeastward to an indefinite point). The effective occupation of the country, the introduction of civilization, and the conversion of the natives to Christianity was beyond the resources of a trading company. These tasks could be carried through either directly by the Russian government or indirectly by some agency acting with government support. In Shelekhov's mind personal interest and the interests of the state were inextricably mixed, or perhaps he consciously cloaked one with the other to make his schemes attractive to the Empress. He was well aware that the interests of the trader were of less concern to Catherine than an opportunity to play the role of an enlightened despot. The first petition, presented in 1789, for a monopoly to be conferred on the Shelekhov-Golikov Company together with a loan of 200,000 rubles from the treasury was refused. The Empress, as marks of her favor, merely bestowed on the partners swords and medals suitably inscribed to be worn by them as evidence of their "services rendered to humanity." It was necessary to win the government with more tempting bait.

Not a whit discouraged by this gentle rebuff, Shelekhov cast about for other means of advancing his project. He had long sought for the management of the company's posts in the North Pacific a man at once thoroughly reliable and loyal in accepting and executing his instructions. Shelekhov had eyed Alexander Andreyevich Baranov, a merchant of Kargopol, who, in addition to other interests, had for some years been engaged in the fur trade in the far north. Baranov had been averse to giving up his independence to enter the employ of another and had declined Shelekhov's offer. But a run of bad luck overtook him about the time of Shelekhov's return to St. Petersburg, and his enterprises all seemed to come to grief. His stores in the north were plundered at Anadyr. His glass factory at Irkutsk, through inadequate supervision, became run down and began to lose money, while a rascally partner cheated him of much of his fortune. He found himself facing bankruptcy, and so, like many another man in a like situation, he was forced to make terms with circumstances. He accepted Shelekhov's offer, and in 1790 he set out for Kodiak to become general manager of all the posts of the Shelekhov-Golikov Company in the North Pacific.

The arrival of Baranov at Kodiak in 1791 was an epoch, if not in Russian history in which it passes unnoticed, at least in that of the northwest coast of America. Born at Kargopol in north Russia, Baranov was inured to the rigors of a severe climate and undoubtedly also thoroughly acquainted from childhood with the life of the woodsman and the hunter. His energy and ambition had carried him to the far outposts of the empire in search of the "pot of gold." Adversity and hardship had not quenched his spirit, and now in middle life, with years of training and experience behind him, he was admirably qualified to carry out the plans which Shelekhov had drawn for his future domain. It is true that, as a member of the merchant class, Baranov had gone without much formal schooling. He lacked the urbanity and polish of the noble. Nevertheless, qualities of heart and mind made him both a faithful servant and an indomitable leader of men. With Baranov in personal command of the posts, Shelekhov was left free to push at the capital the interests of the American Northeastern and Northern and Kurile Company, as the company was officially named.

As far as can be judged from his correspondence, Shelekhov aimed to exclude all his rivals from the fur trade in America and thus to enjoy complete freedom in exploiting the resources and reaping the profits to be derived from this exploitation. To do this, however, it was necessary to induce the government to proclaim the annexation of those regions to Russia so that it could grant a monopoly. Shelekhov found a prototype for this form of commercial activity in the East India Company, which exercised control over British India at that time. The East India Company had been, in its inception, purely a commercial venture authorized by Queen Elizabeth with no purpose beyond commerce. Events, however, had forced the company to assume wider political powers and eventually to take over the control of Bengal. The Hudson's Bay Company's charter was perhaps a more suitable modern pattern, but it is doubtful whether the founders of the Russian company had any save the vaguest information about their British prototype. Shelekhov had taken great pains to lay claim to the territory wherever he had gone and had directed that this policy be continued; but while Catherine was quite willing to profit from such claims, she was loth to support them so openly as to involve her in conflict with Spain. She therefore turned down the request for a monopoly and refused to allow the state to take, even indirectly, a share in the fur business.

Shelekhov then tried a different approach to the problem. He began to advance as the chief concern of his company the conversion of the natives to Christianity and their instruction in the arts of civilization.[1] These aims had not been altogether overlooked by him during his expedition, but he had preferred to omit them from the preamble of his petition in 1788, relying on more substantial arguments. No mention of purposes such as these had been made by Governor-general Jacobii in his support of the petition of the partners. Shelekhov now began to pay court to the Holy Synod to urge them to undertake this praiseworthy work and indirectly to contribute to the expansion of Russian power. He followed this move by a still more ambitious scheme to found on American soil a colony to which a native Russian population would be transported; and to insure the success and prosperity of the venture, he urged that settlements be established on the shore of Prince William Sound. He proposed introducing crafts and encouraging settlers to make a start in agriculture, and he urged that families of peasants should be moved out. In addition, he promised to build shipyards for constructing seagoing vessels out of native lumber. Other necessaries for community life were to be provided. The whole was to be a model settlement to evoke even the admiration of foreigners should they chance to visit the Russian settlers. The primary consideration to be kept in mind by the management was to secure profits. These and other ambitious projects were outlined in letters to Baranov. Shelekhov, on his part, agreed to find the necessary workers, craftsmen, and peasants; and permission actually was granted by decree for him to recruit and send them to the New World with passports for seven years.

Other means were soon found to advance the company interests. In 1794 Shelekhov had been successful in betrothing and marrying his daughter, Anna Grigorievna, to a young courtier,

[1] The proclaiming of this pious motive had direct results, for on February 18, 1796, Gabriel Metropolitan of Novgorod appealed to Platon Aleksandrovich Zubov, Catherine's reigning favorite, on behalf of the Shelekhov–Golikov Company. *Papers Relating to the Russians in America,* 1732–96, University of Washington, Vol. 13.

Nikolai Petrovich Rezanov, who came from the nobility of the province of Smolensk. Rezanov was at this time secretary to Derzhavin, who held the office of secretary of petitions at court. Rezanov, young and ambitious, saw in advancing the interests of Shelekhov a chance to improve his own prospects. Then, having made the interests of the Shelekhov-Golikov Company his own, he found the readiest means to further them was through the reigning favorite, Zubov. It is therefore no mere accident that we find a letter addressed to Zubov by Natalia Shelekhova setting forth the status of the company for which she besought his protection.

Meanwhile, on the distant island of Kodiak Baranov was struggling to hold his ground against rivals. The Lebedev-Lastochkin group had built many posts on Cook Inlet, which they almost completely controlled. Their servants used every means to secure fur and to prevent their rivals from sharing it. This undeclared war caused Baranov no end of trouble. It began in 1791 with the arrival in Prince William Sound of a party of *promyshlenniki* under Konovalov to reinforce the Lebedev-Lastochkin posts. They harassed their competitors in the prosecution of the fur trade, and they also plundered other posts of their own company. A reign of terror not only prevailed in Cook Inlet, which was completely dominated by the Lebedev-Lastochkin interests, but also spread to Prince William Sound. Baranov got little help from Shelekhov, who sneered at "the lion trembling in fear of the mouse." But Baranov, who was on the ground, acquired for his rivals a wholesome respect that he never lost. In later years he confided to Khliebnikov that, if he had commanded the services of the Lebedev-Lastochkin *promyshlenniki,* he could single handed have won the whole of the fur trade for himself. He found his own men disloyal, dishonest, quarrelling incessantly, and complaining. They were totally unreliable, and Baranov commented that when he wanted a thing done, he had to supervise it himself. He had to bear constantly with the querulous and captious criticism of Shelekhov. Nevertheless, to his credit he never swerved in his loyalty to his employer and his devotion to duty.

Shelekhov died in 1795 with his task far from complete. Golikov, who succeeded him as president of the company, gained his first success when he invited and obtained the first tentative merger of the interests of Siberian merchants at Irkutsk in 1795. The death of the Empress in 1796 opened new possibilities. The Emperor Paul had few natural gifts and, having been kept out of public life by his mother, lacked experience with affairs. His distinctly limited mind could grasp only the simplest ideas; his feelings rather than his reason were his guide. It was easy, therefore, for the Golikov interests to persuade Paul through the Holy Synod that they were the bearers of Christianity to this benighted corner of the earth, to emphasize the civilizing role of their company, and to stress the glory that would accrue to the Fatherland to have this task undertaken by a Russian company acting under the protection of the state.

Matters were brought to a head when a rival company organized at Irkutsk applied for incorporation along the same lines as the Shelekhov-Golikov Company. This company was apparently to be known as the Commercial American Company of Irkutsk. Its petition was granted, but it was put under the control of the Imperial College of Commerce, and an order was promulgated that henceforth all companies taking part in the trade with America should be brought under that College. In the preamble, emphasis was laid on the harm likely to accrue to Russia's interests from excessive competition—an indication that events were moving rapidly towards granting a monopoly. Notice was given that henceforth no further charter would be granted for incorporation but all companies trading with America must merge their interests. At Irkutsk on August 3, 1798, the rival Shelekhov-Golikov and Mylnikov groups agreed to unite. Their fusion was approved on July 8, 1799, when the Act of the American United Company signalized this union. After reciting the history of the Shelekhov-Golikov Company, the act mentions a tentative merger achieved in 1797, sanctioned at the time only "on condition that the companies would form a new organization worthy of emulation by other countries, calculated to bring greater benefits to the merchants of Russia." The avowed purposes of the company were:

1. To spread the Christian religion among the natives of America.

2. To engage in trade within or beyond the Russian Empire, to explore new lands, to search for new peoples, to build ships, to colonize the land by Russians, and to maintain friendly relations with the natives.

NIKOLAI REZANOV

The name chosen for the new company was The Russian American Company. The formal charter was finally granted on December 27, accompanied by a series of rules and regulations for the conduct of the company's affairs. Within a few months the headquarters of the company were moved from Irkutsk to St. Petersburg.

The day of the independent trader was now at an end. It had been succeeded by that of a chartered company acting under a state monopoly. The last free trader to send a ship eastward from Okhotsk was Kiselev, a merchant of Irkutsk. His ship, the *Losimi Savvaya,* made its final voyage in 1798. The next year all trading companies that had not united with the Shelekhov-Golikov Company wound up their affairs.

IX

Baranov Lays the Groundwork

WHEN BARANOV TOOK SERVICE WITH THE SHELEKHOV-GOLIKOV Company, it may have been his experience and his proved capabilities that recommended him to his employers, but nothing that Baranov had known prepared him for what he was to encounter. Instead of in the broken, diversified terrain of northeastern Asia with mountain, valley, and treeless tundra interspersed with verdant plain, he was to make his home on the narrow, timbered strips of coast that fringed the islands of the northwest coast of America. Instead of the familiar Siberian landscape his horizon would be bounded by the monotonous stretches of sea on one side and the towering mountains on the other. Instead of the warm sunshine of summer and the invigorating cold of winter, he was to know nothing but interminable fog and rain, months of gloomy, overcast skies. Instead of the docile *yassak*-paying natives, with their reindeer and their cattle, combining pastoral pursuits with the chase, he was to be surrounded by the uncivilized Tlingit or Haidas. Cut off from the rude plenty of the Siberian countryside, he was to be dependent on the sea and the forest for his food. The threat of famine was to hang constantly over him and his companions. The uncharted seas imperiled their lives. The forest and the mountains screened the furtive native lurking to kill the Russians, his yearning restrained by neither tribal law nor the white man's superior force.

Baranov's entry on his new duties was attended by disaster. Setting sail in the *Tryek Sviatitelei,* he went ashore on Unalaska for water. After a short stay, the company put to sea only to be driven back and wrecked on the rocky coast of the island. Through the winter they ranged far and wide over the islands in search of enough food to support life. After constructing *baidars* in the spring, they decided to continue their journey. Baranov directed

Bocharov in one *baidar* to explore the north side of the Alaska Peninsula, while he in one of the others proceeded to Kodiak. Here he arrived on June 27, 1791, still suffering from the fever which had tormented him all winter. Delarov loyally put at the disposal of Baranov all the information he had on the operations of the company and gave a full account of his stewardship. Then he left, in the spring of 1792, for Okhotsk and St. Petersburg to live in retirement on what modest wealth he had accumulated.

Baranov was soon made aware that America was not Siberia. After all, the Chukchi, Koriaks, and Kamchadals had long since submitted to Russian rule. But in America, and particularly on Kodiak, he had to deal with primitive folk, still untamed and little disposed to accept any overlordship. He was surrounded by powerful rival trading companies whose truculence was not checked by the long arm of autocracy. The very land on which the Russian fort stood was still claimed by Spain; if Spain faltered, Great Britain and the United States threatened to take what might fall from the Russian grasp. Baranov found as Kipling, "There's never a law of God or man runs north of fifty-three." He must have asked himself how mortal man could control his destiny in such a land. Yet as soon as he had taken over his new duties, Baranov was astir to accomplish what had been enjoined on him by his employer. His first resolve was to move the Russian settlement from Three Saints Bay on the south coast of Kodiak to St. Paul, a site selected towards the northeast point of the island. He then proceeded to the mainland to stake out for his company claims in the great fur-bearing regions there.

The Lebedev-Lastochkin Company had been one of the first to follow up Cook's and Potap Zaikov's explorations here. In 1786 the *Sv. Pavel* under the *peredovshchik* (senior trader) Kolomin had appeared at Kodiak and had been urged by Shelekhov's men to enter Cook Inlet. This they had done and then had proceeded to make themselves at home there. They had been reinforced in 1791 by a second party in the *Sv. Yuri* (*St. George*), under Konovalov, but for some reason the two did not join forces. Konovalov built another fort and began to harass Kolomin's party, to plunder his supplies, and to mistreat his native workers and force them into his own service. He even began to encroach on the one Shelekhov post in Cook Inlet and to threaten its monopoly of Prince William Sound. Baranov practiced the utmost self-restraint, either out of regard for his employer's interest in the rival company or because of his lack of force to back up a protest. Encouraged by this apparent acquiescence to his actions, the Lebedev leader continued his reign of violence until the arrival of reinforcements from Okhotsk in the *Sv. Ivan* gave Baranov a chance to intervene. Claiming an authority he did not actually possess, Baranov summoned Konovalov, put him in irons, and dispatched him to Okhotsk for trial. The trial did not come off. Shelekhov and the rival company composed their differences amicably. Konovalov was put on board ship and sent back to America with a letter to Ieromonakh Ioassaf requesting him to arbitrate the dispute. The affair ended tamely enough, but the Lebedev company was already on the decline and never made serious trouble again for Baranov, who now proceeded to push the claims of his company to dominant if not exclusive control of the territory adjacent to Kodiak. In addition to asserting his claims to Prince William Sound, he allowed one of his lieutenants, Purtov, in the face of protests from the rival company, to explore the Copper River and to enforce Russian control of the natives in that area. Here he came face to face with a new factor now to give him cause for greater concern than the menaces and encroachments of rival Russian companies.

The treaty that followed the Nootka Sound incident had not settled the rivalry between Spain and England. England had dispatched Vancouver's expedition partly to receive the surrender of the regions which the government thought Spain had ceded under the agreement of 1790 and partly to carry to completion the explorations of Captain Cook. Spain herself, not aware that she had signed away much of her rights, sought to buttress her claims by redoubling her activity, both commercial and official, in these regions. Spaniards and Englishmen therefore vied with each other in examination of the coast, while they both sought, under cover of the amenities of diplomacy, to oust one another.

But a much more decisive voice in settling the fate of the northwest coast was that of the sea captains who arrived on this coast in ever increasing numbers to engage in the fur trade. Baranov, on his first visit to Prince William Sound in the summer of 1792, had met one of these, Captain Moore of the *Phoenix* from Bengal. Despite their rivalry, the two men struck up a warm friendship, attested by the gift to Baranov of an East Indian slave, who served him for many years. Actually many other commercial vessels were plying trade up and down the coast this year. The number continued to increase from year to year.

In 1794, at a difficult stage of his dealings with the Kolosh natives in the neighborhood of Yakutat Bay, Purtov was at least passively assisted by the presence of Vancouver's ships, while active support was given by Captain Butterworth of the *Jackall*, one of three London vessels that had been engaged in the trade for the past two years. The United States, too, was represented; and one of her seamen, Captain Gray, had entered and named the Columbia River in 1792. France also had representatives, but with the outbreak of the war in Europe in 1793, English and French participation declined, and it was the American ships that began to loom large. The "Boston men" soon discovered a profitable three-way system of trading that enabled them to outstrip their competitors. Loading at home with English goods, they cleared for the northwest coast, where, if they had chosen their cargo with care, they disposed of it to advantage in exchange for furs. With this cargo they proceeded to Canton, where they exchanged the furs for Chinese goods—tea, nankeen, and other things much in demand in New England and elsewhere along the Atlantic seaboard. Then they sailed for home, for it was from these Oriental goods that the real profits were realized. In addition to the greater distances they had to traverse, Englishmen were at a disadvantage, for they had to reckon with the monopoly of the East India Company at Canton. Theoretically they might have used methods similar to those of the Americans, but the East Indian monopoly was a fairly effective bar, and the incidence of war gradually drove them out of a lucrative field, which went to the competing Yankees. Baranov estimated that by 1800 the Russians had lost a total profit of 3,000,000 rubles to the redoubtable Boston men. Some means had to be found for excluding them. Baranov must move his headquarters southward and deny to the Americans access to the Alexander Archipelago, whose intricate passages swarmed with the coveted sea otter, from which their most valuable trade was derived.

Meanwhile other enterprises projected by the company had gone forward. An Englishman named Shields, who, after some time at sea, had wandered into Russia and found his way into the company's service, was chosen to take charge of the work. A site at what came to be known as Voskresenskaya Bay (Blying Bay)—modern Resurrection Bay—on the west side of Prince William Sound was selected for the proposed shipyards. Here in 1792 the ways were laid, and a ship was begun. The very tools for working with timber had to be forged from the metal that chanced to be available. Green timber had to be felled in the forest. For caulking, a mixture of pitch and oil had to be improvised on the spot. Finally, however, in the spring of 1793 there slid into the water the *Phoenix,* a somewhat crude vessel of about one hundred tons, the timber still showing the brightness of newly cut wood, its lines anything but beautiful and its structure still incomplete. Its one claim to distinction was that it was the first vessel to be built of native lumber and launched on the northwest coast.

In 1794 there arrived from Okhotsk two ships loaded with provisions, implements, seed, and cattle and carrying 192 passengers—peasants and craftsmen to form the long-projected colony on Yakutat Bay. Shelekhov had petitioned for permission of the government to transport convicts or bankrupt debtors who were qualified in some craft and also peasants, to be released by their *pomyeschik* on agreement to pay the *obrok*.[1] The convicts and peasants sailed in a convoy of two vessels and 450 *baidarkas* for Yakutat Bay, the 450 *baidarkas* to hunt for sea otters in Lituya Bay. From the first the settlement was unlucky. Except for the good anchorage provided, the location had little to recommend it. It lay along a stretch of coastal plain where the rugged St. Elias Range thrusts out icy tongues towards the sea. These spread a dozen ice fields over much of the plain and chill the air and make farming a precarious calling. It lay also within the territory of the dreaded Kolosh. The reluctance with which they agreed to the cession of land was scarcely a good omen. Their behavior towards the Russians had

[1] A *pomyeschik* was a member of the gentry or landholding class. The peasants were serfs (i.e., bound to the soil) and required to render to the landlord dues (*obrok*) and services (*barshchina*). If a peasant wished to leave the estate, it was customary for him to continue to pay *obrok*.

been sullen and resentful. There had been some violence and bloodshed. A sinister dread continued to hang over the settlement. Scurvy and famine was the constant lot of the colonists. The population dwindled as settlers died or gave up the unequal struggle and left for service elsewhere. Finally, in 1804, the Kolosh descended and massacred all but a handful; the survivors were made prisoners and were only recovered through the utmost efforts of Baranov. Yakutat Bay ceased to be inhabited, and its one-time colony became a vague and half-remembered tradition.

The souls of the natives were from the very first the object of Shelekhov's great solicitude. This was perhaps as much due to long Muscovite custom as to the wish to impress the government by hypocritically assuming pious motives. This emphasis on proselytizing the natives and rendering them docile ran through all Shelekhov's reports and instructions to Baranov. Whatever may have been the latter's personal views, he had to provide for the missionaries dispatched to the New World at the instance of Shelekhov. But the quality of the missionary efforts in the last analysis depended on the character of the men sent out and the harmony that developed between them and their compatriots. The three men of whom we hear most—the archimandrite, Ioaasof, and the ieromakhs, Herman (German) and Juvenal—do not appear to have had the qualities needed in their new fields.[2] The first of these must have had the confidence of Shelekhov and his superiors in Siberia, since he was commissioned by them to settle the dispute between Konovalov and Baranov. Concerning the others, there is little evidence that they were endowed by nature to make a success in this venture. Probity, fanaticism, and piety were not calculated to overcome the opposition of those with whom they labored or to disarm the suspicions of those they sought to win to Christ unless accompanied by other and more human traits—discretion, good judgment, and kindliness. These qualities they conspicuously lacked. The company assumed responsibility for them, but they had no understanding of the primitive conditions under

[2] The Valaam Monastery in Finland assumed all this early missionary work. Monks do not seem to have been the most effective bearers of the gospel. Their work may have been faithful, but it does not shine forth with the brilliance of that of Veniaminov, a generation later.

which they would work. Hence they resented the hardships which they were called on to share with the company servants. The appalling living conditions and the violations of the ordinary moral code by Baranov and his men roused their indignation. They openly criticized them to their superiors and secretly condemned them. Moreover, the methods they adopted for propagating the faith among the natives were calculated to enrage rather than to conciliate; and one of them, Juvenal, paid with his life for his missionary work at Lake Ilyamna. They carried on some educational work both at Kodiak and at Sitka, but most of the neophytes were sent to Irkutsk for training until the eparchal seminary was established at Sitka somewhat later. The well-meant enthusiasm of the church for making converts, as well as the efforts of the company for rendering the people docile, had few results, save to induce outward conformity. It required the simplicity, the zeal, and the devotion of Veniaminov to correct later the errors of church policy at the beginning.

The early years of Baranov's service brought well-nigh overwhelming calamities. In his first winter he had suffered shipwreck and had as a consequence been exposed to the full rigors of an inhospitable climate in a strange land. In order to survive, he and his men had had to scour the islands for edible roots, a diet which they had supplemented from time to time by shooting sea lions and seals. He had suffered from fever on his hazardous journey by sea to Kodiak. Hostile natives had menaced not only his establishment there but also every post he ventured to build on the mainland. The rival companies harassed him and tried to oust him from the mainland by intimidation. First, the presence of Spanish ships along the coast warned him of Spain's pretensions; when these vanished, English commercial and war vessels filled him with apprehension. When the war in Europe drove French, English, and Spanish ships from the sea, Americans began to appear in alarming numbers to filch the trade from under his very eyes; and Baranov was faced with its complete loss to the enterprising Yankees unless they could be excluded.

At first Baranov had been complaisant towards foreign traders. He had extended hospitality to the first English captain he had met in Prince William Sound, and they had warmed towards each other. His men had shown every courtesy to the Vancouver expedition. Baranov had been severely censured by Shelekhov for allowing his humanity to override his concern for the company's and the Empress's interests. His reply to his superior is characteristic; he wrote:

> I return to that part of your letter in which you express astonishment at my complaisance in welcoming and entertaining Moore, the captain of the English merchant ship. I am rather astounded at your censure of me which reveals a boundless greed for self-aggrandizement; how can you believe that I could violate the sacred laws of hospitality . . . .
>
> I have always felt bound, of course, to obey the instructions of Her Majesty; I told Moore, and will tell him again and insist on it, that I consider the welfare of my country the object of my special care, without undertaking to bar people from areas which have not been claimed by our government or which are regarded as beyond the boundaries of Russia. I have received no special instructions about the English but shall consider the French the enemies of our state.[3]

One cannot fail to be struck by the loyalty of the servant coupled with the courage with which he rose above narrow national boundaries in meeting the common claims of humanity in these inhospitable regions.

Towards territorial expansion of the Russian empire in America, Baranov at this time was cold. His attitude, of course, ran counter to the purpose which had been expressed again and again by Shelekhov. But unlike Shelekhov he was under no delusion about the value of the land for colonization. In 1798 he wrote in a letter addressed to Larionov, the factor of the company at Unalaska:

> The coast of America, as well as the numerous islands, could long since for the benefit of our country, as well as in our own interests, have been explored and occupied, in one direction to Nootka Sound and in the other to Bering Strait. But why do so when so large a part of it was and still is given over to savagery and ignorance, if our sole purpose is to maliciously prevent others from gaining access to it, or, with no effort on our part, to deprive them of what has been gained by laborious effort, particularly if we have not in mind some aim in the distant future or some benefit to be conferred on posterity.

[3] Tikhmenev, *Obozryenie,* II, *Prilozhenie,* ii, 96.

On the subject of his relations with foreign traders Baranov had second thoughts. The presence on the northwest coast of an increasing number of English vessels had been the subject of acrimonious correspondence between the factor and the company. Though he resisted the suggestion that he should show reserve towards foreigners who appeared in these waters, Baranov could not but be aware that Vancouver's activities were evidence of growing English interest in this region. Moreover, the Englishman Shields, in charge of shipbuilding, became a cause for anxiety in case he should lend himself to English intrigues. However, with the outbreak of the European war, England and the other European states ceased to be an object of concern. On the other hand, the beginning of inroads on Russian trade by the Boston traders now inclined Baranov to heed the earlier admonitions of the company that he should extend his operations to the east and south. In 1793, upon the completion of the ship *Phoenix,* he had sent Shields on a voyage of reconnaissance along the coast between Lituya Bay and the Queen Charlotte Islands.[4] But this activity on the part of Yankee traders finally assumed proportions that could no longer be ignored. The depletion of the supply of furs in areas which could be reached from Kodiak compelled Baranov to look for fur resources in areas still comparatively untouched. His mind naturally turned to Nootka Sound and the adjacent coast where his only cause for anxiety would be the Boston men, who had no territorial ambitions.

"There is now no one at Nootka," wrote Baranov in 1800, "neither Englishman nor Spaniard. It has been left tenantless; when they reappear there, they will endeavor to extend their trade and found settlements in our direction. I have heard from the Americans that they are organizing a special company to form a permanent settlement in the vicinity of the Queen Charlotte Islands towards Sitka; perhaps our head office could secure protection and strengthen their position if they were to petition the Throne. This is very pressing now that Nootka is unoccupied by the English, who are engaged in war with the French. The advantages of these localities are so great that they would guarantee the government millions of profits for the future. Just recall this

[4] *Ibid.,* 120.

one fact that, for more than ten years, English and American ships have been visiting this coast at the rate of six to ten a year. They figure that if they take in less than 1,500 otter-skins, they encounter a loss. There are places along this coast where they will get 2,000 to 3,000 skins. Let us assume that the average number is 2,000; with a minimum of six ships per year, 12,000 skins will leave here, and even if you take a lower number, say 10,000 over a ten year period, the total will be 100,000; allowing 45 roubles for the price of an otter in Canton, this will amount to 4,500,000 roubles, and if one allows an expenditure of 1,500,000 roubles per year on goods, there is left a clear profit of 3,000,000 roubles for the ten year period. What advantages might accrue to Russian subjects alone by every claim of justice! But add to this the fact that from the supplies of furs imported to Canton and from there shipped all over China, our trade at Kiakhta is suffering from a decline in prices or may come to a complete stop. The Americans say that when Kiakhta was closed to trade, they enjoyed extraordinarily favorable conditions and disposed of their goods at an advance of 20 per cent. Wherefore, one must conclude that the conduct of the trade at Canton has an important bearing on that of Kiakhta."[5]

With Baranov, to think was to act. Almost at the same time that the charter incorporating the Russian American Company was being promulgated, Baranov was carrying out the project that had been forming in his mind—the establishment of a new post in the Alexander Archipelago to head off the enroachment of American traders.

The party destined for the occupation of the new post left Kodiak on May 1, 1799, in two vessels and about two hundred *baidars,* crossed to the mainland, and proceeded along the coast eastwards from Cook Inlet to Prince William Sound, where they had a rendezvous with Kuskov. He met them, accompanied by 150 *baidars*. While traversing the exposed stretches of open waters, they encountered heavy seas that swamped some of the fragile craft. Since night was coming on, the survivors made for shore, but the high waves and adverse winds tried their endurance to the extreme limit. Almost overcome by exhaustion from their exertions, they had scarcely stretched out on shore when they were attacked by

[5]*Ibid.,* 84–85.

the Kolosh who had been lurking in the forest. The Aleuts at first scattered, but Baranov rallied them, and a show of resistance checked the assailants and drove them back into the woods, but not before they had killed or carried off into capavity at least thirteen of the company. Fortunately for the Russians their ships appeared offshore in the early morning, and the remainder of the journey was without further incident.

Baranov selected as the point of disembarkation the site of modern Sitka, on the west side of Baranof Island along a stretch of water named Norfolk Sound by Vancouver. This location had been previously reconnoitered by the Russians. It had been sighted by Baranov on a cruise in the *Ol'ga* in 1795. Shields in 1796 had carried out a more careful survey of Norfolk Sound. After that it was frequently visited by parties of Aleuts and yielded extraordinary catches of sea otter. The presence of Boston ships indicated that the place was known to American traders as a fertile source of sea-otter pelts. Baranov, arriving in early summer with three ships —the brig *Ekaterina,* the cutter *Orel* and the galley *Ol'ga*—and his *baidars* met the three native Kolosh chiefs, Skautel, Skaatagech, and Koukhkan, and came to terms with them for the land needed for the post. On the advice of the Boston ship captain, Cleveland, Baranov observed the utmost precautions against surprise by the natives, regularly mounting guard with half the men while the others felled timber and erected buildings for their establishment. Good progress was made and on completion the new fort was given the name St. Michael (not the St. Michael in Bering Sea). During the winter of 1799–1800 Baranov exerted himself to conciliate the local native chief. He bestowed on him a bronze plaque to attest that the place on which the fort had been erected had been given the Russians by the chief, that he had submitted to the Russians, and that in return the Russians had undertaken to furnish him with needed supplies and to protect him against his hostile neighbors.

Baranov thus concludes his account of the reasons that impelled him to found this settlement:

These most significant factors, intimately connected with the welfare of the state, impelled me at an early date to found a settlement on

Sitka and to explore in every way conditions there and at Canton for merchants visiting them, determining however weak our resources might be and whatever the conditions that a start should be made in erecting posts and establishing contacts, anticipating our greatest rewards only after the lapse of considerable time. . . . It would be a great pity if these places should be taken from us by Europeans or some other company. Then we should be robbed of all the advantages now enjoyed and would be left with nothing at all.[6]

Almost at once the factor found himself faced with serious dangers. The natives there, in contrast with those of Kodiak, had been trading freely with foreign ships from whom they had obtained firearms. Baranov wrote:

I said to them [i.e., the American traders] again and again that these goods [cannon and powder] were not suitable things to sell an uncivilized people. Among them, they often caused bloodshed and brought harm on themselves; they even made sudden attacks on ships and have often seized them; it was all the more harmful and wrong, since they threatened to disturb the peaceful relations between the Russian court and the Republic of the United States. But they paid little attention, saying, "We are a commercial people; we look for profits and there is nothing to stop us doing so." . . . The Americans, seeing our solidly constructed buildings, remarked that it was unnecessary for them to build here. They marvelled at our audacity and our ability to endure hardships, the meager and unsatisfying diet, and our drink, which was water.[7]

The chief factor outwardly personified courage and determination, but inwardly he suffered acutely from depression and discouragement. The move southward to Sitka had been calculated to head off the inroads of English and American traders on the main source of sea-otter skins. Already, shortly after the founding of the Sitka post, one of the hunting parties—more than one hundred Aleuts—had died of poisoning from eating of mussels. During the winter Baranov had to deal with contumacy of the Kodiak islanders. Like the Aleuts they had been subjected to compulsory

[6] K. Khlebnikov, *Zhiznopisanie A. A. Baranova (Biography of A. A. Baranov)*, 43–46.

[7] *Ibid.*, 45–46.

labor, and because the number of Russians was quite inadequate for the task of fur hunting, their co-operation was imperative. Baranov managed to keep the fidelity of the chiefs and through them reasserted his authority and secured the return of the natives to the service of the company. But in the spring a fresh calamity overtook the post. The *Phoenix,* under Captain Shields, had been some months overdue. After a severe storm, wreckage was found at different points along the coast, mournful witness to the vessel's fate as she was returning with a cargo from Okhotsk. Since she was the first ship to come out in two years, her loss deprived the stations of the necessities of life, which could not be replaced for at least another year. This disaster came on top of a "winter of discontent." Low in spirits, Baranov had spent the previous months trying to put things right on the mainland, when the arrival from Okhotsk of the ship *Elizaveta,* under Bocharev, with goods and supplies temporarily lifted the load from his shoulders. However, the letters he received were for the most part filled with criticism or censure, and he could detect behind them the gossip and intrigues of his enemies among the functionaries at home, civilians all, whom he despised as stay-at-homes:

> Above all I fear them for their filthy intrigues with officious functionaries, who judge of everything here according to their own fancies. They are dissatisfied with everything and never cease to carp, asking questions on all points; if an arrival, whether he is a resident or a worker; where or how do they live; what is going on and where; it is to such persons that reports are made.[8]

He was, moreover, anxious about English and particularly United States competition, now driving the English from the seas. He was harassed by the dissatisfaction among the Russians and the unrest among the natives. But in the spring of 1801 he was able to make good the loss of supplies on the *Phoenix* by purchasing from Captain Scott, of the ship *Enterprise* of New York, his cargo. Scott brought back word, however, of the outbreak of war in Europe (1799) in which Spain as France's ally and an enemy of Russia contemplated sending an expedition to fall on the Russian settlements in the New World. Then all other troubles were swallowed

[8] *Ibid.,* 51–52.

up in grief for the fate which overtook the settlement of Sitka in the early summer of 1802.

Baranov had left Sitka in the *Ol'ga* on April 20, 1800, turning the factory over to Vasilii Medvednikov to manage during his absence. The ordinary precautions were observed—half of the men being absent by day in the forest or along the shores engaged in work, while the other half kept watch. But the garrison had been seriously reduced, and it was natural because of the need for strong laborers to leave those less able-bodied and less alert on guard at the camp. Moreover, the natives who came and went almost at will were well informed of conditions within the fort, for the native girls, largely recruited from the Kolosh, were not above betraying their Russian lovers. The natives gathered in hundreds more or less openly.

Suddenly on a Sunday in the latter part of June (the eighteenth or nineteenth according to Khliebnikov) just after midday, they rushed the fort to overwhelm the little garrison. The alarm was given, but not in time to allow all to reach the blockhouse. Those in the immediate neighborhood barricaded themselves in it; the rest were either cut off or forced to flee to the forest to hide. Meanwhile, hordes of armed warriors, in full war regalia, wearing the masks of their totem animals, surrounded the blockhouse; the windows were broken and musket fire poured in on the refugees. The women and children seem to have taken refuge in the cellar, but the entrance was battered down, and they fled into the street. Fire applied to the building quickly reached the second story and forced the Russians to abandon this stronghold and jump to the ground. There they were seized by the Kolosh and dragged off. While the rest were making their last stand on the ground floor, fresh reinforcements of savages arrived and forced the door. In the melee that ensued, all of the Russians in the fort were killed, their heads severed, while the Kolosh turned to the serious work of plundering what the fire had spared.

A few of the fleeing Russians had managed to secret themselves in the forest. Stealing down to the shore the next day, one of them descried an English ship and managed to signal to it. Though some of the Kolosh rushed up and compelled him to hide, the next day he was fortunate enough to establish contact with the ship and was rescued. He also conducted his rescuers to a small group of survivors in whose company he had been. Captain Barber of the *Unicorn,* who effected this rescue, was joined by two American ships, one the *Alert* under Captain Ebbets, the other not identified. They decided to seize a number of the natives and hold them hostages until the rest of the captured Russians had been surrendered. This bold act was successful, and the prisoners were then taken to Kodiak and delivered to Baranov.

Before the tragedy two hunting parties had been dispatched from Sitka into the waters of Alexander Archipelago. On returning, one of them under Ubranov was attacked by the Kolosh, captured, and its furs stolen. Ubranov escaped into the forest, and, securing two *baidarkas* which the foe had left intact, he, with a group of Aleuts, made his way back to Sitka. Entering the fort at night, they found it in ruins. They were joined here by others who had escaped, and the party of survivors made their way back to Kodiak.

Kuskov with a much larger party (in 450 *baidarkas*) had set out the previous April from Yakutat. From the first they were harassed by groups of Kolosh who showed themselves insolent and troublesome. Again and again they fired at the Aleuts and on one occasion tried, though without success, to rush their camps. Finally a truce offered by the Kolosh allowed Kuskov to return to Yakutat to replenish his supplies and receive reinforcements. Setting out again, he exercised extreme vigilance. In Icy Strait, which he reached on June 17, he was told by a native that the Kolosh had gathered from far and near to destroy Sitka. He selected six *baidars* armed with the best baidarmen and sent them on ahead to reconnoiter while the party followed. In the Bay of Islands the company was met by the scouting party with the news that Sitka had fallen. Kuskov made his way back to Yakutat in time to get reinforcements and forestall a Kolosh attack on the post before returning to Kodiak. Upon his arrival the number of survivors of Sitka was found to be forty-two out of the original garrison of more than two hundred.

This rising of the Kolosh, the most savage in their history, embraced the whole coast from Yakutat Bay to the Queen Charlotte Islands. Its planning showed a remarkable degree of co-ordination

DAWSON

Courtesy Fish and Wildlife Service

UNALASKA

and secrecy. A population of perhaps fifty thousand persons was involved, made up of groups considerably diverse in dialect and customs. It almost succeeded and probably would have, had not individuals from among the Kolosh, moved by humanity, warned the Russians of this impending attack.

The loss of Sitka was a heavy blow to Baranov. A few days after the receipt of the news, the brig *Ol'ga* arrived from Unalaska with Banner. It brought word of the organization of the new Russian American Company, of the grant of the charter, and of the bestowal of the order of St. Vladimir on Baranov by the Emperor Paul; but even this could not efface the terrible memories from his mind. He set about preparing to restore Sitka early in 1803, sending out *baidars* to Yakutat Bay, where he intended to pick up reinforcements for the attempt. But he was dissuaded by the agent Kuskov, whose advice he always listened to with respect. Yet the disaster continued to gnaw at his vitals. When in the spring of 1804 one of the company's agents, Bubnov, who arrived at Kodiak in a *baidarka,* after his ship, the *Dmitrii,* had been wrecked on Umnak Island, apprised him of his elevation to the rank of collegiate counsellor, he broke down:

> I am a nobleman; but Sitka is lost! I do not care to live. I will go and either die or restore the possessions of my august benefactor.

The attack on Sitka and its capture by the natives is but one incident in the long train of deeds of violence enacted along this coast during the period. Part of the blame is undoubtedly to be laid at the door of the Russians for their oppression of the natives. Perhaps the disaster might have been averted if they had kept their posts properly manned and had observed sufficient vigilance. But the Russians never had enough men to garrison them adequately. Their numbers were further reduced by scurvy and death, and the natives were perfectly well informed about the exact state of defense of the fort through the native women who kept them fully apprised of Russian dispositions. Moreover, as Baranov had previously remarked, the Kolosh were furnished with firearms that were equal or superior to those of the Russians; it was said that they had secured small ordnance which they had learned how to serve. The Russians also claimed that the natives had been instructed in the art of constructing field fortifications by fugitives from American ships. It is known that men were always deserting from the ships that visited the coast, and a number of American ships and at least one British vessel were in the vicinity at that time. Ship captains were also in the habit of putting mutinous sailors ashore on the coast. Deserters from various vessels had been associating with the natives, and while we have no evidence that they actually either collaborated with the Kolosh, or instructed them, the Russians suspected that the natives had had some help from this quarter. Neither the Americans nor the British could have felt regret at the calamity that befell the Russian settlement. It was typical of the savage warfare between white men and natives and of the bitter rivalry between the various groups of white traders. It is almost impossible to assess the blame. The situation, however, that made this sort of thing possible was the complete absence of any definite authority in these regions. Although nominally under the control of the Russian American Company (only since 1799, and the natives had not been apprised of the fact), and through them of the Russian Empire, the natives recognized no authority save that of their own chiefs. The threat to which the increasing numbers of Europeans exposed them was mitigated by the fact that these nations were at variance among themselves. The natives made use of the familiar device of the weak throughout history and tried to play their stronger enemies against one another. In this particular instance they all but achieved complete success.

X

The Beginning of the Monopoly

THE SHELEKHOV-GOLIKOV COMPANY HAD BESTED THEIR RIVALS ON the continent. The Lebedev-Lastochkin traders hung on until 1800, when their last foothold on Cook Inlet was relinquished. The Mylnikov group had merged their interests with those of Shelekhov. Now by imperial decree all other companies were suppressed. But the victory was more of the making of Baranov than of Shelekhov or Golikov.

A new era had dawned for Russia and expectations for the future ran high. Paul's passing had been as violent as his father's, but the world was inclined to overlook this when it contemplated the new sovereign on whom the imperial heritage had descended. Alexander I was handsome and dignified. His early education and training—entrusted to a Swiss exile, Laharpe, with republican sympathies—was in the best tradition of the age of enlightenment. Alexander was inspired with its principles of reason and universal benevolence. Moreover, he had gathered around him a group of kindred souls, reared like himself in the rational spirit, and their enthusiasm went far to reinforce his own.

It was with these associates sitting as an inner council or committee that he began his work of reforming the empire. But in addition to his own intimates, he carried over from the former regime certain persons who had inspired his confidence. Such a man was Arakcheyev, who became Alexander's chairman of the Department of Military Affairs. Another was Nikolai Petrovich Rezanov, son-in-law of Shelekhov, who had probably been instrumental in promoting the Russian American Company and its monopoly. He had won the young sovereign's favor, been elevated to the rank of *Ober-Kammerherr* (supreme chamberlain), and now availed himself of his position of trust to advance his projects in the Far East. The first of these was the dispatch of vessels of the Imperial Navy under command of regular naval officers to strengthen Russia's position in the Pacific; the second, to use the present situation to renew the attempts (suspended since 1793) to establish diplomatic relations with Japan; the third, to get supplies to the colonies in the Pacific, hitherto dependent on Siberia for their food, which had to be brought over the precarious route through Yakutsk and Okhotsk.

These Oriental plans were not exactly new departures. They had been raised successively several times since they had first been mooted by Catherine. Russian foreign policy since the consolidation of the Muscovite empire had been one of expansion outward to the open seas. In Europe the Russians had fairly well attained this end, with the partitions of Poland, the annexation of the Crimea, and the tying of the fortunes of the Grand Duchy of Finland to the destinies of Russia. For the moment Russian purposes in Asia were satisfied with the acquisition of Georgia and detached bits of Persia. Rezanov's scheme was shrewdly calculated to appeal to the imagination of the young emperor, who already was casting his eyes on distant regions to which he might bear the blessings of civilization. Rezanov was therefore entrusted with the mission to Japan and was given the title of "correspondent," with authority to inspect and report on the operations of the Russian American Company. For his diplomatic assignment, Rezanov was armed with the rank of ambassador and authorized to address the Emperor direct. He was to sail on the *Nadezhda,* one of two vessels purchased in England, accompanied by the other, the *Neva.* They were to be commanded respectively by Lieutenant Adam Johann Krusenstern, a member of the Baltic nobility who had trained in and fought with the English navy, and his friend and companion, Yuri Lisianskii, who had seen similar services. On August 7, 1803, the expedition sailed from Kronstadt bound for Japan and the North Pacific.

At the Sandwich (Hawaiian) Islands word was received that Sitka had been captured by the Kolosh and its garrison massacred. It was at once decided to detach the *Neva* under Lisianskii to America while Rezanov pursued his journey with Krusenstern to Petropavlovsk. Here Rezanov arrived on July 14, 1804, and left on September 6 for Nagasaki. After getting in touch with the local authorities, he was forced to wait for the arrival of the Japanese emperor from Jeddo, the provincial capital. The emperor did not arrive until March 30, 1805. A preliminary audience was then arranged for April 4, but not until a second audience was any business transacted. Then Rezanov was informed that no Russian ships would be allowed to put into Japan, and the presents which he had brought with him for the emperor were returned. Thus the negotiations for the opening of commercial intercourse were abruptly terminated. Swallowing his chagrin, Rezanov sailed for Petropavlovsk. From here he took ship with Doctor Langsdorff for America on the *Marya* under Captain Khvostov, leaving Krusenstern to carry out explorations in the north.

Lisianskii, meanwhile, had set his course for the north, and on the morning of July 13, 1804, he entered the Pavlovsk harbor on the northeast coast of Kodiak. Here he received from the resident agent, Banner, Baranov's account of the loss of Sitka and instructions to proceed to a rendezvous in Norfolk Sound. He arrived there on August 15 to find two of the company vessels, the *Aleksandr* and the *Ekaterina,* lying at anchor awaiting the arrival of Baranov. The chief factor during the spring had dispatched three hundred *baidarkas* under Demianenkov for Sitka via Cross Sound. Two company ships, the *Aleksandr* and the *Elizaveta,* sailed for Yakutat Bay, while Baranov left some days later for Norfolk Sound with the *Yermak* and the *Rostislav,* accompanied by the three hundred *baidarkas.* After a perilous trip through Cross Sound and the intricate passages of the Alexander Archipelago, the group arrived off Sitka on September 19. The crews of the *baidarkas* camped along the deserted shore and the four Russian ships lay at anchor not far off, while in the neighborhood an American ship commanded by Captain Joseph O'Cain of Boston lay at anchor to await the issue of the forthcoming struggle between the Russians and the Kolosh and to do business with the victors.

Baranov had now arrived with the main group of the *baidarkas;* a second party under Kuskov from Yakutat Bay straggled in the next day. The whole force of *promyshlenniki* and natives disposed themselves on the beach near the site of the former Fort St. Michael. Towards the end of the month of September the ships, with the flotilla of *baidarkas,* moved out of Krestovskii Bay in the direction of the high bluffs where the Kolosh had erected a formidable fortification. An ultimatum to surrender was rejected by the Kolosh, though they were ready enough to parley somewhat inconclusively. But Baranov would not agree to conditions, and on October 1, on Baranov's insistence and against Lisianskii's advice, an assault was launched. Field pieces had been mounted on boats by Lieutenant Arbusov and taken close inshore to support an assault on the main position under attack. The natives withheld their fire until the Russians had advanced to close quarters. Then at the first volley the Aleuts broke, and the Kolosh, seizing the opportunity, rushed out. The Russians, including Baranov, who had been wounded, were pushed backward until they came under the protection of the ships' guns. Baranov, now weak and dispirited from his wound, gave the command over to Lisianskii and told him to act as he saw fit. The latter moved his ships close inshore to bring his fire to bear on the enemy's position. The next day he opened a bombardment which continued until the enemy sent an envoy to ask for terms. He was informed that their evacuation of the *kekur* (fortified hill) was a necessary preliminary to a parley. The Kolosh gave no answer but during the night evacuated their position and retired, apparently across Chatham Strait, on whose eastern shore they later that winter erected a fort. The next year negotiations were reopened, and on July 16, 1805, the Kolosh formally submitted and signed with Baranov a treaty by which they recognized Russian authority.

Meanwhile Rezanov was on his way. He arrived at Kodiak in the *Marya* and proceeded at once to Sitka. Here he began his inspection of the Russian American Company posts and the activities of the company. It is safe to state that, when he arrived, the fortunes of the Russian settlements were at their lowest ebb. True, the rival companies had been eliminated, but Baranov had now to pit his slender resources against a savage wilderness inhabited by an equally savage people. Russian posts were mere clearings in the forest that clung with a precarious footing to islands or coasts separated from one another by a watery waste. The climate was execrable, especially in winter—the sky always overcast, merely ringing the changes on fog, rain, and snow. The conditions under which the Russians lived were squalid to a degree. The *promysh-*

lenniki, never dainty in dress or diet, eked out a living from what the country supplied. The settlements reeked of rotten fish, of furs half cured, of the offal which was the by-product of the chase; and when to these conditions was added the Muscovite contempt for sanitation or the amenities of civilized life, it is small wonder that the courtier's senses and digestive organs revolted to the point of nausea.

The situation at Sitka was hardly improved by the arrival of Rezanov and his retinue. Since the recapture of the post, the work of restoration had been pressed, but it was necessary to concentrate on the go-downs—the barracks and storehouses and living quarters had been neglected. Those which were there were scarcely proof against the inclemencies of the weather. Moreover, with Rezanov's attendants, some two hundred persons were collected in these incommodious quarters. Food began to run low. The *Elizaveta* was overdue from Kodiak, and all were put on short rations. Moreover, the press of work did not allow men to be released to catch fish, a source of fresh food that would have improved the diet and morale of the garrison. Scurvy, which had been present before, now began to rage. After considerable discussion, it was finally decided by Rezanov, with the approval of Baranov, to purchase the American ship *Juno,* from Bristol, Rhode Island, and her cargo at a price of sixty thousand Spanish *piasters*. The supplies thus acquired partially relieved the situation but could have no more than temporary effect. Rezanov, who had taken over the command, felt overwhelmed by the squalor, misery, suffering, and death. To make matters worse, the inhabitants of Sitka, as in all isolated communities where men crowded together in restricted space, constantly getting in one another's way, suffered from wrangling and feuds. To this situation was added the gloom of winter, the lack of food, the threat of famine, the hard work, the prevalence of scurvy, and the many deaths. All the pent-up rancor accumulated until it broke forth in mutual recriminations and intrigues. Eventually Rezanov was all but driven to distraction, and, when it seemed as though the colony were doomed, he decided to load a boat with furs and other goods and, in defiance of Spanish authority, sail to San Francisco to secure a cargo of grain to relieve the distressing shortage of food.

Accordingly, the *Juno,* under command of Khvostov and with Rezanov and his suite on board, sailed on February 26. Because it had been Rezanov's purpose to select a site for a Russian settlement at the mouth of the Columbia River, for days the *Juno* lay off the bar of the Columbia waiting for a suitable wind to enable her to enter. Water and food began to run low, and Khvostov warned Rezanov that further delay would imperil the whole expedition. Reluctantly, therefore, Rezanov was forced to abandon his plan, and the *Juno* continued her voyage southward to San Francisco.

The ship ran through the Golden Gate under the very muzzles of the Spanish guns; and the chamberlain, as soon as he had identified himself as the plenipotentiary of the tsar, was accorded the appropriate honors Spanish officials on the west coast were instructed from home to observe. But trading was another matter; it was contrary to the law. The priests might have been tempted, but Governor Arillaga, who had ridden up from Monterey, refused to countenance evasion of the laws. Rezanov was in a desperate situation and, according to his own story, had to recourse to stratagem. The young daughter of Argüello, the commandant, Doña Concepción, was extremely impressionable and in the lonely outpost of civilization inclined to welcome the courtly attentions of a suitor as distinguished as Rezanov. Posing (so he says in his letter to the tsar) as a prospective candidate for her hand, the chamberlain succeeded in winning her favor. The surprise and anger of the parents could make no headway against the firm resolve of the daughter to marry Rezanov, and, after a hurried consultation with the clerics, they accepted the Russian as a future son-in-law. From this it was a natural step to circumvent the law to comply with the Russian's plans. Rezanov got his goods; the friars got their furs. On May 10 Rezanov sailed away from the Golden Gate with Spanish grain in the hold and Doña Concepción's heart in his keeping.

When the ship *Juno* reached Sitka on June 8, the situation was found to be somewhat improved, a run of herrings having allowed the garrison to replenish their stores of fresh food, and the scurvy had abated. Rezanov had originally intended to return to California and from there take ship for Manila, China, and India with a view to establishing commercial relations with the East India

Company. But his success in California made the prospect of establishing trade relations with Spanish America more attractive, and he posted to St. Petersburg, ostensibly to obtain through regular diplomatic channels Spain's acquiescence in this trade. The necessary imperial consent and papal dispensation for his marriage may well have been one of his objects; but he fell ill during the journey across Siberia and succumbed at Krasnoyarsk in January, 1807.

It is not a light task to assess the real value of Rezanov's work. His aims were primarily to open trade relations with Japan and to reorganize the administration of the Russian American Company on the American coast. He failed in the first assignment. In America he appeared not only as the plenipotentiary of the tsar, but also as the agent of the directors of the Russian American Company. He practically superseded Baranov and took matters into his own hands. His measures to bring order and efficiency out of chaos at Kodiak and Sitka were as effective as one could expect; he showed tact, judgment, and determination. In the supreme crisis of threatened famine he rose to the emergency and secured from California the needed food. While he was carrying out these tasks, his mind was already busy with other ambitious schemes: to open commercial relations with California, to seize a part of the coast of "New Albion," to trade with Manila and the East Indies and the Hawaiian Islands. These vast projects would have taken decades to realize, but they might have succeeded. Unquestionably the history of Russian America and the Russian American Company might have been vastly different if they had, but one feels that there was no chance for them to be realized in the midst of the ordeals through which Europe was passing. Rezanov's own sovereign, Alexander, had no time to devote to America, preoccupied as he was with other problems. Thus these more ambitious schemes were stillborn. But Rezanov's great energy and undoubted gifts were unequal to the task of even managing the Russian settlements under the existing circumstances. In his practical grasp of the needs of the time, in patience, in ability to make much of little, and withal, in tenacity and endurance, the humble merchant from Kargopol stood head and shoulders above the courtier.

With the departure of Rezanov for St. Petersburg, Baranov resumed full control of Russian interests in America. Because of the continued losses of vessels outward bound from Okhotsk and their cargoes, the posts had to rely on their own resources for food or secure it from other regions more readily accessible. As the connection with Siberia became weaker, Baranov tended to depend more and more on the ubiquitous Yankee and his ships to provide his needs.

In 1803 Joseph O'Cain had arrived in the *O'Cain* at a time when stores were low on Kodiak. Baranov purchased from him goods to the value of ten thousand rubles. The American captain, who had unquestionably been engaged in smuggling goods up and down the shores of Spanish America, had noted the large number of sea otters along the coast, on the Farallones, in San Francisco Bay, and off Lower California. He proposed that Baranov lend him Aleut hunters and that with their assistance he engage in taking sea otters in the south. Somewhat reluctantly Baranov agreed, taking part of O'Cain's cargo as surety. The Yankee captain thus opened a new field of enterprise in which both Russians and Americans were to engage. Other ship captains followed O'Cain's example, and the California coast became a regular hunting ground for American ships attended by Aleut huntsmen with their *baidars*. This "poaching" became the regular practice and was combined with another equally profitable business—that of smuggling, that is, running merchandise ashore in the face of Spanish regulations that prohibited commerce and disposing of it to the missions and presidios.

These were the years when Europe was in the throes of the Napoleonic Wars; Russia was engaged from 1805 to 1807 in the struggle with Napoleon; in 1809 the war with Finland began. Meanwhile Napoleon had intervened in Spain and for five years was himself engaged in bitter conflict with the Spanish guerrillas aided by the armies of Wellington. Then came the campaigns of Wagram, Aspern, and Essling, and finally these isolated struggles fused in the grand finale of the last phase—1812–15. Russia had no energy to give to affairs in America, and communication by sea with the Russian colonies was suspended.

Left thus to his own devices, Baranov solved his problem with characteristic boldness and dexterity. In 1808 Alexander, without waiting for the establishment of regular diplomatic relations with the United States, had dispatched to Washington Andrei Dashkov, Russian consul-general at Philadelphia, and named him "chargé d'affaires near the Congress of the United States." Dashkov arrived in the United States in June, 1809, and immediately endeavored to put relations between the United States and Russia on a sounder basis. He was aware of the straitened circumstances of the Russian posts and had approached leading merchants with a view to supplying them with goods.

John Jacob Astor, who had been for some years in the China trade, was induced to interest himself in the northwest coast. Having no ship of his own available, he purchased one called the *Enterprise* and arranged with John Ebbets of New York to load a cargo. Goods of the kind needed by Baranov were hard to secure, but new shipments were expected to make them accessible later. The *Enterprise* left, therefore, with a nondescript cargo and a letter to Baranov offering to send a better selection as soon as the goods were to be had. Astor also proposed to Baranov a working arrangement between the Russian American Company and the American Fur Company by which the whole fur trade of the northwest coast would be divided between them, and their rivals, particularly, the Northwest Company, would be excluded. Baranov took only part of the goods but loaded the *Enterprise* with furs for Canton. Ebbets carried out his commission to their mutual satisfaction, and on his return Baranov bought the rest of the cargo. Ebbets then made a second trip to Canton to purchase Chinese goods for the return trip. After securing these, he made the return voyage, dropping anchor in New York harbor in 1811. Baranov politely declined Astor's offer of a working partnership, pleading as an excuse that he was shortly to retire; for he was confident that when the war with England came to an end, supplies of food could easily be replenished. Actually it appears that Baranov would not bind himself to limit his purchases to one vendor but wished to buy where it was most to his advantage.

The conditions of squalor and want that prevailed at the American posts led to more than one ugly incident. In 1809 a convict, Naplavkov, found among the company's servants a group of men as desperate as he. Together they entered into a conspiracy to kill the governor. The plot was given away by one of the group,

Leszczynski, who weakened at the last moment and went to Baranov. The men were seized at night in their quarters as they were putting the last touches to their plans. Since there were no courts in America, they were put in irons and shipped to Petropavlovsk for trial. Khliebnikov, who was in charge of the company's interests there, wished to hush the whole affair up, for he was convinced that the fearful conditions tolerated at the North American posts made such occurrences inevitable. He was, however, overruled. The men went to trial, and all received severe sentences.

The appointment of Levett Harris of Pennsylvania to the post of American consul at St. Petersburg provided the first medium of communication between the governments of Russia and the United States. Nikolai Petrovich Rumyantsev, chancellor and minister of foreign affairs and commerce, had availed himself of this to register, on May 17, 1808, the first official protest on behalf of the Russian American Company against the encroachments of the American ships that had so long been a thorn in the flesh of Baranov. The charge was not only that they had violated the alleged monopoly of the company but that they had supplied the natives with ammunition and firearms with which they had harassed the Russian posts.[1]

Dashkov had likewise protested to the United States government against the trade carried on by American ships in firearms and ammunition with the natives in the Russian possessions on the northwest coast of America. The United States government refused to impose an embargo on such traffic on the grounds that: (1) if the Indians were subject to Russia, then it was Russia's responsibility to prevent ship captains from operating within territorial limits; and (2) if the natives were not Russian subjects, then other nations could not be barred from this trade, save in contraband of war during a state of hostilities.[2] The United States government's stand was that such a prohibition could be imposed only as part of a bilateral agreement and would involve fixing some line of demarcation to set the areas within which the ships of the respective countries could operate. Dashkov was not authorized to negotiate such

[1] *American State Papers, Foreign Relations,* V, 439. Romantzoff to Harris.
[2] *Ibid.,* 438–39. Letter of A. Daschkoff to R. Smith, January 4, 1810.

an agreement, nor was the United States prepared at this time to broach a matter which would unquestionably involve the rights of Spain on the west coast.[3] The matter was finally referred to John Quincy Adams, who had arrived in St. Petersburg as United States minister. Adams discussed the matter with Rumyantsev during August, 1810. Rumyantsev made the suggestion that, since Russian ships were barred from Canton, the trade between Russian American posts and China should be carried in American bottoms (an arrangement which would be mutually profitable) and that the United States should have the trade of the settlements, in return for which they should agree to refrain from selling the Indians arms and ammunition. Incidentally, he intimated that Russia's claim to exclusive control of the coast went as far south as the Columbia River. Adams was inclined to hedge on these matters. He was unalterably opposed to this southward extension of Russia's claims and declined to bind the United States on the question of restricting trade with the Indians, in the absence of any definite territorial limits. As the time was not ripe for settling this matter, the question of trade was for the moment shelved until it would be possible to negotiate a general trade treaty between the two countries. However much this was desired by both, the imminence of Russia's war with France continued to postpone the decision, and the actual outbreak of war put it off indefinitely.[4]

Meanwhile Astor had another card to play. Negotiations with Count Friedrich Petrovich Pahlen, the Russian minister in Washington, brought out that the proper course would be to send an agent to St. Petersburg to arrange the matter there with the head office of the Russian American Company and the minister of foreign affairs. For this role Astor chose his son-in-law, Adrian B. Bentzon, who took passage on the ship *John Adams,* which was to take United States Minister Erving to Denmark. Bentzon arrived in St. Petersburg in 1811 and opened negotiations with the Russian American Company. It appears that a tentative agreement was reached for collaboration of the company with the American Fur

[3] *Ibid.,* 441. R. Smith to A. Daschkoff, May 5, 1810.
[4] *Ibid.,* 442–50. J. Q. Adams to R. Smith, September 30, 1810.

Company and for the exclusion of the Northwest Company from participation in the trade.[5]

Astor had also taken active steps for securing his share of the fur trade of the Pacific coast through his own efforts. As early as 1808 he had devised a scheme for an aggressive plan to establish on the Pacific coast a post which could be used as a base of operations against the Northwest Company and which might also, if the Russians were agreeable, be used as a means for promoting co-operation with the Russian American Company. Accordingly, he decided to send two expeditions to the mouth of the Columbia River, one by sea, the other by land. For both of these he endeavored to secure experienced fur traders. Some of the men serving the Northwest Company were persuaded to sever their connections with that company and transfer to Astor's service. The overland party left in June, 1810, proceeding by way of the Missouri River, on whose banks they wintered. The second expedition left in the ship *Tonquin,* under Captain Jonathan Thorn, with "sixty men and all the means which were thought necessary to establish a post at or near the mouth of the river." The *Tonquin* proceeded by way of Cape Horn and the Hawaiian Islands to the Columbia River, which it reached on March 22, 1811. In crossing the bar, eight men were lost, but Thorn got his ship through; and on April 12 a site for a post was fixed about fifteen miles above the mouth of the river. Because of friction between Captain Thorn and other members of the party, Thorn hastened his departure on a trading trip up the coast, leaving on June 1. Sometime in August the ship was attacked by natives and during the fight was blown up, leaving only one survivor. Thus at its very inception Astor's project met with an almost irretrievable disaster.[6]

After dispatching the *Tonquin,* Astor had immediately busied himself with preparations for the sending of a second ship. He selected the *Beaver,* one of his ships especially built for the China trade, and loaded it only partly with the goods designed for the Columbia; half of the space was taken with articles to fill an order apparently forwarded by Baranov through Ebbets. The *Beaver* was under command of Captain Cornelius Sowle, a New Englander of

[5] Porter, *John Jacob Astor,* I, 194ff.

[6] *Ibid.,* 190–91. Washington Irving, *Astoria,* 194ff.

considerable experience in the China trade. The *Beaver* reached Oahu on March 26, 1812, and the Columbia River on May 5, her arrival almost exactly coinciding with that of the last party of overlanders. On July 15 David Thompson, representing the Northwest Company, reached Astoria with a canoe load of men. Parties were sent to the interior to trade, and one group of men detailed to make their way back with mail to the east.

Early in 1813 news of the outbreak of war between English and the United States was brought to the Columbia by John McTavish, who appeared at Astoria on April 11. This changed the situation entirely. During the following summer, when the Astor men once more gathered at Astoria, continued pressure from their British rivals and the hostility of Indians, as well as their hopeless isolation, induced them to sell the fort, their goods, and the business to the Northwest Company. Their decision was perhaps hastened by a rumor of the approach of a British vessel of war. On October 16 the deal was finally completed. The Northwest Company took over the fort, and those employees who did not wish to enter the service of the Canadian company were allowed to leave for home. The last of them departed on the *Pedler,* a ship which had been chartered at the Hawaiian Islands for Astor by Hunt of the American Fur Company for the relief of Astoria but had arrived too late to effect this. Hunt, however, sanctioned the agreement, and on April 3 he embarked with the last of the clerks who had refused service with the Northwest Company.

The *Beaver* sailed from the Columbia River on August 4, 1812, and proceeded to Novo-Arkhangel'sk, where Sowle disposed of the remainder of his cargo to Baranov for $56,000. His pay, however, had to be taken in skins, and as there was not a sufficient supply on hand, the *Beaver* had to sail to St. Paul in the Pribilof Islands in Bering Sea where a cargo of sealskins was taken aboard. From here —contrary to the instructions of Astor, who had directed the captain to return to the Columbia—Sowle sailed for Oahu and thence to Canton, where he arrived on January 1, 1813. Here it was necessary to lay up the *Beaver,* so that Sowle did not return to New York until March, 1816.

Astor's role during the war of 1812 was somewhat equivocal. He was able to teeter on both ends of the diplomatic see-saw. Before the war actually broke out, he had induced the government to wink at his violation of the Non-Intercourse Act in bringing his furs from Michillimackinac under safe conduct from the British. National interests were no concern of his. Profits were his objective, and he played with either side indifferently, while cloaking his maneuvers under high-sounding professions. On the outbreak of war he decided to reinforce and supply the garrison at Astoria and bestirred himself to prepare a ship for this purpose. In his usual thoroughgoing way, he dispatched two—one the *Forrester* under British convoy from London, the other the *Lark* from New York. Not only was the *Lark* under United States escort, but also, on the pretext that she was going to supply Novo-Arkhangel'sk, she was given a passport from the Russian embassy and, through the Russian ministry, secured a safe-conduct from the British admiral, Sir John Borlase-Warren. The *Forrester* sailed from London in a British convoy, and as a final *reductio ad absurdum* there sailed in the same convoy the *Isaac Todd,* a twenty-gun ship fitted out in London by the Northwest Company and provided with a letter of marque for the express purpose of destroying the very fort which Astor's ship was intended to save! Truly, if ever the gods laugh, they had every occasion for mirth.[7]

The *Isaac Todd* sailed around the Horn into the Pacific. Here one of her consorts, the sloop-of-war *Racoon* became separated from the *Isaac Todd* and proceeded on her errand alone. She arrived at Astoria early in December, 1813, where she received the formal surrender of the post. The Stars and Stripes were hauled down, and the Union Jack was run up to signalize the transfer of sovereignty.

Meanwhile, at Novo-Arkhangel'sk Baranov was exerting himself to keep the Russian American Company afloat. The outbreak of war in Europe had severed sea communication with St. Petersburg and the uncertain links through Siberia and Okhotsk were incapable of supplying the northern posts. Hence Baranov had to continue to rely upon his own efforts and the help he could draw from the United States vessels. The practice of hiring Aleut hunters to vessels operating in Californian waters for sea-otter skins had become more and more frequent, to the extreme annoyance of the

[7] Porter, *John Jacob Astor,* I, Chapters VII and VIII.

From an old print

SITKA (NOVO-ARKHANGEL'SK) IN RUSSIAN TIMES

Courtesy Fish and Wildlife Service

SITKA IN 1920

Spanish authorities, but Spain was less and less able to adopt countermeasures, and after 1808 little heed was paid to Spanish protests. Finally in 1809 Baranov decided to send his own ship, and the *Nikolai* was sent south under Bulygin, with Tarakanov as purser. The *Nikolai* went ashore and was totally wrecked at Grey's Harbor. Bulygin died, and most of the natives were taken prisoners by the Indians, but finally Tarakanov made his way back to Sitka. The same year Kuskov left Sitka to rendezvous with the *Nikolai,* but since this vessel had been cast away, Kuskov went on to Bodega Bay where he hunted for sea otters and carried out a reconnaissance of the country, returning to Sitka the following year with two thousand skins.

The information secured by Kuskov confirmed Baranov in his decision to establish a farming settlement on the shores of New Albion. The necessary personnel was assembled, including some convicts exiled to Siberia, permission for whose emigration to America it was necessary to secure. This second attempt at colonization was a failure. Kuskov made the mistake of putting in to Queen Charlotte Islands, and the party was attacked by natives. The third attempt, made in the ship *Chirikov* towards the end of 1811, proved successful. Kuskov landed at Bodega Bay (which he named Rumyantsev) but found that the location, while providing good anchorage, was unsuited for a settlement. Accordingly he selected a tract of land eighteen miles to the north on the Slavyanka River, purchased it from the Indians, and moved his party and their supplies to it. Not until the beginning of 1812 did the settlement really take form, and the name Ross was given it. Within a reasonable time it began to produce livestock and grains, and for upwards of thirty years it continued to provide the northern posts with food.

Meantime, before supplies from Fort Ross were available, Sitka had to be fed. The steady stream of cargoes with which Astor had tried to tempt Baranov into partnership at first had been diverted and then, with the outbreak of the war, had dried up. Before the news of the outbreak of war could reach the Pacific, the first installment on Astor's promises arrived on the *Beaver* at Novo-Arkhangel'sk on August 19, 1812, and, as we have seen, was purchased by Baranov. But before another shipment could arrive, Baranov had recourse to other American ships to replenish his dwindling larder. This was during the term of Astor's tentative agreement, and Baranov had to resort to hand-to-mouth methods all through 1813–14. Succor from home arrived when the *Suvorov,* in command of Captain Lozarev, reached Sitka in November, 1814. But Lozarev was one of those naval officers who found it hard to take orders from a mere merchant. He interfered in the business of the company and assumed an independence which Baranov found difficult to tolerate. A quarrel occurred between Baranov and Wilson Hunt of the Astoria party which all but led to bloodshed, and Lozarev was indirectly involved. Then, one morning when Baranov awoke, he found that Lozarev had put to sea to take his ship and his grievances back to St. Petersburg.

Meanwhile the company had been pressing Baranov to send a mission to the Hawaiian Islands with a view to occupying them. After long hesitation, he decided to make use for this purpose of Doctor Scheffer, the ship's doctor of the *Suvorov,* who had been left behind with the supercargo when Lozarev had absconded. Passage for Scheffer and his party was arranged on the *Pedler,* homeward bound, and in the winter of 1815 Scheffer was dropped off at Kailua Bay. His relations with King Kamehameha (Tomi omi, as he was known to the Russians) were amicable enough. He became personal physician to the king and received grants of land and other favors, but his efforts to establish plantations and develop trade in sandalwood met with considerable opposition from the Americans. He was saved from considerable embarrassment by the timely arrival of two company ships. On one of these, the *Otkrytie* (*Discovery*), he sailed to Atuvai with a view to recovering the *Bering,* which had been cast away on an island and seized as prize by King Tamori. Other proposals made by Scheffer to Tamori were well received; the grant of land he wanted for a plantation was forthcoming, as well as a monopoly of the sandalwood trade in return for help from Russia to overthrow Tamori's rival, King Kamehameha. Scheffer thus aroused King Kamehameha against Russia; moreover, he failed to get the needed support from the Russian government. Confidence of the king in Scheffer waned, and finally he lost the respect and fear of the natives. Then the Russian plantations and fort were attacked. The Russians and the Aleuts were glad to save themselves by flight on one of the company's ships, the *Kodiak*.

(Captain Wadsworth in another, the *Il'men,* had already deserted.) The *Kodiak* managed, despite its unseaworthy condition, to limp into Honolulu, but welcome was lacking here, and Scheffer eventually escaped on an American vessel to Canton, the rest of the expedition making its way back to Sitka some eight months later.

Finally, after the conclusion of the French war, in 1817 the headquarters of the Russian American Company at St. Petersburg sent the twin vessels, the *Suvorov* under Captain Leontii Hagemeister and the *Kutuzov* under Captain Ponifidine, on a round-the-world voyage to Sitka with instructions to Hagemeister to make a thorough inspection of the company's business and posts and to supersede Baranov. They arrived in November, 1817, and proceeded in their task without first apprising Baranov of their full instructions. Eventually, after the inspection of the books and accounts had been completed, Hagemeister used the powers conferred on him to name Yanovskii, a young lieutenant, to Baranov's post. Yanovskii had in the meantime married Baranov's daughter, Irina.

But Baranov presented the real problem. When told that he had been superseded, he toyed with several alternative schemes. Finally Golovnin, captain of the *Kamchatka* which had newly arrived, induced Baranov to return to Russia. So, on December 1, 1818, he embarked on the *Kutuzov* to return to the land he had left more than forty years before. He was not well on embarkation and did not improve during the voyage. At Batavia he went ashore when the *Kutuzov* was delayed. After resuming the journey, he was taken ill of fever and within a day or two was dead. Somewhere in the Straits of Sunda his body was committed to the deep.

XI

The Adjustment of Territorial Claims

THE DEATH OF BARANOV CAME AT A TIME WHEN THE FORTUNES OF the Russian American Company were in the balance. The company's first charter was about to expire, and before it could be renewed, the operations for the past twenty years would of necessity be subjected to severe scrutiny. Moreover, the encroachment of American traders was steadily reducing the catch of sea otters in the Alexander Archipelago and rendering the maintenance of Sitka unprofitable. Pressure brought to bear on the Ministry of Foreign Affairs by the company's headquarters had from time to time led to protests being lodged in Washington and to demands that this poaching by United States traders be stopped. All were to no avail. The United States government always contended that the activities of private traders were not subject to its control, and it refused to act.

Shortly after the expiration of the charter a committee was named to review the activities of the company and to recommend whether or not its privileges should be continued. This committee, coached by the officers of the headquarters at St. Petersburg, urged that the charter be renewed, that the limits of Russia's exclusive claims be defined, and that other Russians or the nationals of other governments be enjoined from trading within this area. Accordingly on September 4, 1821, a *ukaz* was issued whose preamble recited how

> the trade of our subjects on the Aleutian Islands and on the northwest coast appertaining to Russia is subject, because of secret and illicit traffic, to oppression and impediments.[1]

[1] The relevant parts of this proclamation are given in *Alaska Boundary Tribunal, 1903. Proceedings* II, 25–26. (Fifty-eighth Congress, 2 sess., *Sen. Doc.* 162, Ser. 4600); hereinafter cited as *Alaska Boundary Tribunal.*

The rules reserved to Russian subjects

> the pursuit of commerce, whaling and fishery, and all other industry, within an area extending from Bering Strait south to 51° of north latitude on the American coast and from Bering strait to 45° 50′ (the southern tip of Urup in the Kurile Islands) on the Asiatic side.

Foreign vessels were forbidden to approach within less than one hundred Italian miles of these coasts at any point. The charter issued to the company on September 13 secured to it the exclusive privileges of taking fur-bearing animals and catching fish within the waters so described.[2]

The intention of the Russian government, as expressed in these documents, was to exclude United States and English ships from prosecuting a trade in furs within those parts of the North Pacific which were claimed by Russia. The governments of the United States and England were accordingly notified of this purpose.

This unilateral action on the part of the Russians called forth prompt and emphatic protests from both of these governments. Castlereagh's words were guarded but strong: "His Britannic Majesty must be understood as hereby reserving all his rights." In Washington, John Quincy Adams was somewhat more cautious but no less resolutely prepared to challenge Russia's position: "The President has seen with surprise . . . ."

The British government, at the time when it was notified of this action, was preoccupied with two crises in affairs in Europe—the revolt in Greece and the revolution which had just broken out in Spain. Castlereagh, however, found time to draft instructions to the Duke of Wellington, who represented England at the European Congress of Verona assembled in October, 1822, to consider these affairs. But Wellington's representation of the English case was somewhat perfunctory; and the Tsar, having none of the necessary documents with him at Verona, asked that negotiations should be initiated at St. Petersburg by Sir Charles Bagot, British ambassador at the Russian court.

It had been the intention of the Tsar to have the negotiations carried on with the United States government through Pierre Poletika, Russian ambassador at Washington. Because of ill health, Poletika

[2] *Alaska Boundary Tribunal,* II, 27.

was recalled; and Baron Tuyll, his successor, was instructed to ask that the discussions be transferred to St. Petersburg. On the way to his new post he was somewhat unaccountably delayed by a stopover in England, and before he arrived in the United States, the Russian government had seen the advantages of carrying on negotiations simultaneously with both powers at St. Petersburg by the same plenipotentiaries and changed Tuyll's instructions. Thus it came about that Sir Charles Bagot's powers were issued to him on February 20, 1823. Those of the United States ambassador, Middleton, because of the delay explained above, were not issued until July 18, 1823, and did not reach him until October. Powers to the Russian plenipotentiaries, Poletika and Nesselrode, were not forthcoming until February 20, 1824. These dates must be kept in mind, for while negotiations were initiated by both ambassadors prior to the receipt by the Russian plenipotentiaries of their powers, such negotiations were merely preliminary and obviously were binding on neither party.

On the face of it the point in the *ukaz* which both England and the United States were prepared to challenge, and on which they could make common cause, was the arbitrary assumption of Russia of jurisdiction over the seas adjacent to her American and Asiatic possessions. A second point—the advance by Russia of a claim to sovereignty over the American mainland as far south as 51° north latitude (about the north end of Vancouver Island)—would also not go unchallenged. But on this point the interests of the United States and England diverged. Great Britain was prepared to restrict Russia's claims within the limits over which her claims were unquestioned, which was assumed certainly not to extend further south than 59° and which might not go beyond 61°. (There was considerable vacillation on this question.) Two considerations, however, prejudiced Britain's case. In the first place the Russian American Company had occupied Sitka in latitude 57° (approximately) and had made this their headquarters. There was, as a result, some justification in Russia's claims to the Alexander Archipelago. The other complicating factor was that by the Convention of 1818 Great Britain and the United States, having failed to fix a boundary for their possessions on the northwest coast, had agreed that for ten years the whole area west of the Rocky Mountains should be open to the citizens of both countries, without prejudice to the territorial claims of either country. The United States had actually put forward no serious claims to territory north of the forty-ninth parallel, but this Convention was invoked as justification for the claim of the United States to be a party to the settling of the boundary between Great Britain and Russia.

The issue was further complicated by the fact that the trouble in Spain inevitably involved the Spanish colonies in which both England and the United States had a special interest. John Quincy Adams, about the time that he was sending instructions to Middleton concerning the negotiations with regard to the northwest coast, had submitted to Benjamin Rush, the ambassador in London, a list of questions to be discussed with Foreign Secretary George Canning. The problem of the northwest coast was one of them, but for some unknown reason Adams did not see fit to instruct Rush at this time, informing him, instead, that instructions would follow. During the course of his discussions with Foreign Secretary Canning, Rush (probably on a directive by Adams) dropped a broad hint that he would like to go over the situation in the Spanish American colonies with a view to possible concerted action. This suggestion was received without comment, but on the occasion of their next meeting Canning returned to this proposal enthusiastically, and as a result the two were soon deep in working out some basis of common action. The negotiations on this proposal broke down, however, because of Rush's insistence (presumably on Adams' orders) that a necessary prelude to such concerted action must be Great Britain's recognition of the South American governments. For this step Canning was not yet prepared, and the matter was dropped. Then, towards the end of the year, Canning returned to the question of the northwest coast.

Foreign Secretary Canning had from the first been laboring under some misapprehension concerning the attitude of the United States, for Stratford Canning, his cousin and British minister to the United States, had reported (in a letter written on July 23, 1823) a conversation which he had had with Adams on July 12. In this letter there occurs this extraordinary passage: "He [Adams] added that the United States had no territorial claims of their own as high as the 51st degree of latitude."[3] This statement, as it stood, without qualification, was quite misleading. Indeed, there was some evidence from statements of Monroe, Adams, and others that the United States hoped to exclude Great Britain from the northwest coast. And if Stratford Canning had had nothing else to go on, he might have recalled Adams's statement to him during their clash in 1821 over the bill proposed in Congress to send an expedition to occupy the mouth of the Columbia River. On that occasion Adams, angered by Minister Canning's protest (which was quite in order in view of the treaty of 1818), blurted out his conviction that Britain had no rights anywhere on the shores of the North Pacific.[4] What was more serious still, Foreign Secretary Canning completely misjudged the attitude of the United States or the purpose of Adams. He wrote to Bagot:

> That part of the question in which the American government is peculiarly desirous of establishing a concert with this country is that which concerns the extravagant assumption of maritime jurisdiction . . . the other part of the question which relates to territorial claims and boundary is perhaps susceptible of separate adjustment.[5]

Having been put off his guard by Stratford Canning's remark, the Foreign Secretary had completely failed to interpret correctly Rush's advances in August. At that time Rush claimed not to have received instructions with regard to the northwest coast. In any event, the matter had dropped into the background while negotiations were under way for joint action of the United States and Great Britain in South America. Whether or not these instructions arrived subsequently we do not know, but we find Foreign Secretary Canning writing to Bagot on January 15, 1824:

> Upon receipt of Your Excellency's despatch No. 48 reporting the arrival of Mr. Hughes at St. Petersburg with instructions of the Government of the United States to Mr. Middleton, I applied to Mr. Rush for information as to the tenor of these instructions. I then found what I

[3] *Ibid.,* 120–21. Letter of Mr. S. Canning to G. Canning, Washington, May 3, 1823.

[4] J. T. Adams, *The Adams Family,* 180–81.

[5] *Alaska Boundary Tribunal,* II, 123–24. Dispatch of Mr. G. Canning to Sir C. Bagot, July 12, 1823.

had not before been led to expect, that Mr. Rush had himself authority to enter into negotiations with us as to the respective claims of Great Britain and the United States on the northwest coast of America, although he does not appear to have been instructed to invite such negotiations here if we should prefer leaving it to be conducted at St. Petersburg.[6]

It is extremely likely that Adams had wished to come to an understanding with Britain before approaching Russia on the question of territorial boundaries. This would have involved scrapping the Convention of 1818, which had nearly five years to run, a step to which Canning was averse. If Adams had thus secured a settlement, he would have left the boundary to be adjusted between Britain and Russia; if he failed to get a settlement, Middleton was instructed to demand that the United States be made a party to the negotiations, a requirement which made a very awkward situation for Sir Charles Bagot at St. Petersburg.

We are indebted to Rush for a running account of these negotiations with Canning on Spanish colonies, and, after these broke down, on the northwest coast.[7] A series of interviews with Canning, beginning on December 12 but interfered with by Canning's attack of gout, finally cleared matters up and gave Canning a good idea that British claims against Russia were going to be crossed up with those of the United States:

> What can this intend? Our northern question is with Russia as our southern is with the United States. But do the United States mean to travel north to get between us and Russia?[8]

To which Rush replied that "it was even so."

Canning, therefore, was faced with three alternatives: to try to come to an understanding with the United States at the eleventh hour and then fight out with Russia her northern boundary; or to allow negatiations to take their course in St. Petersburg, in order to put Britain in a better position to confront the United States; or to make the Convention of 1818 with the United States a

[6] *Ibid.*, 144–49. Dispatch of Mr. G. Canning to Sir C. Bagot, January 15, 1824.

[7] The other matters were later the subject of negotiations between Rush and special commissioners named by Great Britain.

[8] Richard Rush, *Memoranda of a Residence at the Court of London*, 467–69.

tripartite one including all three countries and by which all the country beyond the Rocky Mountains would be open to the citizens of all three on equal terms. Towards the end of the year 1823 Foreign Secretary Canning had taken counsel of Stratford Canning who had just arrived in London from his post as ambassador in Washington. Stratford's opinion, written shortly after this interview, shows how the minds of both men were working and is worth close examination. From Stratford Canning's letter it is clear that the Foreign Secretary at that time proposed to confine Russia to the north of latitude 61°. It had been, as we know, suggested by Adams that in view of the Convention of 1818 it would be advantageous for the matter of Russia's southern boundary to be the subject of negotiations among the three governments, who would then sign a tripartite pact. Stratford Canning then advised against such an agreement, which would admit tacitly the claim of the United States to a division of the whole territory (i.e., west of the Rocky Mountains) lying between the parallels of 42° and 61° north.

He then discusses an alternative plan suggested by his cousin in their conference:

1. To obtain from Russia by separate negotiation at St. Petersburg a disavowal of her twofold obnoxious pretension; her so-called maritime claim and her attempted extension of her southern boundary south to the fifty-first degree north latitude.

2. To settle by a negotiation, also separate, with the American plenipotentiaries in London a good boundary line between the territories of the United States and Great Britain from the Rocky Mountains west to the Pacific.

3. To return to Russia and settle separately with her. Or in the alternative of her proving uncompromising, to leave things as they were in the hope of reaching a better settlement later.

Stratford Canning uttered the warning that Russia would not withdraw her extreme pretensions without settling the question of territorial boundary. This could not be settled without the concurrence of the United States; and such concurrence would almost certainly necessitate an adjustment of England's dispute with the United States. The great prize on the west coast was the outlet to the Columbia River. The only way to secure a satisfactory settlement would be to come to terms first with the United States; then agreement with Russia would be easy.[9] Whatever may have been the intention of the Foreign Secretary at the time, the advice contained in the letter was not taken. On December 2 President Monroe delivered his memorable message to Congress in which, among other things, he said: "That the American continents . . . are henceforth not to be considered as subjects for future colonization by any European power."[10] On January 15, George Canning wrote his final instructions to Sir Charles Bagot to conduct his negotiations on both the issues entirely separate from those of the United States ambassador, because of the divergence of their interests.

Instructions to Middleton, the United States ambassador, had been forwarded on July 22. Preliminary sounding of the Russians had begun as early as 1822; delay had followed because of the uncertainty of whether or not the ambassadors of England and the United States would negotiate jointly with Russia. The real reason for the delay, however, seems to have been that plenipotentiaries for Russia had not yet been named. The departure of the Russian court from the capital in the autumn of 1823 further postponed matters. Finally the decision not to act in concert had been reached. The court had returned, and the appointment of Pierre Poletika and Count Nesselrode was made on February 20, 1824.

Middleton began his conferences with the Russian plenipotentiaries early in April. For his guidance he had received in the dispatch of July 22, 1823, a number of enclosures doubtless composed under the direction of Adams. One of these, called "Observations on the Claim of Russia to Territorial Possessions on the Continent of North America," contains this passage:

> With the exception of the British establishments north of the United States the remainder of both the American continents must henceforth be left to the management of American hands . . . the United States

[9] This letter is contained in the *Bagot Papers,* Vol. 37, Correspondence *re* Russian *ukaz* of 1823, 47–48, letter of Stratford Canning, Berkeley Square, to George Canning, December 24, 1823.

[10] *American State Papers, Foreign Relations,* V, 246, message of President of the United States at the commencement of the first session of the Eighteenth Congress, December 2, 1823.

can in no wise admit the right of Russia to exclusive territorial possession on any part of North America south of the 60th degree of north latitude.[11]

But, in his instructions to Middleton, Adams said:

With regard to territorial claims . . . we are willing to agree to the boundary line within which the Emperor Paul granted exclusive privileges to the Russian American Company, that is to say, latitude 55°.

As to Great Britain's claim, Adams suggested:

As the British ambassador at St. Petersburg is authorized and instructed to negotiate likewise upon this subject, it may be proper to adjust the interests and claims of the three powers by a joint convention.[12]

At the outset Middleton served notice on Bagot that in the matter of territorial settlement the United States would not recognize any decision reached by Russia and Great Britain separately, but would insist on being a party to negotiations concerning the boundary. This stipulation was according to the terms of the Convention of 1818, and to it Sir Charles Bagot agreed.

In his conferences with the Russians Middleton had something to bargain with, and he made adroit use of it. In the first place the speech of President Monroe had announced an uncompromising stand on the claims of any European powers to occupy American soil. Adams, as we saw above, had no intention of interpreting the statement literally but thought Russia should keep north of 60°. To get a withdrawal of her maritime claims, he was prepared to concede a territorial boundary as far south as 55°. Whether Russia was frightened by the Monroe Doctrine we do not know, but this offer to retreat from its extreme claims was a tempting one, and it was not difficult for both sides to come to terms. A satisfactory treaty was hammered out by April. According to it, the parallel of latitude 54° 40′ north was fixed as the southern limit of Russian territory on the coast, and the northern limit of settlement of

[11] *Ibid.*, 445–46.

[12] *Alaska Boundary Tribunal,* II, 47–51. Letter of Adams to Middleton, July 22, 1823.

citizens of the United States.[13] All parts of the Pacific Ocean were to be open to the subjects of both powers, without discrimination, for purposes of trade and fishing, with the stipulation that the citizens of neither country were to resort to a part of the coast occupied by the other power without permission. For ten years the ships of both powers were to be free to frequent the coastal waters. Traffic in firearms and liquor was forbidden.[14]

The conference between Bagot and the Russian plenipotentiaries opened on February 28 and ran concurrently with those of the United States Ambassador. It was agreed by Bagot and the Russian plenipotentiaries at the outset of their negotiations that:

> the question of strict right should be provisionally waived on both sides and that the adjustment of our mutual pretensions should be made upon the sole principle of the respective convenience of both countries.[15]

Bagot had looked forward to the negotiations with considerable confidence. He thought he had taken the measure of both his adversaries and that neither of them was a man of independent judgment, but that, in the last analysis, everything would be referred to the Emperor. He seems to have underestimated both the ability and the astuteness of both men. As negotiations progressed, he found himself caught more and more in the consequences of decisions already reached. He had started out originally by challenging Russia's right to territory south of 60° of latitude; then had modified his challenge on instructions from Canning to the extent that he was prepared to take Cross Sound (approximately 57° 50′) as the dividing line. But he was soon embarrassed by the United States offer of 54° 40′. The acceptance of this boundary by Middle-

[13] It was found that 55° parallel of latitude would have cut Prince of Wales Island in two. To avoid this, the boundary was run to the south of the island in order to give it all to Russia.

[14] On hearing of the United States' offer of the line of 54° 40′ as Russia's southern frontier and 51° as United States' northern limit, Canning had written: "It does not seem uncharitable to suppose that the object of the United States in making a selection, otherwise wholly arbitrary, of these two points of limitation for British dominion, was to avoid collision with Russia themselves and to gratify Russia at the expense of Great Britain." *Alaska Boundary Tribunal,* II, 146. Dispatch of Mr. G. Canning to Sir C. Bagot, January 15, 1824.

[15] *Alaska Boundary Tribunal,* II, 154. Letter from Sir C. Bagot to Mr. G. Canning, March 17/29, 1824.

ton made any other boundary between Great Britain and Russia almost impossible. This would have left the way open to vessels of one nation to circumvent the treaty effectively by using the territorial waters of the other. Without knowing the cause, Bagot found the attitude of the Russians becoming stiff and uncompromising. By this time the Russians had set their heart on a strip of mainland coast beginning in or near latitude 54° 40′ and running north to the one hundred and thirty-ninth meridian so as to place a barrier between the Russian American Company and the operations of the Hudson's Bay Company.[16] Therefore, Bagot was driven from one concession to another. He finally agreed to accept the "55th degree of latitude as her boundary on the islands"; but on the coast the fifty-sixth parallel was to be the boundary; a line passing out through Sumner Strait would join these two parallels, Baranof and Sitka Islands going to Russia and Prince of Wales Island to Great Britain. This offer was rejected by Russia in favor of her original proposal, a frontier that would pass south of Prince of Wales Island (54° 40′) and would then traverse Portland Canal to the summit of the mountains assumed to border the coast and then along the summit of these mountains to the one hundred and thirty-ninth meridian of longitude. Bagot claimed that to concede this would exceed his powers, and negotiations were broken off at this point.

Bagot then referred the dispute to London. An instructive letter from Nesselrode analyzed the whole question from the Russian point of view. In this letter Nesselrode pointed to the Convention of 1818 as indicating the weakness of the position of Britain; by that convention she had admitted (or so he claimed) the United States to an equal share in the territories west of the Rocky Mountains. She had, therefore, no exclusive sovereignty. Russia had come to terms with the United States, the other member of the partnership; there was therefore nothing for England to do but to acquiesce in this settlement and to conform. The logic was unanswerable. It was Canning's mistake to have attempted to come to a settlement with Russia without first having come to an understanding with the United States.

16 See letter of Count Nesselrode to Admiral Mordvinov April 11, 1824, *Alaska Boundary Tribunal,* II, 166.

Having been duly instructed by Lieven, Canning prepared to yield but sought to obtain some compensation—the right to trade at Novo-Arkhangel'sk. He also endeavored to restrict the *lisière* (coastal strip) within the narrowest bounds by having it follow the foot of the mountains, a line which the most superficial consideration would show to be impracticable to negotiate. The treaty as redrafted was now forwarded to Bagot to present to Nesselrode with no discretion. But Russia, who had apparently agreed to opening Arkhangel'sk in perpetuity to English trade, now withdrew her offer on the grounds that the privilege had not been granted to the United States. She also insisted on her original line following the crest of the mountains. Bagot thereupon returned the treaty unsigned. He left St. Petersburg in the summer of 1824, profoundly regretting that he had not been instrumental in reaching an agreement on a matter which he considered of capital importance.

The British cabinet gave the matter consideration throughout the autumn of 1824 and finally decided to send Stratford Canning to St. Petersburg with a draft of a treaty. His instructions were: "If the present project is agreeable to Russia, we are ready to conclude and sign a treaty." Canning carried out his instructions faithfully, and on two matters he was able to get some last-minute concessions. Bagot had suggested in a letter to Foreign Secretary Canning as early as March 10, 1824, that, since Russia was inclined to be so arbitrary on the question of Prince of Wales Island, it might be possible to secure some compensation further north by inducing Russia to move the boundary to the north of Mount St. Elias some distance to the west. This suggestion had been overlooked in the draft forwarded to Bagot in the summer, but the Foreign Secretary remembered it later and instructed Stratford Canning to press to have the boundary north of 59° moved from the one hundred and thirty-ninth meridian (the one usually mentioned) to the one hundred and forty-first.[17] The other modification was with respect to the *lisière,* where it was conceded that the line (which was supposed to follow the crest of the mountains) should never exceed a distance of ten marine leagues from tidewater. This was yielded with somewhat bad grace by Lieven.

[17] The result of this afterthought was to secure to the Dominion of Canada the Klondike gold fields, which would otherwise have lain to the west of the boundary.

The settlement of the dispute over the northwest coast was based neither on any abstract title nor on "mutual convenience." Spain had had the most clear-cut claim, but a Papal Bull had no standing with heretics outside the Roman Catholic fold. It was of little use to invoke "mutual convenience" since the governments were ill informed on actual conditions in these remote regions. None of those participating in the discussions had ever been to the northwest coast. The maps used were imperfect and antiquated. The British placed their reliance on the maps of Vancouver, who, gazing from the deck of his ship, had fancied the serrated peaks that formed the eastward horizon were a continuous and well-defined ridge. A group of diplomats sitting around tables on the other side of the globe, working under handicaps with defective, out-of-date maps could hardly produce satisfactory boundaries. Canning's quip of "bobbing for whale *ipsis in faucibus Beringi*" was mildly satirical of the air of academic unreality that hung over the negotiations. The convention was but one incident of a diplomatic game in which the participants were playing for stakes not always on the board.

Considered by itself, the issue was less one between the Anglo-Saxon powers and Russia, as it seemed to be, than a phase of the struggle between Great Britain and the United States for the possession of the continent. It is questionable whether Russia could ever have made a serious bid for power in the North Pacific against either of her rivals. She had an insecure foothold on the continent. The original Shelekhov-Golikov Company had never penetrated further east and south than Lituya Bay (approximately 58° 30′ north).[18] Baranov had been subsequently instructed to extend his operations to the south and east, but when he did so, such extension was made from commercial motives and not out of deference to

[18] This was the extreme limit of the concession granted in 1798 when the government sanctioned the merger of the rival companies in the North American trade. The so-called Act of Union, August 5, 1798, is given in *Polnoe Sobranie Zakonov,* 1799, text 19,030. The charter of 1799, however, carried the boundary forward three and one-half degrees. An English translation of this charter is in *Alaska Boundary Tribunal,* II, 23. The claim to the American coast as far south as 55° north latitude was, however, not recent. It appeared first in the time of Catherine having been advanced by Müller by virtue of Chirikov's discovery. See *Doklad Komiteta ob Ustroistvye Russkikh Amerikanskikh Kolonii,* Vol. 1, App. 279.

Courtesy Fish and Wildlife Service

RUSSIAN ORTHODOX CHURCH ON ATTU

Russia's political aspirations.[19] Russia's tenure was constantly threatened by native risings. Russian occupation Baranov continued to regard as provisional.[20] At the very time negotiations were under way in the capital, the board of directors had already authorized abandonment of Sitka, a fact carefully suppressed during the discussions.[21] Moreover, up to 1825, Russia had relinquished one by one most of the mainland posts. The methods by which the Russian American Company obtained its furs tended to exhaust rather than to preserve its resources and thus to render its occupation transitory.

The "non-colonization" principle, which formed part of the Monroe Doctrine, already foreshadowed by Adams and proclaimed by the President, played relatively little role in the actual discussions. It was, however, implicit in the attitude of Adams and others. Bagot's anger against Adams was perhaps due to the latter's skill in cloaking, as Bagot believed, a policy of exclusion with the mantle of a righteous crusade against tyranny. Yet Rush believed that this novel "pretension on the part of his government was intended as a set-off against the maritime pretension of the Russian *ukaz*."[22] The principle had not been adhered to in the settlement with Russia, and Adams was probably ready for a deal with Canning. It is apparently this inconsistency between extravagant claims and the profession of moderation on Adams' part that explains the charge of "duplicity" Bagot made in his private letters to Canning. Adams, aspiring to the presidency, could ill afford to sheathe so trusty a sword as the policy of manifest destiny.[23]

19 *Records of the Russian American Company*. Instructions from the board of directors to the governor of the colonies, April 18, 1802.

20 Baranov's views are given in a letter on Kodiak to Larionov at Unalaska, March 3, 1798, given in P. Tikhmenev, *Istoricheskoe obozryenie obrazovaniya Ross. Am. Kompanii* (*Historical Survey of the Formation of the Russian American Company and Its Activity down to the Present*), II, Pril. 120.

21 *Records of the Russian American Company*. Letter from the board of directors to the chief factor of the American Colonies, Muraviev, February 28, 1822.

22 *Alaska Boundary Tribunal,* II, 147. Dispatch of Mr. G. Canning to Sir C. Bagot, January 15, 1824.

23 See also my article, "Drawing the Alaska Boundary," in *The Canadian Historical Review,* Vol. XXVI, No. 1 (March, 1945), 1–24.

XII

Scot versus Muscovite

TOWARDS THE END OF 1825 THE DECEMBRIST REVOLT STIRRED RUSsia to its depths. A secret society had been formed in 1817 by a group of young men drawn together by the common experiences of war and common aspirations. Most of them belonged to the class of landed nobility—the class that had been called into existence to serve the state but which during the course of the eighteenth century had been freed from that obligation, though still continuing to have first claim on posts in the tsar's service. Members of it had for the most part enjoyed a superior education and had traveled widely, but their experiences little fitted them for the dreary round of the barrack square or the dull routine of composing endless "most devoted reports" for "Your Most Esteemed Excellencies."[1] They longed to exchange the ornamental role they occupied for one of freer participation in the serious work of government. The more radical members hoped to remold Russia according to the models of constitutional government then prevailing. In the twenties, the movement found many converts among the aristocrats. But it was quite out of touch with living realities in Muscovite life. Neither the peasants, whose lot the Decembrists sought to ease, nor the soldiers who were to be their instruments had an understanding of their aims. For those of other than their own station in life many of the nobles had nothing but contempt. Thus walled off from other classes, the society tended to be aloof and dilettante.

While there was much in the movement that was mad and quixotic, it was inspired by high and generous impulses. Many of its leaders were men of outstanding gifts. Among them was a distinguished poet, Ryleyev, who suffered the supreme penalty. The brother of Aleksandr Pushkin, the poet, was implicated. If birth,

[1] Honorific terms much affected in official circles in tsarist times.

high attainments, and nobility of character could have availed, some measure of success might have been achieved; or perhaps as partial compensation for failure some answering spark of generosity might have been wakened or some emulation of their purpose kindled to life in the Tsar. But nobility weighed nothing with the autocrat when it went hand in hand with defiance of authority. The supreme virtue in a subject was submissiveness.

Positions in the administration of the Russian American Company were at this time regarded as bureaucratic posts. A number of those implicated in the conspiracy had been in the company's employ. The poet, Ryleyev, had been particularly prominent. Zavalishin had written copiously of the company's affairs. He had constituted himself an advocate of expansion and entertained an ambitious project towards this end. A third, Somov, more obscure, during the course of the investigation came before Nicholas for questioning. He admitted that he had worked in the company's service, a statement which drew from the Tsar the scornful exclamation, "A fine company you have got together there."

A special commission held a most searching investigation of the conspiracy, and afterwards a tribunal was created to fix guilt and adjudge penalties. Five men were condemned to feel the full weight of the autocrat's vengeance, among them, Ryleyev. Of the others involved, hundreds passed into exile in remotest Siberia. Russia had had a long history of palace revolutions, and Nicholas regarded this uprising as but another chapter in this story. To render his throne secure, the movement must be stamped out.

It was natural that the Russian company should feel the weight of imperial disfavor. It was whispered that the company was to lose its franchise. In the great house at 72 Moika, where directors had made high wassail with friends and where officials resplendent in epaulettes and gold braid had presided in state, the atmosphere was now one of noiseless activity. Gravity and industry prevailed in place of ostentation and gaiety. One saw only clerks in sober habits, poring over their ledgers or laboring at the graceful flourishes with which they embellished the official correspondence. The ringleaders passed to their doom, months went by, and the terrible scenes on Senate Square became a half-forgotten memory before Nicholas regained his normal composure and laid aside his distrust and suspicion. The Persian and Turkish wars gave Nicholas the opportunity to appear before his people as an inspired leader and to regain something of the popular favor he had forfeited through these severities. He signalized this *rapprochement* with his people by certain acts of grace, among which letters patent of November 28, 1828, confirmed the privileges of the Russian American Company. Four months later, on March 29, 1830, these were announced in a proclamation of the Senate.

With the death of Baranov the old order in America had passed away. The governors who succeeded him—Hagemeister, Yanovskii, Chistyakov, and Wrangel—were officers of the Imperial Navy, on detached service with the company. They brought with them naval traditions and looked to the navy rather than to the company's service for advancement. Since officers in the armed services were drawn from the aristocracy, it was now rank and birth, breeding and education, that were the doors to preferment. Respectability and decorum were the new watchwords. Gone were the roistering days of the old *promyshlenniki,* prodigal of life, contemptuous of danger, who had plundered and murdered the natives, had robbed them of their women, had exposed themselves recklessly to every hazard, had endured the ravages of scurvy, and had suffered shipwreck or perished at sea. Dividends for shareholders and pensions for officials were the new objectives; decorum the virtue insisted upon. Much, it is true, had been gained. Squalor, drunkenness, and brutality were frowned on. Moral laxity was forbidden, and lawful wedlock was required. Patterning itself after Europe, the bureaucracy became enlightened and liberal; at the same time it lost something of its pristine vigor and simplicity.

We are indebted to Sir George Simpson of the Hudson's Bay Company for a shrewd glimpse into the operations of the Russian American Company in America. He visited Sitka in 1842, and none of the details were lost on his practiced eye and penetrating judgment. He noted the sharp cleavage of rank between the strictly civilian employees and those from the armed services and the upper strata of the *Table of Ranks.*[2] He was astonished at the

[2] An elaborate scale devised under Peter by which the state services were arranged into fourteen successive and ascending *chins* or ranks. There were sharp differences in caste, recognized in America as in others of the Tsar's dominions.

generous pay and the still more lavish scale on which the company employees lived, so lavish indeed that most of them had already heavily mortgaged their future by contracting debts. He was impressed with the good order and discipline among the servants. Above all he was struck by what to him seemed to be the excessive numbers of persons required to carry on the modest operations of the company. "For the amount of business done," comments Simpson, "the men as well as the officers appear to be unnecessarily numerous, amounting this season to nearly five hundred, who, with their families, make up about one thousand two hundred souls as the population of the establishment."[3] But if the thrifty Scot was astonished by the extravagance in the colonial administration, what superlatives would he have found for the headquarters in St. Petersburg? At best those living in America had a lonely life, deprived of the amenities of civilization and the society of friends and relatives, for which their ample pay could be only slight compensation. There was little to say for the magnificent remuneration and generous pensions bestowed (for very inconsiderable services) on the many retired "generals and admirals" (in the scornful words of Veniaminov) who made up the board of directors at St. Petersburg.

Across the North Sea the Russian American Company's formidable rival, the Hudson's Bay Company, had amalgamated in 1821 with the Northwest Company and thus had taken on new vigor. After 1826 its interests in North America were directed by a man who would bear comparison with Baranov. The little Scot, George Simpson, who had been sent to America to preside over its destinies as chief factor, like Baranov, was a man of broad views. In tenacity he was the Russian's equal; in resourcefulness perhaps not much his inferior. The wide, free realms beyond the Rocky Mountains, that were now added by the new charter to the company's imperial domain, fired his ambition to secure in so vast a field an outlet for his enterprise and energies.

The members of the Hudson's Bay Company, in entering this region, plied every advantage to displace their United States rivals and even to capture trade from the Russians. The new industrial ascendancy of England enabled them to invade Sitka itself with cheaper and better goods and to take much of the trade. After 1830

[3] Sir George Simpson, *Narrative of a Journey Round the World,* II, 190.

they became particularly aggressive on the coast. In 1832 Peter Skene Ogden founded a post at the mouth of the Nass River and visited Sitka with a cargo to tempt the Russian factor with English goods. Ogden took pains to deny rumors that the English company intended to move up the Stikine River. Nevertheless, the following year he appeared at the Nass with two ships—the schooner *Vancouver,* under Captain Alexander Duncan, and the *Lama,* under Captain McNeil. Leaving Nass in August, he ascended the Stikine to a point fifteen miles inland (supposed to be beyond the frontier), where he reconnoitered a site for a post. During the winter following his visit, Wrangel, becoming apprehensive of this move, decided to forestall it by establishing a post himself at the mouth of the Stikine near Point Highfield. For this purpose a party was dispatched during the season of 1834 under the command of Moskvitinov.

A Russian fort, which the British could be forbidden by its commandant to approach (as he might legally do under the treaty), might very effectively exclude the British from the navigation of the river. Wrangel planned thus to use the provision of one article of the treaty to circumvent another.

The schooner *Dryad,* under command of Captain Kipling, arrived with a Hudson's Bay party under Ogden on June 18, 1834, and came to anchor in the sound. Though Moskvitinov was in actual command of the fort, it was to Lieutenant Zarembo of the brig *Chichagov* that Wrangel looked to carry out his instructions. Wrangel had chosen the occasion to be absent from Sitka, leaving his immediate subordinate, Captain Etholin in charge. He had taken precautions to draw up a proclamation in English to notify both the Hudson's Bay Company and the United States skippers that the provisions of the conventions with their respective countries by which they were permitted to frequent these coasts for ten years had lapsed, and that henceforth they would be barred from these waters. It was explained that, while the British unquestionably had the right to navigate any rivers that traversed the *lisière,* they could not pass a post without the permission of the commandant. In addition, Wrangel had enjoined on Zarembo that he was to use every means *short of force* to dissuade the Hudson's Bay party from proceeding up the river. The argument he was to use was that to force passage over Russian protests would constitute a violation of Article XI of the Convention.[4]

Although Wrangel thought he had made certain that the Russian position would be quite clear to the English, there arose the inevitable misunderstandings. Of course the social amenities were punctiliously preserved. Invitations were exchanged between the commanders. There were goings and comings between the *Dryad* and the *Chichagov* and between the *Dryad* and Fort Dionysius. There were official visits and ceremonial calls; the Tsar's health was pledged in champagne, the King's in rum. But the diplomatic deadlock could not be broken by convivialities. It is now apparent that lack of interpreters capable of explaining the Russian views was the cause of much misunderstanding. An Indian with some smattering of English and a Russian who had picked up a few Spanish words on the California coast were unequal to the task of explaining the subtleties of Wrangel's reasoning. Phrases such as "My captain speak you go away" might convey a rough idea of Wrangel's purpose and might give the Englishmen pause, but they hardly met the requirements of diplomatic intercourse. When the Englishman became angry and persistent, an appeal to Sitka was tried (which meant of course, Captain Etholin). An express was dispatched with a letter from Ogden to the commandant, and the party settled down to the dreary wait for a reply.

Having reached a deadlock in his dealings with the Russians, Ogden next tried his hand at winning over the Indians. Their chiefs, Seix[5] and Anacago, had somewhat truculently supported the Russians by denying the English right of entering the Stikine. Ogden reported that:

> . . . they [Chiefs Seix and Anacago] assumed a tone I was not in the habit of hearing, and requested to know if we had come here with the intention of erecting an establishment, and that although the Russians had one, they had no objections to our building one in the Sound, but

[4] The correspondence between Etholin and Zarembo indicates clearly that the use of force was not contemplated. *Records of the Russian American Company* (Correspondence of the Governor, Correspondence sent). Letter from Captain Etholin, Sitka, June 8/20, 1834.

[5] The chief whom Campbell called "Shakes" and the Russians "Shekzh."

were determined to prevent us if we attempted to proceed up the river, as by doing so we would injure their trade with the interior . . . .[6]

He therefore decided to vary his diplomatic methods and invited the chiefs on board to ply them with rum. But he had the indelicacy to water the rum down two-thirds (as he naïvely admits) instead of the one-third which was customary with the Russians. This ruse could scarcely go undetected, and Ogden's sharp practice was a sizable blunder, if we may judge by the fact that the chiefs, on leaving, reiterated in still more emphatic language their resolve to stop the British from entering the river.

The express to Sitka merely brought confirmation of Zarembo's original instructions. Another interpreter had accompanied the express on its return to help smooth matters. Etholin wrote:

As an English interpreter, for want of a better, I am sending you Dahlstrem. Although he is not a "professor" in the language yet perhaps you can manage to make yourself understood by Ogden.[7]

The "professor" merely made the confusion worse. Ogden was persuaded that the Russians intended to fire on his party if they attempted the ascent of the river in open boats; and even if the Russians did not, the Englishmen would certainly be attacked by the Indians, a natural deduction to be drawn from the menacing bearing of the natives. Ogden can scarcely be blamed for declining a contest on what appeared to be most unequal terms. So, inwardly raging at his discomfiture, he called off the expedition and sailed back to Fort Nass and Fort Vancouver to report to Dr. McLoughlin, Hudson's Bay factor at that post.

The incident immediately suggested to McLoughlin a bill for damages from the Russians, and he forthwith listed losses incurred for which compensation might be claimed from the Russian American Company for violating Article XI of the treaty by refusing the British the right to navigate the Stikine. But the "Honorable Company" had an alternative, namely, to open posts in the desired territory from the rear. It had for many years had a firm footing in the

[6] *Letters of John McLoughlin,* 317–22.

[7] Records of the Russian American Company (Letter from Etholin to Zarembo, June 20, 1834.)

Mackenzie Valley. At Fort Simpson[8] a considerable tributary from the west seemed to offer a prospective route for reaching this region from the east, and in 1834 the first attempt was made by J. McLeod, who was in the employ of the company at that post. Entering the mouth of the Liard, McLeod began to make his difficult and perilous way up against its constantly increasing current. The river in its lower course runs somewhat sluggishly across the timbered lowlands that border the Mackenzie. Above, where it crosses the cordillera, it is forced to scour a troubled channel through the northern Rockies and the southern end of the Mackenzie Mountains; in its upper reaches its tributaries spread through the interior plateau and drain the northern Cassiar, a land of solitude and of mystery. Tribal feuds, perhaps, have made the red man shun it as a land accursed; myths and legends cling to it. The story of its hot springs and "tropical valley" have helped to cast a spell.[9] The Liard's powerful current and impassable rapids have barred it to all but the most intrepid. The foaming waters of its canyons have taken their toll of white men and red. The very names that cling to its natural features are of ill omen—the Devil's Portage, Rapids of the Drowned, Whirlpool Canyon, and Hell Gate.

McLeod managed with his Indians, trackers, and canoemen to surmount these fearful obstacles. He portaged the rapids and lined his canoes through the swirling waters of the upper reaches. The canyons were traversed, and he succeeded in passing the mountains into somewhat quieter stretches. Here he established Fort Halkett at the mouth of the Beaver River. This was not, however, to be the limit of his exertions. Pursuant to instructions, he pushed on to where the Liard begins to branch out into a number of tributaries that constitute its headwaters. He chose one of these coming from

[8] Fort Simpson on the Mackenzie River at its confluence with the Liard River is to be carefully distinguished from the fort of the same name near the mouth of the Skeena. Eventually, to avoid misunderstandings, the latter was designated Port Simpson.

[9] Parties traveling through the Liard country to the Klondike in 1898 and 1899 had found a valley where the growth indicated unusual local conditions. The story grew until there were said to be jungles of tropical ferns and enormous evergreens three hundred feet in height. With actual reconnaissance the "tropical valley" has turned out to be a limited area where hot springs have created exceptionally favorable conditions for vegetation, prolonging to some extent the normal growing season for these latitudes.

the south, ascended it to its source in a lake which he called Dease. From the upper end of the lake he passed over to the Tanzilla and so reached the Stikine, where, after sweeping down from the north, that river gathers the waters of its head streams to make the final assault on the coast mountains before reaching the sea. For some reason McLeod turned back here, perhaps because of the hostility of Shakes's coastal Indians.

Fort Halkett seems to have been maintained as an outpost of Fort Simpson, but no serious attempt was made to open this route until after the failure of Ogden to get through from the mouth of the Stikine. In 1838, however, the company decided to renew the effort and chose for this purpose young Robert Campbell, one of its most energetic and resourceful officers. Campbell, chosen to advance Hudson's Bay rule into these regions, was already a seasoned veteran. Hence to him the Liard was just another river.

In the spring his party were on their way, tracking through the gorges and paddling up the quieter stretches. Passing the mountains, they turned into the mouth of the Dease River, emerging in Dease Lake from which it flows; from its upper end they portaged over to the river flowing southwestward to which McLeod had given the name Pelly. Here they met coastal Indians under their chief, Shakes, or Seiks (Seix), or Shekzh,[10] who traded with the Hudson's Bay on the coast and whom Campbell entrusted with a scribbled note for the factor at Fort Simpson (on the coast). The astonished factor, John Work, could scarcely believe his eyes when his old enemy, Shakes, landed a couple of days later at Fort Simpson and handed him the paper entrusted to him by Campbell, soiled but still legible. The great turbulent river which McLeod thought he had discovered was clearly the Stikine.

Kuprianov, who had now succeeded Wrangel as governor at Sitka, was dismayed by the success of the English in gaining access to the area between the northern Rockies and the sea, and he forthwith informed McLeod at Fort Simpson (on the coast) that he had been instructed by his government to open the navigation of

[10] There are several variants of his name—Shakes (Campbell), Seix or Seiks (John Work), Shekzh, according to the Russians—all somewhat futile efforts to reproduce the Indian sounds. "Shakes" seems to have prevailed. Years after the American occupation, his venerable figure could be seen around Wrangell. See John Muir, *Travels in Alaska,* 35, 36, 200, 201.

the Stikine to the English. But Simpson was not satisfied with the retreat of the Russian. He resolved to press the claim of the Hudson's Bay Company to the limit. McLoughlin had already furnished an elaborate bill of damages with which he might confront the Russians. Lord Durham, British ambassador to Russia, had by the end of 1837 been instructed to file the claim with the Russian authorities and continued to press it. The Russian government was much embarrassed by Durham's persistence. Nicholas had scored over England in 1833 when he had secured from the Sublime Porte an alliance with exclusive privileges to pass his warships through the Straits. Now, these diplomatic alliances having served their turn, he needed other allies. Louis Philippe, whom he hated as a usurper, now so threatened Russia and her ally, Turkey, by his open encouragement of Mehemet Ali that Nicholas sought the favor of England. The Russian American Company had always been suspect, and the new embroilment on the coast of America merely confirmed the Tsar's low opinion of it.

When Simpson wrote to Wrangel suggesting a lease of the coast as a solution of the misunderstanding, the question in due course was referred to the Emperor. Nicholas directed the company without further ado to accept Simpson's offer. Simpson and Wrangel, who represented their respective companies, met at Hamburg, and on February 6, 1839, drew up and signed an agreement whereby the *lisière* from Cape Spencer south to 54° 40′ was leased to the Hudson's Bay Company for ten years; the Hudson's Bay Company was to deliver to the Russian American Company as annual rental two thousand seasoned land-otter skins, procured on the western side of the Rocky Mountains; in addition, all the land-otter skins collected on the western side of the Rocky Mountains (not to exceed two thousand in number) were to be sold to them for twenty-three shillings each. The Hudson's Bay Company was to provide the Russian posts with the goods they required, thus eliminating their United States competitors, and to make delivery at Fort Simpson on the west coast or at such other place as the Russians should direct.

The plans of the Hudson's Bay Company to drive United States ships from the waters north of 54° 40′ were furthered by measures taken by the Russian government itself. Wrangel's warning issued to United States shipowners on the expiration of the special privileges granted by the treaty of 1824 was given wide publicity in the United States. United States ships, like those of the Hudson's Bay Company, were barred from the coast claimed by Russia. But the warning was unheeded. Vessels continued to sail in defiance of it, and one, the *Loriot* under Captain Blinn, was intercepted in 1836 and ordered away under threat of force.

United States shipowners had hoped that the right of access to the coast above 54° 40′, secured them for a period of ten years by the treaty of 1824, would be automatically extended at the end of that time. It seemed possible, as Middleton had suggested, to construe this right of access less as a privilege granted by Russia than as a limitation to completely free access, voluntarily agreed to by the United States; when the time had run out, rights hitherto enjoyed would then be restored.

The Russian government declined to take this argument seriously, maintaining on its part that the treaty secured to Russia full sovereignty above 54° 40′, on which they now would accept no limitation.

A lively exchange of notes between the two governments continued for some years over the *Loriot* case, but nothing could budge Nesselrode from the position he had taken. He refused to admit any liability for damage suffered by the owners, nor would he hear of any extension of trading rights. A note of Nesselrode of March 9/21, 1838, finally disposed of the case; and the United States was chagrinned to see the trade of the northwest coast go to its rival and to submit to a diplomatic rebuff which it had no means of averting.

By 1849, the date of the lease's expiration, gold had been discovered in California. The influx of population to the west coast created an unprecedented demand for food and almost all articles of human consumption. The Russian American Company's shelves at Sitka were cleared of out-of-date and shopworn goods, which were shipped off to San Francisco. All that could be got in exchange was gold. The Russians, therefore, had no recourse but to turn to the London company for a renewal of the agreement for ten years. Five years later, when war broke out between Russia and the western powers—England and France—both companies were dismayed at the prospects. Nicholas, moreover, with a British blockade of the Baltic and Black seas in prospect and his Pacific naval forces directly menaced by Anglo-French squadrons, could ill afford ships to guard Sitka. He therefore directed the company to seek an agreement with the Hudson's Bay Company to neutralize their respective possessions in the New World. The Hudson's Bay Company agreed, and the British government approved the arrangement, with the stipulation that it would not extend to the naval forces. During the Crimean War, therefore, Sitka and the American possessions were left alone, though the Asiatic posts of the Russian American Company suffered.

In 1859 sale of the colonies by Russia was in the air, the company's third franchise was about to expire;[11] hence the imperial government refused to allow the agreement to be extended beyond January 1, 1862. When this time came around, the Civil War was raging in the United States, and the matter of the sale was still undecided. It was found necessary to authorize the extension of the agreement to June 15, 1863. Since Russia was then herself in the midst of a crisis, the lease was prolonged to June 1, 1865; at that time a further extension was sought and obtained to January 1, 1867. Shortly thereafter the deed of cession to the United States was signed and ratified.

With the Hudson's Bay Company now squarely across the path of any eastward expansion and the fur reserves of the Alexander Archipelago dwindling, the Russians turned to the more northerly part of their possessions. Little more of the coast of Bering Sea was known than had been discovered by Cook, but the end of the Napoleonic Wars had seen the search for the Northwest Passage revived. In 1823 Sir John Franklin worked westward from the Mackenzie River by land and Captain Beechey in the *Blossom* tried to beat his way east along the Arctic coast. Franklin pushed west from the mouth of the Mackenzie River but was forced to turn back about the time that Beechey's progress was frustrated by ice when he was within one hundred and fifty miles of the other ex-

[11] The company had received a renewal of its charter in 1841. This was the most elaborate and far reaching of the legislative enactments covering the company's privileges and obligations. It remained in force until the cession. *Polnoe Sobranie Zakonov,* Vol. XIX, Part I, text 18, 290, 612–38.

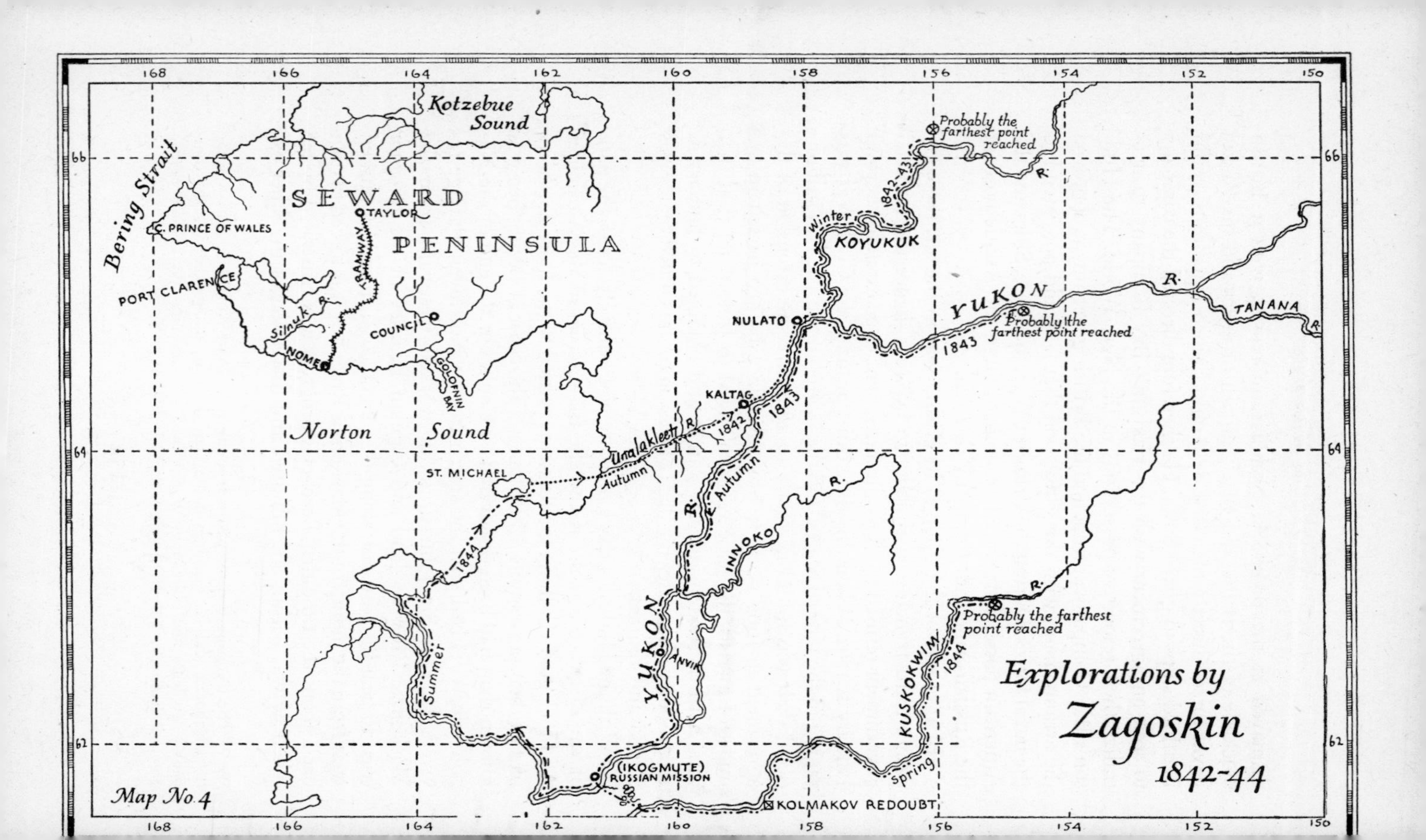
Explorations by
Zagoskin
1842-44
Map No. 4
Bering Strait
Kotzebue Sound
SEWARD PENINSULA
C. PRINCE OF WALES
PORT CLARENCE
TAYLOR
TRAMWAY
Silnuk R.
NOME
COUNCIL
GOLOFNIN BAY
Norton Sound
ST. MICHAEL
Unalakleet R.
Autumn
1842
KALTAG
1843
NULATO
Winter
KOYUKUK
1842-43
Probably the farthest point reached
R.
YUKON
R.
Probably the farthest point reached
1843
TANANA
R.
Autumn
R.
INNOKO
R.
YUKON
ANVIK
1844
Summer
(IKOGMUTE)
RUSSIAN MISSION
KOLMAKOV REDOUBT
Spring
KUSKOKWIM
1844
Probably the farthest point reached
R.
168
166
164
162
160
158
156
154
152
150
66
64
62

pedition. The younger Kotzebue in 1815 had commanded a ship which pushed up through Bering Strait and had discovered and explored Kotzebue Sound. Wrangel in 1820 led an expedition which sailed into the Arctic to enlarge geographical knowledge in that region. In 1833 Wrangel, now governor of the Russian colonies, sent Teben'kov north to map the coast, to reconnoiter the mouth of the Kvikhpak (the Yukon), and to establish a post at its mouth. As the delta is a quite unsuitable location for a post and lacks commodious anchorage, he selected a part of Norton Sound about one hundred miles to the north where there was a suitable site on a low island, which also provided a sheltered roadstead. Here he erected the Mikhailovskii Redoubt (commonly called St. Michael's). The lower Yukon and the Kuskokwim rivers were then attempted. Kolmakov ascended the latter and built a post which he called Fort Kolmakov. The Russians, having entered the Yukon, built Ikogmute (or the Mission, as it came to be known) about one hundred and fifty miles from its mouth. By 1841 they had reached the mouth of Nulato, where Glazunov built a fort, called Nulato, just below the Koyukuk. In 1843 Lieutenant Zagoskin was commissioned to ascertain by what means the trade of the middle Yukon was being diverted to the Seward Peninsula and across Bering Strait to the Chukchi. In carrying out this task, Zagoskin proceeded northward along the coast, then ascended the Unalakleet River, and crossed a divide to the river which he descended to the Yukon. He reached Nulato, and seems to have gone up the Koyukuk some distance, then to have come back to the mouth. Here he remained until the break-up. He then ascended the Yukon in a *baidar*. His craft was not suited for river travel; high water made tracking laborious and thus increased the difficulties of his journey. By the end of June he had, according to his observation, reached a point 64° 56′ 07″ north latitude and 154° 18′ 45″ west longitude. From here he turned back. His description of the locality is obscure and the observation is questionable. About all we can say is that it is possible he was near the mouth of the Tanana. He returned to Nulato and, passing over to Kuskokwim, ascended that river some distance before turning back to St. Michael's. As far as we know from official accounts, the place he reached is the extreme point the Russians reached on the Yukon River, but it is

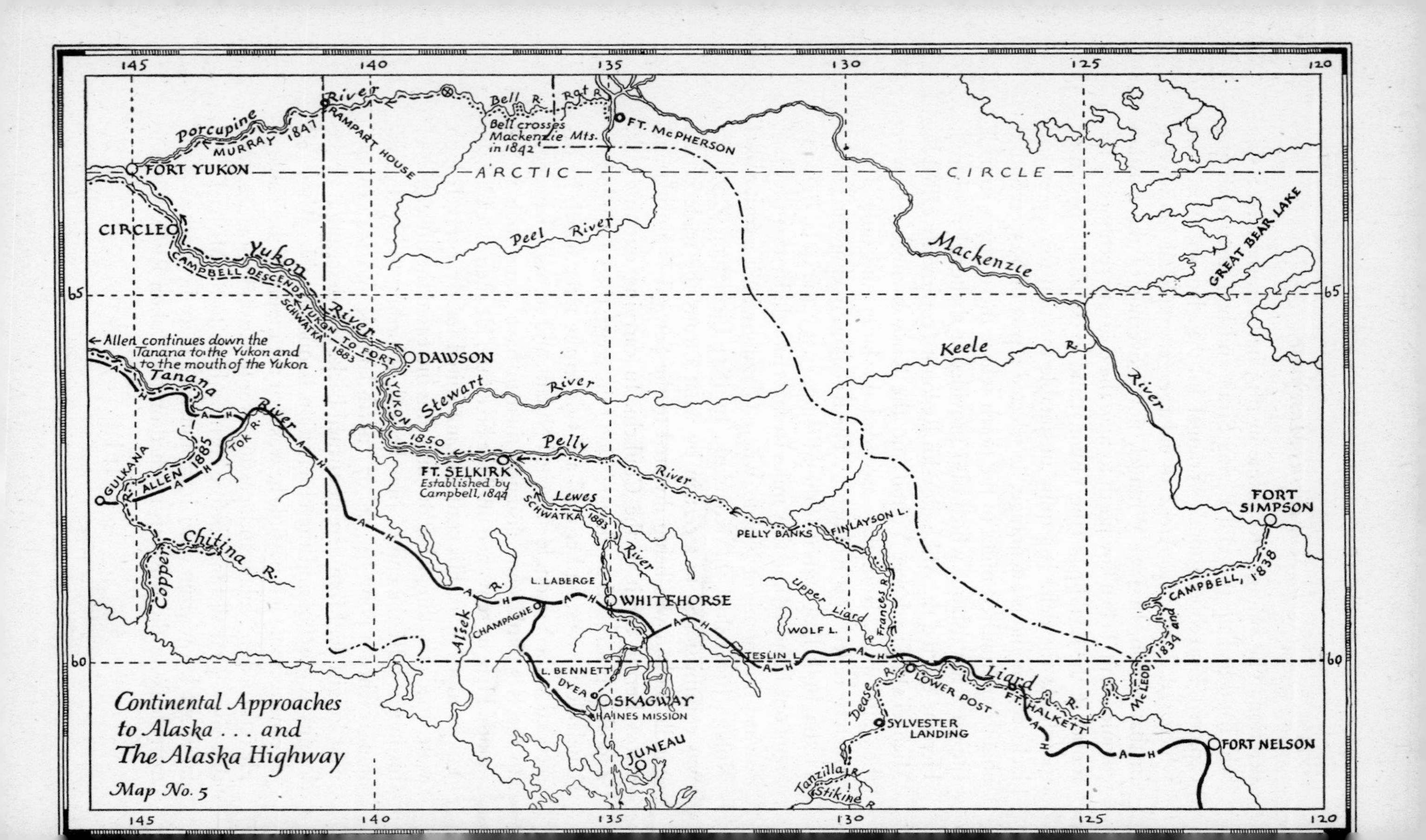

Continental Approaches to Alaska . . . and The Alaska Highway

Map No. 5

Courtesy Fish and Wildlife Service

FISHING

Courtesy Fish and Wildlife Service

DIPPING SALMON

believed that one of the employees of the Russian American Company ascended the river to Fort Yukon.

Meanwhile, the ramparts of the Yukon Valley were breached from the east. After Campbell's reconnaissance of the upper Stikine, he still hoped to find the great river said to flow into Bering Sea. The company had already established Fort Liard on the lower Liard and Fort Halkett on the upper Liard. In 1840 Campbell was authorized to carry out a purpose he had long cherished—exploring to the northwest. This time he followed a left-bank tributary of the Liard River, which he named the Frances, following it to its source in Frances Lake. He established a post on the shores of this lake, but he encountered considerable difficulties. Disappointed in his hopes of securing fish in the same abundance as on the Mackenzie, he was forced to abandon the post temporarily and send his men downriver. He, himself, managed to cross the divide north of Finlayson Lake and to come out on the banks of an unknown river to which he gave the name Pelly. (The name no longer applied to the Stikine after its identity with McLeod's "Pelly" River had been established in 1838.) Here Campbell located a post which he called Pelly Banks. In the spring of 1843, after having assembled supplies from the Liard, he launched his canoes on the Pelly and descended that river to its junction with a large tributary from the south which he named the Lewes. The natives plied the explorers with stories of a terrible fate that awaited them if they essayed to go on. So, after descending a short distance, he was dissuaded by his men from attempting to prosecute the journey further.

In 1847 the company authorized Campbell to proceed once more down the Pelly River and build a post at its confluence with the Lewes. Meanwhile, the middle Yukon had been reached by way of the lower Mackenzie. In 1842 C. T. Bell, the Hudson's Bay factor at Fort McPherson, had made a reconnaissance across the Mackenzie, but the threatened desertion of his guide forced him to turn back. In 1847 his work was taken up by Murray, who ascended the Peel and, crossing over to the Rat River, reached the Porcupine River on whose banks La Pierre House was built. His party finally descended the Porcupine River to its junction with a large river which the Indians called the Youcan or Youkon. Here, in the midst of a vast network of islands and intersecting channels, the so-called Yukon Flats, was established a post which came to be known as Fort Yukon.

In 1850 Campbell achieved his ambition of traversing the main river from Fort Selkirk down, eventually reaching Fort Yukon and thus linking his discoveries with those of Bell and Murray. The Hudson's Bay Company was now firmly planted on both the upper and middle reaches of the Yukon. But in 1852 the enterprise suffered a severe check when Chilkat Indians, in retaliation for their loss of trade, coming up the Chilkat River, over the divide, and down the present Dalton Trail to the Yukon, plundered and destroyed the post at Fort Selkirk. It was not rebuilt.

The Russian colony of Ross, founded near Bodega Bay on the west coast of California, had been the extreme outpost of Russian expansion southward. Its settlement had grown out of the sea-otter hunting in San Francisco Bay and along the California coast begun by Captain Joseph O'Cain in 1803. The immediate inspiration had come from Rezanov, who had had far-reaching plans for which such a location would serve as a base. It was occupied at a time when Russia had been, at least technically, at war with Spain (by virtue of her alliance with Napoleon); but in the year following, the situation altered, for Russia had changed sides. After the Congress of Vienna, Alexander became a pillar of legitimacy and could not, at least openly, flout this principle by countenancing aggression against Spain.

In 1821, however, began a series of very complicated diplomatic moves. The Spanish people rose and compelled their king to restore the charter of 1812. In consequence of this, the Tsar succeeded in securing the assembling of the previously mentioned European conference held at Verona in 1822, at which it was decided to authorize the French to dispatch an army to Spain to restore the absolute sovereignty of Ferdinand. The Tsar thus constituted himself the champion of Spanish royal power.

Meanwhile, in 1821 Mexico had thrown off the yoke of Spain and had received from the United States recognition as an independent power. There is some evidence that the Russian American Company wished to exploit the situation by taking forcible possession of California.[12] Spain had been unable to do more than protest against the retention by Russia of this post. Even before the setting up of Mexican sovereignty, the local authorities had sent various commissions to reconnoiter and inform the Russian commandants time and again that the settlement was a violation of Spanish sovereignty. The Russian commandant, Kuskov, had merely referred the complainants to his superior at Sitka. After Mexico had secured its independence, Mexican officials took up the quarrel with even less success. The central government was impotent, and the local authorities had even less force to rely on. The Russians, therefore, took advantage of this weakness to extend their possessions, and in addition to the main settlement at Fort Ross and the post on Bodega Bay they established others, among them Khliebnikov's (or Vasilii's) Rancho and Don Jorge's Rancho. The Mexicans replied by the establishment of settlements of their own—north of San Francisco—the missions San Rafael, San Francisco, and Santa Rosa. In time, too, other persons, including United States citizens, swelled the local population.

After 1818 the supply of fur had begun to diminish sensibly, and the Russians turned to agriculture and the crafts, in which some of the settlers were skilled. Cattle obtained from the Spaniards had multiplied. These colonists supplied the northern posts with grain and meat and the local Spanish settlements with various articles of iron, leather, and wood made by their craftsmen. Pine pitch was manufactured for use at Sitka, while some ships actually were constructed here. As the Mexican government was eager to obtain recognition, hopes were entertained that a deal could be made whereby in return Mexico would agree to make territorial concessions. In 1836 Wrangel, who was about to give up his post as governor, secured permission to return home by way of Mexico City in an attempt to come to an understanding; but he was unable to secure any concessions from the Mexican government.

When Wrangel's mission failed, it was obvious that Russia could not acquire part of California without incurring risk of war with the United States. The company therefore decided to

[12] Murav'ev-Amurskii is authority for the statement that the company requested the government to seize California but that their request was refused. See Barsukov, *Graf Nikolai Nikolayevich Murav'ev Amurskii,* I, 322–23.

withdraw. The first thought of its directors was to sell the property to the Hudson's Bay Company, which was trying to extend its foothold on the west coast; but the London company feared complications with the United States. Then attempts were made to sell to the Mexican authorities, but relations with that government had not been happy because the Russians had constantly flouted their regulations with regard to customs duties and passports. In addition, the Mexicans knew that there was a good chance that the property would fall to them in the course of time anyway.

Kostromitinov, acting as agent of the Russian American Company, in the end made an offer to sell the movable goods and livestock to John Sutter of New Helvetia on the Sacramento. The price was $30,000, with an initial payment of $5,000, the second and third payments to be made in coin and wheat at $2.00 the *fanega,* the last and final in coin.[13] Actually Sutter bought five establishments: Fort Ross (the headquarters), Kostromitinov Rancho, Khliebnikov Rancho (Vasilii's Rancho), Chernich Rancho (Don Jorge's), and Bodega Bay (with its warehouses). He purchased everything except the land, the various establishments remaining as security for final payment. Sutter drove the cattle and took all the movable property to New Helvetia. The ranches were leased to various tenants and finally passed out of his hands through Mexican land grants. Perhaps Sutter still had a nominal claim; if he did, it was ultimately extinguished because he was unable to enforce it.

One beneficent transformation in the character of Russian occupation in America was in ecclesiastical activities. The early history of the Orthodox Church in America had been one of dismal failure. In accordance with Muscovite tradition and Byzantine precedent, the missionary was regarded as primarily an emissary of the state. Shelekhov's original motive had been to use the church to promote Russian influence and render the natives submissive. That the life of the *promyshlenniki* and the servants of the company was inconsistent with gospel teaching did not trouble even

[13] At the time of the gold rush Sutter had not finished paying, and, as the miners had destroyed his wheat land, he had to make the last payments in gold, a commodity of no value to Russia, whose chief need was for supplies of food for the northern posts.

Baranov. But with the advent of Veniaminov to Unalaska in 1823, this situation was changed. Born of humble parents named Popov of the Irkutsk countryside, the future metropolitan was a "lad of parts." He was admitted to the ecclesiastical seminary at Irkutsk, where his scholastic ability was soon recognized. He was given the name of Veniaminov (son of Benjamin) by the rector. On graduating, he volunteered for missionary service in the Aleutian Islands. Accompanied by his wife and aged mother, he made the arduous journey down the Lena to Yakutsk and overland from that place to Okhotsk, thence by ship to Unalaska. Here for many years he ministered to his flock with zeal and won their affection and undying loyalty. In addition to his pastoral duties, he was an ardent student of their language, their mythology, customs, and traditions.

Out of this interest came a series of publications—his dictionary of the Aleut language and a study of the history and ethnology of the Aleutian Islands. In 1840 the Holy Synod decided to create out of Russia's possessions in the North Pacific a see to be known as the Diocese of Kamchatka, the Aleutian and Kurile Islands. Veniaminov was named bishop. In accordance with ecclesiastical practice he took monastic vows and underwent tonsure. He also adopted the name of Innokentii, by which he was known in later life. In 1850 he was raised to the rank of archbishop of Kamchatka, and a suffragan bishop was named for Sitka. Henceforth his ties with America became more tenuous until in 1867, when he was named metropolitan of Moscow, they came to an end. Nevertheless, his interest in the native population, not only of America but also of Asia, continued unabated through his life. His work in these fields made a notable contribution to Russian scholarship.

Innokentii made a profound impression on his contemporaries, not only in Russia where he was widely known and loved by people of every station but also in America among the islanders to whom he was attached by the strongest ties of affection. Foreigners were drawn to him by his simplicity, his quiet humor, and his deep human sympathy. To Sir George Simpson, who visited Sitka in 1842 and met Veniaminov, we owe the following characterization:

On Sunday next the first after Easter, the Bishop of Sitka who . . .

had just returned from Kodiak, preached a farewell sermon on the eve of departing . . . for the Asiatic part of his diocese. . . . I cannot refrain from rendering a small tribute of praise to his character and qualifications. . . . His appearance with something of awe, on further intercourse, the gentleness which characterizes every word and deed, insensibly molds reverence into love; and at the same time, his talents and attainments are such as to be worthy of his exalted station. With all this, the bishop is sufficiently a man of the world to disclaim anything like cant. His conversation, on the contrary, teems with amusement and instruction; and his company is much prized by all who have the honour of his acquaintance.[14]

But these activities did not exhaust Veniaminov's energies. He opened new stations—one at Atkha, one on Kenai Peninsula. Following the advance of the company to the shores of Bering Sea, he organized a station at St. Michael's Redoubt, and from here missionaries began to move into the Yukon Valley. Ikogmute (or the Mission, as the Russians called it) was founded on the lower Yukon in 1844. A mission was also opened on the Kuskokwim. Work was zealously prosecuted also among the savage Kolosh Indians. By 1848 Veniaminov was able to state that Christianity had been brought to the greater part of the native population of Russian America.[15] He saw that for permanent results in raising the natives to a higher plane of life education was a prime requisite. Parochial schools were organized in many of the parishes. His chief pride was the ecclesiastical seminary which he established at Sitka in 1857, on which he lavished untold care and effort.[16] His zeal on behalf of education was in the tradition of the great churchmen.

Veniaminov was an ardent patriot and lent his position as prelate, as well as the organization which he controlled, to further the aims of the Russian government in extending Russia's territory and advancing Russian interests. His friendship with Murav'ev-Amurskii and his close co-operation with him in estab-

[14] Sir George Simpson, *Narrative of a Journey Round the World,* II, 190.

[15] Veniaminov was thinking evidently only of those who could be reached from the coast. The Russians made little advance into the interior and it remained for the Church of England and other protestant churches to Christianize them after the occupation of the country by the United States.

[16] Ultimately moved to the Asiatic mainland.

lishing a hold in the Amur Valley amply attest his zeal in furthering national interests. But his patriotism was not exclusive or narrow. When his countrymen sinned against the laws of humanity, he was the first to draw attention to the fact. No foreigner could have passed a more severe judgment than Veniaminov's scathing indictment of Russian conduct during the early days of the occupation of the Aleutian Islands.

XIII

A Change of Masters

BEFORE TRACING THE DECLINE IN THE FORTUNES OF THE RUSSIAN American Company, we must turn to the great happenings that were reshaping the Far East. In 1840 trouble broke out between the East India Company and the local Chinese authorities in Canton. Hostilities ensued between Great Britain and the Chinese Empire, and as a result China was forced to sign the humiliating Treaty of Nanking by which it was opened to western enterprise, and Great Britain, and later other Western powers, received valuable privileges. This treaty revealed to an astonished world that the great god had feet of clay—that the Celestial Empire was impotent to resist the powers of the West. The significance of this was not lost on Russia. That country had been turned back from the Amur in 1689 by the Treaty of Nerchinsk, and since then Russian conduct towards China had been one of respect towards a powerful neighbor who must not be antagonized. The sudden revelation of Chinese weakness wrought a marked change in Russia's attitude and set in motion a policy of steady encroachment at the expense of China.

Apparently this change was foreshadowed as early as 1844.[1] Innokentii, censured in 1852 by the *Ober-Prokuror* of the Holy Synod for discussing openly the proposed annexation of the Amur

[1] According to Golovin in *Doklad Komiteta ob Ustroistvye Russkikh Amerikanskikh Kolonii* (*Report of the Committee on the Organization of Russia's American Colonies*), 62–63. "In 1844, by instructions from the Emperor, the Company [i.e., the Russian American Company] was invited to participate in the acquisition of the Amur region. The co-operation shown by the company in this instance was recognized in the following pronouncement by the Governor-General of eastern Siberia to the Siberian committee on April 4, 1859, 'the part which the Russian American Company played at the very beginning in the Amur business had the greater significance in that the activity of the company laid the foundation for future developments.' "

Valley country and the transfer of the cathedral seat from America to the Asiatic mainland, had this to say in his own defense:

As early as 1845 I was initiated into the Amur secret; and from then on till the summer of last year [1851] I guarded that secret in my correspondence; but having received a letter from His Highness, the Metropolitan of Moscow, in which he openly spoke about the mission to the Amur and the Gilyaks; and more especially, having a copy of an *Ukaz* of the Holy Synod in which the words were quoted from the report of Your Excellency to the Emperor, I assumed that now I might write openly of the matter in my communications.[2]

In 1846, as a prelude to the movement southward, the board of directors of the Russian American Company, under pressure from the government, occupied the port of Ayan south of Okhotsk, on the sea of Okhotsk. The ecclesiastical organization also was brought into the picture, and by June 1 of that year a church had been opened at this place. The proposal was now openly made that the episcopal see should be moved here from Sitka. The Russian American Company was also urged to extend its operations to the Gilyaks on the lower Amur.

To inaugurate so ambitious a policy of expansion of Russia's sphere of influence, the government must choose a suitable agent. The man selected for the task was Nikolai Nikolayevich Murav'ev, who was named in 1847 to the post of governor-general of eastern Siberia. According to his official instructions, gold mining and trade with China through Kiakhta were to be the ostensible objects of his concern, but there is no doubt that secretly he was directed to prepare for the advance of Russia's frontier to the Amur. With this appointment events in the Far East moved rapidly. In 1852 a Russian squadron under Nevel'skoi began a reconnaissance of Sakhalin Island, the Gulf of Tartary, and the mouth of the Amur River. Following Nevel'skoi's work of exploration, the Russians decided in 1852 to occupy de Kastries Bay, where the post of Alexandrovsk was founded. Lake Kidzi also came within the Russian sphere; on the Amur, Nikolayevsk and Mariinsk had already been founded in 1851.

The threat of imminent war in Europe revealed all too clearly

[2] Innokentii, *Pis'ma* (*Letters*), I, 347–48.

the precarious condition of Russia's possessions in the Pacific. With an eye to securing them against attack, Murav'ev induced the Russian government to apply to the Chinese government for permission to send troops down the Amur River to reinforce posts on the lower river and to transport supplies for Russian squadrons in these waters. Permission was not forthcoming. In the winter of 1853–54 Murav'ev urged the Russian government to undertake this action without Chinese permission, and in the spring of 1854, permission not having been secured from Peking, this authority was forthcoming from St. Petersburg. Murav'ev embarked his Cossacks, his suite, munitions of war, and supplies on river transport. The convoy left Shilinsk on May 27 and arrived at Nikolayevsk at the river mouth on July 9. Murav'ev thus tore up the Treaty of Nerchinsk, by which Russia had recognized the Amur Valley as under China's exclusive sovereignty.

The year 1854 was a critical one for Russian interests in the North Pacific. Up to this time the special powers with which Murav'ev had been armed and his command of all naval and military forces had sufficed. Whenever a crisis had arisen, he had been able to surmount it by tact and diplomacy. The assistance of the church, assured by his cordial personal relations with Innokentii, had furthered these plans. But it was another thing to secure the co-operation of the Russian American Company. The board of directors was five thousand miles away in St. Petersburg. The governor of the colonies was as far away across the Pacific in Sitka, and only local *prikazchiks* (agents) without authority looked after the company's interests on the Asiatic mainland. In 1854 Murav'ev therefore proposed that the company should be reimbursed for its losses but released from all obligations on the mainland, its sphere of activities in Asia henceforth to be restricted to the island of Sakhalin. To carry out his program, a new chartered company—the Amur Company—was called into existence. In contrast with the Russian American Company, its headquarters were to be in Irkutsk, and it was under the more or less direct control of the governor-general.

The prospects of a general European war and its spread to the Pacific led Nesselrode on January 23, 1854, to suggest that the Russian American Company reach an agreement with the Hudson's

Bay Company for the neutralization of their respective possessions on the American mainland. A feeler put out to the London company at the Tsar's direction was welcomed by it. The British government sanctioned the agreement on March 22, 1854, but refused to allow this neutralization to cover Russian shipping. Nicholas was intensely eager to secure such an arrangement in order to release his squadrons for service in Europe. He therefore directed that the offer with this modification be accepted by Russia. Official sanction was forthcoming on March 31, shortly after the declaration of war.

On the whole the agreement was kept by both sides. The board of directors, in conveying the news, informed the governor of steps being taken to circumvent the British refusal to extend the agreement to cover naval forces. There is some evidence also that a fraudulent bill of sale of the Russian colonies to the American Russian Company was drafted by the Russian American Company's agents in San Francisco. But fear of the consequences should Britain refuse to permit such transfer led to the plan's being dropped.

Meanwhile Murav'ev's prompt dispatch of reinforcements and supplies enabled him to garrison and supply Russia's Asiatic ports. The result was that at Petropavlovsk in Kamchatka the defenders were able to repel a determined attack by the warships of the Western powers. Towards the end of June one allied squadron on the other side of the Pacific put into Sitka but, after being satisfied that the garrison was observing its neutrality, departed. Another squadron visited Ayan on the sea of Okhotsk, where were found only a few stragglers, the majority of inhabitants having fled. Archbishop Innokentii, however, who turned up, was persuaded somewhat reluctantly to accept the hospitality of Sir Charles Elliott, the commander, on board his flagship. He was astounded at the courteous treatment he received at the hands of the English, whom he found it difficult to regard as enemies. The English visited Petropavlovsk a second time in the hope of catching the Russian squadron that had taken refuge there. It had, however, been withdrawn to the Amur. Efforts to trap the Russians in the Gulf of Tartary also failed. The Russians were familiar with the shallow waters and so were able to escape into the mouth of the Amur. In spite of all this feverish activity little actual material damage was done by the British and the French.

The end of the Crimean War was a turning point in Russia's affairs. The weakness of her social system and political structure and the backwardness of her economic methods, that had led to her collapse, made internal reforms inevitable. Moreover, her foreign policy had to take account of her complete helplessness. Russian naval power was hopelessly outclassed. In the North Pacific only the resourcefulness of Murav'ev, as well as some good fortune, had enabled her to escape disaster. Events had demonstrated the need of reducing commitments in this area. The first step was to get rid of her American colonies, a policy openly advocated by Murav'ev. In 1853 he had written in a report to the Emperor:

Twenty years ago the Russian American Company approached the government with a request for the occupation of California, which at that time hardly belonged to anyone; at this time, they communicated their fears that, within a short time, the region would become a prize for the American United States. In St. Petersburg, they did not share this fear and maintained that it would take a hundred years, and yet for the past year, California has been in the Union. It was impossible not to foresee the swift expansion of the United States power in North America; it was impossible not to foresee that these states, having once secured a footing on the shores of the Pacific, would soon surpass all other maritime powers and would acquire the whole northwest coast of America. The supremacy of the North American states throughout North America is so inevitable that we need have no regrets that we did not establish ourselves in California twenty years ago—sooner or later we should have lost it; by yielding peacefully, we might have been able to secure in exchange other advantages from the United States. Now more than ever, with the invention and development of railroads, we ought to be convinced that the United States are bound to spread over the whole of North America, and it is impossible not to keep in mind that sooner or later we shall have to surrender our North American possessions. Moreover, in contemplating this, we ought also to keep in mind something else that is inevitable for Russia, if not to control the whole of eastern Asia, at least to hold sway over the whole Asiatic coast of the Pacific. Unfortunately we allowed the English to invade this part of Asia— . . . but the mistake can be rectified by a close alliance between us and the United States. . . . In order to provide, on the one hand, a strong and suitable base for our American Company in place of the coast of America, and, on the other hand, to bring about a speedier and more certain development of our power on that part of the shores of the Pacific which belongs to us, it is essential at this time to allow the Russian American Company to establish itself on Sakhalin whence its trade with Japan and Korea will develop.[3]

Nicholas, a man of strong prejudices and a stickler like his brother—Alexander I—for legitimacy, had perhaps hardly been enthusiastic for an alliance with a power whose origins had been in an act of revolt against authority. But death removed Emperor Nicholas in 1855, and with his departure much of the old order collapsed. In foreign affairs and in domestic matters there was a demand for changed policies, and new men came to the front. These outer changes sprang from the profoundly altered ideas of the people. Whether from policy or conviction the new monarch reflected these liberal ideas. This could not but affect the fortunes of the Russian American Company, which had long been under fire. On the one hand it had been criticized by adherents of the old order because an institution which enjoyed partial exemption from the state's authority was an anomaly in an autocracy; while, on the other hand, as a monopoly it challenged the principles of the nineteenth century *laissez faire,* now coming into favor in Russia.

But perhaps it was practical influences that sealed its doom. Murav'ev-Amurskii had had the ear of the former Tsar, of the heir-apparent Alexander, and of the Grand Duke Constantine Nikolayevich. His far-reaching views and the depth of conviction with which they were held, his boundless energy and the success which had attended his efforts to carry out governmental policies gave him an enormous prestige with the group that surrounded the young Emperor. His views always commanded a respectful hearing. In an autocracy like Russia the higher circles quickly adjust their point of view to that of the monarch. After Alexander's accession it seems to have been taken for granted that the American colonies would be disposed of. Early in 1857 we find a minister (probably Gor-

[3] Ivan Barsukov, *Graf Nikolai Nikolayevich Murav'ev-Amurskii,* 322–23.

chakov) submitting to the Grand Duke Constantine a memorandum "on the cession of our American colonies to the Government of the United States." This letter suggests two things: (1) sending to America a committee to report on the activities of the company; and (2) sounding out the United States in such a way as to draw an offer from her if possible. The letter suggests that the government was to come to a decision. The matter advanced another stage when the Ministry of Foreign Affairs approached the Emperor's chancery suggesting in a memorandum the value that should be placed on the colonies in case of sale.[4] Late in the year the Russian minister in Washington, Edouard de Stoeckl, became alarmed when the Mormons on the western frontier had defied the federal authorities and rumor had it that they contemplated emigrating to British or Russian territory. President Buchanan, to whom Stoeckl appealed for information, replied, "It is for you to settle the question; for us we shall be glad to get rid of them." When this was reported to the Emperor, he added this notation in his own hand to the dispatch: *"Cela vient a l'appui d l'idée de régler dès à present la question de nos possessions américaines."*

1858

The next year Stoeckl was approached by Senator Gwin of California (perhaps sent by Buchanan) concerning the possibility of Russia's selling Alaska. We may infer that Stoeckl, too, had been casting about for a suitable channel of communication with the President. Representations had been made to Stoeckl that interests on the west coast would gladly take over the lease of the Hudson's Bay Company and pay the Russian American Company more than the English company paid. These suggestions were forwarded direct to Cassius Clay, who would thus deal directly with the company in St. Petersburg on behalf of those making the offer. Meanwhile, the negotiations for purchase were broadened to include the Secretary of State, who hitherto had been purposely left in the dark. The last occasion on which possible sale was discussed was July, 1861. The outbreak of the Civil War convinced Stoeckl of the hopelessness of going further in the matter, and he recommended that for the time being it be dropped.

By the attack on Fort Sumter the public life of the United States

[4] Apparently embodying suggestions made on April 9 in a memorandum of Baron Wrangel.

was plunged into turmoil, and it was inevitable that Russo-American relations should be profoundly affected. In general the attitude of the various European powers towards the North and the South was determined in part by their sympathies in Europe. The rise of the kingdom of Sardinia under the leadership of the House of Savoy threatened the European balance of power. During the course of the sixties, that balance was to be still further menaced by the emergence of a new Prussia. For the moment most of the European states chose sides in the new grouping of powers in accordance with national interest. England was engaged in a duel, more or less concealed, with Russia in the Far and Middle East and therefore needed allies. She had linked her fortunes during the preceding ten years with France, and in general the two powers marched in step.

Napoleon III, on the other hand, had abandoned his policy of coercion at home for one of conciliation towards the forces of opposition. This required a vigorous foreign policy that would not alienate Roman Catholics by too vigorous championing of the enemies of the church. The American Civil War and the diplomatic problems that it raised began eventually to overshadow all other issues. The secession of the Southern States confronted the European countries with one question that demanded an answer. Should they declare their neutrality in the armed struggle and should they further recognize the belligerency of the South?

The first step of most of the powers was to issue a declaration of neutrality. But the question of recognition of belligerency—all but equivalent to a recognition of *de facto* independence—gave them pause. This issue was one of extreme delicacy. Each power was inclined to leave the question open and to allow events themselves to determine the answer—a tendency that could not but be viewed with alarm in the United States.

An acute diplomatic crisis arose with Lincoln's proclamation of the blockade, since it injured foreign commercial interests, especially those of England. To this the South replied by the threat to issue letters of marque. This produced an awkward situation. The United States had signed the Convention of Paris to outlaw privateering, but like others had neglected to ratify the treaty (either with or without the so-called Marcy amendment). Now, in view of the action of the South, the leaders of the North were tempted to withhold ratification. Eventually, however, Lincoln decided to adhere to the Convention. But the blockade continued to create difficulties for the administration. Great Britain's trade was suffering, her cotton factories were closed, her workers in want, and prices of food were soaring since the import of grain had ceased. There was considerable unrest; and parliament, critical of the government's policy of neutrality, demanded positive action.

France, England, and Spain were drawn into the ill-fated venture in Mexico, though England and Spain—realizing the dangers of intervention—withdrew, leaving France to carry on alone. The great struggle raging in America overshadowed all other issues and roused bitter partisanship for both sides. Stoeckl openly professed Russian sympathy with the North but declined to commit his country to any overt act that might be regarded as unneutral. Seward had to content himself with assurances that it was to Russia's interests that the Union be preserved and that she would do nothing to imperil it.

In a situation already tense the Trent affair brought all the irritation and clash of interests to the surface and threatened to involve the North in war with England. It appeared that Seward was about to have the wish he had expressed a year before—war with England. But the good sense of Lincoln asserted itself, and in England more moderate counsels prevailed. War was averted by the North's surrender of the Confederate emissaries to the British.

The year 1862 was a critical one for the North. The hopes of an early victory had evaporated in 1861, but the people had girded themselves for renewed effort. A vigorous campaign was launched beyond the Appalachian Mountains for the control of the western rivers, but in the East indecision and incapacity prevailed. McClellan was driven back from Virginia. The North was invaded, and the invading forces turned back only at Antietam on September 17. The long-drawn-out hostilities raised the confidence of the South and dashed the hopes of the North for an early victory. Talk of mediation of European powers, silenced for a while, revived. Finally an attempt was made to secure joint action by Great Britain, France, and Russia (which probably would have meant war). Russia balked, and her action prevented the European concert.

Courtesy Bureau N.W.T. and Yukon Affairs

RUNNING MILES CANYON

Photograph by E. J. Hamacher

SHOOTING WHITEHORSE RAPIDS

On the heels of one crisis came another. The British government had permitted the building in English shipyards of Confederate cruisers, ostensibly as peaceful commercial vessels but actually to prey on Northern commerce. One of these, the *Alabama,* put to sea secretly without permission of the port authorities and, having taken on board at sea her complement of men and arms, began her career as a privateer. This action further strained Anglo-American relations. Eventually the government of Lord John Russell recognized that it had been at fault and agreed to accept financial responsibility for the havoc wrought to Northern commerce by the *Alabama.*

Meanwhile, Russia had her own problems. The Poles, who had been deprived of their autonomy in 1834, had been restive under Nicholas' policy of repression. After the accession of Alexander II, they thought they saw in the new regime prospects of a revival of their independence. The Russian government partially met their aspirations by extensions of privileges, but these half-measures did not satisfy the Poles, and Russia found it necessary once more to institute active measures of repression. But neither force nor concession availed to head off a campaign of widespread disorders directed by a central secret committee from Warsaw. The struggle was doomed to collapse unless the Poles could secure help from abroad. No European government espoused their cause. Germany lent Russia her moral support, and Russian authorities eventually discovered and broke up the quasi-government, and the revolt collapsed. Poland was brought under more rigid control than ever, the purpose of which was to bring about the absorption of the Poles into the general body of Russian life.

When the situation was most tense, France and England endeavored to make capital out of it by invoking the Act of the Congress of Vienna and demanding that the Polish question be brought before a European congress. Alexander, confident of Prussia's support, bluntly refused. When a crisis seemed imminent, the Russian government decided to send the greater part of its naval forces to sea in advance of actual hostilities to be ready to strike at English and French commerce. The Baltic fleet was put on a war footing, and on July 17/29 a force of six ships—frigates, corvettes, and clippers—sailed from Kronstadt under command of Lesovskii, recently named rear admiral. They reached New York in October. Simultaneously the squadron in far eastern waters under command of Rear Admiral A. Popov also moved. It had been the intention of the minister of marine to send it to the China coast, but Admiral Popov, apparently trusting to his influence at court, and without awaiting instructions, sailed direct to San Francisco.

It is questionable whether these naval forces were ever in a position actually to menace French and English commerce. Lesovskii continually complained of the fact that the *Aleksandr Nevskii* leaked badly and that the *Oslyabie* was unseaworthy. Popov, in turn, informed Lesovskii that the vessels in the Pacific squadron would be a liability rather than an asset to the Atlantic squadron should they effect a junction with his. Nevertheless, the incident had immediate and striking repercussions, coming as it did shortly after the great victory of Gettysburg and the capture of Vicksburg. It seemed to a people distracted by three years of war one gesture of friendship in a world of enemies.

What wonder that Lesovskii's men were joyfully welcomed in New York? There was a continuing round of banquets and speeches, whose recurring burden was the identity of interests of the Russian and the American peoples. The press took up the cry. The emphasis on Russian-American friendship grew until it was whispered that it was about to take the more definitive form of a treaty. The Russian government was not averse to the spread of what soon became a historical legend—a confirmed belief that Russia and the United States had a secret understanding to support one another in the event of the outbreak of war in Europe. The story was never denied, and, like a ghost refusing to be laid, it kept coming back intermittently to life for the next half-century.[5]

A factor that was not without influence on Russo-American

[5] The legend that Russian warships were dispatched to the United States in October, 1863, to demonstrate Russian and American solidarity persisted in the United States until it was finally dissipated by Frank Golder in an article in the *American Historical Review* in July, 1915. The true facts with regard to this incident were, however, common knowledge in Russia long before, the correct version having been given to the world for the first time in the *Voennaya Entsiklopediya* (*The Military Encyclopedia*) II, 385, in an article by N. Kallistov. See *Istorik Marksist,* 1936, No. 3, 104–12 for the secret instructions given to Lesovskii; also E. Ephimov's review of James Robertson's *A Kentuckian at the Court of the Tsars* in *Istorik Marksist,* No. 3 (1936), 149–59.

relations during and after the Civil War was the telegraph line which was proposed to be constructed across British territory and Russian America to Bering Strait and thence by Bering Strait across Siberia to Nikolayevsk at the mouth of the Amur River. This scheme was fathered by Perry McDonough Collins of Hyde Park, New York, a one-time resident of San Francisco. After the Crimean War his imagination had been fired over events and future prospects in the Far East. He secured an appointment as commercial agent of the government for the Amur (a merely honorary title). Armed with this he secured in St. Petersburg permission to proceed across Siberia and to visit the Amur country, just then being opened. Everywhere he traveled his restless mind gathered information regarding the new land and its possibilities. Impressed with its resources, he promoted a number of schemes—a railway to cross Siberia, a telegraph line from St. Petersburg to Nikolayevsk to meet one to be built by Americans across eastern Siberia, Bering Sea, Alaska, and British territory. A new company, the Amur Company, fostered by Murav'ev was to undertake the Russian part of the project. At the time when Collins returned by ship to San Francisco, the first Atlantic cable laid in 1858 had failed. Hence Collins was able to interest the Western Union Telegraph Company in a scheme for a telegraph line across British America, Alaska, and Siberia to Europe. Hiram Sibley, the president of Western Union, lent encouragement and active assistance. In 1863 Collins returned to Europe and succeeded in inducing both Great Britain and Russia to grant him a concession. Congress, however, when approached, at first (in 1862) declined to assist him. Later, when he had succeeded in organizing a company, Congress was induced to give financial backing.

Charles S. Bulkley, a former military engineer, who during the Civil War had been in charge of telegraph construction in the Southwest, was put in charge of the whole project. The line was begun from Portland, Oregon, and pushed northward to New Westminster, which was reached early in 1865. Parties reconnoitered in advance of construction, and a route was surveyed up the Fraser River and its tributaries to Fort Fraser, Fort St. James, over to the Skeena, and thence by the headwaters of this river to the headwaters of the Stikine River. It was planned to go north from here to the headwaters of the Yukon. Meanwhile, other parties were sent to Siberia. It was proposed to carry the line across Bering Strait, over the Chukchi Peninsula to the Gulf of Anadyr, across that gulf to the Anadyr River, and so on across the base of the Peninsula of Kamchatka and south along the coast to the mouth of the Amur. Some assistance was given by the Russian government in the way of furnishing transportation. The government of the United States, on the other hand, was somewhat niggardly in extending help.

One party under Major Robert Kennicott proceeded to the mouth of the Yukon to survey a route up that river. Kennicott had brought his party across the Tehuanapec Isthmus and up the coast. He proceeded from St. Michael's to Nulato. Here, while engaged in preparations for his task, he died very suddenly early in 1866. Others carried on the work in the Yukon Valley. Unfortunately for the venture, the second Atlantic cable was successfully laid in the summer of 1866. When confirmation of this news was received, the Western Union suspended its Alaska project and recalled its crews. Much of the equipment was left to rot and rust in the wilderness. Abandoned telegraph poles or shaky wire bridges the natives have strung across the gorges of northern streams are about all that remain of this undertaking. It is now a mere memory.

While the money gambled by Western Union was lost, some tangible benefits accrued from the venture. For the first time interest was roused in the United States in these little-known parts of the continent. George Kennan, who accompanied the parties into Siberia, gave the world its first account of the exile system in Siberia in his book, *Siberia and the Exile System,* published in 1891. A number of books were written on Alaska. The work of these pioneer authors had much to do with bringing Alaska to the notice of the world. It may indirectly have facilitated its purchase by the United States.

In eastern Asia the last act was now to be played. Attempts of the local Chinese authorities or the government in Peking to secure the evacuation of the Amur were fruitless. At length, during the allied invasion of China in 1858 when Peking was occupied by the English, Murav'ev induced the local Chinese officials, helpless as they were, to sign a new treaty at Aigun giving Russia all territory north of the Amur and providing for joint control (by Russia and China) of the south bank from the mouth of the Ussuri River to the sea. The Russian government sought later to have these concessions confirmed by the Peking government. Their ambassadors, Admiral Putiatin in the Treaty of Tien Tsin and Ignatiev in the Treaty of Peking (1860), not only secured such confirmation but obtained in addition exclusive control by Russia of the south bank (from the Ussuri to the sea) with an extensive strip of coast running southward to the borders of Korea. This gave Russia an important harbor on Peter the Great Bay where Vladivostok was founded.

Meanwhile, in 1862 the third charter of the Russian American Company lapsed, and the question of its renewal came up for consideration. Two men were named to tour the colonies, making investigations and reporting to the government. Captain Golovin of the Imperial Navy and Sergei Kostlivtsov, active state councillor, were chosen. The Council of State, meanwhile, on May 1, 1861, had extended the privileges of the company until July 15, 1863. Golovin and Kostlivtsov made their investigation and on their return reported to a special committee. It then submitted their recommendations: that the charter of the company should be renewed for twelve years dating from 1862; that the administration of the colonies be reorganized; and that thoroughgoing reforms be instituted. Only its monopoly of the fur trade was to be retained by the company, all other rights to be surrendered. Control of the company over natives, Creoles, and Russians was to cease. These people were to be free to move where they wished and to earn their livelihood where they saw fit, class distinctions were to be abolished, and the same taxes were to be paid by all. Creoles were to owe the company service only when they had been educated at company expense. All connection between the governor and the company was to be dissolved. In addition, two special protectors were to be appointed for the native population. In these recommendations two opposing principles were invoked—that of individual liberty on the one hand and that of paternalism on the other. Courts, hitherto lacking, were to be introduced.

These recommendations did not please everyone. Voices were raised even in the committee against the sacrifice of company interest. The proposed reforms are merely of academic interest now, in view of the cession of 1867. More practical problems to be faced concerned outstanding contracts with the Hudson's Bay Company, the American Russian Company, the company agents in San Francisco, and others. These had some time to run—that with the Russian American Company had been drawn up in 1854 for twenty years; and the Hudson's Bay Company lease, due to expire in 1865, was renewed until January 1, 1867.

The Civil War in the United States was now ended. Both the United States and Russia felt an immense relief at emerging from the perils and tribulations with which they had been beset. They felt drawn together by a common interest. The emancipation of the peasants in Russia in 1861 seemed to contemporaries a counterpart of the emancipation of the Negroes. This feeling of solidarity received its most striking and spontaneous manifestation on the first anniversary of the assassination of Lincoln, when the members of both houses, the President, and the chief officers of state attended a memorial service in the halls of Congress. George Bancroft, the historian who spoke, referred to the dangers through which the countries had passed and the cordiality of the relations between the United States and Russia. The emancipation of the serfs in Russia and of the Negroes in America was also stressed. The same sentiments were expressed at a banquet given by the merchants of Moscow to the United States ambassador to Russia, Cassius M. Clay, and the first secretary of the legation, Jeremiah Curtin. Besides their mutual good will, the speeches breathed a common hostility to their enemy, Great Britain.

An attempt made on the life of Alexander II on April 4 in the garden of the summer palace in St. Petersburg gave the United States further opportunity to demonstrate this friendly feeling. A joint resolution of both houses of Congress on May 16, 1866, congratulated the Tsar on his escape and requested that the President transmit a copy of it to the Emperor. Gustavus Vasa Fox, the retiring assistant secretary of the navy, was authorized to convey this message. A warship, the *Miantonomoh,* with a suitable escort was put at his disposal. Fox and his party were greeted effusively by the Russian government and the populace. The general atmosphere during the early months of 1867 could not have been more cordial.

In the winter of 1866–67 Stoeckl, the Russian ambassador, returned to St. Petersburg on leave of absence apparently with a view of relinquishing his post. He was taken into the confidence of the government and participated in the deliberations of a committee called to decide the future of Russia's American possessions. The Grand Duke Constantine Nikolayevich, the friend and supporter of Murav'ev-Amurskii, who had long advocated a policy of expansion on the continent of Asia, presided. Constantine's mind was already made up. All the committee was expected to do was merely to give effect to this decision. But other factors helped. Liberal feeling in Russia was opposed to a monopoly and to arbitrary powers such as the company had exercised in these distant regions. The chaos into which state finances had fallen during the Crimean War made it imperative that unnecessary drains on the state's monetary resources should be stopped. The maintenance of the company's credit had for some years required a yearly subsidy of 200,000 rubles. The experiences of the Crimean War warned the government that Russian naval forces were unequal to the task of defending these American possessions. It was finally decided, therefore, to sell them if the United States could be persuaded to buy. Stoeckl was directed by the Emperor to return to Washington and angle for an offer from the United States government.

In February, 1867, Stoeckl arrived in New York. On reaching Washington, he immediately broached the matter delicately. He dropped the hint to Seward that Russia would entertain any reasonable offer. President Johnston was approached by Seward, and by the middle of March Stoeckl was told that the President was prepared to pay $5,000,000; Stoeckl, in reporting the interview with Seward, expressed his hope of getting $6,000,000 or possibly $6,500,000, a definite sum fixed by Reutern, Russian minister of finance.[6]

[6] Before leaving St. Petersburg, Stoeckl had been furnished with certain essential information: first, an estimate of the value of the company's holdings in America; and second, their extent. The first statement was prepared by Baron Wrangel. Wrangel submitted two separate estimates, one, on the assumption that the property would be sold to another Russian company, Russia to retain sovereignty. For this case he set the figure at 7,500,000 rubles, enough to pay off all company obligations and enable the company to pay 100 cents on the dollar. The other estimate assumed that the sale would be to a foreign power, for which case he set the figure at 20,000,000 rubles. The nominal value of the ruble was about 75 cents, but the

Armed with these directions, Stoeckl endeavored to induce the Americans to raise their offer. On March 25 he informed the Emperor by cable that the United States had increased the figure to $7,000,00 provided the sale were not encumbered with any outstanding obligations.[7] Seward also insisted that payment should be made in New York and not in London, and to offset this change, he agreed to raise the price to $7,200,000. Stoeckl accepted. Since the Russian had not received his formal powers as a plenipotentiary, Seward, who felt the need for haste, urged Stoeckl to secure these by cable so that the treaty could be submitted to the Senate at once. Thus an unprecedented step was taken, and authority was obtained by cable.

The necessary authority was received at Washington late at night on March 29 when Stoeckl and Seward were spending the evening together. They summoned their aides immediately and, working on until morning, completed and signed the final draft of the treaty. This act was reported to St. Petersburg, and a summary of the treaty sent over the wires. Ratification was secured in the Senate by a final vote of 37 to 2 on April 9. On May 10 the treaty was ratified by the Emperor.

The treaty provided for a payment of $7,200,000, payable in New York. No obligations of the Russian American Company were

---

term "silver ruble" was a misnomer, since it was actually a paper ruble (secured by silver) whose subsequent value fluctuated.

The defining of the boundaries of Russia's American possessions was necessary, since up to this time no line had been drawn between her Asiatic and her American territory. This task was entrusted to Admiral Krabbe. The latter selected a point in midchannel between St. Lawrence and the mainland for a starting point; from here a line was drawn nearly southwest until it intersected the one hundred and seventieth meridian, whence it was continued in a direction nearly east by south to the point where the one hundred and eightieth meridian intersects the fiftieth parallel of latitude; from the original starting point the line was drawn northeast (approximately to the center of Bering Strait) and then north between the Diomede Islands to the Arctic. This is today the course followed by the international date line where, in passing through Bering Sea, it deviates from the one hundred and eightieth meridian.

[7] This referred specifically to the lease of the Alaskan coast to the Hudson's Bay Company, which was due to expire on January 1, 1867; the agreement with the American Russian Company of San Francisco, which must be terminated; and the contract with the Finnish Whaling Company, which also must be written off. On these points Seward was adamant.

taken over. The archives of the Russian American Company at Sitka were turned over to the Department of State.[8] Public property—that is, property of the company for company use, such as barracks, warehouses, hospitals, and schools—was turned over to the United States government. Private homes with their land became the property of individuals; and churches were turned over to the Greek Orthodox congregations.

Under special agreements the United States government named a commissioner, General Lovell Rousseau, to take over Russian possessions—a military force under command of General Jefferson C. Davis accompanied him. The Russians appointed Captain Peshkurov as Russian commissioner. Both commissioners proceeded to Sitka, where, on the afternoon of October 3, 1867, the ceremony of handing over was completed in the presence of Prince Maksutov, his wife, and members of the Russian colony. The two-headed eagle was hauled down, and the Stars and Stripes went up to signalize the passing into foreign hands of Russia's American possessions.

The treaty had now cleared the first hurdle—that of the Senate—but since it involved the payment of money, it had to come before the House of Representatives as a money bill. Delays occurred, and it did not come up until 1868. The impeachment of Johnston naturally imperiled a bill originating with his administration, and by the time the bill was submitted there were grave doubts whether it would pass.

The fate of the bill was prejudiced by some claims held against the Russian government by one Benjamin Perkins for contracts awarded him during the Crimean War. Perkins claimed that he had not been paid. The matter got into the courts, and Perkins seems to have accepted a small sum in settlement. But either he went back on his word or else trumped up another claim, for he now demanded $800,000 to be paid from the purchase price of the Russian colonies. The Perkins claimants had strong backing in the House and were in a position to block passage of the bill. Matters dragged on through the spring and early summer. Stoeckl dreaded

[8] Taken from Sitka to Washington, they remained for years in the archives of the State Department. They have now found their way into the National Archives, but those for the years from 1802 to 1817 are missing.

the diplomatic complications that might arise should the agreement be repudiated. Eventually, however, after endless delays and bargainings, the appropriation bill was passed on July 14, 1868, and the money was paid.

There is now little question about the means by which passage of the bill was secured. There is not much evidence that any of the senators were bribed to ratify, even though ten days elapsed between signing and ratification and Stoeckl was not one to remain inactive when great issues were afoot. But the situation is different with the House. Evidence has accumulated that persons within and without the House accepted money. Certainly Stoeckl's language and his success in managing influential people strongly suggest that such means were used to secure votes. It was not unknown for Russian diplomats to have funds at their disposal to create a favorable public opinion.

The full amount paid did not reach Russia, even if we allow a generous deduction for exchange. This difference has never been accounted for. There is no evidence to suggest that this was an offset for the expenses of the Russian squadrons dispatched to the United States during the Civil War as has been claimed. That was another matter and had no connection with Alaska. If part of the purchase price of Alaska remained in the United States, it was for a different purpose.[9]

The diplomatic repercussions of the sale were considerable, especially in Great Britain. On April 1 the British government was apparently apprised of the transaction (since the news did not arrive officially through the embassy until the second, it must have been learned from some other source). Lord Stanley, the foreign

[9] See William A. Dunning, "Paying for Alaska," *Political Science Quarterly* (Vol. XXVII, No. 3), September, 1912, 384–98; and Frank A. Golder, "The Purchase of Alaska," *American Historical Review* (Vol. XXV, No. 3), April, 1920, 411–25.

Most of the documents relating to the sale of Alaska are contained in a collection secured from the Russian Archives by the United States Embassy in Moscow in 1936. Following is the reference: "U. S. Embassy, Russia, Papers relating to the cession of Alaska [enclosures No. 2 and 3 to Dispatch No. 2115 of December 2, 1936, from the United States Embassy in Moscow], 1856–57 [*sic!* 1867]."

The dispatches of Stoeckl that deal with the passages of the appropriation bill through the House of Representatives are not in this collection, though they were seen and used by the late Professor Golder in the above-mentioned article.

secretary, immediately wired to Sir Andrew Buchanan in St. Petersburg to get full particulars. Gorchakov, Russian minister of foreign affairs, granted an interview and, in reply to Buchanan's question, confirmed the news. He took the opportunity to deny that it had any political significance. He claimed that the company had been recently in receipt of an annual subsidy of 200,000 rubles to enable it to keep in operation; that its stock had sharply declined in the market; and lastly, that the Crimean War had proved conclusively that Russia's American possessions were extremely vulnerable. To this Sir Andrew rejoined:

> I said it might have been considered a friendly act on the part of the Russian government if she had afforded Her Majesty's Government or the Government of Canada, an opportunity of purchasing the territory which had been sold, but that their not having done so was materially unimportant as I felt assured it would not have been bought.[10]

"Her Majesty's Government approve the language you held in your conversation with Prince Gorchakov," was the stiff reply of Stanley.[11]

It is impossible to escape the feeling that for many years events had been shaping that made the sale of Russia's American colonies to the United States a foregone conclusion. The general situation at the end of the Civil War was peculiarly favorable. But it was the sharpening of their antagonism against their common enemy—Great Britain—that brought the Russian and the United States governments together rather than any identity of interests. Seward's antipathy to Britain was such that in 1861 he would have welcomed a declaration of war against her as a means of healing the breach in the home front. Though Cassius Clay, the American ambassador at St. Petersburg, had no part in negotiating the treaty, his Anglophobia was well known. Back of the more recent developments was the old aspiration summed up in the phrase "manifest destiny," now strongly accentuated by the passions unleashed by the war.

[10] Hudson's Bay Company, *Certain Correspondence of the Foreign Office and of the Hudson's Bay Company copied from the original documents, London, 1898, by Otto J. Klotz.* Dispatch from Sir Andrew Buchanan, St. Petersburg, to Lord Stanley, April 4, 1867.

[11] *Ibid.* Draft (of a dispatch) from the Foreign Office, April 16, 1867, to Sir Andrew Buchanan.

Sir Frederick Bruce in Washington was convinced that the United States would make these grievances a pretext for annexing the whole of the west coast.[12] It seems to have been the belief of most prominent Russians that the proper course for Russia was to aggravate this antagonism. As Stoeckl had said during the early stages of the Civil War:

Let us remain passive spectators of these internal dissensions of the two branches of the Anglo-Saxon race. Humanity can only gain from it.[13]

The cession was a strictly guarded secret up to the very last, to so great a degree that probably not a dozen persons in either country shared it. Russian diplomacy has always shrouded its moves in mystery, and this negotiation was no exception. But in 1867 when Stoeckl was prepared to abandon this time-honored practice in favor of a campaign of publicity in order to win over the Senate, it was Seward who dissuaded him. Is it too much to assume that his purpose was to forestall Great Britain and prevent interference from that quarter?

Stoeckl had anticipated some of the obstructions to be encountered in negotiating the treaty and in securing its ratification. He had been at great pains to impress on Gorchakov the severity of the ordeal he faced in attempting it. Accordingly, on the signing of the treaty, the Tsar directed Reutern, minister of finance, to pay Stoeckl the amount of 25,000 rubles in recognition of his services. But in reality the difficulties had far surpassed even Stoeckl's expectations. In addition to laying the groundwork for a treaty that would meet the monarch's exacting demands, he had gone beyond these by a wide margin in the amount received. He had then seen the treaty safely through the Senate, and the following year he had faced unforeseen difficulties in getting the appropriation through the House. Outwardly he professed gratitude for the government's honorarium; secretly, he was chagrined at the slight value placed on his services. In the end, worn out, he asked to be relieved of his post and assigned to some sphere of activity where he might seek at least partial repose from his arduous labors.

[12] *Ibid.* Dispatch of Sir Frederick Wright-Bruce to Lord Stanley, April 2, 1867.

[13] M. M. Malkin, *Grazhdanskaya Voina v. S. Sh. A. i Tsarskaya Rossiya* (*The American Civil War and Tsarist Russia*), p. 66, n. 2.

XIV

Alaska's Evolution

THE PROVISIONS OF THE TREATY OF CESSION WERE CARRIED OUT IN the autumn of 1867, even before the money was paid over. Unfortunately the controversy that arose over payment, combined with other domestic issues of the Johnston regime, injected bitter political partisanship into Alaskan affairs that prejudiced the future interests of Alaska.

Alaska had been taken over by General Rousseau as commissioner for the United States government, and a military force of about five hundred men distributed eventually in five different posts were left, under command of General Jefferson C. Davis, to assume charge and to maintain peace and order. Almost simultaneously with the cession there arrived at Sitka from Pacific coast ports a rather nondescript population of adventurers, bound north in search of fortune—small business men, speculators, shipowners —the flotsam and jetsam of humanity that make up the class of persons we call (perhaps euphemistically) pioneers. All were enthusiastic and hopeful for the future. Almost without exception they believed that the new territory would provide the greatest opportunities any new territory had ever provided.

At the very beginning of American occupation two factors operated to prevent this. The treaty of cession had provided that the former Russian population who wished to leave would be repatriated; that those who remained were to be allowed three years to elect whether to remain permanently or return to their native land. Most of them, deprived of their employment and finding no new opportunities, were compelled ultimately to leave the country, so that by 1870 few Russians remained in Alaska. The second factor was the taking over of the resources of the Russian American Company by a San Francisco group—the Alaska Commercial Company. Immediately after the treaty of cession had been signed, a number of San Francisco business men organized a firm under the name of Hutchinson, Kohl and Company and sent a representative north to Sitka to purchase from Prince Maksutov the property of the Russian company on the Pribilof Islands. Parties were then sent north to begin sealing operations. They found rivals, and for some years there was almost armed strife among the companies competing for a share in this lucrative business. This situation led inevitably to the taking of an excessive number of seals and to rivalry that bordered on lawlessness. Eventually the government decided to put an end to the strife by leasing to one company the exclusive right to take seals. As a result, in 1870 the lease for twenty years was let to the Alaska Commercial Company of San Francisco, which had taken over the rights of Hutchinson, Kohl and Company. Thus the fur business in Bering Sea, in the Aleutian Islands, and finally in the Yukon Valley passed to this new company, which continued a regime not materially different from that of its Russian predecessor.

The first legislative provision for the new territory was the so-called Customs Act of July 27, 1868, by which United States laws regarding customs, commerce, and navigation were extended to Alaska.[1] It also prohibited the sale, importation, or use of firearms and of distilled liquors. Offenders were to be prosecuted in any United States court of the states of California, Oregon, or Washington. The army was charged with the defense of the country and the prevention of native risings, but the only department of the government actively responsible for administration was the Department of the Treasury, represented at Sitka in the person of the collector of customs.

From the very beginning, efforts to introduce some form of civil government were defeated by the suspicions that such government would interfere with the seal interests. In other words, Alaska gradually reverted to a company possession, save that now

[1] The name "Alaksu" was originally applied by the Aleuts to the mainland lying to the east of their islands, which is, of course, the Alaska Peninsula. The Russians always referred to their possessions as "Russia's American colonies" or "our American colonies." After the cession some new nomenclature was necessary, and it was decided to adopt the Russian "Alyaska" in a slightly modified form—Alaska. This name appeared for the first time in the above-mentioned Customs Act of July 27, 1868.

it was the Alaska Commercial Company instead of the Russian American Company that spread its influence everywhere. Outside of this, Alaska had no government. Its soldiers might drill or idle in barracks; their authority was *nil* and the effect of the military occupation insignificant. Gradually, one after another the outlying posts were abandoned, and finally in 1877 the last of the soldiers left. There were immediate threats that the natives would rush into the vacuum left by the army. The people of Sitka in alarm appealed to the British naval authorities, who dispatched the *Osprey,* under Captain A'Court, from Esquimalt in the summer of 1878 to furnish protection. Fortunately an American vessel, the *Jamestown,* was shortly afterwards sent northward. The navy then joined forces with the Department of the Treasury to provide at least some semblance of authority in these distant regions.

Complete stagnation had marked the years 1867 to 1879. The new regime saw a gradual change for the better, and in southeastern Alaska the pulse of a new life was making itself felt. The early attempts at establishing self-government had broken against the barriers of poverty and economic depression. In 1869 the first "City Provincial Government" was organized among the residents of Sitka, with a mayor and a council. An appeal was directed to Congress to remove the disabilities from which the country had been suffering since the cession and to provide some form of civil government. In answer to this appeal a series of abortive efforts were made to remedy the deficiency, but the original impulse was too weak to overcome the inertia or the active, though obscured, opposition of the interests. Nothing came of the plans, and Alaska sank back for another ten years into the custody of the Treasury with the somewhat inert co-operation of the Department of War.

In 1879 when the navy took over, new and encouraging factors were making themselves felt; nevertheless, the first attempt at forming a "Provincial Government" broke down, partly from inexperience and dissensions among the population, and the government was dissolved. By now mining activity was looming on the scene. Some efforts at mining had been made in the vicinity of Sitka, where gold deposits had been known even in Russian times to exist. Miners from the Cariboo gold-mining region had gradually worked their way up the Fraser River and over the divide into the upper Peace and Finlay rivers. From here it was a natural transition to the valley of the Liard and Dease rivers. The Dease River and Dease Lake were known from the time of Campbell and earlier to be accessible from the sea. The Skeena River also was prospected. Many miners found their way along the coast to the Stikine. By 1874 the Cassiar district (i.e., the region tributary to the Stikine and Liard rivers) was producing one million dollars in gold a year. In 1879 John Muir found gold from Sitka northward. He also ascended the Stikine, crossed over to Dease Lake and Dease River, with its tributaries, and talked with miners working on the creeks. It was but natural that prospectors disappointed in their luck along the rivers should spread north through the coastal regions; and in 1880 two miners—Juneau and Harris, from Sitka—prospecting along the Gastineau Channel, found placer deposits and quartz ledges on Gold Creek and Silver Bow. Immediately a rush to the new fields began, and a town sprang up here to which the name Harrisburg (later Juneau) was given in honor of one of the original discoverers. Eventually, at this point two great groups of mines developed—the Alaska Juneau mine at Juneau and the Treadwell mines on Douglas Island.

These developments could not but affect the political growth of the country. Difficulties with regard to land and mining rights led to a renewed attempt to revive a provisional government. This effort failed, but during the following year appeals from Sitka led to the collector of customs' being summoned to Washington to try to reach some solution. Again the movement collapsed. Renewed disturbances over the townsite of Harrisburg suggested to the miners the summoning of a convention at Harrisburg in August, 1881. This convention was strictly nonpartisan, attended by representatives of the three chief settlements—Sitka, Harrisburg, and Wrangell. It proceeded to elect a delegate to Washington, the choice falling on the collector of customs at Sitka, Mr. M. D. Ball. At the capital Mr. Ball found himself without a definite status. In any event, both Senate and House decided that the time was not ripe for a change and refused to take the question up. Again Alaska was left without a government.

But the seed had been sown on ground not entirely sterile. Other influences came in to reinforce the move begun by the miners

SKAGWAY

Courtesy Fish and Wildlife Service

INDIAN VILLAGE WITH FISH RACKS

of Harrisburg. The Presbyterian church in the person of Sheldon Jackson came to the support of the agitation. Jackson had long been in charge of missions of the Presbyterian church west of the Mississippi, and in 1877 was approached to launch a mission in Alaska. It was begun tentatively at Wrangell in that year, and in 1879 the first actual Presbyterian church was opened there. Jackson was exceedingly active in promoting missions, not only by Presbyterians but by other denominations as well. He soon saw that provisions for law and order were the conditions requisite to the success of the missions and that these could be insured only by a civil government. He threw his influence into the movement. Congress could not but respond to these forces. The Senate Committee of Territories in 1883 finally reported a bill which emerged as the Organic Act of 1884.

This act made Alaska a district, a geographical division strictly *sui generis,* with a civil governor. It became also a judicial district, with a judge, a marshal, a district attorney, four commissioners, and four deputy marshals. The laws of the state of Oregon were, "as far as applicable," to be in force. Alaska became a land district, though the general land laws were not to be applied. The churches, however, were assured of 640 acres at each mission, and the rights of Indians were reserved. Provision was made for registering mining claims with the four commissioners, who became *ex officio* registrars, the clerk, *ex officio* receiver, and the marshal, *ex officio* surveyor-general. The Secretary of the Interior was authorized to establish schools as he saw fit and was provided with twenty-five thousand dollars for this purpose. In regard to the liquor traffic, Alaska was treated as Indian country: the sale, importation, or manufacture of liquor except for "medicinal, mechanical, and scientific purposes" was forbidden. On the negative side the country got neither delegate nor legislature. It was hoped that this rather sketchy enactment would provide citizens with "reasonable protection of life, liberty, and the pursuit of happiness."

During the next thirteen years an effort was made to conduct the affairs of this frontier outpost in accordance with this legislation. The governor was appointed by the federal government. It was assumed that he would live in Sitka, but since he had little more to do than make out a report, he contrived to spend the time in Washington or in regions of more salubrious climate and more agreeable surroundings. Reports usually pressed for reform and more earnest consideration by Congress of the problems of transportation, the natives, and taxation. The second governor, Lyman E. Knapp, was a man of considerable ability; and he earnestly stressed the needs of the country, especially for territorial government. The fourth governor, Sheakley (1893–97), was more reconciled to the existing order; but he did denounce the ineffectiveness of the existing prohibition laws and strongly recommended provision of some form of municipal government. (There were now some three hundred communities that might perhaps be dignified by the name of municipalities.)

Prohibition, education, and law enforcement were the chief problems by which the widely-scattered communities of the North were plagued. On one of these—education—some progress was made. After the twenty-five thousand dollar appropriation had remained unexpended in 1884, the matter was referred to the Secretary of the Interior and the Bureau of Education. As a result of their recommendation, it was decided to name a general agent of education. The man chosen was Sheldon Jackson, head of the Presbyterian missions, who continued for some years to combine the two offices. His headquarters were in Sitka. As a result of friction that developed there, it was decided to choose a commission, of which the agent would be a member, to supervise education. In 1890 the agent was moved to Washington to the Bureau of Education.

There was a feeling in the newer towns of Alaska that the interests of the whites were being ignored in favor of those of the Indians, who were the special objects of the solicitude of the evangelical missions. Experiments were made with local boards and superintendents to eliminate friction in the administration of local schools. In 1893 the government chose to reduce the appropriation, and many of the schools were in low water.

By 1890 acute distress was beginning to be felt by many of the natives, particularly those living along Bering Sea. Ever since the eighteen thirties whaling had been actively carried on in the North Pacific. The whalers had worked into the Sea of Okhotsk and finally into Bering Sea, the whales gradually retreating northward into the Arctic. When whales were scarce, some of the ships turned to walrus hunting. The result was the disappearance of much of the game on which the Eskimos had lived. The natives, then armed with modern repeating rifles, began to decimate the caribou, and these animals gradually disappeared from the coast. Thus game of all kinds was scarce, and distress was widespread. These conditions led Sheldon Jackson and others to think of finding some substitute for the wild life on which the natives had until now relied for sustenance. The idea occurred to Jackson of introducing the domestic reindeer to sustain the Eskimos as they did the Chukchi and the Tungus on the Asiatic coast. He broached the question to Congress in 1890 but was unable to secure action in time to enable him to put his plan into effect that season. He therefore turned to private friends, to whom he depicted the privations of the natives and from whom he asked contributions to enable the project to be started at once. In response to his appeal a sum of two thousand dollars was forthcoming. Thus freed from the necessity of awaiting government action, Jackson sent agents to the Asiatic coast to persuade the natives to part with their herds. The sale of their reindeer was a strange idea to the Chukchi, who were not accustomed to business deals. Indeed, money meant nothing to them. Their superstitious fears also had to be overcome. Some slight success was achieved. Vessels sent out laden with goods usually returned with reindeer attended by the Chukchi, who were by degrees becoming accustomed to this odd system of barter. At any rate a beginning was made with a few dozen animals brought to the mission stations on Seward Peninsula. Chukchi herdsmen accompanying the reindeer were sometimes put under contract to help train Eskimo herdsmen. But the greatest difficulty experienced was in persuading any to remain beyond the terms of their contracts. It was also found extremely difficult to accustom the Eskimos to this novel occupation. During the winter of 1890–91 it was suggested to Jackson that herdsmen recruited in Lapland might be superior to the Chukchi as instructors for the Eskimos. Lapps were accordingly imported with a few of their own reindeer, and the tasks of rearing and looking after the herds and training the Eskimos were entrusted to them. The Lapland reindeer were not found so suitable for North America as their Chukchi counterpart, but the Lapp herders were an unqualified success.

Gradually the numbers of the herds and of the animals in the herds increased. This work was, of course, subsidiary to missions and educational work, and the herds were usually attached to the missions. The Eskimos, as time passed, grew accustomed to this new way of life. Government biologists and animal husbandmen were lent to assist in the supervision. Eventually abattoirs were provided, and arrangements were made for shipping carcasses down the coast. A market for reindeer meat was found in the Puget Sound cities. About 1934 a herd of considerable size was sold to the Canadian government and moved to the mouth of the Mackenzie River to help improve the lot of the natives there.

At the time when the original Presbyterian missions had been launched in Wrangell, Sheldon Jackson had approached the other denominations with a view to dividing the territory. The Roman Catholics were at Holy Cross Mission in the lower Yukon, the Episcopal church at St. Michael's and Anvik in the delta, the Methodists in the Aleutian Islands, the Baptists on Wood Island, the Swedish Evangelical church at Yakutat Bay, the Friends on Douglas Island and at Kake, and the Moravians on the Kuskokwim. From these beginnings, almost all of the churches branched out, for the most part into contiguous areas; but, as newer fields opened, these, too, were apportioned in a manner that made missions somewhat of a patchwork on the map but which effectively prevented overlapping.

One of the most interesting Indian settlements was that of Metlakatla near the mouth of the Skeena River. In June, 1857, there had arrived from England, William Duncan, a representative of the Church Missionary Society, to begin work among the Tsimshean Indians at Fort Simpson on the northwest coast. Duncan arrived by steamer at Fort Simpson on October 1 and after some preliminary study of the Tsimshean language began his work of proselytizing. In 1859 he decided to remove the converted Indians from the corrupting influences of the fort and the pagan Indians who congregated there. For this purpose he selected a site for a new settlement at Metlakatla, about seventeen miles south of Fort Simpson. Here he gathered several hundred Indians, of whom he became not only the spiritual head but the acknowledged leader and guide in material affairs as well. A village of thirty or forty houses, with a church, grew up. The community purchased a schooner to engage in co-operative fishing; the settlers learned the manufacture of textiles. The settlement prospered and became a model on account of its law-abiding character in the midst of a howling wilderness; sobriety and industry prevailed. Schools and education were provided. Foreign crafts, in addition to native ones, made the village an oasis of civilization in these northern wilds.

Duncan was the life of the community. As white settlement came up the coast, the episcopal see of Columbia was organized with headquarters at Victoria; and Duncan's somewhat unorthodox missionary settlement became subject to its jurisdiction. Orders were issued to introduce Church of England ritual, which Duncan had neglected. These orders were resented. In 1879 the diocese of Caledonia was carved from the see of Columbia, and William Ridley was named bishop with his headquarters at Metlakatla. Never was a situation fraught with greater possibilities of trouble. Ridley was a person of narrow views, self-righteous, intolerant, and inclined to insist on the dignity of the cloth. But had he been a paragon, he would have found it difficult to adjust himself to the situation. Duncan had been unchallenged head of the community for twenty years. He had seen his work prosper, and his success had given him extraordinary prestige. He was not inclined to brook interference or to accept either advice or direction. There were inevitable clashes, some minor, some over more vital issues. Finally Duncan was dismissed from his post, but he continued his interest in the community. When the government of British Columbia undertook to deed to the church land which the Indians claimed as their own, there was violence. Ships had to be sent north to restore order, and the courts had to intervene on more than one occasion. Duncan interviewed Sir John Macdonald to induce the Dominion government to protect the Indians' interest. His appeal failed, and a majority of the Indians decided to apply to the United States government for a sanctuary in Alaska. The United States agreed to provide one, and Annette Island was set aside as reservation for the use of the Indians who had migrated thither with Duncan in 1887.

The vast interior of Alaska had begun to yield its secrets. In 1869 Lieutenant Charles P. Raymond, authorized by the army and acting for the Treasury Department, proceeded to Fort Yukon to determine its exact location. If, as was presumed, it lay to the west of the one hundred and forty-first meridian, he was to require the Hudson's Bay Company to withdraw. Raymond traveled on the brig *Commodore,* from San Francisco, which carried on its deck a small steamer, the *Yukon.* At St. Michael's this small steamer was launched and used by Raymond to ascend the river. Fort Yukon was reached without mishap. There Raymond found the agent, John Wilson, in charge of the post, and the Reverend William Bompas of the Church of England, who had arrived recently. Raymond served notice on Wilson that he was on United States territory and that the post must be moved. The Hudson's Bay Company transferred to a new location up the Porcupine, to which they gave the name Rampart House. Some time later this, too, was found to be in United States territory, and a second move upstream to a New Rampart House was necessary.

Even after Alaska had been transferred to the Treasury Department, the army did not lose its interest. A reconnaissance of the basin of the Yukon had long been projected. Congress had declined to make an appropriation in 1883 for this purpose, but despite lack of congressional support the army went through with the scheme. Lieutenant Frederick Schwatka, a geographer and explorer of some prominence, was chosen for the task. His instructions were to proceed to the headquarters of the Yukon River by way of Lynn Canal and the Chilkoot Pass and to traverse the whole length of the river to Bering Sea. Schwatka left Portland on May 22 and arrived at Pyramid Harbor on June 2. Here arrangements were made to have supplies transported up Dyea Inlet and Dyea River (by boat), thence packed by Chilkat Indians over the steep Chilkoot Pass to a lake near the summit which Schwatka named Lindeman Lake. From the scrubby timber that is found in these Alpine regions, the men constructed a rude raft to carry them on their long journey. They made their way across the lake and down a swift watercourse to a second lake, which was named Lake Bennett after James Gordon Bennett. After reinforcing their awkward craft by adding two logs along the side, they pushed it out into the waters of Lake Bennett, which was crossed with the aid of a makeshift sail. From Lake Bennett they passed through Nares Lake and on to twin lakes, to which Schwatka gave the names Tahk-o and Bone. These are now known as Taku Arm and Windy Arm, respectively, of Lake Tagish.

The group worked their way out into a river, which they descended into Marsh Lake. From here the waters fell in a swift and powerful stream heading northward on its great voyage to the sea. Some sixty miles below Lake Marsh Schwatka entered the gloomy, mile-long canyon of which his guides had warned him and to which he gave the name Miles. He had little choice in the matter of running the canyon. His raft was his only means of travel, and he had to go through. The men poled out into midstream until the force of the current caught the raft. It was swept into an entrance flanked by sheer basalt cliffs and borne along between their perpendicular walls at awesome speed. The canyon broadened into a whirlpool which spun the raft around and dashed it against the cliffs. Two outer logs were torn off. The plight of the party seemed desperate. But even as the men hesitated, any decision about what to do was taken out of their hands, and their raft was impelled into the middle of the stream on a swelling crest formed by the waters as they were dashed back from the canyon walls. An unseen hand seemed to hold them to the center of this narrow chute from which they were powerless to diverge. At its lower end they were spewed out of the canyon to be swept along on a current scarcely less rapid or dangerous than that of the canyon itself. Shoals, sandbars, and shallows followed in swift succession; then came Squaw Rapids, where the river makes a sharp right-angle turn and foams over ugly boulders that rushed forward to seize their craft. Finally they reached White Horse Rapids, where the whole volume of the river pours through a narrow flume in a basalt ledge and three great combers, rising to toss the craft along on its crests, threatened to overturn it and plunge it into the depths. With a convulsive leap, however, their raft rode free at last and was shot with its crew and cargo, dripping but safe, into a quiet eddy beyond.

From here Schwatka's trip was less stirring. Fifty miles below the rapids they entered the last of the lakes—Laberge, named for an employee of Western Union, Mike Laberge. Then down the next stretch, the Thirtymile River, they rushed to the junction with the Teslin. Some two hundred miles lower another rapids was named by Schwatka, Rink Rapids,[2] from which point the river becomes relatively placid though still swift. At Fort Selkirk Schwatka's route converged with that traversed by Campbell, in 1852, in his descent of the river to Fort Yukon. As he progressed further, Schwatka entered the territory reached by the traders from the lower Yukon—Fort Reliance, Belle Isle, and Fort Yukon. Passing through the Yukon Flats, he emerged into the now reunited river, winding once more through hills, passing the Ramparts and the mouth of the Tanana, eventually reaching the post of Nuklukayet. Here the party transferred their equipment from the raft to a *baidarka*. Later a steamer overtook them, and they completed the journey to St. Michael's in relative comfort. At St. Michael's Schwatka secured passage to San Francisco on the *Leo,* homeward bound from Point Barrow with Lieutenant Ray of the International Meteorological Station.

The following year (1884) Lieutenant W. R. Abercrombie of the Second Infantry was selected to follow up Schwatka's expedition by an exploration of the Copper River country, hitherto unvisited by white man since the purchase. The stories of native copper found there had acted as a magnet; and efforts were made again and again to pass the swift rapids, the glaciers, and the dangerous canyons of the Copper River's lower course to reach the localities from which came the copper, to become acquainted with the *Mednovskie*—the Copper people—as they were known to the Russians. It is difficult to identify precisely the Russian expeditions. Prince William Sound had apparently been entered by the Russians about 1783 (by Zaikov). Teben'kov speaks of the *promyshlennik* Tarakhanov who took furs in this region, and also of Samoilov and his *artel'*,[3] who were active here about the time that Baranov came to America (1790).

[2] Miners had already named it Five Finger Rapids and the name has stuck. Rink Rapids is the name now applied to a less tumultuous but still dangerous stretch of water some six miles further down the river.

[3] *Artel',* a name applied to various forms of co-operative enterprises in Russia, is here used of a group of *promyshlenniki* organized for taking furs. It is to be noted that co-operative farms in the Soviet Union were first organized on *artel'* lines. Samoilov was one of Shelekhov's men whom we hear of about the time of Baranov's

Later names connected with the Copper River country trade were Patochkin in 1798, Bazhenov in 1803, and Klimovskii in 1819. From then on interest in the Copper River languished until 1843, when Teben'kov (now governor) sent two parties into the country —one to ascend the Copper River to its confluence with the Chitina and up the Chitina to the copper country, the other to ascend the Copper River to explore the river which unites the Copper with Lake Plavezhnoi. These parties appear to have been led by Grigoriev. One of the purposes, that of exploring Lake Plavezhnoi, was achieved; but the ascent of the Chitina was impossible because of the swift current.[4] Another attempt to reach the sources of the Copper River was made under Governor Teben'kov, who sent Shturman Serebrennikov into the country for this purpose. Serebrennikov went up the lower Copper River past Woods and Abercrombie canyons in 1847 and wintered at the *Odinochka* of Taral.[5] Leaving for the upper river, he came to grief. It is believed that he was murdered by natives some time about June 5.[6]

The object of the expedition (like that of Schwatka's) is given in Abercrombie's report (Compilation of Narratives of Exploration, 383):

At the date above [1884] little was known of the interior of Alaska. The conflicting interests between the people and the Indians of the territory were likely in the near future to result in serious disturbances, hence it was deemed important that all possible information as to the facts should be obtained for the guidance of the military branch of the government. I was instructed to make my objective point the district of the country drained by the Copper and Tanana Rivers and ascertain as far as practicable the number, character, and disposition of all Indians living in that section of the country. I was to learn the manner into

arrival. He was left by Shelekhov at Kodiak in 1786 to extend exploration and fur trade in Prince William Sound.

[4] Lake Plavezhnoi is the present Lake Tazlina and the river that drains it into the Copper, the Tazlina River.

[5] *Odinochka,* a *singleton,* is the Russian word used in Alaska for posts that were little more than roadhouses.

[6] A map obtained by Sir Charles Bagot from the Ministry of Marine at St. Petersburg in 1802 bore a notation that Baranov had ascended the Copper River above five hundred versts. There is no other evidence that the governor of the Russian American Company ever ascended the Copper River.

which the natives were subdivided into tribes and clans, the district or country they inhabited, their relations to each other, and especially their disposition toward the Russian Government in the past, as well as the feeling which existed among them toward the present government, and the white people who were making their way towards that region. I was further instructed to examine their modes of life and means of communication from one part of the country to the other, the amount and kinds of material of war in their possessions, and from whence obtained. I was also expected to inform myself as to the character of the country and the means of sustaining a military force, should one be needed in the Territory.

Abercrombie proceeded to Sitka, where he endeavored to complete outfitting. He was unable to secure proper river-transportation facilities and was forced to rely on a *baidarka* and an old Russian ship's boat. Proceeding to Nuchek by sea, he landed his supplies and loaded his river craft. Leaving here, he and his party entered Prince William Sound and went through the channel between Hinchinbrook and Hawkins Islands eastward to the Copper River Delta, through which they succeeded in passing at high tide. They engaged some local Indians to help in the ascent of the river. The river was now (June 21) at a high stage of water from the melting glaciers. Spread out over its wide flat, choked with glacial deposits, it bore on its current icebergs parted from the numberless glaciers that entered the lower valley of the Copper River. The fearful swiftness of the stream bearing these icebergs along or rushing through and around them, when grounded in its shallows, the many bars and mud flats, the flooded banks—all tested to the limit the mettle of the travelers. Finally two of the larger glaciers entering the valley—Childs and Miles—presented a serious obstacle. The party endeavored to make their way over one of these—Miles Glacier, flowing in from the northwest—but had to give up the attempt. Abandoning their *baidars,* they made their way on foot past the face of Childs Glacier, carrying a canoe. On making a crossing of the Copper River, they encountered a prospector, John Bremner, from the interior. It was now August 30, and Bremner warned them that the only feasible route to the interior was one that had to be traversed on foot. Because Abercrombie hesitated to make this effort so late in the season, on September 1 he turned back and dropped downstream to tidewater. Proceeding up the coast, the party reconnoitered two inlets, Port Valdez and Port Fidalgo. Entering Port Valdez, they attempted to locate a trail over Valdez Glacier. After somewhat indifferent success, they returned on September 14.

The next year (1885) Lieutenant Henry T. Allen of the Second United States Cavalry was directed by the commanding officer of the Department of the Columbia

> to proceed to make a reconnaissance of the Copper River and the Tanana River valleys . . . to reach the mouth of the Copper River at least in March so as to ascend the river on the ice. In all other things Lieutenant Allen was left to his own discretion and judgment.[7]

Allen left Portland on January 28 and reached Sitka on February 10. Considerable confusion and delay occurred in getting transportation to Nuchek, the starting point of the expedition, but this was eventually secured in the U.S.S. *Pinta,* under command of Lieutenant Commander Nichols. The party reached Nuchek on March 18, proceeded through the delta of the Cooper River on boats, completing the first part of the journey, and finally reached the first stage—the Indian village of Agalnik. Here they engaged Copper River Indians as guides and began the ascent on the ice. Because of the lateness of the season (March 28), water was running over the ice in this part of the river, but as they reached the interior, they found the spring less advanced and the ice firm, with considerable snow on the ground.

Passing the glaciers which had caused Abercrombie so much trouble, they entered the canyons, Abercrombie and Wood, above which they arrived at their first settlement, the *barabarra* (native house) of Taral. Here the Chitina River enters from the east. Allen decided to proceed up this valley. Diverging from the main stream to follow one of its tributaries, the Chettystone, they encountered here the leading native of the district, Nicolai. They were now in the copper country. Evidence of the presence of the metal was seen

[7] *Compilation of Narratives of Exploration,* 411. Lieutenant H. T. Allen's report.

everywhere. Nicolai offered to build a *baidar* of moosehide, with which to descend the Chettystone, and to accompany the party as pilot. As the ice had gone out, the descent was begun on April 28. When they reached the Chitina, they found the river was not yet clear of ice. Their progress was delayed so that they did not reach Taral until May 4. From Taral they began the ascent of the Copper, tracking upriver. They were accompanied by Nicolai, who was a great help to them in dealing with the natives, several of whose settlements were passed. The Indian chief left them at the mouth of the Tazlina.

After entering the upper Copper River Valley, the party had suffered much from hunger. No game has been encountered, and supplies were running low. On May 30 the party abandoned their *baidar* above the mouth of the Chistochina and began their toilsome march across the Alaska Range. Still following the course of the Copper River, they continued to make progress under the guidance of a crippled Indian. At the last Indian camp they engaged native porters and began the direct ascent of the mountains. From Lake Suslota they climbed a pass to which the name Miles was given. Just before they reached the summit, the first salmon arrived, relieving their hunger. On June 6 they crossed a low divide through the Alaska Range out of which flow three of the most important rivers, the Tanana, the White, and the Copper. From the divide salmon was plentiful, and game also was encountered. On June 10 they reached Nandell's on the Tanana. Following the Tanana to Tetling's, they constructed there a *baidar* with which to descend the Tanana. On June 14 the descent was begun, and after a somewhat dangerous and exciting run, on June 26 at 2:30 A.M. they reached Nukilerai and Nuklukayet, two posts at the junction of the Tanana and the Yukon rivers. At Nukilerai the party were informed by natives "*kooshat nato, chai nato*" (Russian for "no food, no tea"). St. Michael's was reached on August 29.

This journey was little short of momentous since it was the first successful attempt made to pass from the Prince William Sound country directly to the Yukon. It proved the comparative ease with which, despite the difficulties of the ascent of the Copper River, the Alaska Range could be crossed. It also proved that there was considerable going and coming, not only between the natives of the upper Tanana and the Copper, but also between the Indians of the Copper River and the Yukon. Many of the natives on the upper Copper had traded at Fort Reliance and Fetutlin. The idea of a road from Prince William Sound to the interior now began to take form.

In 1886 Alaska became the subject of acute diplomatic controversy. The issue centered around the sealing on the Pribilof Islands in Bering Sea to which the seal herds resort during the summer months to bring forth and rear their young. The right to carry on operations here had been leased in 1870 for a period of twenty years to the Alaska Commercial Company of San Francisco.

The fact that the herds spend only a part of the year at the rookeries on St. George and St. Paul islands somewhat lessened the value of the company's monopoly. The herds leave the islands during the autumn months and head south. While returning in the spring, they are exposed to attack in the open sea. Pelagic sealing, as the taking of seals in the open sea is called, had been practiced ever since the purchase of Alaska, but in the eighties it assumed alarming proportions that seriously depleted the herds.

To prohibit sealing operations in the open sea, the Alaska Commercial Company, by virtue of its lease, appealed to the United States government to protect its monopoly. To what extent this was possible under international law was doubtful, but the Treasury Department had in 1881, in letters addressed to the agents of the company and to the collector of customs at San Francisco, expressed the view that the United States would be within its rights in putting a stop to this practice.[8] In 1886 Daniel Manning, secretary of the treasury in the first Cleveland administration, issued instructions to officers in charge of revenue cutters in the Pacific to seize any ships conducting sealing operations in Bering Sea. Accordingly, a number of Canadian vessels were seized and taken into Sitka. The territorial court, Judge Dawson presiding, condemned the vessels and ordered them sold.

Strong protests were immediately lodged by the British government against such seizures in the open sea. Unfortunately the Treasury Department had acted without consulting the Depart-

[8] *Fur Seal Arbitration,* IV, 85–86. Letter from Acting Secretary H. F. French of the Treasury Department to D. A. d'Ancona, collector of customs, San Francisco, March 12, 1881.

ment of State, and the latter was for months without official information on the incident. The British continued to press for the release of the vessels and their crews. Bayard, secretary of state, had received somewhat contradictory advice concerning the rights of the United States, but he seems at this time to have been convinced that the seizure and condemnation was counter to international law, and he therefore induced Cleveland to intervene. The President directed that a telegram be dispatched to Sitka ordering the discontinuance of proceedings against the vessels and their masters' and their crews' release. But no notice of this order was taken at Sitka, the collector of customs there affecting to doubt the genuineness of the President's order; therefore, the court sentences were carried out, and the papers forwarded to Washington.

It does not appear that any move was made by the attorney-general to correct this action or to implement the order of the President. The Department of State sought to turn the occasion to account to bring about a comprehensive international agreement to regulate seal fishing in the North Pacific. In this desire, despite the friction caused by the seizures, there seemed to be some promise of success. Lord Salisbury had already expressed himself in favor of action of this sort when the arrival in London of a communication from the government of Canada held negotiations up while the Canadian case was being prepared for submission to the imperial government.

Indignation was openly expressed in United States circles that Canada's intervention had blocked a settlement on the eve of success. But the delay allowed new evidence to be gathered that threw fresh light on the incident. It was now shown that the seizures in Bering Sea had been inspired by the Alaska Commercial Company, who were active lobbyists in Washington. Moreover, one of their agents at Sitka had coached the judge in his handling of the case. The Department of State, while not conniving at the original seizures in 1886, had not been willing to intervene actively to get this action reversed. Nor would it give the British ambassador any guarantee that incidents such as this would not recur. It was urged that the only way that Britain could guard against further seizures would be to come to some understanding for measures to protect the seal herds in the Pribilof Islands.

Matters thus dragged on until after the election of 1888, when Benjamin Harrison became president. In the last session of Congress a bill was sponsored by Mr. Dunn, chairman of the House Committee on Marine and Fisheries, extending the prohibition of taking fur seals (or other fur-bearing animals) within Bering Sea under the law of 1870. It was rejected by the Senate but after undergoing some modification was finally passed and was approved by the President on March 2, 1889. The new provision included and applied to all "the dominion of the United States in the waters of Bering Sea." This action of Dunn's, doubtless sanctioned if not approved by President Cleveland, ran counter to the policy of the State Department, which had accepted the view that sealing could not be stopped in the open sea.

However, the ball was passed to Harrison and his new secretary of state, James G. Blaine. It was obvious by now that the issue had ceased to be one involving only the protection of the seal herds by international agreement but had resolved itself into the question of whether the United States could board and seize vessels in the open sea. It would seem that the two countries had exchanged their traditional roles. The United States was now found on the side opposite to her historical position, while Britain was now championing the freedom of the seas. The act passed by Congress attempting to settle the matter by unilateral action could have no standing in international law. Eventually, much to the chagrin of the United States minister in London, Salisbury, prodded by the governor-general of Canada, declined to settle the question of an international agreement until the issue between the United States and Britain was cleared up. Seizures had continued (upwards of twenty ships were seized), and resentment soared.

The United States at last very reluctantly agreed to arbitrate the matter and at the same time signed a *modus vivendi* to regulate sealing for the year 1891, pending a decision. Experts were sent north to study the habits of the seals, their study to provide a basis for regulations to be adopted for the protection of the animals. Delay in securing immediate ratification by the Senate (not until March 29, 1892) of the arbitration treaty necessitated the renewal of the *modus vivendi* for 1892. Finally the members of the tribunal were named, and the agents and other officials were appointed to their several tasks. The tribunal met at Paris early in 1893 and gave its award August 15, 1893.

The new Secretary of State, like many other men in government circles, was convinced of the strength of the position of the United States. This conviction seems to have rested on the assumption that Russia had exercised exclusive sovereignty in Bering Sea, as evidenced from an examination of the documents. On June 30, Blaine in a note to the British ambassador emphatically stated that Russia's exclusive rights in Bering Sea had been acquiesced in by Great Britain and that such rights had been transmitted unimpaired by the treaty of cession of 1867.[9] While admitting that the United States had in 1822–24 protested against the Russian *ukaz* of September 4, 1821, he claimed that the protest was directed only against interference with United States ships along the coast between the fifty-fifth and fiftieth parallels of latitude. In other words, he endeavored to prove that Russia's exclusive sovereignty in Bering Sea had never been challenged by either the United States or England and that it therefore had not been involved in the treaties of 1824 and 1825.

On November 2, 1892, the agent for the United States, Mr. John W. Foster, informed the British agent, Sir Charles Tupper, that it had been discovered that some of the documents that had been printed in support of the American case had been falsified in translation. He asked for permission to withdraw these translations (which had been published) and to substitute correct translations. It was discovered that Ivan Petrof, who had been chosen to make the translations, had thought to advance his interests and recommend himself to the government by contributing to its success through his translations. The incident passed off without otherwise affecting the course of events. Since photostats of the originals were also printed, the falsifications could scarcely have escaped final detection.

One would like to know to what extent Blaine and the State Department had formed their opinions from these wrong translations; or to what extent, if any, documents that would not support the American case had been withheld from their attention. One of

9 *Fur Seal Arbitration*, II, App., 224–35. Letter from Mr. Blaine to Sir Julian Pauncefote, June 30, 1890.

Courtesy Roger Dudley, Seattle

A DREDGE

Courtesy Roger Dudley, Seattle

RECOVERING GOLD BY SLUICING AND HYDRAULICKING

the most pertinent documents was a dispatch of Henry Middleton to John Quincy Adams reporting a conversation he had had with Speranskii regarding the *ukaz* of September 4, 1821.[10] Since Speranskii unquestionably was the most eminent jurist in Russia at the time and had probably drafted the *ukaz,* any statement of his merits attention. Mr. Middleton wrote:

To. Mr. Speransky, governor-general of Siberia, who had been one of the committee originating this measure I stated my objection at length. He informed me that the first intention had been (as Mr. Poletika afterwards wrote you) to declare the northern portion of the Pacific Ocean a *mare clausum,* but that idea being abandoned, probably being abandoned on account of its extravagance. They determined to adopt the more moderate measure of establishing limits to the maritime jurisdiction on their coasts such as would secure to the Russian American Fur Company the monopoly of the very lucrative traffic they carry on.[11]

This document does not appear at all among those produced during the arbitration. At least it is not to be found in *Fur Seal Arbitration*. It may not have been purposely suppressed, but perusal of a document containing such a pronouncement by one of the principal actors would have put the Secretary of State on his guard. No reference seems ever to have been made to this neglect of a document that would have disposed summarily of the American claim.

As the case proceeded and the United States discovered that the documents would not substantiate the position taken, an attempt was made to shift ground and claim special property rights in the seal herds, which could only be safeguarded by enforcing prohibitory measures in Bering Sea. But the tribunal refused to admit these rights.

[10] Mikhail Mikhailovich Speranskii was named deputy minister of justice under Alexander in 1809 and became the Tsar's confidential adviser. He advocated far-reaching reforms, but his program was interrupted by the French wars. Speranskii was dropped in 1811 for reasons which are obscure. He later became governor-general of Siberia. Under Nicholas he was charged with the codification of the laws. Under his direction were prepared the *Polnoe Sobranie Zakonov Rossiiskoi Imperii* and the *Svod Zakonov*. In recognition of these services he was created a count.

[11] *Alaska Boundary Tribunal,* II, 42–44. Dispatch, August 8, 1822.

The final award went against the United States on four of the five points submitted to the tribunal. The fifth theoretically was in her favor, to the effect that the rights of Russia passed unimpaired to the United States (without defining what these were); but actually, since the United States lost on the other counts, this then was immaterial. The United States, however, succeeded in securing an agreement on regulations for the control and the protection of seal fishing in the North Pacific, while damages to the extent of $425,000 were paid by the United States to the owners of vessels that had been seized during the course of the dispute.

XV

The Sourdoughs

FIVE YEARS AFTER THE TREATY OF CESSION THE FIRST ASSAULTS ON the remote fastnesses of the upper Yukon were made by straggling adventurers through the back door from the Mackenzie River Valley. It seems to have been a peculiar train of fortuitous circumstances that brought the first sourdoughs into Alaska by this roundabout route.

What prompted the movement is difficult to trace. At this early date the only vestige of gold in the Yukon Valley of which we have knowledge is that claimed to have been found by a Hudson's Bay Company employee not far from Fort Yukon, probably on Birch Creek, in the year 1862 or 1863. It is not likely that news of this find became generally known even in Hudson's Bay country, since that company has never been interested in mining. At any rate, in the year 1872 a group of miners left Manson Creek on the Omineca River in northern British Columbia with a vague idea of going down the Mackenzie River and across to the Yukon. Following the Finlay to its junction with the Parsnip and then the Peace River where the latter strikes across the main range of the Rockies, east of the mountains they turned up the Halfway River, one of the left-bank tributaries. The Halfway was followed to its source. From here their supplies were dragged on sleds across to the Sikanni Chief and down that river to its junction with the Fort Nelson. The latter was then followed to its confluence with the Liard, where they wintered at Lower Post.

In the spring of 1873 the group resumed their journey down the Liard and the Mackenzie to its mouth; thence, ascending the Peel and its tributary, the Rat, they crossed the divide to the Bell and the Porcupine. They passed in succession Lapierre House, New Rampart House, and finally Fort Yukon at the mouth of the Porcupine, now occupied by the Alaska Commercial Company, where they arrived on July 15. A few days later they were followed by some acquaintances from the Liard River post. It was these two parties who combined forces and did most of the pioneering in the Valley. The most notable members were Arthur Harper, who seems to have been an experienced prospector, Leroy Napoleon McQuesten, and Alfred H. Mayo. These three became the "grand old men" of the early days, while the others almost at once entered the service of the Alaska Commercial Company and gradually faded out of the picture.

Harper began prospecting. He ascended the Yukon River, searched the White River (for copper), and later the Stewart and Fortymile. Eventually he was forced by financial straits to abandon the search for gold and in 1875 entered the service of the company. His prospecting days were over.

The route to the Yukon via Chilkoot Pass had long been known to the Indians and used by them in their lucrative trade with the Stick or Tagish Indians of the interior. While its existence was no secret, the Chilkoot Indians regarded it as a route exclusively their own, and no others were allowed to use it. Until 1878 they managed to exclude even the whites, but in that year George Holt was able to secure the consent of the Chilkoot and Chilkat Indians to traverse it. Holt apparently reached the lower end of Marsh Lake and crossed over to Teslin Lake, whence he returned, reporting the presence of coarse gold. Holt was followed two years later by a party under Edward Bean, which prospected the Teslin River, and from then on travel into the interior was uninterrupted. Probably the natives were reconciled to this trespass by the profitable monopoly of the business of packing across the summit.

Gold nuggets picked up by Indians or traders found their way to the outside world, and news of this got around in mining circles. In 1882 an expedition organized by Ed Schieffelin of Tombstone, Arizona, reached the mouth of the Yukon, which river they ascended on their own steamer. Schieffelin was interested primarily in lode mining, and, though placer gold was found, he gave up the search, for he believed that transportation problems and the severe climate would render mining unprofitable in these regions. He sold his boat and returned to Arizona. By this time a party under Joseph Ladue left Juneau (founded in 1880) and arrived over

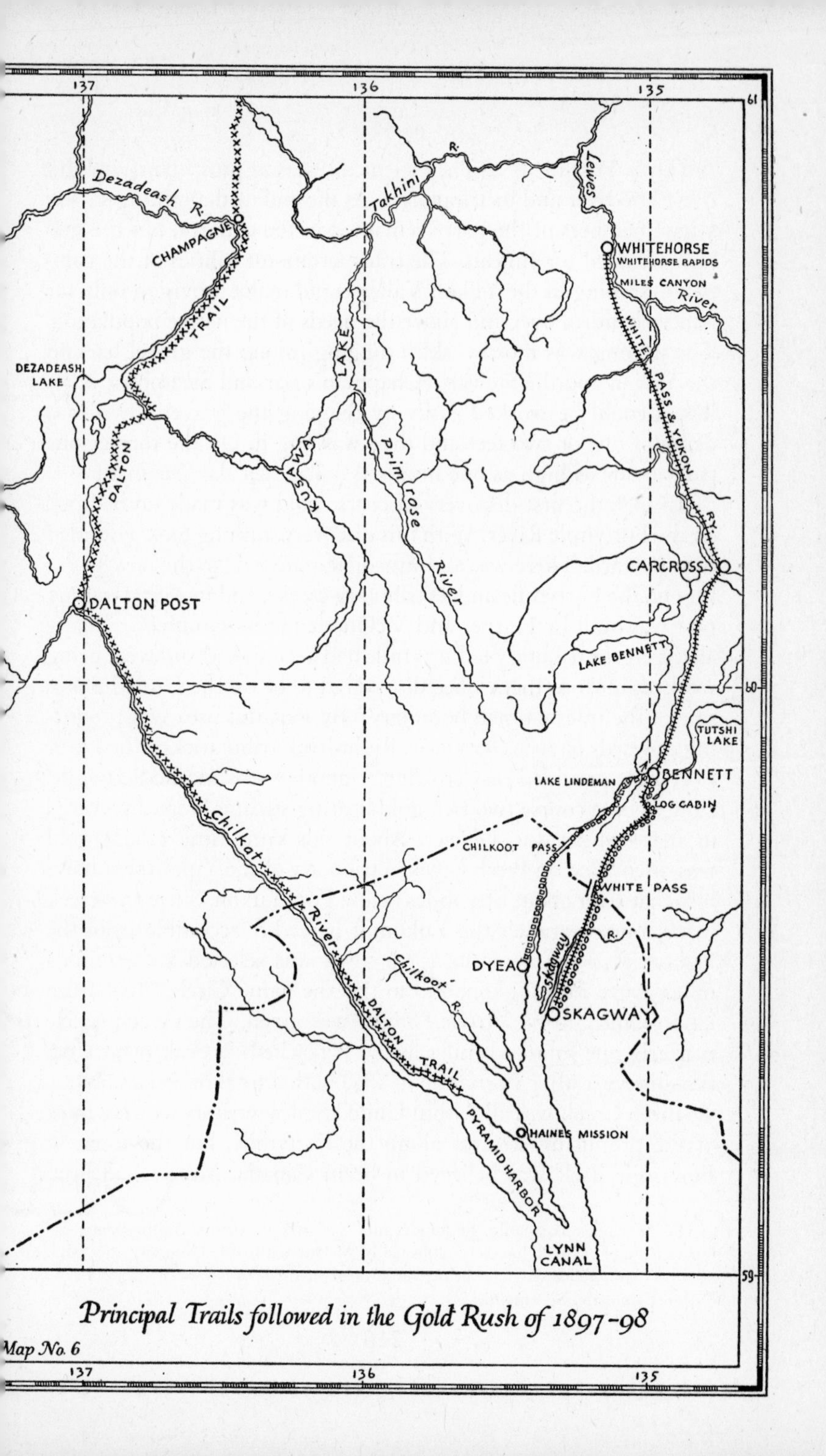

Principal Trails followed in the Gold Rush of 1897-98

Map No. 6

the Dyea Pass in 1882. They spent the season prospecting up and down the river and its tributaries. At the end of the mining season a few members of the party remained in the country, but the majority headed for Juneau. The transportation facilities of the companies trading in the Yukon Valley could make provision only for a mere handful over and above the needs of the native population. The mining was mostly "skim digging" along the gravel bars on the Yukon and the Stewart (Chapman's Bar and Steamboat Bar). These could be worked easily by thawing the gravel down to a depth of one or two feet and then washing it. On the former one party made as high as one hundred dollars per day per man.

In 1886 the first discovery of coarse gold was made on bedrock on the Fortymile River. With this discovery, mining took a decided turn upward. There was an immediate stampede to the new workings on the Fortymile and its tributary creeks, and in 1887 a trading post was built by Harper and McQuesten at its mouth. Gradually all the creeks tributary to Fortymile had been staked and were being worked, most of them since discovered to be on the United States side of the international boundary.[1] By 1895 this area was producing upwards of $600,000 a year. Right-bank tributaries of the lower Fortymile provided easy crossing to another stream, the Sixtymile, along whose course two rich gold-bearing streams were discovered in 1892—Miller and Glacier. About this same time (1892) gold was discovered on Birch Creek, a tributary of the Yukon that flows into that river about fifty miles below Fort Yukon. Since this creek in its course parallels the Yukon, it is readily accessible from the Yukon. A convenient site for a town was selected about ninety miles above Fort Yukon, and to this the name Circle City—from its proximity to the Arctic Circle—was given. The Arctic Circle is nearly one hundred miles away. It reached its peak of production one year after Fortymile in 1896 with a total of $700,000.

Birch Creek was all within United States territory as were most of the producing streams along the Fortymile, but the town of Fortymile itself was believed to be in Canada. Miners had been

[1] The names Fortymile, Sixtymile, and Seventymile denote approximate distances from old Fort Reliance (established by McQuesten in 1874) on the right bank of the Yukon, about six miles below the present site of Dawson. Sixtymile is above, but Fortymile and Seventymile rivers are lower down.

entering the Yukon Valley by crossing the Chilkoot Pass and descending the river. The governments of the United States and Canada had so far ignored this flow of population. Alaska had rocked along since 1884 on the alleged self-government provided by the Organic Act of that year; Canada's share of the Yukon Valley was nominally under the administration of the government of the Northwest Territories. Actually no control was exercised. The uncertainty as to the exact boundary and the discoveries made in areas through which it was believed the line passed threatened complications. In view, therefore, of the growing interest in these regions and of the uncertainty as to the boundary, the Canadian government decided in 1887 to send north an expedition to secure information about the country and to fix at least a tentative boundary. Dr. George M. Dawson of the Canadian Geological Survey was placed in general charge of the expedition, while Mr. William Ogilvie accompanied the party to do the work of surveying.

Dr. Dawson and his party proceeded to Wrangell and from there embarked on a river steamer for the ascent of the Stikine River to Telegraph Creek. From that point they moved their supplies across country by pack train to Dease Lake, where they had already arranged for the construction of three boats. When the last ice had disappeared they crossed the lake and proceeded down stream to "Lower Post" at the junction of the Dease and Liard rivers.

At this point the original expedition split up. Mr. R. G. McConnell with a boat and two men proceeded down the Liard to Fort Simpson on the Mackenzie; from here he descended by river steamer to the delta and thence crossed the height of land to the Yukon. With the rest of the men and boats Dawson began the ascent of the Frances River to Frances Lake along the route first traversed by Campbell in 1840. He succeeded in reaching the limit of canoe navigation and in passing over to the Pelly River, which he descended in a canvas canoe to Fort Selkirk. Here he began the building of a new boat for the ascent of the Lewes. Ogilvie arrived on August 13 and turned over to Dawson his reports and maps, which the latter took with him on his return to the "outside." Dawson's and McConnell's were the first scientific expeditions into the upper Yukon and their reports gave the world the first reliable information on the geology of the country traversed. In addition, Dr. Dawson's report contained invaluable material on its early history.

Mr. William Ogilvie, meanwhile, had proceeded north to Lynn Canal. Here, having arranged for the transport of his supplies across the pass and for the building of a boat, he used the time of his enforced wait to make a traverse over Chilkoot Pass to Lake Bennett. He thus provided an accurate basis for a survey of the river down to the international boundary. Then he went on to Fortymile and wintered there. The winter was spent in determining the position of the one hundred and forty-first meridian at its crossing of the Yukon and the Fortymile rivers. A line slashed for some distance through the bush on both sides was checked in 1889 by the United States government and found reasonably correct. It was provisionally accepted by them.

On his return in January, 1889, Ogilvie asserted that as most of the miners were United States citizens, they preferred United States mining laws, and recommended that since any attempt on the part of the Canadian government to interfere in the affairs of the country would be resented, the Canadian government should refrain from asserting its authority. At the time of Ogilvie's report neither Fortymile Creek nor Birch Creek had really got into production.

By 1893 production had greatly increased and the influx of population was so great that action could not be further put off. Moreover, Bishop Bompas of the diocese of Selkirk reported that during the previous winter—1892–93—approximately two hundred miners had entered the Yukon and that their presence without restraint of law was threatening to demoralize the Indians. Similar reports were made by the trading companies. Mr. Ogilvie, then at Juneau, supported the move for adequate law enforcement; and it was decided to send two representatives of the Northwest Mounted Police from Moosomin—Inspector (Lieutenant) C. Constantine and Sergeant Brown—to make a reconnaissance. Constantine proceeded to Victoria, Juneau, and, crossing Chilkoot Pass, proceeded downriver to Fortymile, where he appeared as the first representative of law and order. Customs duties were collected from the trading companies on goods in stock. He returned to Ottawa by way of St. Michael's and San Francisco and recommended the establishment of a post at Fortymile. This recommendation was approved by the commissioner.

The following spring found Constantine en route to the North with a party of twenty officers, noncommissioned officers, and men to establish this post. Upon arriving at St. Michael's from Seattle, the party and their supplies embarked on the boat of the N.A.T. and T. Company for the trip upriver. Fortymile was reached on July 24, and the construction of the post was begun. The Mounted Police had been created in 1873 for the somewhat similar purpose of asserting law in the Canadian west and along the long border that separates the Canadian prairie provinces from the northern tier of states. But whether experience with Indian tribes and the cattlemen was a preparation for dealing with the polyglot population that had entered the Yukon Valley was another matter. Only success could justify what was then regarded as a rash venture.

Hardly had the police taken over when extraordinary developments occurred. Word of the new finds of gold on Fortymile and Birch creeks had spread to the "outside," and the new diggings had drawn miners from other parts of the Yukon. Their numbers were beginning to be swelled by arrivals from the Alaskan coast, from British Columbia, from California—in fact the whole Pacific coast—and from much of the interior that harbored a more or less floating class of prospectors and adventurers. Miners began to spread themselves over the Yukon Valley and along the tributaries of the Yukon River. Among them was a Nova Scotian, Bob Henderson, who had abandoned the life of the sea for the search for gold. Henderson had been "grubstaked" by Joseph Ladue, then trading at the Sixtymile. He had made his way up a hitherto unprospected stream—Indian River—that flows into the Yukon from the east about twenty miles below the Sixtymile. He had worked this stream and one of its tributaries, Quartz Creek, in 1894 and 1895. In 1896 he passed over the divide to a stream flowing northward to the Klondike. Returning to Sixtymile to replenish his stores, he was compelled by the low stage of water in the Indian River to use the Klondike on his return. At the mouth of the Klondike he encountered a party of Indians, among them a white man, George

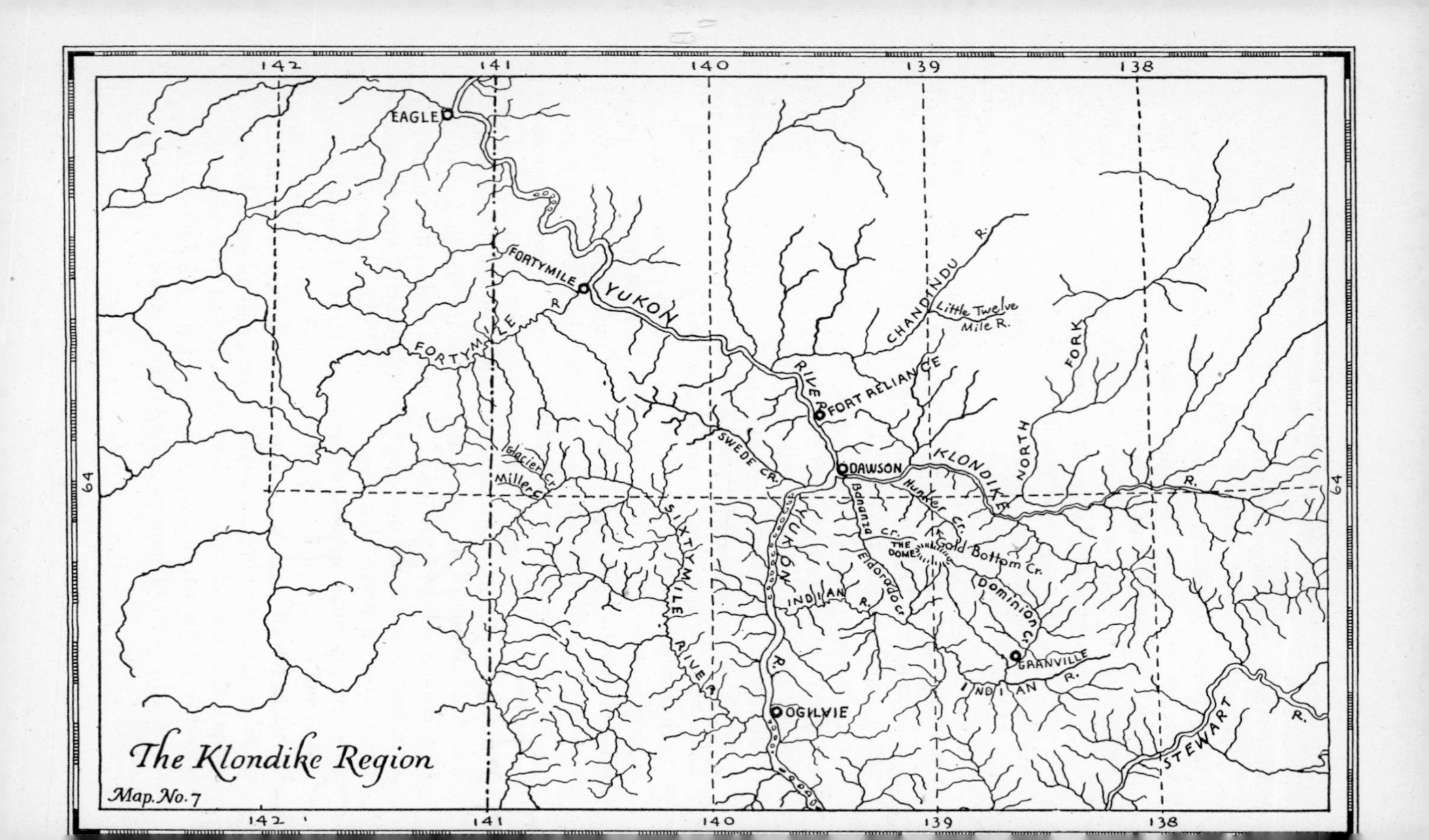

The Klondike Region

Map. No. 7

Washington Carmack, who was married to an Indian woman. Henderson urged Carmack to try his luck on the stream where Henderson had found "pay"—Gold Bottom. Henderson continued his journey, going up the Klondike and then up what is now Hunker Creek to his own prospect.

Later during the summer Carmack and his Indians, who had gone out on a timber-cutting expedition, combined it with a search for gold. They went up the Klondike River and Rabbit (Bonanza) Creek and on the way did some panning, with excellent results. They finally reached Henderson's location on Gold Bottom, but though they staked, they were disappointed with the prospects there. On the return trip, while working their way down Bonanza, at one place they found unbelievably rich "pay." Waiting only to confirm it, they staked four claims, Carmack getting two—Disvery and No. 1 below. Hurrying downstream to the mouth of the Klondike, they made up a raft of logs, on which they floated down to Fortymile where they recorded their claims with Inspector Constantine.

Then began the Klondike stampede.[2] The discoveries of Henderson on Gold Bottom Creek (a tributary of Hunker) had already created mild flurries in the gold camps up and down the river. Carmack's sensational news, in spite of the natural distrust of the professional miner for the amateur, sent the excitement to a high pitch. It was said that even the drunks were loaded into boats in the hope that they would sober up before reaching Dawson and be ready to join the stampede. At Fortymile there was a general exodus. The news was somewhat slower in reaching Circle City; but when it arrived, a similar clearing out of the diggings on Birch Creek followed. Sixtymile (some fifty miles above the mouth of the Klondike) heard of the strike only with the arrival of an upbound river steamer, but since this same steamer had already brought to the new gold field its load of stampeders from the other camps, the miners from upriver were already late and found the claims on the two promising creeks—Bonanza and Eldorado—taken up. Their only recourse was to go beyond these limits to areas which ultimately proved to be comparatively poor. Henderson, on

[2] The actual discovery was made on August 17, 1896, though the claims were not recorded for some days because of the time consumed in reaching Fortymile.

Gold Bottom, despite Carmack's promise to inform him of a strike, heard nothing of it until weeks later, and he, too, was left definitely out in the cold.[3]

But to discover the existence of gold is only one step, and that one perhaps the easiest, in the making of a gold camp. Before production could begin, many obstacles had to be overcome. Supplies had to be assembled to enable the miners to work their claims. The pay streak had to be located by sinking shafts to bedrock and running a number of experimental drifts to determine where the gold was. This involved stripping off the overburden of muck and vegetation, then working down through the frozen gravel. The methods of doing this had been developed on Fortymile and Birch creeks. The overburden was not a serious problem since it seldom exceeded a few feet in thickness, but the gravel through which miners must work was frozen and extended down twenty to thirty feet. At that time the only known way to excavate was to build fires, on the surface in the case of a shaft or against the face in the case of a drift. When the fire had burned itself out and the smoke had cleared, the miner could then enter the shaft or drift, as the case might be, remove the thawed material, then rebuild the fire and start again. This operation was continued until bedrock was reached or the pay streak had been found.

Many of the miners were inexperienced and much of the labor was unskilled, but work went forward throughout the fall and winter. Log cabins were erected on the claims; timber for building and for firewood was cut and hauled. Lumber for sluice boxes was secured from the Ladue's sawmill at Dawson. With limited supplies of labor and material, progress was slow; but as the winter wore on, enough shafts had been sunk to trace in a general way the course of the pay streak, and a considerable amount of gold-bearing gravel had been taken out. With the thawing of the snow, the runoff enabled the gravel to be washed; and the spring clean-up of

[3] A movement was later launched to give Henderson, in view of the contribution he had made to this discovery, some compensation. He was granted a pension by the Dominion government, but it was made conditional on his undertaking not to engage in further prospecting. Eventually this "slippered ease" palled on the old prospector. In 1927 he threw up the pension to resume his pursuit of gold mining on Vancouver Island and continued to follow it until his death, at an advanced age, several years later.

1897 gave startling results—compared with previous production in the Yukon Valley. The A.C. and N.A.T. and T. boats arriving from the lower river with supplies took back a load of gold. This was trans-shipped to ocean-going vessels, which reached the West Coast ports by the early summer. The arrival of these cargoes of gold in San Francisco and Seattle was the first authentic news the world had received of the gold strike. Its effect was immediate and startling.

The world was still feeling the effects of the depression that had begun in the seventies and had become most acute in the nineties. It had been partially alleviated by the discovery of gold on the Witwatersrand, South Africa, but this was "reef" or lode mining; and since the ore, abundant as it was, was low grade, large-scale development had to wait on the building of railroads and the discovery of cheaper methods of mining. These conditions were not met until 1895. Then railway rates began to drop, and the cyanide process, recently introduced, further cheapened production; but the full effects of these changes were to be felt only gradually.

With the arrival of the first gold-laden steamers at San Francisco in 1897, men started to Alaska from the mining camps, the ranches of the West, and the offices and factories in cities on the West Coast. As the news spread to the Middle West, to Canada, to Europe, and to the Antipodes—losing nothing in the telling—the movement grew to unheard-of proportions. At this time the most fabulous finds had not been made. The mines began producing in 1897, but it was not until the clean-up of 1898 that the richness of the pay streak on Bonanza and Eldorado creeks was fully demonstrated. Pans as high as $212 in value were taken. (Forty cents a pan was the highest yield recorded in California.) Again excitement, which had practically subsided, soared. Even the most skeptical were convinced. Reality overtook the most fantastic exaggeration. Now there were no more claims on the original creeks, and newcomers had to go farther afield. Hillsides and benches without any prospect of water, which hitherto had been scorned by the stampeders, were staked and distant creeks taken up without the slightest preliminary prospecting. Still the rush continued without signs of abating. Estimates place the population of the gold fields at the peak at 35,000 to 40,000, but a census taken in 1898 by Superintendent Steele of the Northwest Mounted Police estimated the population at that time as something over four thousand persons with an equal number on the creeks. This census, of course, did not include those prospectors going and coming and the population of Whitehorse and the more remote diggings.

The problems created by this unprecedented influx were staggering. Fortunately Canada had anticipated the situation by sending the Mounted Police north in 1895. A general election in 1896 brought a new government into power under Wilfrid Laurier (later Sir Wilfrid). His minister of the interior was a zealous young Westerner, Clifford Sifton. The Yukon district was at once carved out of the Northwest Territories, and preliminary steps were taken to create a separate administration for it. When word of the discovery of gold and of the inrush of miners reached Ottawa, it was decided to name a commissioner and to provide him with a staff to administer the country. For this post Sifton decided to recall from retirement Major James M. Walsh of Sitting Bull fame, who twenty years before as an officer of the Mounted Police had performed unique service in winning the friendship of that chief and inducing him to return with his Sioux to the United States. Major Walsh was given full authority over the Mounted Police and all officials of the territory and empowered to alter or amend mining regulations. Successive Orders-in-Council provided collectors of customs, land agents, and a gold commissioner. A Yukon Judicial District was created and provision was made for a judge to be sent in to the territory by the federal government.

With these steps the new government of the "district," as it was then called, or the territory, as it came to be later, was started on its way. Commissioner Walsh arrived at the coast in the early fall, hoping to reach Dawson before winter. He was, however, overtaken by the freeze-up at the Big Salmon River, where he was compelled to go into camp for several months—an unmixed blessing, since the most acute problems were those that developed in the southern part of the territory. Major Walsh had under his eyes the beginning of the great rush that swept into the Yukon Valley. One of his first measures was to issue an order that no one was to proceed downriver to the new gold diggings without at least three pounds of food per day for a full year, or approximately one thousand pounds. All boats were checked at a post established on the Tagish River. They were assigned a number, which was painted on them, and it was required that they report to the Mounted Police on arrival at Dawson. Until other provision was made, the Mounted Police collected customs duties on incoming goods, and posts were set up at the summit of the Chilkoot Pass and the White Pass, after it came into use.

Everywhere was excitement as tingling as an electric charge! Many of the incoming prospective miners were from the United States, and many of them were aliens, there being but a sprinkling of Canadians. Questions of nationality had hitherto not arisen. Indeed, the sourdough was inclined to take scant note of national lines. There had been no frontiers and no customs officials since it would scarcely have paid to collect duties; but the sudden influx brought agents of both governments, each to enforce its own authority and to exact payment of customs duties. Offices were set up on the beaches, and goods being landed were subjected to United States duties if they had originated in Canada. At the summit they were examined again, this time by Mounted Police constables. If they had originated in the United States, duty must be paid before they could be taken into Canada. Common sense would have dictated that the Canadian goods should have passed through United States territory in bond; and, indeed, Major Walsh urged this course and offered to extend a like privilege to the United States goods going through Canada. But United States customs officials, while agreeing, insisted that such goods in bond must be accompanied by a convoy through to Bennett, the cost of which was to be borne by the owner of the goods, thus imposing heavy and unnecessary expense on the miners. On horses bought in Canada, if used for transport across United States territory, a duty of thirty dollars each had to be paid. Major Walsh was directed to establish customs posts at both summits (Chilkoot Pass and White Pass), where the weather most of the year was execrable. The police who acted as customs officers suffered great hardships, and incoming travelers were subjected to inconvenience and delay while they unpacked and submitted their outfits to examination. Since the goods were always rechecked for customs at Tagish, through which all traffic was bound to pass, it does seem that nothing was gained by this decision. Indeed, it was necessary to maintain two additional posts.

One thinks instinctively of the diplomats who sat around the table in 1825 and disposed of territory on paper. If they had in imagination conjured up the scene in 1897 and 1898, would they have awarded the interior to one power and given to another a quite useless coastal strip which could serve only as a barrier to traffic? The governments were not always wholly at fault. Sometimes the local officials, jealous of national rights and personal prestige, were to blame. Pressure was exerted by coastal cities to force the purchase of goods on their own side of the line.

There was some resentment that the new gold fields were claimed by Canada, and that, at least for a time, a post of the Mounted Police was established in the newly built town of Skagway. Some loose talk about seizing the territory and holding it for the United States spread alarm in Canada. The police force, despite reinforcements, was still pitifully small. Hence it was decided to send in an additional militia force of several hundred officers and men, known as the Yukon Field Force. It was hastily raised, equipped, and sent in via the Stikine, arriving in the Yukon early in 1898. Fort Selkirk was chosen as the location for these men.

A sensational press, avid for the bizarre and the romantic to tickle the jaded palates of their readers, eagerly played up the more extravagant side of these events. Not too discriminating newspapers and boards of trade in ambitious municipalities saw their towns as jumping-off places for these argonautic expeditions and coveted the profits that would accrue. The merits of each town and city were properly advertised as a starting point for the new gold fields. Ignorance of the North gave scope for this sort of thing. There was no one in authority to contradict the claims. Newspapers farther afield helped to spread misinformation.

Every train headed west was crowded with passengers and freight to be dumped on the waterfronts of the Pacific coast ports. Every craft that was seaworthy was pressed into the northern service. Loaded to double their capacity, ships nosed their perilous way through the dangerous waters of the Inside Passage or the no less dangerous Gulf of Alaska. If they kept afloat and escaped the reefs, they transferred their cargoes by lighter, scow, barge, raft, or wagon

ourtesy Roger Dudley, Seattle

CHILKOOT PASS

through the surf to the beaches on Pyramid Harbor, Dyea Inlet, and (after the White Pass was opened) at the mouth of the Skagway River. Passengers scrambling ashore sorted out their goods as best they could from the general hodgepodge. They made all haste to forestall the rising tide and remove their supplies to safety over the slippery, rock-strewn foreshore beyond the reach of the tide. Only then might they seek out a place to pitch a tent back in the forest or amid the mud and rocks along the shore, where man and beast had worked the soil into a bottomless ooze.

If the travelers had money, they brought draft animals to carry their goods; otherwise, they moved them on their own backs by stages up the narrow river valley to the foot of the steepest mountain slopes. The road, churned into slush in winter and seas of mud in summer, caused men and horses to strain and struggle. If they did not drop from exhaustion, a false step or a slip on the treacherous rocks might result in a broken limb; if they were on the steep slopes, a swift descent carried risk to life itself. The Chilkoot Pass, bad in its lower reaches along the Chilkoot River, became in its upper stretches a killing mountain slope where loads had perforce to be carried on the back. The labor required to lift a ton of supplies from Sheep Camp to the summit was prodigious. At the Scales the frowning mountains, which here overlook the pass, bear on their summits an ever growing burden of snow. A sudden hot day would loosen it and send it roaring down, threatening to bury the unwary travelers in its track. A disaster of this nature occurred on April 3, 1898, when over fifty people were overtaken by a swift avalanche and crushed or suffocated under mountains of snow.

The White Pass, opened in 1897, was less direct but had easier grades. Much of it lay through forest over river flats and up gulches where the muck was deep. During the summer in these sunless gorges it became a morass where animals died by scores, almost hundreds. The name—Dead Horse Gulch—perpetuates the memories of dreadful scenes. Eventually the road became blocked, and traffic was stopped. Grading and corduroying were done to improve it before travel could be resumed. But those who had passed were little concerned to advance the excellence of this road. It was left to those who came after. Parts of the road clung precariously to the narrow gorge of the river. The fifteen miles from tidewater to the summit was one long agony—by no means improved by the abandoned equipment and animals with which it was littered.

Once over the summit the traveler found himself on an uneven, rocky plateau, deep in snow in winter, in summer its unevenness marked by a sucession of depressions, the water spilling from one to another. Mountain slopes only slightly less forbidding than they had appeared from tidewater flanked the depressions. The drainage of the potholes eventually drew together into small lakes, the small lakes into larger ones. The first of these lakes of any considerable size—Lake Lindeman—was the initial halting place. Most people preferred to push on with their goods to a second and much larger one—Lake Bennett—where timber was available for boat-building and where better camping sites were to be had. Here they camped and constructed the craft on which they might float themselves and their goods down to Dawson.

Whipsawing of lumber and putting the boat together was likely to take some weeks. To the cheechako this was cruel work and sorely tried both muscles and temper. If this ordeal was surmounted, he loaded his cargo on his usually clumsily constructed boat and began his voyage. When the wind blew from the stern, he could raise a sail and take his ease; but more frequently he had to ply the oars, especially when he came to one of the lakes—Bennett, Nares, and Tagish. When he reached Tagish Post (on the Tagish River), he registered with the police and was given a number to paint on his boat. Then he was on his own. Down the Tagish, through Marsh Lake into the Fiftymile River, through the wild waters of Miles Canyon, Squaw Rapids, and finally through the flying mane of the White Horse Rapids, and then he had comparatively placid waters. Only the wind on Lake Laberge was likely to give him trouble. If the gravel bars did not reach out to grasp his scow while the pilot slept, if the running ice of the fall did not crush his boat, within a week or more he would round the last bend and see the rock slide that scars the mountain above Dawson. Keeping as close as he dared to the right bank, he would pass the mouth of the Klondike and be borne along by its tumultuous waters to scramble ashore in a welter of confusion—grimy, weary, and stiff. Here amid scenes of ant-like hurrying, even squalor, most men felt a surge of exultation as they breathed an atmosphere charged with hope and excitement. At last they were part of the great stampede.

The numbers engaged, the countless risks involved at every step, the inner fever that drove each on with scant regard for his fellow traveler, and the feeble control exercised by either government made chaos inevitable. Officials at the summit could not cope with the crowds continually reinforced by newcomers, each adding to the turmoil. The police and customs officers worked day and night. Fog settled down on the passes. Men felt their way blindly over the summits and crowded on those ahead. Blizzards raged, burying the camps, the piles of goods, and the tents where the officers worked—all under one vast blanket of snow. But nothing stopped the movement. Weather cleared, and the crowd went on to the lakes where the sound of the saw and the hammer echoed through the mountains week in and week out. The boats vanished down the lakes, but still the camps at the summits and on the lakes received fresh recruits. The tide of men and goods and animals seemed endless.

The earliest crisis that developed was a food shortage. The few river boats that had hitherto plied the river made leisurely trips in summer, never more than two, and were able to supply the limited needs of the small population of miners, prospectors, and fur traders. The sudden influx of population put an intolerable strain on the local food supplies. With reasonable foresight miners were secure on this point, and they never took chances. But the cheechakos who swarmed in during the winter of 1896–97, accustomed to meeting their needs from the corner grocery store, had no understanding of conditions in a country remote from civilization. After Major Walsh's arrival in the autumn, he immediately announced that no one would be allowed to enter the country without a year's supply of food, and this regulation was enforced.[4] Prior to this ruling, thousands had already entered the region without any check, and as winter came on ugly rumors got abroad of an

[4] This order was later declared *ultra vires* since it infringed the constitutional rights of the individual to go where he pleased, and was withdrawn. By that time the need of it was over. It is generally held that, without regard to its constitutionality, it was a salutary measure.

impending famine in the upper Yukon. Stories reached Washington, and Congress, catching the alarm, appropriated two hundred thousand dollars to provide relief. How to get food in during the winter when navigation was suspended was the problem. Supplies arriving from the lower river on the last boats were earmarked for Dawson, but miners at Circle and Eagle held up the steamers and took what they required (paying Dawson prices). Then, as the river had dropped to an unprecedented low level, the last boats could not get beyond Fort Yukon. Captain Constantine of the Mounted Police at Dawson had publicly urged those persons without supplies for the winter to leave and even furnished free transportation to some. The greater number of those attempting to descend the river had been caught in the ice between Fort Yukon and Circle and had not got beyond the fort. Here trouble developed.

Fortunately the United States had sent into the country some officers of the army, Captain Ray and Lieutenant Richardson, and their presence at Fort Yukon proved salutary. They were unarmed with authority except of a most general nature. Nevertheless, they used what they had to prevent wholesale looting of the steamers and persuaded the miners to agree to an orderly distribution of supplies as needed and to make good their value. If a man could not pay, he was allowed to work out the cost. Some even were permitted to spend the winter prospecting. By these means violence was averted. Conditions were equally bad at Circle City, but eventually adequate supplies were received. At Dawson, because of the prompt measures taken by Captain Constantine, no shortage occurred. And so the first crisis in the history of the Klondike was successfully surmounted.

Relief of another kind, however, was already on its way. Congress had turned to the Reverend Sheldon Jackson and had authorized him to import some five hundred reindeer from Lapland with their herdsmen. The animals were to be shipped across the Atlantic, sent by train across the continent, and then carried on steamers to southern Alaska, whence they were to be given to the gold fields. Incessant delays occurred; the reindeer did not do well on their diet of hay, and moss had to be brought from their native land. Climate, terrain, and forage on the Alaska coast proved unsuitable.

Eventually they were worked along the Dalton trail, their numbers constantly diminishing. Long before they approached the gold fields, the need for them had vanished, and they were taken north and added to the herds of Siberian reindeer on Seward Peninsula.

Of other alternative routes whose claims were recklessly advanced, one was over the Valdez Glacier, up the Copper River, and over the Alaska Range. This was tried by thousands. During the season of 1898 approximately thirty-five hundred persons are estimated to have swarmed into this region, Klondike bound. Captain W. R. Abercrombie, who had reconnoitered the Copper River country in 1883, was sent north to find a road, if possible, from Port Valdez to the Yukon. Abercrombie's instructions were to secure at Haines Mission reindeer for transport. When he arrived at that place, he learned that the reindeer, which were some distance inland, were in so emaciated a condition that a sea voyage would be fatal to them. He reached Port Valdez April 20 and 21, and landing on the beaches, he broke his expedition into parties and divided the supplies and equipment among them. On May 4 he began the ascent of Valdez Glacier. He employed men to pack the supplies, but a few days' trial convinced him that the work was entirely too arduous for them. He therefore abandoned his intention and decided to return to Seattle for pack animals and equipment. Early in July he was ready to renew his attempt to reach the interior. He first tried to follow the Lowe River and cross the Coast Range through Thompson Pass; in fording the river, his horse was swept from his feet and both animal and rider narrowly escaped drowning. He then gave up this project and decided to cross the glacier and Bates Pass. Incredible exertions of men and beasts were needed to surmount the glacier. Crevasses lurked under the snow at their feet. Fog descended and blotted out the trail. Howling gales bearing snow swept down from the mountains and shut out every landmark. At night they made their camp and strung out the picket line on the glacier to tether the horses. Their grain was portioned out on the ice. The men were served cold rations and a small tin cup full of whiskey. Thus wet and cold, they spread their blankets on the snow and turned in. Their sleep was broken by the intermittent roar of masses of ice detaching themselves from the glaciers higher up in the surrounding valleys and hurling themselves down into the valley below.

Thus they made their painful and perilous way to the summit, which they reached at the end of the second day. The most dramatic change took place in their surroundings. Abercrombie describes them thus:

> After some five or six hours' travel in the howling storm where it was impossible to hear or see a comrade, a high and rocky cliff was finally rounded and the expedition beheld the most beautiful sight I ever witnessed. The change was almost magical. Two yards after passing behind the shelter of this rocky cliff there was a perfect haven of rest and sunshine, while out of the pass rushed the howling storm, like water out of the nozzle of a fire hose. Throwing ourselves on the snow in the sunshine at full length, we enjoyed the rest which only men can enjoy who have been battling for their existence. As if understanding the situation, the poor miserable pack-ponies, their manes and tails all clotted with ice, lay down in the soft snow and grunted with satisfaction as the rays of the sun peeled the coating of ice off their bodies. After resting here a short time, and eating lunch, the expedition proceeded down the glacier to the timber line. Here the camp was made for the night in a grove of stunted cottonwoods and willow.[5]

The Abercrombie party then proceeded until they reached Klutina Lake. They followed along the banks of this body of water to the Klutina River, down which they travelled to its junction with the Copper River. They then turned up the Copper River Valley which they traversed, following the cutoff across Mount Sanford to the Slahna. They then ascended this stream to Mentasta Pass, finally reaching the Tok River which flows into the Tanana. From here they turned back and proceeded down the Copper River. Abercrombie notes meeting men reconnoitering a route to take cattle into the Klondike. At the mouth of the Tazlina River he reorganized his expedition for a boat trip and thus made the descent to the coast by way of the Copper River and the delta. He arrived at the camp at Port Valdez on October 16.

Abercrombie, when he had reached Valdez towards the end of

[5] Captain W. A. Abercrombie, "A military Reconnaissance of the Copper River Valley," *Compilation of Narratives of Exploration in Alaska,* 563–90.

April, had found that hundreds of stampeders, drawn by rumors or newspaper accounts of an all-American route to the gold fields, had begun to arrive with their kits. Later he found them strung out from the beach to the foot of the glacier, met them on the glacier, often overcome with snow blindness, and saw hundreds more at "Twelve Mile Camp" beyond the glacier on Lake Archer. They had cabins at the foot of Lake Archer, at Copper Center. The most advanced camp he found was in Mentasta Pass, the gateway to the Tanana and the Yukon. He reported that many who had crossed the glacier, when they learned of what lay ahead, became apprehensive of being cut off by snow on the glacier and began to drift back to the coast. Few of those who went in made it through to the Yukon. Those who did blazed a trail for others to follow.

The next year Abercrombie was sent back with a fully equipped expedition to survey and cut a trail through from Valdez. He reached Valdez on April 21. He was shocked at the appearance of those who had remained throughout the winter:

> They seemed to be badly demoralized; and from a hurried conversation I had with six or seven of them I was led to believe that hundreds were dying of starvation and scurvy beyond the coast range in the Copper River valley. . . . Many of the people I had met and known the year before were so changed in appearance with their long hair hanging down over their shoulders and beards covering their entire face that I do not think I recognized one of them. Most of these then in the settlement of Valdez had little or no money. . . . That they had passed a terrible winter was beyond all question of doubt; that many of their companions had died of scurvy and had been frozen to death was in evidence at the little graveyard that had sprung up since my departure the year before.

Abercrombie commented on the signs of mental derangement present. One manifestation, he notes, was an almost universal belief in a "glacial demon," who waylaid them on the glacier, looking for a chance to pick off isolated individuals. One man told him how he had failed in an attempt to guard his son from the demon's attack amid the crevasses half way up to the summit, and that the boy had succumbed. He had brought back his body and buried him in the freshly opened burial ground at Valdez. The bystanders found nothing unusual in the recital, which they confirmed. Those unfortunates were the backwash from the tide that had swept into the valley the previous year fired with enthusiasm and buoyed with hope but withal inexperienced and unskilled. Abercrombie set about succoring them and trying to furnish them with at least the necessities of life and to relieve sickness until the time when they could be evacuated.

During the season Abercrombie's party surveyed, cleared, and graded about ninety miles up Lowe River through Keystone Canyon and over Thompson for a road for pack horses. Preliminary work was done for a hundred miles further down to the crossing of a tributary of the Copper, the Tonsina. This took them quite through the Coast Range and marked the first stage in the road which was finally carried through to Eagle on the Yukon and which later formed part of the Richardson Highway leading from Valdez to Fairbanks.

Another overland route that appealed to many was that up the Stikine River to Telegraph Creek, thence northward over the route of the Western Union parties to Teslin. In summer the Stikine could be ascended by boat; in winter supplies could be hauled over the ice. But the journey was full of peril from the treacherous ice in winter and swift currents in summer.

For those to whom time was of little account and who wished to avoid the danger and labors of toiling up the summits and building and guiding their own craft down the Yukon, the route by St. Michael's recommended itself. It was accessible by sea from any West Coast port; river steamers then would carry prospectors with their goods up the two thousand miles to the gold fields. There were drawbacks, however. Bering Sea was not clear of ice until June, and vessels were frequently held for weeks at its entrance in the early summer. River boats could not leave St. Michael's ordinarily until the arrival of vessels from the south, even though the river might be clear of ice. At times wind delayed for days their departure from safe anchorage for the run of seventy-odd miles across Norton Sound to the mouth of the Yukon. The journey upstream was toilsome. One hundred miles a day was considered good going; halts for "wooding-up," for running aground, or for loading and unloading supplies involved further loss of time. By the time the middle course of the river was reached, the water was frequently dropping. A whole season (and that the only season for prospecting) might be consumed; this route was ordinarily left to those who could afford to wait, for vessels from St. Michael's never reached Dawson before July 15.

Those who followed the indirect routes arrived much too late to stake claims on the rich ground and usually turned to other ways of making money. Indeed, few of those who arrived even in 1897 got claims on creeks of the original strikes. These were staked in the fall and winter of 1896. But the flood of newcomers that swept into Dawson in 1898 flowed far beyond the Klondike gold fields; they worked out into remoter areas of the Yukon Territory and over into Alaska. Some went into the profitable work of transportation. Some opened grocery or general merchandise stores. Some started newspapers, built toll roads, or created booths along the roads to the gold fields. Some took "lays" or worked for others on the creeks. They were as likely to succeed in this as the original stakers. Money was flowing in to the North, and anyone who could divert some of it to his own pockets had a chance to succeed.

Now other currents began to deposit their flotsam and jetsam on the Dawson waterfront. Towns in the Canadian northwest had advertised themselves as the waterway to the gold fields—notably Edmonton. Travelers gathered there in 1897 and 1898 to essay the long trip northward, either by the Mackenzie and the Porcupine rivers or overland through the Peace and the Liard valleys. The former route, long used by the Hudson's Bay people, was largely by water. It was a time-consuming journey, and there was some risk in negotiating the rapids of the Athabaska and Slave rivers. From the delta of the Mackenzie an easy grade carried one over the mountains to the Porcupine; or the route could be varied by ascending the Wind River and crossing over to the Stewart.

The Peace-Liard route was a matter of saddle and pack horse. It recommended itself to those who were attempting to drive horses or cattle through. The first parties had already left to endure its heart-breaking experiences, when the Mounted Police were instructed by the minister of the interior to send a party over this route and report on it. Inspector J. D. Moodie was selected for the task. He left Edmonton in the fall of 1897, proceeded to Fort St. John on the Peace River, which he left during the winter to make his way by the Halfway, Opica, and Finlay rivers to Fort Grahame on the Finlay. He was forced to delay the expedition while he went south via McLeod Lake and Fort George to Quesnel on the Fraser to secure horses to continue his journey. (He had sent his first horses back from the Rocky Mountain divide). This consumed several weeks and meant a long overland trip on his return with the horses before he could resume his journey up the Finlay to Sifton Pass, down the Kachika (known variously as Muddy, Black, or Turnagain) River, and finally over the mountains to Sylvester Landing on the Dease River. Pushing on from here with horses, he descended the Dease and Liard rivers to the Frances River, ascended the Frances to Frances Lake and Finlayson Lake. Horses were killed or sent back. With dogs he crossed the summit between Finlayson Lake and the Pelly, procured a Peterborough canoe from a Klondike-bound traveler, and launched it on the Pelly. A number of portages were necessary on account of rapids. For this purpose he found the canoe too cumbersome and was forced to discard it for a canvas boat he had brought along. He cached most of his supplies and thus made his way through the canyons. Thirty miles above Selkirk he was obliged by running ice to abandon his boat and make his way overland to the post. He arrived at Selkirk on October 18, 1898, one year after starting, and catching an up-bound river boat the next day, reached Skagway and the outside world within a few days. His trip proved (if that were necessary) that the route was not feasible as an entrance to the Yukon. But his report was not in time to head off parties of travelers. Moodie overtook and passed hundreds making their toilsome way over these unexplored and trackless solitudes to their distant goal. For cattle or horses, shortage of feed, the heavy growth of timber, and the innumerable streams that had to be forded or swum made the route all but impassable.

Meanwhile, a railway was under construction from Dyea to Dyea Canyon and an aerial tramway from Dyea Canyon to the summit of Chilkoot Pass, to be completed by January 15, 1898. This did much to improve and speed up transportation and to relieve the situation. After the first winter private enterprise took care of the situation. Vessels were being rushed to completion on the ways at St. Michael's, and shipyards along the coast were being ransacked for craft which could be pressed into service on the Inside Passage; even old wooden ferryboats and river boats that could brave the North Pacific crossing were put on the Yukon River run. By 1898 the lower river was well supplied; some river steamboats were taken over the summit and put together on Lake Bennett to make the run down as far as the Canyon. Once the peak had passed, the restriction on travel to those who had one year's supplies, enforced by Major Walsh, operated to maintain a proper balance between the population and the food supply, at least on the upper river.

One final improvement in the situation was the completion of a railway from tidewater over the White Pass beyond Miles Canyon to the foot of White Horse Rapids. Capital was provided by Close Brothers of London, but the work was carried through by United States engineers and contractors. Construction began on May 28, 1898. By February 18, 1899, the summit had been reached. On July 24 rails reached Lake Bennett; and on July 30, 1900, service began between Skagway and Whitehouse. By 1901 Dawson had also been linked with the outside world by a telegraph line paralleling the Yukon River to Atlin and then across British Columbia to Telegraph Creek and Quesnel.

In general the richer creeks were staked in 1896 by persons already in the country. The townsite of Dawson was laid out within a few weeks by Joseph Ladue, who transferred his headquarters there. Inspector Constantine established a post at Dawson, and the next year police headquarters were removed thither. The Alaska Commercial Company and the North American Trading and Transportation Company also moved there and began to prepare for the rush. By January 1, 1897, there were fifteen hundred people at Dawson City, probably mainly stampeders from the neighboring gold fields in Alaska or from the coast. It was not until the steamers of the A.C. and the N.A.T. and T. company arrived at San Francisco in the summer of 1897 that the real rush started.

The real stampede came in 1898, when word of the fabulous richness of the gold fields had been conclusively demonstrated. How many came that year is not known exactly, but Inspector

Steele reported that thirty thousand persons had passed Tagish. Dawson became overnight a crowded, raw, frontier city of frame warehouses and stores hastily thrown up, of log hotels and banks, police barracks, with tents sprawled over the hastily cleared flats or straggling up the hills into the still virgin forest that crowned them. Along its streets, knee deep in mud, straggled pack trains. Along its waterfront were boats of almost every description, ranged three and four deep. In the most pretentious buildings facing the river there were already running dance halls, saloons, and gaming houses. Crowds of miners and prospectors, clad in the appropriate garb of the frontiersman, rubbed shoulders with women of the underworld, with boatmen, with gamblers, and with the heterogeneous mass of persons lumped together under the somewhat derogatory term—cheechako. It was a mad, good-natured crowd, yet serious and determined. All were bent on a great adventure.

Large-scale production of gold began in 1898. In six months the total taken amounted to $3,072,000 for the whole of 1898.[6] For the first time claims on Bonanza and Eldorado creeks began to yield phenomenal returns. The next year (1899) the railway had reached Whitehorse, and heavy machinery could now be hauled across the summit and brought downriver in scows. The first boilers to be used in thawing and to provide motive power came in that fall just ahead of the ice. By 1903, when royalty was paid on $12,113,000, the peak had been reached and passed.

By this time up-to-date and efficient methods had superseded the crude process of ground sluicing or washing in sluice boxes. The use of steam engines for hoists and dumping and for pumping water up to beach and hill claims, the construction of dams, flumes, and ditches to bring water from distant streams for hydraulicking —all allowed more economical working of low-grade deposits but involved heavy capital expenditure. This started the elimination of the poor man working the individual claim and forced the grouping of claims. The process of differentiating the enterprising, ambitious men from the more easy-going began in the early days but became much accentuated as the original discovery creeks, Bonanza and Eldorado, with their tributary gulches were worked out. The

[6] The change in the fiscal year explains why we have only figures for the first six months.

creeks beyond proved less rich, and the deposits were more scattered. Over the Klondike divide on Dominion and Sulphur creeks the deposits, while very extensive, were much lower in value. Transportation and other costs therefore made it impossible for them to be worked profitably except on a large scale by the most efficient methods.

The granting of concessions containing the whole watershed of a stream without proper safeguards led to some criticism of the government. Alexander Macdonald was one operator generally regarded with a certain degree of mistrust since his operations involved the grouping of claims. Finally when A. N. C. Treadgold, M. H. O. Ewing, and W. Banwick secured an extensive grant and water rights in 1901, there was an immediate outcry among the miners, led by the Dawson press. A royal commission was named to investigate the granting of these enormous claims. The commissioner, Mr. Justice Breton, thought that grants such as this might lead to abuses and urged that they should be surrounded by proper safeguards concerning development so that they would not prevent the land from being staked by individual miners. The Treadgold concession had already been thrown up voluntarily. Since the forces at work were powerful, the movement continued unchecked.

Dredges were tried out in 1905 and from the first proved successful. They were operated by electric power generated by boilers and turbines, the boilers being fueled with wood. But exhaustion of timber and the rising cost of cordwood led to experiments with hydroelectric power. An electric power plant was installed on the Twelve Mile River (which appears on official maps as the Chandindu River), and a power line carried electricity across country to the Yukon Consolidated Goldfields' ground on Bonanza. Other dredges were put on Eldorado and Hunker. The introduction of more and larger dredges forced the development of the power on the north fork of the Klondike, power being transported to Dawson and Dominion Creek. This generous water supply, which held up well in winter, allowed dredges to operate nearly up to Christmas.

For hydraulicking purposes for white channel gravels on the hills and benches, the local water supplies, dependent on the spring runoff and chance showers in summer, began to prove insufficient. This led the Yukon Gold Company to construct a ditch ninety miles in length from the headwaters of the Twelve Mile River, an operation that cost $7,000,000. It was in working order by 1909.

These developments enabled production, which had fallen to $2,820,000 in 1908, to increase once more until it eventually reached $5,301,000 in 1914. After World War I production declined rapidly until by 1925 it had shrunk to $625,000. The increase in the mint price of gold, introduced in 1933, as well as the reorganization of the Yukon Consolidated Gold Corporation (the only large company operating in the Yukon, the Yukon Gold Company having withdrawn in 1925) brought an increase until 1938 when production was $2,545,000 (Canadian funds).

Slight compensation was found for this falling off by the opening of silver lead mines in the Mayo district. They were first discovered in 1914, and some work was done by the Yukon Gold Company on Keno Hill. The Treadwell Yukon Company began development in 1920 on Keno Hill. A concentrator was installed, and work was also done on Galena Hill and on neighboring properties. The resultant concentrates and ores were shipped out to the smelter at Solomon Mines, Idaho. The fact that they could be shipped by the primitive and costly transportation system available at that time indicates the richness of the ores. But with the drop in the price of silver and lead in the thirties, there was an inevitable decline, and eventually these mines, too, ceased production.

New methods for thawing the ground, substituted for the time-honored wood-burning process, were at once cheaper and more efficient. The first of these was the introduction of "hot points," that is, driving pointed and perforated pipes down to bedrock. These were then joined and hooked up with a boiler, and the steam was forced through the pipes and out into the gravel under heavy pressure. This system was superseded by the use of "cold points." In the latter case, using much the same equipment, engineers introduced cold water instead of steam. This was much cheaper, though more time might be required.

The great economy of manpower involved in these operations and the gradual exhaustion of gold has been attended with an exodus of settlers from year to year—not only in mining population but in professional and business classes as well. The airplane has aggravated the situation, for it has facilitated ingress and egress of both workers and managers, who have largely become an absentee exploiting class. Yukon Territory has few other resources—farm land is scarce, it has no great fishing industry, and timber in the interior has slight commercial value. The population continued to decline, therefore, until the advent of the Alaska Highway, and the new pipe line has brought population into the southern part of the territory and given business generally a new lease on life.

The Yukon had already become a district separate from the Northwest Territories when in 1897 it was made a judicial district with a commissioner of its own. On June 13, 1898, the Yukon Territory Act passed by the Dominion Parliament made it a territory with its own local government. This was to consist of the commissioner and a five-member council to be appointed by the government. To start it off, all Northwest Territory ordinances were to be applicable *mutatis mutandis* unless otherwise provided. Some Dominion statutes like the Lands Act were to be applied. Later, in 1903, the council was increased to ten, of which five were to be elected. In 1908 the whole council was made elective; in 1910 the number was reduced to three, where it now stands. In 1900 Dawson was incorporated, but this did not work out well, and its charter was later revoked by the council. Whitehorse and Grand Forks were given the status of unincorporated hamlets with minor officials of their own, but actually were administered by the council. A Public Service Ordinance of 1902 established a territorial government with certain officials of its own—a road inspector, a superintendent of schools, and a treasurer.

Except during the first feverish days of the gold rush, Canada's problems have been simpler than those of the United States. The settlement was more concentrated and population going in or out had only one route to funnel through. Hence law enforcement was less hampered by vast distances and by settlements widely separated and completely alien to one another as in Alaska. The problems had to do largely with the administration of gold-mining laws and provision for the needs of a few communities. Nevertheless, there appear to have been inevitable confusions in the administration at the beginning because of the unprecedented influx of people and the novel conditions which involved hasty improvisation.

During the first year of the Territory's history the arrival of the officials from the outside was delayed. Major Walsh, the commissioner, did not arrive in Dawson until May, and at the end of his year in office he left for the outside in July. Other officers, including the gold commissioner, arrived towards the end of 1897 and organized the gold commissioner's office and the courts. Unfortunately the overwhelming demands caused frightful congestion and chaos in the gold commissioner's office which led to long-continued and bitter complaints. Major Walsh's relations with the Dominion government had not been too happy. He had been persuaded after considerable urging to take the post, but since there was no telegraphic communication, decisions were made by the minister without consulting him. Moreover, the confusion with regard to the gold commissioner's office as well as in the handling of mail was unjustly laid at his door. But on the whole as the tide of immigration receded, these difficulties tended to disappear.

In one respect Yukon Territory enjoyed a distinct advantage over Alaska. The enforcement of law was in the hands of a federal body—the Mounted Police. They had first arrived in 1895 and within a few years had a large proportion of their total strength concentrated in the Yukon, while back of it was the Yukon Field Force. The Mounted Police enjoyed an enviable tradition established on the plains in the early days. The men sent north were the cream of its recruits. Amid the chaos of the gold rush they were the one stable element in an otherwise disordered scene. Without pretensions they maintained a high standard of excellence and scrupulous fairness in the discharge of their duties. This was done with good humor and without fuss or gunplay. United States citizens, who were naturally allergic to redcoats, at first were inclined to distrust them. They ended by becoming their most ardent admirers. There was frequent clamor to have a similar federal force established for Alaska but without success. Failure to do so was not solely due to the unwillingness of the larger country to borrow from its smaller neighbor but rather to the United States tradition which prefers to rely on local initiative in law enforcement.

XVI

Post-Klondike Period

THE ACTIVITY STARTED BY THE KLONDIKE DISCOVERY COULD HARDly be restricted to Canadian territory. Even during the winter of 1897–98 a food shortage in Dawson sent its overflow population drifting down the Yukon to the older camp at Circle and the trading post at Fort Yukon. Here some slight efforts at prospecting were carried out, but in the spring most of the "drifters" went on down the Yukon to Rampart, where a mining camp sprang up in 1898. This became a thriving center—Minook and Hess creeks, with their tributaries, continued for some years to be steady producers of gold.

But it is to Seward Peninsula that we must turn for the most sensational events. Here where North America thrusts its most remote westerly headlands towards their Asiatic counterpart, the Chukchi Peninsula, to form Bering Strait is the land of the Eskimo. Along these shores he had from time immemorial hunted with spear and kayak the whale, the walrus, and the seal. The white man's first visit was in 1732 when Mikhail Gvozdev, coming from northeastern Siberia, made the first Russian landfall in America. Later expeditions had passed it by. Kotzebue had skirted it to reach and explore Kotzebue Sound in 1815. Kromchenko subsequently surveyed Golofnin Bay and Norton Sound. In 1833 Teben'kov was sent by Governor Wrangel to occupy St. Michael's. Russian expeditions which followed worked up the Yukon and the Kuskokwim.

But it was not until the Western Union began to survey its telegraph line through Alaska and across Bering Strait that Seward Peninsula was explored. One of the company's parties, led by Baron Otto von Bendeleben, seeking a route from Golofnin Bay to Port Clarence on Bering Strait had ascended the Niukluk and, traversing the height of land, went down the Kruzgamepa (Pilgrim). His party is said to have found colors in the Niukluk River. Shortly after, when news of the successful laying of the Atlantic cable was received, the Western Union recalled its expedition. If gold had been discovered, it was forgotten, and the country returned to its primeval peace.

A quarter of a century later traders in Bering Strait heard from the natives of the finding of galena, and a prospector, John C. Green, with a party reached these deposits and staked claims in 1881. Green organized a company, called the Alaska Gold and Silver Mining, Milling, and Trading Company, to develop the ground. (This was later the Russian American Milling Company.) Incidental to these mining activities, placer gold was apparently located on Fish River. The company discontinued operations, but one of its employees, John Dexter, opened a trading post at Golofnin Bay. He seemed to have maintained a sharp lookout for gold during the years that followed. The Congregational church, in the meantime, had started a mission at Cape Prince of Wales, and the Swedish Evangelical church located stations at Port Clarence and Golofnin Bay. Here in 1891 Sheldon Jackson established his reindeer herds to provide a livelihood for the natives. As late as 1897 it was neglected by the gold seekers, who pushed on north to Kotzebue Sound, a more favored prospect. Only when disappointed here did they as a last resort turn to the Seward Peninsula.

Meanwhile, one of the countless parties outfitted in San Francisco when the fever first kindled made its way thither. Daniel B. Libby had been with the original von Bendeleben party in 1866. When he heard of the Klondike strike, in spite of his years, he was fired with a longing to visit the scenes of thirty years before. He sought out friends and communicated his enthusiasm to them. They found a backer who grubstaked them, and, chartering a ship, they came north to St. Michael's with an outfit. Here in August, 1897, they landed on Golofnin Bay. They did not have to rely wholly on their own efforts to guide them. Besides King and Green of the Omalik mine, a Norwegian, Johannsen, on the eve of the Klondike discoveries had panned gold on the Niukluk, but hearing of the finds on the Yukon, he had gone off to look for his pot of gold elsewhere. This was in 1894. Three years later an Eskimo, Tom Guarick, taught by John Dexter, the trader at Golofnin Bay, to pan, came back from a hunting trip on Ophir Creek with an ounce of gold. When the Libby party came ashore, the Eskimo offered to guide them to the location. The find was confirmed, and the members of the party staked and proceeded to organize the Eldorado Mining District and appoint a recorder. Thus came into existence Council City, the first producing camp on Seward Peninsula.

However, one of the members of the party, H. L. Blake, was not satisfied with the results. On a trip from Council City to the post at Golofnin Bay at Christmas, 1897, he had talked with a native, Too Rig, on Fish River. Too Rig had showed him gold he had picked up in the country to the west in the vicinity of Cape Nome. Blake thereupon agreed to hire the native to guide him to the spot. He purchased supplies, secured a reindeer team from the mission, and accompanied by the missionary, N. C. Hultberg, he set off. They arrived at the place designated (apparently the valley of the Snake River), and after unsuccessful efforts at prospecting through the snow, they gave up and decided to return the following summer.

Blake then made up a party of himself, Hultberg, J. L. Haggalin, John Brynteson, and Christopher Kimber and left Council City in June, 1898, to resume prospecting. They made their way along the coast in a whaleboat; during a storm they attempted to run into the mouth of Snake River, but their boat was swamped and many of their supplies lost. After getting ashore and saving what they could, they began prospecting Snake River and a creek to which they gave the name Anvil Creek. Supplies ran low, and they agreed to proceed up the coast to a native settlement at the mouth of Sinuk. Here word of a find on this river diverted them from their original intention and induced them to ascend the Sinuk River.

At this point Hultberg was said to have feigned sickness (actually he had been lost and almost perished on Snake River) and insisted on leaving the party to return to the coast. He made his way back to Golofnin Bay, the whole party returning somewhat later, towards the end of July. Apparently Brynteson and Hultberg talked things over and agreed that the country around Cape Nome looked good to them. Brynteson found two young men working as day laborers in the Council City gold field, both restless and eager to try their fortunes elsewhere. These were Jafet Lindeberg and Eric O. Lindblom. Lindeberg, a native of Norway, had been brought out by Sheldon Jackson to relieve one of his men stationed on the Siberian coast to arrange purchases of reindeer, but the Chukchi drove off the agent, and after it was decided to abandon the post, he was released to work in the mines. Lindblom had shipped at San Francisco on a whaling bark, the *Alaska,* to see the north country. When the ship put in to Port Clarence, he deserted (probably he had intended to do so when he shipped) and made his way across country to the gold fields with some natives.

The three—Lindblom, Lindeberg, and Brynteson (a native of Sweden)—secured a boat and provisions at Golofnin Bay and set out on September 11. Putting in to the mouth of Snake River, they ascended that stream prospecting. They also prospected Anvil, Glacier, Dry and Rock creeks, as well as Snow Gulch. On each of these streams gold was found. As prospects were best on Anvil Creek, the three jointly staked Discovery claim on that creek, and in addition, each staked another claim in his own name. In addition to these, they staked a claim on each of the other creeks for themselves, as well as some for friends by power of attorney—a practice which prevailed at that time in Alaska. This gave them a total of thirty claims.

On their return to Golofnin Bay with the story of their success, there was at once a stampede from the trading post and from Council City. A general exodus took place. Powers of attorney were widely used, and the new creeks were plastered over with locations for the stakers, their relatives, and their friends. At once a new mining district called the Cape Nome District was organized, and A. N. Kittleson, who had been recorder at Council City, was chosen recorder. Word spread up and down the coast to St. Michael's, and even Dawson, fifteen hundred miles away heard of the strike. By the middle of May, 1899, Anvil City, as the new settlement at the mouth of the Snake River was known, had 250 persons. Vessels from the outside could not reach the new camp until after the middle of June, because of ice in Bering Sea, but they took word back to Seattle and San Francisco, and the rush from the West Coast was on.

Meanwhile, an ugly situation had developed in the new gold

fields. The original stakers included employees of the missions and reindeer stations—all Scandinavians (Norwegians, Swedes, and Lapps, and not naturalized). The law at the time held that no alien might locate a claim on United States soil. On the other hand, no one was authorized to question such a claim but the state itself, which might, if it found the entry unauthorized, eject the claimant. The claimants had made good this deficiency by appearing before L. B. Shepherd, United States commissioner, and declaring their intentions of becoming citizens, a step which hitherto had been held to satisfy the law. The later comers, notably the Libby party and particularly H. L. Blake, Brynteson's partner on the prospecting trip of the early summer of 1898, begrudged them their claims. Blake, on his return from St. Michael's whither he had gone on business, was deeply chagrined to learn that during his absence gold had been found in quantities on the very ground he had previously prospected.

When the richness of these claims was known and Blake discovered that the practice of staking additional claims under power of attorney had blanketed all the ground on these creeks, he and his associates became bitter. Blake finally persuaded himself that he had been the original discoverer and that he was entitled to one of the rich claims; therefore, along with his companions he restaked or "jumped" some claims on these grounds. Carelessness in staking fostered irregularities. The proper method was to drive in six stakes —two at the extreme upper and lower limit of the claim on the bank of the stream and four others at the corners. Since the ground was frozen, stakes could not be driven in but had to be held upright by mounds of stones or earth. In addition, the coast at Nome has no timber except stunted willow, and the difficulty of obtaining stakes of the requisite size from driftwood led the prospectors to have recourse to the native willow. Each branch was split and a paper inserted on which was recorded the name and the date. The rapidity with which such evidence disappeared or was obliterated greatly facilitated "claim jumping." By the winter of 1899 confusion had spread. The original creeks had been exhausted by generous use of power of attorney. Latecomers had to go farther afield or go to work. It was much easier to restake a claim, and the practice became general. By the summer of 1899, with nearly two thousand people in Anvil City, less than half were actually mining. There was neither work nor (at least they so persuaded themselves) claims left. Hence discontent grew rapidly among the idle workers who had been convinced they had a grievance.

This threatening condition of affairs led to the dispatch by Captain E. S. Walker of a detachment of men from St. Michael's under command of Lieutenant Spaulding to head off any trouble. Lieutenant Spaulding had no authority and could do little except by persuasion. When it was decided to call a miners' meeting, in accordance with the immemorial practice of mining camps, to declare all existing locations void and throw the ground open for relocation, Lieutenant Spaulding decided to anticipate trouble and to intervene. It was reported to him that crowds of men were stationed on the slopes of Anvil Mountain, and as soon as the resolution passed, they would be apprised by the firing of a beacon and thus could forestall others. Spaulding thereupon broke up the meeting. Later he ordered that matters be adjusted by the civil authorities whom he would support. Since almost every claim in the district was the subject of dispute, it was a futile gesture.

When tension was at its height, things took an unlooked for turn. An old prospector who was ailing spent his time panning gravel along the beach. To his astonishment he discovered gold. As soon as this news got out, the idle miners rushed to the beaches with improvised equipment to try their luck. All that was required was a shovel, a wheelbarrow, a bucket fitted with a long handle as a ladle for dipping up sea water, and the material for making a "rocker" or a "long tom," variants of the device long used for separating gold from gravel. Within a short time two thousand miners were at work.

The land laws of the United States provide a strip of sixty feet along the beach that is not open to entry. The groups of persons who had staked tundra claims adjoining the sea protested that their claims included the beach and warned the miners that they must pay a royalty of fifty cents a day for the right to wash gold. When the miners refused to pay, the company appealed to the commandant. The miners were warned off, and when they failed to comply with his orders, all who were at work—upwards of three hundred men—were taken into custody. There was neither jail to confine them nor civil magistrate to try them nor funds to provide for their maintenance pending trial. The men were released, whereupon with one accord they all went back to work at the beaches.

Practically all the miners made wages as long as panning lasted; some cleaned up thirty to forty thousand dollars. It is estimated that one and one-half million dollars in gold was taken out. Certainly the want and unrest was relieved. This development even brought a temporary wave of prosperity. The beaches far and near were prospected. Returns, though uneven, were generally gratifying. Eventually ancient shorelines were also located extending back to the hills; but since these could not be brought within the legal definition of "beaches," they were worked as ordinary tundra claims.

Soon, however, these were exhausted, and once more the tension became acute. Early in 1900 word of troubles in Alaska reached Congress, and as the Spanish War had been terminated successfully, it turned to domestic matters. The territory of Alaska was provided with a code of laws and was divided into three judicial districts, with two judges in addition to the one already stationed at Sitka. For the second district (which included Nome) Judge Arthur H. Noyes of North Dakota was selected.

These changes failed to bring peace. The motives of the lawmakers at Washington may have been above question, but sinister forces seem to have been at work somewhere behind the scenes. On July 21, 1900, Judge Noyes and the officials of the territorial court arrived at Nome. One of the judge's fellow passengers on board the ship carrying him to Alaska was Alexander McKenzie, a political figure from North Dakota, already interested in one of the companies active at Nome which had bought the interests of a number of the claim jumpers. Within a few days after his arrival and without allowing the owners a hearing, Judge Noyes appointed McKenzie receiver of a number of claims whose titles were in dispute (between McKenzie and the original stakers) and directed him to take possession and operate the mines. A second order instructed the receiver to seize everything at the mines, even personal property and gold already recovered. The judge also failed to require an adequate bond from McKenzie; no provision whatever was made for securing the interests of the owners or for preventing the disposal of the gold. Noyes refused to hear the protests of the owners or to permit an appeal to a higher court.

The ease with which apparent success was obtained in this case suggested the same course regarding approximately twenty other valuable claims. The owners were impotent to protect their own interests. Mining activity on the Seward Peninsula practically ceased. To develop a claim and prove its value was to risk losing it. Even prospecting came to a standstill.

Fortunately the company that had the largest interests and which had been singled out as the first victim, the Wild Goose Mining Company, had in its manager, Charles D. Lane, a man of resource and courage. When Noyes would not hear his company's protest or allow an appeal to a higher court, Lane sent papers with sworn affidavits and instructions to his solicitors in San Francisco to begin proceedings in the Ninth Circuit Court to secure an appeal. As a result Judge Noyes was directed by the Ninth Circuit Court to stay all proceedings in his court and McKenzie to cease all action in the suits pending and to turn back to the defendants all the property seized.

This order did not end matters, however. McKenzie refused to comply with the writs, and he evaded restoration of the gold. Judge Noyes, too, declined to obey the instructions of the higher court. He actually called on United States troops to guard the bullion in the bank to prevent its being restored to its rightful owners. Again Lane dispatched a man to San Francisco while McKenzie's exploitation of the mines went on. On October 15 on one of the last boats to reach Nome that year there arrived two deputy marshals sent by the Court of Appeals who took McKenzie into custody and released the gold. The deputies took back with them certified copies of the court records, obtained only with great difficulty. McKenzie was tried by the Circuit Court of Appeals and sentenced to six months in Alameda jail for contempt of court. But he was shortly released by the personal intervention of President McKinley. The President confided to one of the judges that he had been subjected to intense pressure by politicians on McKenzie's behalf. The court deferred to the President's wishes, and on the grounds of ill health McKenzie was released.

Noyes, however, continued to defy public opinion as well as to flout the established practices of law. A vigilantes committee threatened violence, but at last the long winter came to an end. The first boat in June brought a citation for the judge to appear before the Court of Appeals in California. Noyes was found guilty of contempt of court and fined one thousand dollars. His assistants were sent to prison.

Through the efforts of the press the story gradually leaked out, and a senatorial investigation was set on foot. The evidence shocked the Senate, and it was in part expunged from the Congressional Record. The Attorney General thereupon ordered a search of the departmental records, and in these was found sufficient evidence to justify the dismissal of Judge Noyes. Judge James Wickersham was directed to proceed from Juneau to Nome to break the log-jam of litigation at that point. After the congestion was relieved and the tangle unraveled, Judge Wickersham was relieved by Judge Alfred S. Moore.

Responsibility in the case is very difficult to assign. But both points where Congress intervened—first in the drafting of the Civil Code and second in the insertion in the Code of Civil Procedure of amendments declaring entry by aliens illegal—suggest some complicity between interested persons at Nome and someone in the halls of Congress. Both Noyes and McKenzie had strong political backers, even President McKinley having intervened on McKenzie's behalf.

Nome thus got off to a bad start. Yet despite its bad name, law and order were maintained. Even before the law permitted organization for a municipality, it had a mayor and council and provided for local needs by voluntary subscription. As soon as the necessary law went through, the town became incorporated as Nome. (The name Anvil City had been dropped in 1899.)

There had been indifferent progress to the end of 1900, but during the winter 1900–1901 high-bench and tundra claims were developed. In 1901 finds were made in the northeastern part of Seward Peninsula. The slight decrease in output of gold for this year was due to certain special factors. The great rush of 1900 had slackened in 1901, but the year 1902 saw renewed activity through restoration of confidence in the courts. In this year systematic efforts were made to lower costs by the introduction of fresh supplies of water, installation of proper equipment, and the employment of properly trained experts to direct operations. In addition, railways were provided to furnish transportation to outlying diggings, and high-level ditches were constructed. The results of these improvements—the recovery of confidence after the reign of lawlessness and corruption in the early stages, the extension of the Nome field to include the whole of the Seward Peninsula, the introduction of efficient methods and facilities for extracting the gold, the expansion of transportation, the attraction of capital, and the employment of men with technical training—is reflected in the expanded output. Beginning with the modest figure of $2,800,000 in 1899, the output increased to $4,750,000 in 1900. It stood over the $4,000,000 mark thereafter until 1906, when it shot up to $7,500,000, after which it began to decline. But in 1930 the output still stood slightly over $1,000,000.

The city went through a turbulent period to emerge as a substantial, prosperous, and orderly community. Its accessibility had been a handicap, since any wastrel who had the price of a ticket could join the crowd of gold seekers on their way to the shores of Bering Sea. As there was no winnowing place like Chilkoot Pass to sift out the weaklings, they all came. Usually the first experiences were enough to satisfy such persons, and they bought their return tickets and disappeared over the southern horizon. It is estimated that thirty thousand persons arrived during the course of the first summer but that sixteen thousand left, frightened off by high prices, the dread of coming winter, and lack of work. Nome's population finally leveled off at approximately four thousand, with as many more prospectors on the creeks—a figure which was maintained for the years of the city's prosperity. The population in 1939 was about fifteen hundred. Nome, while second to Dawson in its productivity (the Klondike gold fields are said to have produced well over $200,000,000 while the total output for the Seward Peninsula has been in the neighborhood of $90,000,000), never rivaled the fabulous richness of the Klondike, but its producing area was much larger and had a longer-sustained high production.

Before Nome had reached its peak, another area of placer gold had been discovered. In 1898 a prospector, Felix Pedro, from the

Fortymile had wandered into the country between the Yukon and the Tanana rivers and had located gold, but had returned to Circle shortly afterwards, probably for supplies. Three years later, with a band of companions, he had tried to find the lost creek. In their quest the party had been unsuccessful and had gradually worked their way over towards the Tanana Valley. About this time an old river captain, Barnette, who had taken a boat up from St. Michael's and had lived at Dawson for a number of years, decided to take a steamer and goods up the Tanana to trade. His objective was the point where the trail between Valdez and Eagle crosses the Tanana. He doubtless hoped to locate the rumored copper deposits at the head of the White River. Reaching St. Michael's in his boat, the *Lavelle Young,* he ascended the Yukon to the Tanana, then ascended the Tanana. He either lost his way and entered the Chena mouth by mistake or else was unable to get further up the river. At any rate he wintered in the so-called Chena Slough.[1] Felix Pedro and his companions, Tom Juarack and Bert Johnson, had reached this general vicinity, and on the verge of starvation they located Barnette and appealed to him for supplies. After their wants were met, they returned to prospecting and on July 27 located gold on Gold Stream.

Barnette meanwhile had gone out, bought a smaller vessel with a lighter draught and had her "knocked down" and shipped to St. Michael's. Here he put her together and took her upstream loaded with supplies, intending to proceed as originally planned to the headwaters of the Tanana. But on arriving at Chena Slough, he learned of the discovery of gold. He thereupon decided to stay. Story of the find was carried to Dawson. There was an immediate stampede from that camp, eight hundred men leaving Dawson for the new field. Few were bona fide miners, and most of them, after looking the country over, left. Actually mining did not begin until 1904. Meanwhile, a small town grew up around the post built by Captain Barnette, and to it the name Fairbanks was given, in honor of Senator Charles W. Fairbanks who became vice-president in the election of 1904. In 1903 Fairbanks had a population of 800, which increased to 5,000 in 1904; to 6,000 in 1905; and to 8,000 in

[1] *Slough* is the word applied in the North to one of the secondary channels of a river.

1906. Gold production, begun with $350,000 in 1904, increased to $3,500,000 in 1905 and to $9,175,000 in 1906. In 1908 it was estimated that the population was 3,500 with 15,000 on the creeks, while gold production was $9,250,000.

Fairbanks is somewhat unique in a number of ways. It perhaps has had the most consistent and substantial history of any mining camp. Its topography is quite different from that of the Yukon, being one of low relief, wide valleys, and gentle slopes. The gravels are covered by a deep overburden of muck which makes stripping laborious and expensive. The richest ground was soon exhausted, and there was some decline of activity. Eventually, however, in 1925 a new company was organized. Flumes were built to bring ample supplies of water in for hydraulicking. After spending, it is said, about $15,000,000 in development, operators resumed production on a considerable scale. The work was already showing a profit when the rise in the price of gold brought about in 1933 gave a great stimulus to activities here, as in other parts of Alaska.

But the conditions that have made the Tanana a difficult mining country have made it a good country for farming. Much of the middle and lower Tanana consists of areas of alluvial land. These, when cleared and broken, are capable of considerable agricultural development.

In 1922 Fairbanks became the terminus for the Alaska Railroad, built by the government from Seward on Resurrection Bay. Because of ice conditions in the upper part of Cook Inlet, the winter port was located at Seward on Resurrection Bay. The main terminal and summer port is at Anchorage. This has given Fairbanks an importance no other town in the interior has. It also became the terminus of the Richardson Highway from Valdez built by the Alaska Road Commission.

Cheechakos bound for the Klondike entered the Copper River country in 1898 and 1899. Instead of continuing to the Yukon, many turned their attention to the possibilities of the Copper and Chitina river valleys. Placers were located, but because of glaciation there are few major deposits of gold. Copper was the chief attraction in this region. In 1885 Lieutenant Allen had visited the Chitina River Valley and had established the first relations with the native Chief Nicolai, whom Allen calls "autocrat of the Chettyna River and fishing rendezvous Taral." The following year Nicolai conducted a party of whites to the copper deposits on the Chitina, and in 1900 Bonanza claim was staked.

For years there was considerable activity—prospecting and preliminary development—but until communications were opened, the ore could not be shipped. Such an undertaking was only possible for powerful financial interests. A syndicate was organized by J. P. Morgan and Simon Guggenheim to undertake (in addition to other projects) the development of Bonanza and Kennecott copper claims in the Chitina Valley. A townsite named Cordova on Cordova Bay was selected for the railroad terminal, thus bypassing Valdez, which had long aspired to be the metropolis of the Copper River Valley. In 1908 began the construction of the railway. It followed the course of the Copper River, going through Abercrombie and Wood canyons. It crossed the river on a bridge between Childs and Miles glaciers. At one place the track passed right along the front of a glacier where the subsoil rests on ice. The river was bridged again and again. At Chitina the railway turned up the Chitina River to the copper deposits. Here was built the town of McCarthy, the center for the mining regions. At one point where the track crossed Hidden Creek, it was exposed to periodic floods released when the water dammed up behind the Kennicott Glacier broke through. But these difficulties were all successfully surmounted.

A camp that experienced a brief surge of prosperity and at one time threatened international complications was in the Porcupine Creek area. Here a little corner of Alaska surrounded by British Columbia is accessible only from the Dalton trail that runs up the Chilkat River from Haines Mission. Miners entering this region were at first told they were in British Columbia. If true, this would have deprived them of their claims since that province does not permit aliens to stake. Eventually the boundary settlement of 1903 removed the complications and allowed development of the few productive pockets scattered over this region.

Throughout this period of ups and downs in placer mining, lode mining pursued the even tenor of its way, especially in southeastern Alaska. The Treadwell mines on Douglas Island near Juneau went into production in 1882 and by 1905 had produced a total of $26,556,470. Production was maintained at a level of over $3,000,000 through the early part of the century. But in April, 1916, a disastrous cave-in occurred and all of the mines but one—the Ready Bullion—were flooded by sea water. This mine also closed down in 1922. Meanwhile the mines of the Alaska Juneau Company on the mainland, which had given only modest returns, began to show increased activity. Greatly improved methods of handling the ore and the opening of new bodies resulted in the output's exceeding in value the million dollar mark in 1921. The increase continued steadily until in 1937 it amounted to $5,308,472. It is to be noted, of course, that part of this increase is due to the increase in the price paid by the government for gold, beginning in 1933. The production of lode gold in 1937 amounted to $7,718,000, which compares favorably with the total of $11,000,000 (1936) for placer production.

XVII

Self-government

THE RAPID EXPANSION OF MINING AND THE INCREASE OF POPULATION involved momentous consequences and rendered obsolete Alaska's system of government. We have seen the alarm occasioned by the reported imminence of famine in 1897–98 which caused Congress to vote $200,000 for relief, to dispatch military officers and the reindeer expedition to the gold fields. The alarm turned out to be false, and Congress lost interest, becoming absorbed in other matters—the Spanish American War and the election of 1900. The experience of the gold rush brought one concrete proposal, that of Captain Ray that the Yukon Valley be separated from the rest of Alaska and be given a semi-military government. Captain Ray evidently took for his model the administration of the Canadian Yukon, where the role of the Mounted Police was paramount, but his suggestion found little favor.

A change of administration at Washington just prior to the Klondike gold rush had brought in its wake a new governor, James Sheakley being superseded by John Green Brady.[1] As the Spanish War drew to its close, events impelled Congress to take some action. The area to the north of the sixty-first parallel of latitude was erected into a military district under the secretary of war, with St. Michael's as a military reservation. Troops were also stationed at Skagway.

Some decision had to be reached in the vexing question of natural resources, on whose disposal there was still no legislation. Various interested groups were besieging Congress with petitions

[1] Governor Brady was a protégé of the Reverend Sheldon Jackson and had been brought to Alaska by him in 1885 as a missionary. He had severed his connection with missions the following year to enter business at Sitka, had been in politics, and was warmly interested in Alaska. He was always regarded as close to the missionary interests and as governor, from 1897 to 1904, he was nominally the delegate from Alaska.

for the grant of special privileges. The Alaska miners had hitherto managed their own affairs, with neither help nor interference from the government, by means of miners' meetings. Obviously this policy of neglect could not meet the new situation. The country's attention was turning towards this still undeveloped treasure house, and groups were reaching out eager hands to despoil it. To meet this need, the "Homestead Act" of 1898 was passed. This act, sometimes known as the Carter Act, made provision for granting homesteads but under certain special limitations. A private survey was required, and the area granted was restricted to eighty acres. There was some criticism of this act on the ground that it was the interests of the canning companies, who sought to safeguard their shore rights, that it served rather than the rights of the individual settlers.

The next problem attacked was that of the enforcement of law, notoriously lax during the gold rush when it had been left entirely to the local initiative. There was one judge in the whole territory—at Sitka—assisted by a marshal, district attorney, four commissioners, and four deputy marshals. The laws were the Oregon Code (as far as applicable) and the Statutes-at-Large. Of either of these up-to-date revisions were lacking. Moreover, certain local conditions made the Oregon Code inapplicable; yet nothing had been done to correct this. The powerlessness of the authorities in the absence of a system of law enforcement was abundantly clear during the reign of Soapy Smith in Skagway in 1898. The Department of Justice, therefore, insisted on a new criminal code for Alaska, which was provided by Congress in 1899. A system of taxation was also introduced. The sale of liquor (forbidden by the Organic Act) was legalized but only with payment of a high license fee. Businesses, irrespective of their nature, were subjected to a similar tax; railroads were to pay one hundred dollars per mile for each mile operated; canneries, four cents for each case of canned salmon and ten cents for each barrel of salted salmon; gold mines, three dollars per stamp. All taxes were to be deposited in the Alaska Fund payable to the United States Treasury. No provision was made for self-government.[2]

[2] Every student of Alaskan history is indebted to Jeanette Paddock Nichols for her study, *Alaska: a History of its Administration, Exploitation, and Industrial De-*

ALASKA JUNEAU MILL

Courtesy Fish and Wildlife Service

CANNERY IN SOUTHEASTERN ALASKA

Self-government

Public opinion was beginning to be aroused in Alaska at what was considered neglect by Congress and the Executive. The inability of the municipalities to organize for any purpose at all and the failure of Congress to provide any form of self-government for the territory stirred the public. A call went out from the Chamber of Commerce of Skagway for a nonpartisan convention.[3]

John G. Price of Skagway was named delegate to Washington. In response to the demands he pressed, Congress took action. A civil code finally emerged, completely recasting the territory's judicial system. Alaska was divided into three districts, the courts for which were to be established at Sitka, Nome, and Eagle, each with a full staff of clerks, marshals, and attorneys and charged with the duty of appointing commissioners. Outlying districts were to have deputy district clerks. Perhaps the most decisive gain registered was the law which allowed communities to be incorporated for self-government, though with considerable restriction on their taxing and borrowing powers. Schools were provided for both in towns and in areas outside of towns. The towns were to have 50 per cent of the receipts they paid into the Alaska Fund for the support of their schools. No progress was made either in the matter of an election or of a delegate to Congress or of securing self-government. The law provided that as soon as suitable grounds and buildings could be provided, the capital should be removed from Sitka to Juneau.

These and other open sores still galled the public—boundary difficulties, the narrowly circumscribed powers given incorporated towns to tax and bond themselves, rising resentment against the

velopment during its First Half Century under the Rule of the United States and the account she there gives of the political development of the territory from the time of its purchase. In recounting the story of the struggle for self-government, I have found her work invaluable and gladly acknowledge my debt to it.

[3] Nonpartisan conventions were the customary means to secure a hearing at Washington. One had been called together in 1881 by the residents of Harrisburg (later Juneau) to impress on Congress the need of organization of the territory. This had led to the Organic Act of 1884. A second in 1890 had sent Captain Carroll of the Pacific Coast Steamship Company to plead the cause of Alaska (though the lobbyists proved too strong for him).

This indifference to ordinary partisan politics carried with it as a consequence an inability to work through the party conventions and perhaps retarded needed reforms. It reflects the personal and sectional nature of Alaska politics, which have seemed only remotely connected with national issues.

missionary dominance of education, and hatred of the absentee industries that monopolized much of Alaska's wealth without making an adequate contribution. At length this ferment led to the inauguration of 1902 in the panhandle of a "Territorial Club" movement which hoped to bring the issue of territorial government to a head. The movement was not successful because of the opposition that developed. Failure of the territory to attain unanimity doomed to defeat the bill to give Alaska an official delegate, and Congress adjourned without taking action.

Nevertheless, the sitting of the Alaska Boundary Tribunal, President Roosevelt's visit to Seattle in May, 1903, and a visit of a senatorial committee to Alaska in the summer of that year all provided an unofficial sounding board for northern grievances. The discussions finally culminated in another nonpartisan convention —the fourth—an offspring of the previous convention of 1899, to meet in Juneau in October. Transportation difficulties delayed some delegates. On their arrival they learned that the convention had gone on record against territorial government. They immediately convened and passed a resolution in its favor. This movement, like the previous one, foundered on the rock of factious strife.

There were, however, two promising signs on the horizon. One was the revival of the old "Territorial Club" movement of 1902 under a new name, "The Citizens' League," formed to insure a united front on the question of home rule. The other was a congressional committee (proposed by Senator Beveridge) and sent north in response to a resolution fathered by him to secure full information on the needs of the territory. The recommendations of the committee members were against the grant of self-government; in lieu of it they proposed an extensive program of road building for the mining camps, similar to that undertaken in Yukon Territory by the Canadian government, and they laid special emphasis on a military highway to be built from Valdez on Prince William Sound to Eagle on the Yukon River; and the providing of a fourth judge and a delegate to represent the territory. These positive gains were somewhat offset by the suggestion that, while in favor of a delegate for the territory, they believed the delegate should be appointed. But even these modest proposals were either lost (as that for judicial reorganization) or whittled down into unrecognizable form (as that concerning roads, which merely provided for a survey).

The natural dissatisfaction with these negative results, ascribed variously to Governor Brady or to the lobbies in Washington, was somewhat forcibly expressed by various public bodies. The convention of the Arctic Brotherhood and the American Mining Congress each called on the government to meet Alaska's aspirations for self-government. Even the Democratic National Convention of the year 1904 accepted a plank for territorial government. But perhaps the most dramatic event was a mass meeting of residents of Valdez, who, in the name of sixty thousand American citizens in Alaska, demanded "that Alaska be annexed to Canada."[4]

Partial relief, however, was in sight. The Supreme Court in 1905 ruled that by the treaty of cession of 1867 Alaska had been incorporated into the United States and therefore was constitutionally an integral part of the United States. This put the demands of Alaska people for representation in an entirely different light. Henceforth representation was their right as American citizens. An immediate result was the adoption of the term "territory" instead of the dubious "district" in use since 1884. Far more important was the decision of the people to close ranks and to make a direct approach rather than through senatorial subcommittees, or official go-betweens such as the governor.

A convention assembled in Seattle consisting of all who, by stretching the term, could lay claim to being considered Alaskans. Factions were still rife, and there was little agreement on the question of a representative in Congress; nevertheless, some degree of harmony was reached. Three delegates were chosen to appear before Congress to press demands for representation. Roosevelt tipped the scales in their favor when in his message to Congress he appealed for such representation. Both houses readily accepted a bill to grant Alaska representation in the House of Representatives, the delegate, who had no vote, to receive the same salary and privileges as other delegates. He was allowed fifteen hundred dollars for traveling and other expenses; the election was to be held on the

[4] Probably occasioned by an agitation recently launched in Yukon Territory for altering the Yukon Territorial Council, hitherto in part appointive, to one wholly elective.

second Tuesday in August; the first election, that of 1906, to be for two men, one to sit for the remainder of the Fifty-ninth Congress and the other to be member for the whole of the Sixtieth. Minor legislation amended mining laws and, with a view to encouraging the establishment of private hatcheries by the canning companies, remitted four cents per case on the pack for every thousand fry liberated.

The choice at election fell on two men, Frank Waskey of Nome for the short term and Thomas Cale of Tanana for the longer one. The regular politicians felt compelled to put up party candidates, but the combined Nome-Tanana forces easily routed them. At this time chance brought it about that the long-smoldering dissatisfaction with the governor, John G. Brady, came to a head. Charges against Sheldon Jackson in connection with his administration of the schools and the reindeer service naturally involved the Governor, who was a close confidant. Roosevelt resolved to make a clean break with the hierarchy of the Presbyterian church; and instead of reappointing Brady, he named Wilfred B. Hoggatt of Juneau as his successor. On the question of a legislature, the President decided to consult the delegate and the Governor on their arrival in Washington concerning the needs of Alaska. The result was a sharp clash of views, Waskey coming out for home rule, while Hoggatt not only opposed it but even cast aspersions on those who supported it. Roosevelt transmitted Hoggatt's letter to both houses of Congress. The President's concurrence in the views of the Governor resulted in considerable loss of face by the territorial delegate. It also added fuel to the already fiercely burning flame of Alaska politics.

Meanwhile, sides were being chosen for the coming election. In November, 1907, the Republican politicians in the panhandle, straining at the leash, arranged a party convention. As an expression of public opinion it failed; the interior blew cold on party matters and did little more than give half-hearted acquiescence by proxy. The delegates assembled, however, and the cause of home rule was brought up.

By now a new and vital element had intervened—Judge James Wickersham of the third judicial district. Wickersham had been named to succeed the notorious Arthur H. Noyes of Nome, and the bold and impartial decisions he rendered at Nome made him justly popular among the miners. His perambulating court, as he moved throughout his vast judicial district from Valdez to Rampart, from Rampart to Circle, and Circle to Eagle on the Yukon, presented the effect of a good-will tour, a sort of traveling Chautauqua. They provided the occasion for the miners to foregather, ostensibly to hear the judge dispense justice, but actually to exchange gossip of the creeks. He had made himself popular with the majority of the sourdoughs, though some of his adverse decisions had made enemies. He had at first been on affable terms with Governor Hoggatt. He was solid with the Roosevelt administration and remained so throughout his political life. A judgment rendered in a mining case estranged Senator Nelson, who succeeded in blocking in the Senate Roosevelt's recommendation of confirmation of Wickersham's appointment. But the President's abiding friendship enabled him to continue in office by successive recess appointments. Eventually despairing of confirmation, Wickersham resigned to plunge into the troubled waters of northern politics. He began his political career by an attack on "the state of Alaska's administrative affairs," a blast sure to arouse the hostility of Hoggatt and endanger his relations with the Administration. It is easy to see, therefore, why proposals to extend self-government came to naught.

While matters were shaping for a warm campaign, events took an unexpected turn. The Morgan-Guggenheim syndicate, planning to develop its properties in the Chitina River Valley, had decided to abandon Valdez as a terminal and to create their own on Cordova Bay. The people of the former town, as a result, lent a ready ear to an agitator who was promoting a rival company to build a railway from Valdez to the interior. When the abandoned Morgan-Guggenheim right-of-way in the Keystone Canyon was entered by workers, they were fired upon as trespassers and one of their number killed by a deputy marshal. The incident aroused intense feeling against the Morgan-Guggenheims in particular and all capitalists in general. The Governor was charged with complicity in the outrage. This furnished an admirable election issue, since it was a simple matter to ascribe the postponement of home rule to these sinister forces.

The approaching election campaign of 1908 assumed a unique character in Alaska. The sourdough's interest in national issues was lukewarm, but he realized that to secure self-government he had to enter the party arena. He nevertheless insisted on playing the game in his own way. Wickersham and Cale combined forces and managed by outwitting the rival Republican faction to seat their delegation in the national convention. This gave them a decided advantage. In the election Wickersham came out as Independent Republican running on an anti-Guggenheim and, in common with his opponents, a home-rule platform. He had the somewhat perfunctory blessing of the Administration. He was successful, but his success was due rather to his own reputation and the tremendous drive he put into the campaign than to the support of the Administration.

When Taft came to power in 1908 two factions of the Republicans were tearing at one another's vitals, and the Alaska problem seemed insoluble. Governor Hoggatt and Delegate Wickersham were denouncing one another. Wickersham delivered his first broadside by castigating his opponent as a tool of the Guggenheim's—a charge that embarrassed the Administration. Secretary of the Interior Ballinger suddenly ordered all federal officials back to their posts to terminate this unseemly wrangling. The easygoing Taft disliked unpleasantness and sought to sooth ruffled feelings by all-around conciliation. Some measure of harmony was reached between Wickersham and his old foe, Senator Nelson, but Taft undid a good deal of what had been achieved by his poor judgment in the appointment as Hoggatt's successor of a journalist, Walter E. Clark. Clark had the wrong backing to recommend him to Alaskans. He had shown himself tender toward Taft's friends in preference to Roosevelt's and was suspected of representing the big interests. But in Alaska protestations are not always to be taken at their face value. Within a short time the lion and lamb, since they had to live together, were lying down in uneasy amity.

Wickersham's first venture at Washington was unimpressive. He sponsored a series of rather innocuous measures of reform in the mining laws, a bill to provide buildings for the capital at Juneau, and a bill for an emasculated system of territorial government. Wickersham's record on this score was not consistent since, while a judge, he had opposed autonomy. The bill drew the ironic remark from former Governor Hoggatt that it guaranteed the right to meet and to pass resolutions. Perhaps the most telling stroke of all came from across the border when the Canadian *Dawson News* undertook to urge Alaskans to assert their historical right of representation as their Canadian cousins had done—a paradoxical reversal of roles.[5] But the disillusionment felt by Northerners was forgotten in the enthusiasm called forth by the Alaska Yukon Pacific Exposition held at Seattle in 1909 and the President's promise to attend. "Big Bill" Taft, when he met the real pioneers of the North, would surely put things right. The Arctic Brotherhood inducted the President into the mysteries of their order and even violated precedent by doing so on the "outside." But Taft struck a sour note when he drew on his Philippines' experience to propose that Alaska should be administered by a federal commission in the manner of a colonial dependency. Angry and unanimous protests burst from the press at the suggestion that they should receive the same treatment as the peoples of the Philippines and Puerto Rico. Even Wickersham was shaken, and he admitted ruefully that they would have to start all over again and re-educate the President.

The year 1910 was to be a troubled election year. Judge Wickersham had to lay the groundwork for his campaign. He went to Washington, his head swimming with proposals on issues now in the public eye. Monopolies seemed to offer the best foemen for his trusty sword. But his problem was by no means simple. The fur-seal monopoly touched the sourdough only remotely. Fishing likewise was largely an absentee industry with which he was hardly concerned. Mining scarcely fell within the category of monopolies, yet Wickersham boldly decided to treat it as such. He came out as the champion of the small miner and sponsored a bill to reduce placer claims to forty acres. He was unable to do away with miners' associations or to abolish power-of-attorney—both long-standing

[5] The somewhat lofty tone of the Canadian press was due to Yukon Territory's having just attained, through the amendment to the Yukon Territorial Act, a council whose members were all elected. The Yukon Council, however, handled only local affairs such as schools, roads, and public health. By far the greater proportion of the services received were provided by the federal government, for which, indeed, the territorial revenue would have been quite inadequate. It was self-government but only to a limited degree.

grievances. Then when he touched on railroads and coal, he broached matters that divided the whole country. The public domain had been regarded from time out of mind as something to be developed by the individual (thus perhaps indirectly to benefit the country). Men who had crossed the mountains and the plains, undergone the hardships and privations of pioneering, and fought Indians regarded some portion of the public domain as their just reward; and generally public opinion had grown accustomed to this view. However, as the natural wealth seemed to approach exhaustion, its disappearance ceased to be a remote contingency. A new conviction took hold that what remained should be reserved for the country as a whole. Lands might be still allotted to individual homesteaders. Forest, water power, coal lands, and mineral deposits whose development called for capital should not be granted indiscriminately to corporations, but should be used where possible for the benefit of society as a whole. In the case of railroads, the day of lavish land grants to aid their construction was over; the alternative to this, a policy of guaranteeing bonds which had been substituted, was now in turn falling into disfavor. Obviously railroads in Alaska could not be built without some form of government aid, and since public opinion was set against it, no politician was willing to risk his political life by championing so unpopular a measure.

The coal question soon became a political storm center. Gifford Pinchot, chief forester under Roosevelt, had won the President over completely to his program of conservation of natural resources. To protect the public interest, the President had made extensive withdrawal of public lands from entry, and even strained the existing law to do so. In the case of the coal lands the situation was somewhat unique. Congress was loath to alienate these lands. The fate of eastern coal lands was a solemn warning of the consequences of such a policy. The general coal law was therefore extended to Alaska in 1900, but as there had been no previous survey, the law, which assumed one, was unworkable. In 1904 it was amended to allow location of individual claims of 160 acres on unsurveyed lands. This law attached one important condition, namely, that the individual had acquired these for himself (and not for a third party) and that he proposed to work them for his own benefit.

Clarence Cunningham had years before prospected the Bering River coal fields in the Prince William Sound region. He had located and surveyed a number of claims for himself and others with a view to making entry. When the act of 1904 was passed, matters advanced another stage, and by 1907 some twenty-six of these claims were ready for the issuing of the patent. Charges of fraudulent practices in securing entry for these coal lands began to reach the General Land Office and led to a careful re-examination of the Cunningham coal claims. This was time-consuming and led to interminable delays. It involved extensive traveling and required endless communications with other departments. Even the forestry branch was involved, since the lands lay within the Chugach National Forest. Eventually it came before Commissioner Ballinger, and he without hesitation directed that the patents be issued. But Commissioner Ballinger left the Roosevelt Administration at the end of 1907; his successor took his time in giving effect to this order. When representations were made against the order by some of his subordinates, he reopened the issue and postponed action until a new investigation could be completed. Meanwhile, damaging admissions made by Cunningham to the effect that the original claimants had always contemplated the development of the claims as a unit by a company effectually blocked the grant of title.

A new turn was given to events by Congress' enacting on May 28, 1908, a bill which provided for the grouping, up to a total of 3,560 acres, of coal claims, entries to which had been made under the Act of 1904 by separate entrants. Some officials of the Department of the Interior interpreted this new act as validating all prior claims irrespective of the intentions of the claimants to circumvent the act. Indeed, a ruling such as this was given in the Department of the Interior. But Attorney General Wickersham gave a contrary opinion. The opponents of the grants within the Department of the Interior feared that the patents would be issued in spite of this, because of the well-known sympathy of Ballinger (now secretary of the interior under Taft) with the rights of capital, and hence they decided to use other means to head it off. The first was a direct approach to the President by Glavis of the Department of the Interior and Shaw of the Forestry Bureau. Their communication reviewed the whole case and impugned the motives of Ballinger. At the same time the press was let into the secret of the tussle going on in the department.

President Taft's reply was to dictate a letter to Ballinger completely vindicating him. He was directed to discharge Glavis. Pinchot had already been informed of developments and made scarcely veiled hints about the issue at the Conservation Congress in Spokane in August. Thereafter matters moved rapidly into the limelight of publicity, and the President was soon under attack. On December 16 Congressman Hitchcock of Nebraska introduced a resolution calling for an investigation of the Land Office, and on December 21 President Taft was requested by the Senate to submit for the consideration of that body all the papers which formed the basis of his letter of vindication to Ballinger on September 13. In January an arrangement was reached between both houses for a full investigation of the whole department and of the Forestry Bureau. As a result of Pinchot's somewhat dramatic action in publicly aligning himself in this investigation with the officials involved, he was summarily dismissed by Taft. While the committee conducted a searching inquiry into the case, it degenerated into a pro-Administration and anti-Administration feud, the Democrats and one "insurgent" censuring Ballinger and charging him with breach of trust, while the majority report of the Republicans vindicated him. No action was taken by the Senate, and Ballinger quietly resigned in March, 1911.

The Cunningham coal claims brought a rift between Taft and Roosevelt and caused a split in the Republican party. In Alaska it was given a characteristic twist. The suspicion was that Cunningham proposed to sell his claims to the Alaska Syndicate. This was known to be a creation of Morgan and Guggenheim, whose interests ramified into the field of transportation, fisheries, railroad building, and copper mining. Thus Alaska politicians made Guggenheim their whipping-boy. The interests were blamed when a United States marshal was found guilty of incompetence and discharged. When Senator J. Beveridge of Indiana and Representative E. L. Hamilton of Michigan sought to implement President Taft's scheme for an appointed committee to govern Alaska, the Guggenheims were suspected of trying to use this means of getting coal lands in collusion with the War Department. When Borah came out against Taft's scheme, the administration proposal was unostentatiously dropped.

The resentment against the Beveridge Bill as well as the political situation in the United States played exactly into the hands of Wickersham. He secured Democratic endorsement in the election of 1912 and was likewise chosen to be the candidate of the "insurgent" Republicans. The Republican candidate, not having specifically repudiated Guggenheim connections, was charged with being their tool. A visit of Attorney General Wickersham and Secretary of Commerce Nagel was regarded as an attempt of the Administration to intervene in local politics and did not promote the Republican cause. Local issues and local politics played almost an exclusive role. Wickersham was elected in August, though there was strong suspicion of corrupt practices, but the result was not questioned because of his overwhelming majority.

The year 1911 was scarcely less turbulent than the preceding ones. Valdez recruited the help of Seward and Fairbanks in promoting its pet scheme of annexation to Canada—a useful bogey suggested by the approaching completion of the Grand Trunk Pacific Railroad to Prince Rupert at the southern end of Dixon Entrance and used to frighten the government into granting home rule. At Cordova, the terminus of the new Copper River and Northwestern Railway, the importation of Canadian coal for operation of the road, while steam coal was lying almost at their doors, suggested a "coal party" in emulation of Boston's more famous "tea party." This bit of horseplay to needle the Administration drew sharp words from the Secretary of the Interior but went unpunished. Meanwhile, chance played into the hands of the supporters of home rule. The new Progressive bloc kept a close lookout for evidence of loose spending or other malpractice. They discovered evidence of fraud, by which the government lost on coal contracts—a charge that involved the Alaska Syndicate. Harsh words were exchanged between Delegate Wickersham and Attorney General Wickersham, whom the former charged with allowing the statute of limitations to run out. When Taft ordered the restoration to entry of 12,800 acres of land in the Chugach Forest on the ground that it had no timber but gave needed access to the sea, a story, which later proved to be false, spread that it had been a deal between the President's brother and Ballinger. Pinchot, on a visit to Alaska, received only a lukewarm welcome. Alaska was willing to use the help of the conservationists in making the Administration squirm but at heart had little use for their program of tying up their resources.

The President, however, was beginning to weaken. His favorite scheme for an appointed commission had gone awry in 1910, and he knew that the only alternative was an elective legislature. Moreover, he had been baited by the insurgents and the conservationists; and in spite of his exasperation he probably felt that it would be better to cut his losses and buy off his noisiest opponent. The new secretary of the interior pronounced in favor of home rule at Seattle and again in Washington, and to the delight of the sourdoughs his views were endorsed by the President. The fight for a legislature had been won.

By the end of 1911 it was a foregone conclusion that the territory would get a legislature. As the President was in favor of it, the Republican standpatters could do little but fall in line. The Democrats had already gone over to the cause, and the Progressives were solidly in favor of it. All that remained was to find a scheme all could agree on. The Senate Committee on Territories and the House Committee were each furnished with such a scheme. During the course of the hearings it became evident that a compromise was inevitable. The lobbies resisted any attempt to give the legislature extensive powers of taxation. No liquor or gaming laws were to be passed by them. The federal government was not to be called on to make up any territorial deficit; nor was the "Alaska Fund" to be transferred to the territory.

At the opening of Congress in 1912 Taft in his message advised the leasing of coal lands, and the construction and operation of a trunk line of railway to the interior. His secretary of the interior agreed but was in favor of at least a partly elected commission in place of one wholly appointive as Taft wished. Governor Clark was flatly against a legislature.

During the election campaign in Alaska (election day was to be the second Tuesday in August under the delegate bill of 1906), Wickersham remained in Washington and consulted with the congressional committee. There were five candidates, but Wickersham had no difficulty in distancing the field, since at that time on the question of territorial rights he had a solid Alaska behind him.

The bill finally reached its last stages and was approved on August 24, 1912. It provided a bicameral house (the Senate committee had wished a unicameral legislature) of eight senators and sixteen representatives to be elected at large from the four judicial divisions, two senators and four representatives from each. The legislature was forbidden to "alter, modify, and repeal" measures relating to game and fish or to legislate on saloons or gambling.

XVIII

The Alaska Boundary Again

In 1861 two prospectors, Choquette and Carpenter, from the Cariboo came north along the coast and turned up the Stikine River. As they ascended it, they prospected and found gold in its bars. News of this in the Cariboo (now declining) started a stampede. The coast was still under lease to the Hudson's Bay Company. The Russian American Company was nervous at this influx of population in view of the prospect that it would shortly revert to Russian hands. After its second ten-year lease to the Hudson's Bay Company had expired in 1859, relations with that company had been on a year to year basis. Sale to the United States had been talked of, but the company wished to be prepared to anticipate any situation that might arise. Hence it dispatched an expedition in 1863 to the Stikine. This party ascended the river and found a number of miners engaged in mining along its lower course as well as considerable ground that had been worked out.

The sale of Alaska in 1867 enabled the Russians to unload on the United States all the boundary complications foreshadowed by these developments. The anticipated trouble did not arise until 1876. After a deceptive nine years of tranquillity, two incidents suddenly touched off the dangers lurking in the uncertain situation. In 1872 Thibert and McCulloch, two miners, had worked up the Stikine and crossed the height of land to Dease Lake where they had discovered pay. This started a new rush. The novel conditions necessitated modification of older mining methods. When miners had learned to apply these, production rapidly increased. Fresh discoveries continued to be made, and by 1875 production of the Cassiar region is said to have reached a total of one million dollars. The Stikine was the natural gateway to these new fields, and there was reason to believe a trading post established in 1876 on this river by Choquette was in United States territory. At any rate the

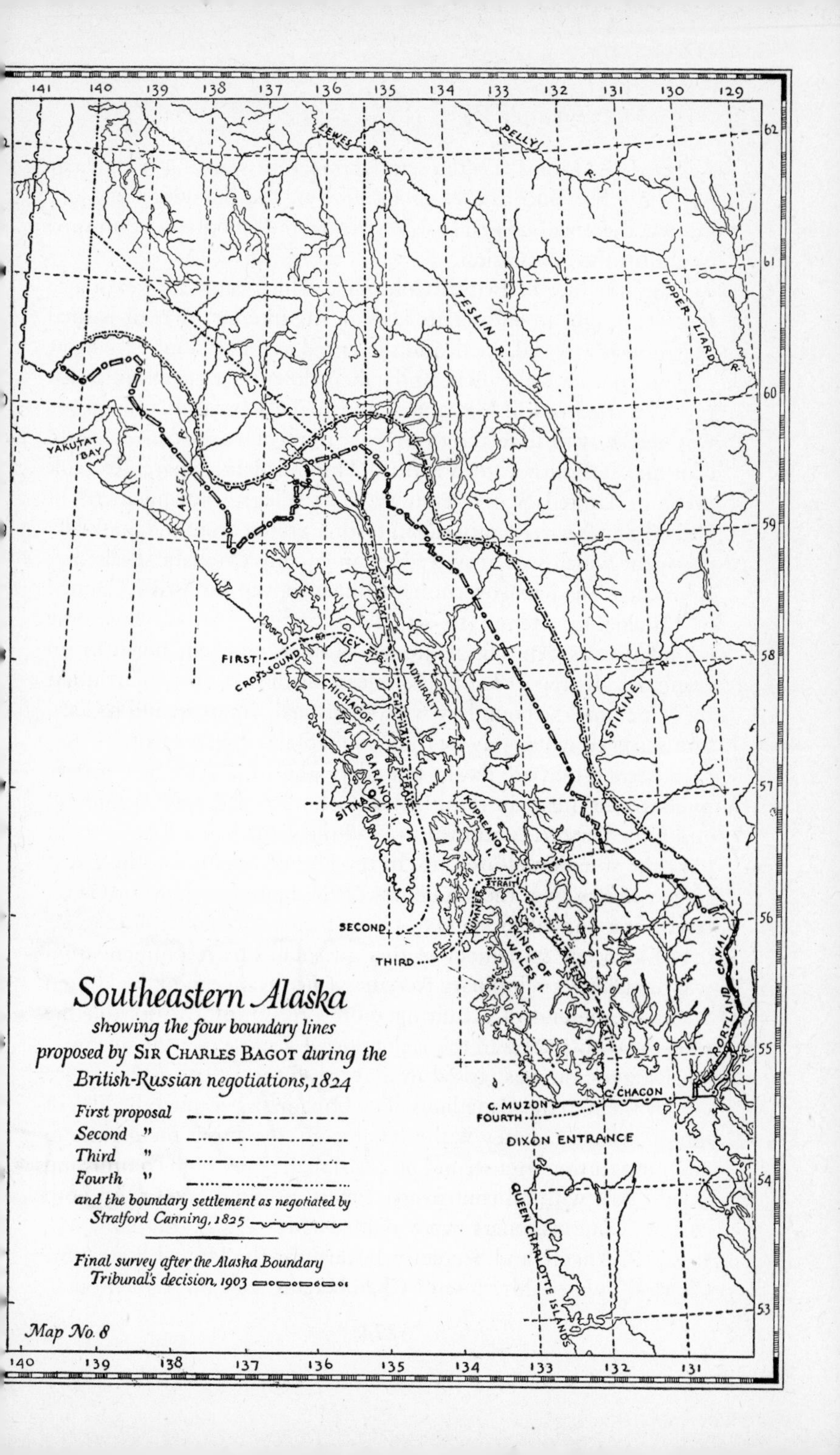
LEWES R.
PELLY R.
TESLIN R.
UPPER LIARD R.
YAKUTAT BAY
ALSEK R.
LYNN CANAL
FIRST
CROSS SOUND
ICY STR.
CHICHAGOF I.
CHATHAM STRAIT
ADMIRALTY I.
BARANOF I.
SITKA
KUPREANOF I.
STIKINE R.
SUMNER STRAIT
SECOND
THIRD
PRINCE OF WALES I.
CLARENCE STRAIT
PORTLAND CANAL
C. CHACON
C. MUZON
FOURTH
DIXON ENTRANCE
QUEEN CHARLOTTE ISLANDS
Southeastern Alaska
showing the four boundary lines
proposed by SIR CHARLES BAGOT during the
British-Russian negotiations, 1824
First proposal
Second "
Third "
Fourth "
and the boundary settlement as negotiated by
Stratford Canning, 1825
Final survey after the Alaska Boundary
Tribunal's decision, 1903
Map No. 8

collector of customs at Sitka sent Choquette a warning to move or pay duty, but since the exact location of the boundary was not known, there was no real basis for action and Choquette continued in undisturbed possession.

The province of British Columbia, which came into existence in 1866, sought to enforce its laws in the interior. A man named Martin was arrested, tried, and sentenced at the mining settlement of Laketon, or Laketown, and taken downriver in custody. En route he tried to kill his captors and make a break for liberty. It was necessary to seize and overpower him before the convoy could continue its journey to Victoria. This incident apparently took place in United States territory. The alleged infringement of United States sovereignty called forth a protest from the State Department which was answered by an equally emphatic disclaimer from the Canadian government. But it moved the Privy Council of Canada to attempt to set about finding exactly where the boundary was. An official, Joseph Hunter, was sent north to investigate. His report led to the release of the prisoner, Martin. At the same time the boundary was provisionally marked and its location accepted tentatively by the United States government.

A second move to fix the boundary, this time with greater definiteness, was made in 1885. British Columbia had not lost interest, and some persons continued to prod the Canadian government to have the situation cleared up. In the United States, too, there was some concern over the vagueness of the boundary line. In Cleveland's first annual message to Congress, on December 8, 1885, he urged a speedy settlement of this question. His recommendation was to make a "preliminary reconnaissance by officers of the United States, to the end of acquiring more precise information on the subject" with a view to the "adoption of a more convenient line." This suggestion was passed by Bayard to the British government and by them to the Canadians. The Canadians accepted the idea of the preliminary survey without agreeing to commit themselves to anything further. But second proposal that a joint high commission should deal with all controversial matters found favor with both parties. Commissioners were named—Mr. W. L. Putnam, Mr. James B. Angell, and Secretary Bayard for the United States; Sir Charles Tupper, Mr. Joseph Chamberlain, and Sir Lionel Sack-

Courtesy Fish and Wildlife Service

ESKIMO KAYAKS

Courtesy Bureau N.W.T. and Yukon Affairs

STEAMER ASCENDING FIVE FINGER RAPIDS

ville-West for Great Britain. Owing to delays involved in securing authority and appropriations, matters dragged on until 1890. By the time these were obtained, Cleveland and Bayard were no longer in office. It was therefore thought wise to make a fresh start. The joint commission was not renewed, but after considerable discussion a new agreement was signed in 1892 to make a preliminary survey after which "they [the governments] will proceed to consider and permanently establish the boundary line in question." Dr. Mendelhall (and after his retirement, Mr. W. W. Duffield) acted for the United States in making this survey. Mr. W. F. King acted for Canada. Sharp disagreements between the commissioners made it apparent that certain highly controversial points would have to be settled before further progress could be made. Interest, however, was beginning to wane in the matter. It finally disappeared below the horizon of practical politics.

The discovery of gold in the Klondike and the stampede of gold seekers to the new fields made the boundary at once an acute issue and led to a revival of the negotiations now in abeyance, this time with a new sense of urgency. John Hay went to London as United States ambassador in 1897, and the Alaska boundary was one of the contentious points in Anglo-American relations that he was charged to try to settle. By the time discussions had begun, relations between the two countries were somewhat altered. The Spanish War and growing complications in Africa had brought together the powers which had been rather estranged as a result of the Venezuela crisis. Moreover, though Salisbury was still prime minister and Joseph Chamberlain colonial secretary, a new figure appears—the suave and subtle Arthur Balfour, secretary for Ireland. Balfour was known to be a friend of the United States. On the American side, thanks to the victory of the Republicans, there was a whole galaxy of new figures—John Hay, who returned in 1898 from London to become secretary of state, Senator Henry Cabot Lodge from Massachusetts, and Henry White, who succeeded Hay in London.

So marked is the change of tone in the negotiations at this time that we may well pause to consider them. On December 27 John Hay wrote to John W. Foster that Canada and the United States did not enter the lists as equals. "It is far more to Canada's advantage than ours to be on good terms with us." Similar ideas are expressed by Henry White in a conversation with Balfour in March, that the attitude of Canada toward the United States was the chief obstacle to the establishment of harmonious Anglo-American relations. If Canada should be complaisant toward United States desires, "the chances of cordial and hearty co-operation between our governments would seem to me much more probable." White added that Canada probably would not change her views except under compulsion. These two threads run through the negotiations in the years that followed. First, towards Canada the tone is peremptory; second, England is constantly warned that pressure on Canada is the price to be paid for United States friendship.

The British proposal for three jurists, one to be appointed by each power and the third by the other two, after a conference in Washington was abandoned in favor of a joint high commission. All the questions at issue between the two governments were to be considered. These were arranged under eleven heads. The commission sat at Quebec from August 23 to October 10, 1898, and then adjourned to meet in Washington from November 9, 1898, to February 20, 1899. Its deliberations were not attended with success.

The discussions centered around Lynn Canal, the Canadians attempting to prove that they were entitled to the upper end of that body of water under the treaty of 1825. A suggestion of Lord Herschell, proposed as a compromise, that a harbor and a corridor across the coastal strip be ceded to Canada, was countered by the United States representatives with a proposal for a fifty-year lease but without the grant of sovereignty. Senator Lodge was angered at Herschell's espousing the cause of the Canadian commissioners, and he wrote to Henry White, United States ambassador in London:

Mr. Chamberlain gave me clearly to understand that Lord Herschell was sent out to mollify and . . . bring to reasonable terms the Canadians who are difficult to deal with. . . . But Lord Herschell goes far beyond them. He is making most of the trouble in the Commission; he is sharp; often violent . . . and if it had not been for him we might have done something ere this with the Canadians. . . . If the Government does not want to wreck the negotiations either in the Commission or in the Senate, they had better give Lord Herschell a pretty broad, strong and speedy hint.[1]

How outrageous! Lord Herschell, instead of furthering the United States' cause, was actually siding with the Canadians. White must certainly speak to Chamberlain about it. This was not the understanding.

Lodge's strange impeachment of a man for defending the cause he was pledged to fight for found no sympathy with Chamberlain, who stood by the British representative. Lord Herschell continued on his stubborn way, and it was his strong advocacy of a port on Lynn Canal and his insistence on its being embraced in the proposed arbitration that led to its rejection by the United States representative. The British government strove to break the deadlock by tying up with this contentious matter the Clayton-Bulwer Treaty, which the United States wished revised, hoping that it would be easier to settle outstanding differences if they were taken up together. This the State Department declined to do. On December 16, in view of the impossibility of arriving at a compromise, Lord Herschell made a proposal for arbitration of the whole question. His suggestion was countered by the United States commissioners with the proposal that, pending further action in the Alaska boundary dispute, the commission should proceed to the other questions on the protocol. This was rejected by the Canadians, and, as an alternative solution, it was again proposed to refer the Alaska boundary to arbitration. To justify the refusal of the United States to arbitrate, Senator Fairbanks offered the somewhat lame excuse that "British claims to the headwaters of Lynn Canal had not been presented to the United States prior to the signing of the protocol," an explanation which Lord Herschell found unconvincing. Negotiations thereupon were suspended. Lord Herschell died suddenly on March 1 and the British government named Chief Justice Sir Charles Russell as his successor, but since there was no reason to believe that he would be more pliant than his predecessor, Hay allowed the commission to lapse.

When it had become clear that negotiations had broken down,

[1] White MS, cited in Tansill, *Canadian American Relations, 1875–1911,* 173–74.

Hay strongly pressed the British government for a *modus vivendi,* which he believed was "imperatively required." The bargaining was carried out by the new ambassador in London, Rufus Choate. It presented no special difficulty. Provisional boundary was fixed at three points; two at the summits of the White and Chilkoot passes; with reference to the third there was a difference of opinion about where the boundary should be on the Dalton Trail, and it was finally fixed along the Tlehini River, so as to leave the miners in Porcupine Creek district within United States territory. During the negotiations over this point, a hint for a proposed lease to Canada of land along the Lynn Canal was considered but abandoned in view of probable Senate opposition. Hay now turned to the revision of the Clayton-Bulwer Treaty, which Great Britain had hoped at one time to group with that of the Alaska boundary. Hay justified his refusal to combine this with the Alaska boundary question on the grounds that such revision was a matter of course. This explanation did not satisfy the British, but in view of the fact that the House was threatening a bill to build the canal without consulting England, so grave an infraction of a treaty was forestalled by altering it to suit the United States.

Meanwhile events had overtaken negotiations. England had become involved in war with the Boers; McKinley had been assassinated and had been succeeded by Theodore Roosevelt. Roosevelt was well-disposed toward England and directed Hay, when he raised the question, not to revive the Alaska boundary issue during the war. He moved, however, towards a settlement on his own terms. Root was directed to reinforce the garrison in Alaska "quietly and unostentatiously," and the President hinted broadly to the British to look for the wielding of the "big stick." After the Boer War ended, Hay again broached the matter to Roosevelt. The latter promptly rejected the British proposal for an odd-numbered group of commissioners (five or seven) and came out for six, three from each side. He also warned Hay that this was not to be an arbitration: "I think I shall instruct our three commissioners when appointed that they are in no case to yield any of our claim"—a prophecy that was faithfully fulfilled. In addition, by various means, work was begun on Sir Wilfred Laurier to bring him around to the United States' way of thinking.

The succession of Balfour to the post of prime minister in 1902 gave the United States government an opportunity to press the question with better chance of success. In October, 1902, Laurier on his return from London finally gave way on the question of the even-numbered commission. Roosevelt then drew up a convention to submit to the British government. Lodge combed it through carefully and deleted any reference to "arbitration." The treaty provided for a judicial tribunal of six members to be composed of "six impartial jurists of repute who shall consider impartially the questions submitted to them." There was some effort made at the last minute in England to make this specific and provide for three justices of the United States Supreme Court, while in Canada independent jurists "not the subjects of either state" were requested. This last condition was rejected by Hay as a form of arbitration. The former suggestions which would have safeguarded the selection were not pressed; and in the event, even "impartial jurists" were not named.

When it was announced that Roosevelt had chosen Elihu Root, Senator Lodge, and Senator Turner (of Washington)—at least two of them rabid partisans in the Alaska boundary matter—there was a good deal of derisive laughter in the United States press and a storm of protest in Canada which the British government was unable to assuage. Great Britain, however, proceeded with the preparations for the tribunal and appointed Sir Louis Jetté, lieutenant-governor of the Province of Quebec, Mr. Justice Armour, puisne judge of the Supreme Court of Canada (on his death, Mr. Alan B. Aylesworth, a barrister of Toronto succeeded to the post), and Lord Alverstone, lord chief justice of England. A last minute hitch occasioned by the Anglo-German blockade of Venezuela was averted by England's reversal of policy in that area.

Roosevelt now had his tribunal and drove hard. When the British wished an extension of time for the presentation of their case, Lodge protested. All the United States representatives had to be back in the country in December for meetings of Congress, the Cuban Treaty had to be ratified, and so on. Quite unconscious of the outrage of ordinary diplomatic amenities, Lodge was for breaking off negotiations and running the boundary as the United States government saw fit. Roosevelt tried to calm Lodge, though he actually agreed with him as he showed in a letter to Chief Justice Holmes.[2] When Lord Alverston proved difficult, Choate, apparently by Roosevelt's direction, intervened with a threat:

> ... the duty and the responsibility of the President were perfectly clear ... he could not hesitate to assume the full responsibility of the government over the disputed territory, and must continue to treat it all, as it always has been treated as United States property, and this he must do openly and emphatically, ... that only by the decision of this tribunal, which would be final, without any action of the Senate, could Canada get anything whatever of what she claimed.[3]

It seems incredible that the Chief Executive should intervene in so abrupt and peremptory a tone in the deliberations of an international tribunal, in an attempt to influence a judicial decision, unless we bear in mind that Roosevelt regarded the tribunal merely as a sop to Canadian self-esteem. As Lodge admitted, the decision would "be reached by the Commissioners and it does not depend on the arguments."[4]

The dispute was referred to the tribunal in the form of a series of seven questions which they were called on to answer. These seven really included only two vital issues: should the line follow the north or the south channel through Portland Canal (the answer to this would determine the ownership of four islands); and should the line be run from the fifty-sixth parallel of north latitude to the one hundred and forty-first meridian, in such a way as to give Canada access to the heads of some of the deeper inlets or should it exclude Canada from access to tidewater.[5]

The only item of real importance to Canada was the possession

[2] He said that he would ask Congress to give him authority "to run the line as we claim it, by our own people, without any further regard to the attitude of England and Canada." Letter from President Roosevelt to Justice Holmes, July 25, 1903. Roosevelt MS, cited in Tansill, *Canadian-American Relations, 1875–1911,* 243, n. 52.

[3] Dispatch of Ambassador Choate to Secretary Hay, October 20, 1903. Choate MS, cited in Tansill, *Canadian-American Relations, 1875–1911,* 258–59, n. 98.

[4] Letters from Senator Lodge to President Roosevelt, September 29, 1903. *Selections from the Correspondence of Theodore Roosevelt and Henry Cabot Lodge, 1884–1918,* II, 59–62. Cited in Tansill, *Canadian-American Relations, 1875–1911,* 251, n. 79.

[5] Other matters, including the actual width of the strip, were in dispute, but they were not material.

of a port on Lynn Canal. It was not specifically included in the agenda as a separate matter but was involved in the decision as to the proper method of measuring the ten-league width of the coastal strip. This issue was clear cut. The Canadians held that it was unreasonable to run the boundary around the head of deep inlets like Lynn Canal but that it should be measured from the general line of the coast; the Americans felt that its extreme width should be measured from the head of all inlets, even the deepest. Alverstone took a position half-way and clung to it tenaciously to the end. But from the first it was agreed by the majority to bar Canada from the sea. The other point of disagreement was how the line should be run through Portland Canal: should it run along the channel to the north of the four islands near its mouth (the Canadian contention), or should it run through the channel to the south (the American contention). On this matter, under pressure from his government (in turn under pressure from the United States delegation), Alverstone compromised; and the ownership of two of the islands in Portland Canal passed to the United States. Bitterly resentful of the decision, Canada's representatives refused to put their signature to the award.

There was intense indignation in Canada at the outcome of the negotiations. It seems to us now, in looking back over events, that the treaty of 1825 was drafted with an entirely false conception of the coast line. This was realized as soon as the first attempt was made to run the line. Dall somewhat hesitantly had suggested a new treaty, and that seems to have been Cleveland's idea in agreeing to the negotiations in 1895.[6] But once gold was discovered, a settlement on the basis of mutual convenience was ruled out. It became at once a live issue. The President had to reckon with the opposition of the Senate, extremely sensitive to public feeling on the West Coast. The treaty, therefore, had to be sold to the Senate and to commercial interests on the West Coast, and they would tolerate no concessions.

All that could then be done was to try to interpret a bad treaty. As John Hay had said, this could be done in one of three ways: by negotiation, by arbitration, or by force. The first had obviously

[6] Letter from Wm. H. Dall to Dr. G. M. Dawson, April 24, 1884. *Alaska Boundary Tribunal,* III, 323–24.

failed. The last, even if it did not entail bloodshed, would have been attended with some odium, and in any event could not have guaranteed the United States a clear title in international law. With regard to the second, Roosevelt seems to have agreed with Thrasymachus that "justice is the interest of the stronger," and could not bring himself to accept adjudication by an impartial tribunal. He tried therefore to combine the two last alternatives—to write the decision beforehand and then to constitute the tribunal so that its acceptance was a foregone conclusion. By this he was driven to shifts that made a mockery of this quasi-judicial procedure. The British, and to some extent the Canadians, acquiesced in a departure from strict arbitration by neutrals, and thus, made parties to a travesty of justice at the start, could not effectively protest at a later stage. At Washington there was never any doubt of the outcome. The worst that could happen would be a tie, and Roosevelt had forestalled that by informing the British that in that case he would occupy the disputed territory and draw his own line.

On the other hand it is difficult to see how a strict interpretation of the treaty could have been favorable to Canada's claims. Since it involved no vital interest for either country, would the American government not have been better advised to accept arbitration, not only as a "good neighbor" but from the consideration of enlightened self-interest? But the practice of making political capital out of international dispute was too deeply rooted to expect either Lodge or Roosevelt to resist it. An impartial judicial decision would have denied them a resounding personal triumph.

XIX

Prospice

THE ATTAINMENT OF SELF-GOVERNMENT ENDED THE TERRITORY'S worst growing pains and ushered in a period of comparative political calm. A steady development of its economic resources went far to insure a measure of prosperity and led to some increase of population.

The most rapid development was in lode mining, especially that of the copper deposits in the valley of the Chitina acquired by the Morgan and Guggenheim interests. Production began in 1911 just in time to take advantage of the high prices occasioned by World War I. Profits were realized on a fantastic scale so that when the Kennecott mine closed down in 1936, it had become almost legendary in the history of mining. The Treadwell mines on Douglas Island near Juneau continued to produce until 1916 when they were flooded by the sea and operation ceased. But the Alaska-Juneau mines on the mainland uncovered some veins which, owing to the ease and cheapness of extraction, turned out to be enormously profitable. This production went far to offset the decline occasioned by the disaster that had overtaken their competitors.

The grant of territorial status was shortly followed by the launching of two important transportation projects. In 1913 the Alaska Highway Commission undertook to finish the highway from Valdez to Fairbanks on which work had been done intermittently since the beginning of the century. Shortness of the season hampered the work but by 1923 it had been carried through to completion. It was named Richardson in honor of Colonel Reese Richardson. A highway only second in importance was the Steese Highway to connect Fairbanks with the Yukon River at Circle.

Of even greater significance was the building of a railway to the interior, hitherto held up by obstacles that seemed insuperable. As has been stated, the conservation movement had made the public peculiarly averse to the granting of public lands for railroad construction. The usual alternative to this—the guarantee of railroad bonds was equally distasteful. Gradually it became evident that the only way out of the impasse was for the government to build a railway itself. In 1912 President Taft named a commission to carry out a survey and to submit to the executive a comprehensive report. This was not available in time for action by the outgoing president, but in 1914 President Woodrow Wilson authorized the construction of a line and appointed a commission of three engineers to supervise the work. Surveying parties were organized and sent out in the spring of that year to locate a possible route or routes. On the basis of these Wilson selected Seward on Resurrection Bay as the tidewater terminus. The road was to cross the Kenai Peninsula to Turnagain Arm on Cook Inlet, which it was to skirt. It would then ascend the valley of the Susitna and after crossing the Alaska Range would reach the crossing of the Tanana River (the present Nenana) at a distance of 407 miles from tidewater. Construction was begun in 1915 and carried through to completion, President Harding driving the last spike in 1923. Subsequently the road was extended to the town of Fairbanks twenty miles up the river from Nenana. Branch lines were also built: one to tap the Matanuska coal fields, a second from Seward to Kern Creek, and a third from Matanuska to Chikaloon. Some narrow-gauge branch lines were added to the system by construction or purchase.

The arrival of the railway in the valley of the Yukon was a landmark in the history of Alaska. Hitherto access to the interior had been possible by ascending the river from its mouth or from Skagway over the White Pass Railway to Whitehorse and so on downriver. The element of time made the latter route the most popular one, but in following this route to reach the gold fields of the Yukon Valley, travelers had to cross Canadian territory. The new railway served the Tanana River in addition to the lower Yukon, river steamers connecting at Nenana for Ruby, Russian Mission, and Marshall (the latter in the Yukon Delta). The Steese Highway from Fairbanks to some extent served the upper Yukon, though traffic continued to come through Skagway during the season of river navigation.

The building of the railroad and the Richardson Highway gave a great stimulus to tourist travel. For a generation Alaska had attracted sight-seers, but they had not ventured far from the coast. Either they took the inside passage to Skagway, viewed the relics of Soapy Smith, and turned back to civilization; or, boarding the steamers of the Alaska Steamship Company, they visited Sitka and crossed the Gulf of Alaska to Seward. The White Pass Railway succeeded, shortly after World War I, in inducing the sight-seeing public to hazard short trips to the interior; to Bennett, to Carcross and Lake Atlin; some bold souls went on to Whitehorse and a few even to Dawson. But now by arrangements between the steamship companies operating on the coast it was possible to route passengers by railway and river steamers from Skagway to Whitehorse thence down the Yukon to Dawson and Tanana, up the Tanana to Fairbanks and so by the Alaska Railroad back to tidewater at Seward. The direction could be reversed but the slow journey upstream was considered tedious and discouraged tourists. Beginning in 1924 this phase of the transportation business grew each season to greater proportions. The traveling public could now see the interior of the Yukon and Alaska in comparative comfort. It swelled to a considerable volume the amount of money in circulation in these northern communities.

Development even took place in the field of agriculture. In the early days of the gold rush a beginning had been made. The high prices of all foodstuffs, especially dairy products, was always an inducement to those who had no other source of income to experiment in farming. Around Fairbanks there is a heavy overburden of soil and here dairy farming and truck gardening took root. The wide Matanuska Valley had extensive areas of land which by clearing were easily made available for settlement. Its sheltered location gave it some advantages in the way of climate over the Tanana and Yukon river valleys. By 1914 some homesteads had been located here which found the market for their produce in the nearest mining camps. The building of a railroad and highways made it possible to transport farm products to the nearest towns either in the interior or on tidewater. An agricultural station was established by the Department of Agriculture and under its able director, Dr. G. C. Georgeson, made useful contributions. It was later taken over and operated by the University of Alaska.

World War I left Alaska comparatively untouched. Sourdoughs did more than their share of the fighting. In the Yukon Territory a machine-gun company was raised and sent overseas to do good work with the Canadian forces. Indeed one Yukoner made history. Colonel Joe Boyle had originally owned the Boyle concession and, at the beginning of the war, managed one of the largest companies operating on the Klondike and its tributaries. Though over the age limit, he managed to persuade the authorities at Ottawa to accept him for service. On arrival in England, for want of other suitable employment in the theaters of war, he was sent to Russia. He arrived there on the eve of the October Revolution and rendered the Bolsheviks some useful service; then he plunged into the troubled seas of international intrigue. Becoming interested in the Rumanian cause he carried off a daring coup. By getting possession of the Rumanian crown jewels and seizing a special private train, he loaded the jewels packed like potatoes in baskets, ran them through five separate fighting fronts, and delivered them intact in Bucharest. His at once became a name to conjure with in the Balkans, and he subsequently served as mediator between both sides in arranging the treaty in which Bessarabia was ceded to Rumania by the Russians.

But apart from the achievements of her fighting men Alaska did not figure in the war. The general economic disturbance checked her growth, while the industrial boom that followed the war drew her population away. As the United States Geological Survey says (Bulletin 933-A-1940):

> During the post-war period Alaska suffered through the fact that in the States scales of wages and opportunities for the employment of capital seemed to offer more advantages and as a result there was more or less fluctuation in the mineral output.

An effort was made to offset the decline by consolidation of holdings and the installation of expensive equipment such as dredges, draglines, and hydraulic monitors with abundant heads of water to reduce the cost of mining lower-grade deposits by large-scale operations. This was true at Dawson in the Klondike, where many of the companies withdrew and mining operations were concentrated in the hands of one company. At Nome and Fairbanks, the United States Smelting and Mining Company undertook operations involving heavy investment which could be recovered only after considerable lapse of time; these were the building of dredges and thawing of ground, stripping off the overburden; the digging of ditches and the building of flumes to carry water for hydraulicking. The results of all these were that while the annual production of placer gold for Alaska had shrunk to $2,982,000 in 1927, by 1932 it had increased to $5,522,000 and by 1940 had reached the astounding figure of $18,852,000. (It is to be noticed that part of this rise is accounted for by the increase in the price offered, beginning in 1934, for gold.)

The act of 1912 recognized the right of the people of Alaska to manage their own affairs, including their schools. The situation in the territory with regard to education had been anomalous. The provision for education made in the Organic Act of 1884 had remained at first a dead letter for want of some agency to promote it. But eventually the line of least resistance had been taken and the administration of the education appropriation had been entrusted to the head of Presbyterian missions, Sheldon Jackson. This had inevitably made education a subsidiary of missionary activity among the natives, a situation which was galling to the white population. The civil code of 1899, which permitted towns to become incorporated, had allowed the establishment of community schools jointly supported by the taxpayers and the federal government. This rudimentary organization was somewhat expanded, and most of the settlements thus provided with school facilities for the greater part of the white population and the natives or half bloods living as whites. The natives who still followed their former way of life continued to be provided with education by the Office of Education.

But mining communities tend to be short lived. The closing down of work and the departure of most of the white population left some of the erstwhile prosperous communities, considerably shrunken, to provide schools for those who lingered on like the wreckage left behind by a flood. Since this remnant usually contained a large proportion of natives and half bloods, few of whom paid taxes, there was a constant clamor that the schools should be taken over and administered by the Office of Education instead of continuing to be a charge on the handful of taxpayers. The dual control of education assumed that the whites and the natives were distinct groups that could be dealt with separately. Actually there was considerable merging of the groups and their interests, with the result that in matters of education there was conflict and overlapping. From time to time there was agitation for the educational services to be combined under one management.

In general it may be said that the decade after World War I was one of stagnation or even decline. The territory could not compete with continental United States in attracting newcomers nor even in holding its own people. By 1926 the white population, which in 1910 had been 36,000, had shrunk to 27,000. The territory continued to suffer from competition with the "outside" all through the prosperous twenties. Only when depression struck and unemployment became general did the pendulum begin to swing the other way. A few of those who had left the North for the fleshpots were glad to return to find employment in canneries or in the new developments taking place in the placer gold fields. But eventually the depression began to make itself felt even in the North, and branches of the various federal relief agencies had to be set up to take care of the destitute. Mining at best is an uncertain and precarious way of life in which there are few prizes. Many reach "the threshold of old age" with failing powers, with no provision for old age, and without relatives to support them. The problem of relief is bound to be especially acute in mining camps. For the incapacitated it is usually met by some form of old-age pension. But even the able-bodied were in many cases destitute and must be given work or, in lieu of work, relief. This was, as elsewhere in the United States, the immediate task to which President Franklin Roosevelt addressed himself during his first administration.

New Deal philosophy, however, was already looking ahead for more permanent solutions of the problems with which society was confronted. In Alaska, since problems were somewhat unique, the results necessarily differed from those attained in the United States.

The first and most important of the policies initiated was raising the price of gold. This seems to have been intended as a mildly inflationary measure to stimulate general business rather than mining. But there can be no doubt of its immediate and beneficial results on mining. Much placer ground with low values had been abandoned since the costs of working would not allow a profit. It was now possible to resume operations on these defunct workings or even to open new ones when there were reasonable prospects of high returns from gold for the future. Companies like the United States Smelting, Refining and Mining Company that had already spent huge sums on preliminary work at Nome and Fairbanks now found themselves handsomely repaid for their outlay and justified in making considerable further expansion. The Alaska-Juneau Mine at Juneau, which had swung into production in the period after 1918, was also able to profit from the higher prices. In Yukon Territory, the Yukon Gold Company, a subsidiary of Guggenheim, had disposed of its holdings both in the Klondike gold fields and in the Mayo silver field and had left the Yukon Consolidated Corporation in full possession. The low-grade deposits more and more forced the latter to restrict operations, and production shrank to a mere trickle of $600,000 a year in place of the flood that had rolled through Dawson at the peak. A struggle for control which went on within the company hampered operations but eventually led to reorganization and the resumption of production on a larger scale.

The increase of almost 75 per cent in the price of gold was a marked stimulus to placer mining. Production of placer gold, which had reached the sum of $3,347,000 (1928) on the eve of the depression, had climbed to $11,000,000 by 1936. Similarly, lode production was increased, though in this case, as we have already noted, the upsurge was gradual, contingent upon long and expensive development work that had preceded. By 1938 it had swelled to $7,000,000. Not all of this increase is due to the higher prices paid. Some part of it is contributed by the new workings that have come into production under the same stimulus.

Even more characteristic of the New Deal philosophy was the experiment made in bringing settlers into the Matanuska Valley. A start in farming had been made here back in the early part of the century, but many of the homesteads taken up had been abandoned. The continued high prices of foodstuffs in the mining camps, which must be imported from "outside," suggested to some one the possibility of bringing in at government expense farmers forced off land in the United States. On certain of the cut-over lands in Michigan, Minnesota, and Wisconsin there had been a series of bad years because of drought and other conditions and consequent crop failures. Many formerly independent farmers were on relief. It was decided in 1934 to select about two hundred of the more desirable families to make the experiment. The Federal Emergency Relief Administration procured land in the Matanuska Valley for the settlers either by clearing or by taking possession of abandoned homesteads. Advance agents were sent in to arrange transportation, to select land, and to make some preliminary preparations for welcoming the newcomers and their families. On arrival the settlers found workmen already on the ground with tools and material for the construction of the most necessary buildings. The colonists were also themselves employed to assist in the building operations and thus were enabled to earn additional funds as well as to provide shelter for themselves and their stock in the winter. Wells were dug and fuel secured. By freeze-up the community was pretty well under shelter. During the winter buildings were completed and preparations were begun for next season's operations of clearing and sowing.

Every effort was made to guarantee the settler satisfactory conditions by providing for long-term purchase of farms. The project was later turned over to the Department of the Interior (which is the agency of the government most intimately concerned with Alaska). The financing of the individual purchaser was operated through the Alaska Rural Rehabilitation Corporation of Palmer, which sells both improved and unimproved farms. The Matanuska Valley Farmers' Co-operating Association was organized to handle the marketing of the products, most of which are disposed of at one or other of the mining centers or the coastal towns.

The settlers were provided with good schools, community halls, churches, and every advantage of a settled society. Communications through the valley are good. But many of the settlers have found life in the North uncongenial. It may be the long winter, the relative isolation, or the primitive conditions. Some who had become depressed were allowed to depart southward, their places to some extent being taken by newcomers. There has been a comparatively high turnover in personnel. The purchase of land, buildings, equipment, and supplies had involved debt. This money can-

Courtesy Public Roads Administration

PEACE RIVER BRIDGE ON THE ALASKA HIGHWAY

Courtesy Public Roads Administration

ALASKA HIGHWAY ALONG KLUANE LAKE

not be recovered until the land is in production. While a new settler may take the place of the family departing and so take over the debt, there have been inevitably heavy losses, some of which will have to be assumed by the government and written off.

There has been controversy over the scheme and its administration. Two opposing philosophies are here in conflict, that emphasizing individual enterprise and that advocating government direction of economic activity. People of the North are inclined to be individualists and extremely self-reliant. While not above government patronage when it can be obtained, they are prone to look askance at the promotion of schemes by direct government subsidy. These new settlers enter into competition with the older ones who have raised themselves by their own unaided efforts. The latter would be more than human if they did not feel some resentment.

On the other hand, schemes of colonization must be judged by long-term results. In the westward expansion of the United States the lure of cheap land was sufficient to advance settlement, but colonization has sometimes been promoted elsewhere by government assistance. In spite of the suspicion with which such schemes are regarded, there seems to be room for a policy of direction and assistance to would-be immigrants. Its only chance of success, however, depends on a rigid selection of applicants and a winnowing out of the unfit.

A third somewhat revolutionary innovation of the Roosevelt Administration has been legislation with regard to the natives. Under the Russians the whole population had been divided into six classes: (1) those serving the Russian American Company under contract; (2) colonial citizens, that is, those who had completed their term of service in America and had elected to remain (most of them in receipt of pensions); (3) the creoles or half bloods in the company's employ; (4) dependent tribes of sedentary people —Aleuts and Kodiak Islanders; (5) dependent natives such as the Kenaitsi or Chugachi (tribes living around Cook Inlet and Prince William Sound); (6) the independent tribes such as the Kolosh (Tlingits), the Haidas, and the Athapascan tribes of the interior.

The law of 1868—the Alaska Act—took no account of these separate categories and so left matters in considerable confusion.

In 1873, however, this act was amended to apply to the district Sections 20 and 21 of the Intercourse Act of 1834, which prohibited the introduction and disposition of spirituous liquors in certain areas. Did this make Alaska Indian country? It was frequently urged that it did, and the way in which the territory was administered certainly supported this argument. But no clear answer was given. Prohibition was finally removed in 1899. The natives, at least potential citizens, had passed under the tutelage of church missions. With the establishment of the post of educational agent in 1884, they came under the Bureau of Education. But this organization was concerned primarily with schools and the economic status of natives only incidental to their education. Eventually it was the Bureau of Education that had to bestir itself in 1890 to save the Eskimos from starvation by importing and distributing among them Siberian reindeer. That was about the extent of the responsibility assumed by the federal government. The natives—Eskimos, Aleuts, and Indians—were not on reservations and indeed were opposed to them, much preferring to move around at will. Moreover, it is doubtful if reservations in the ordinary sense of the word were suited to their mode of livelihood.

Time altered this. The continued influx of prospectors and miners and the depletion of the wild life on which the natives depended to some extent for their livelihood necessitated a change, to which the Indians finally reconciled themselves. In 1934 Congress passed the Indian Reorganization Act (approved June 14)

> to conserve and develop Indian lands and resources; to extend to Indians the right to form business and other organizations; to establish a credit system for Indians; to grant certain rights of home rule to Indians; to provide for vocational education for Indians; and for other purposes.

By the Composite Indian Reorganization Act for Alaska, Sections 1, 5, 7, 8, 15, 17, and 19 were made applicable to Alaska with this provision:

> that groups of Indians in Alaska not heretofore recognized as bands or tribes but having a common bond of occupation or association, or residence within a well-defined neighborhood, community, or rural district, may organize to adopt constitutions and by-laws and to receive

charters of incorporation and Federal loans under Sections 16, 17, and 10 of the Act of June 18, 1934 (48 Stat. 984).

According to John H. Crider, writing in the *New York Times* on December 10, 1944, the first use of this power was made by the Department of the Interior in 1943, when seven reservations totaling 1,540,910 acres to include exclusive fishing rights in coastal waters were set aside for 1,470 Indians. These are:

Reservation	*Acreage*	*Population*
Shishmaref	3,000	266
Wales	7,200 land	194
	14,000 water	
Akutan	72,000 land and water	68
White Mountain	640	202
Karluk	35,000 land and water	175
Unalakleet	870	465
Venetie	1,408,000	100

(The natives of Arctic Village, Christian Village, Robert's Fish Camp, Kachik and vicinity.)

In addition to the above, proposals have been made for sixteen additional reservations with a total of 3,729,420 acres. Two of these Kiukwan and Hydaburg are in southern Alaska and involve withdrawing from national forests areas of 12,800 and 296,000 acres respectively.

Feeling, considerable and heated, developed in the territory over this policy, especially over the proposal to withdraw large areas from the Tongass and Chugach Forest Reserves for the benefit of the natives. Alaskans to a man are opposed to what they call this plan "to turn Alaska back to the Indians." Even Governor Ernest Gruening came out against the proposal, as well as Honorable Anthony Dimond, the former delegate from Alaska. In response to complaints received Judge Hanna, a former representative from New Mexico, was named to conduct hearings on the proposals in Alaska and to submit findings to the executive.

It appears that if this step had been proposed in advance of settlement and before interests of one kind or another had become established, there would have been little criticism. But delay in bringing Alaska Indians into line with the general Indian policy at the very beginning has led to an unfortunate situation and raised a storm of protest from those areas likely to be affected.

Of far greater import for the moment to Alaska was the impact of war. The blow that descended on the United States Navy and naval base at Pearl Harbor on December 7, 1941, created an unprecedented situation in the North Pacific; and for the first time in nearly a century this distant outpost of civilization was the scene of hostilities.

At the outbreak of the European war in 1939 the only military establishment in Alaska was Chilkoot Barracks at Haines Mission, all but inaccessible since it could be reached only from Skagway irregularly by sea. The Washington Treaty of 1922 had forbidden fortifications in the Aleutian Islands. The treaty expired in 1936, but it was not until 1939 that the first appropriation was made for Alaska's defense (a cold-weather army experiment station at Fairbanks). In 1940 an appropriation was made for a naval (submarine) base at Dutch Harbor. Other naval and air bases were built at Sitka and on Kodiak Island.

Meanwhile the army had begun to take seriously the prospect of war. Over the vast stretches of Alaska the ordinary branches of the service would be comparatively useless if tied down to primitive means of communications. The air arm therefore assumed a far more important place than in other theaters of war. The army exerted great efforts to make up for lost time in overcoming the territory's extreme vulnerability. Air bases were provided at Fairbanks and Anchorage, and intermediate stops were built for landing on the way to and from the United States, such as Yakutat Bay, Juneau, Ketchikan, and Wrangell, to link with those of the British Columbia coast.

On December 7, 1941, the Japanese made their attack on Pearl Harbor in the Hawaiian Islands and Manila in the Philippines. The situation in the United States changed overnight. Alaska now found itself in the front line with pitifully inadequate defenses. It was not until the early months of 1942 that the army took steps to secure the safety of Alaska and the Aleutian Islands. Permission was finally given Major General Buckner to establish fields for land-based planes; and with a view to secrecy miscellaneous supplies were rushed north for a mythical company, Blair and Caxton, supposed to have canneries along the Alaska Peninsula and the Aleutians. Sites were chosen at Cold Bay on the Alaska Peninsula and the island of Umnak (the island just west of Unalaska in the Aleutians). Bases at these places were hurriedly completed and were ready early in the summer.

Meanwhile the first blow fell. On June 2 an unidentified surface force (apparently steaming up from Paramushiru in the Kuriles) was reported by a reconnaissance plane some four hundred miles south of Kiska. The following morning at daybreak carrier-based planes of this force attacked Dutch Harbor and did some slight damage. On the next day, towards evening, the second and much the most severe attack was made. But army fighters and medium fighters from the Umnak air bases finally arrived and drove the Japanese off with considerable casualties. Bombers, feeling out in the fog for the surface craft, scored a number of hits, one of them on a carrier. The invasion force thereupon retired, effectively covered by the blanket of fog.

Thus thwarted in their efforts to make an all-out attack on Dutch Harbor, the Japanese fleet played hide and seek in the fog with American planes along the Aleutian chain and finally ran into Kiska, the only harbor west of Unalaska. They also occupied Attu and silenced the weather radio station there. Reconnaissance made within the next few weeks indicated that Kiska had been occupied in force and that permanent installations, including air fields, were in process of erection. Attu likewise was fortified. In this way the mainland and the sea approaches to Alaska were directly menaced and a strategic position seized from which the Soviet Union could be cut off from United States aid.

Meanwhile reinforcements poured in to the islands from Japan, and it appeared that the Japanese had come to stay. The first answer of the United States was to establish a secret air field in the Andreanof Islands within effective bombing distance of Kiska. This move was successful, and army and navy planes continued all winter to chase Japanese planes in and out of the fog, and on days when conditions would permit it, to swoop down through the holes in the clouds to bomb Kiska and Attu. At times destroyers sneaked in for a few minutes of concentrated bombardment—a dangerous practice amid the tide rips of these fog-blanketed, rock-infested waters.

On May 11, 1943, supported by United States warships, troops were landed on Attu and began the task of eliminating the Japanese garrison. By June 4, after prolonged and bitter fighting, all Japanese troops on the island had been killed or captured. American casualties were 1,535, including 432 killed; Japanese casualties were 1,791 killed and eleven captured. Beginning on July 6, Kiska was then subjected to intermittent bombardments from both the air and the sea. During the first two weeks of August this attack was stepped up into an intensive and concentrated barrage. United States and Canadian troops were landed on Kiska on August 15 only to find that the Japanese had evacuated the island. *Domei,* Japanese news agency, reported that Japanese forces had been transferred late in July to a new post. Anti-aircraft fire had been last reported on August 13. Thus ended the last campaign on American territory.

Out of the war two important projects emerged—the highway from the United States to Alaska and the pipe line to supply gasoline for the highway from oil wells at Norman Wells, Northwest Territories.

The idea of linking Alaska with the rest of continental United States was not a new one. Back at the beginning of the century E. H. Harriman had proposed building a railway to Bering Strait to link with one to be constructed by the Russian government. But with the development of the internal combustion engine, the idea of a motor road had come into favor. Preliminary steps had been taken in 1929 when international highway associations were organized at Fairbanks and Dawson. The project was finally taken up by the government. An international commission named in 1930 reported favorably on the plan in 1933. In 1938 United States and Canada each named five members to an international commission to subject the proposal to serious study and to bring in recommendations.

The commission reported in favor of building the road without committing itself to any one route, two being considered. Route A was to take its departure from Hazelton (the most northerly point on the British Columbia road system) or near there and proceed in a generally northwest direction, inside (that is, east of) the Coast Range; Route B was to start from Prince George and follow the Rocky Mountain trench and its northerly extension to Frances Lake and the Pelly River.

Meanwhile air routes had already been established through this wilderness. The Yukon Southern Airways, operating a service from Edmonton to Whitehorse, had laid out emergency landing fields along the route at Fort Nelson and Watson Lake. Later this line was bought out by the Canadian Pacific Railway. In the winter of 1940–41 the Dominion government, in view of the war emergency, assisted the company to build winter roads into their fields for hauling supplies. Thus these fields became available to United States fliers bound for Alaska and Siberia.

After Pearl Harbor the rush of events created near-panic in high government circles for the safety of Alaska and the military and naval forces stationed there, now seriously threatened with interruption of sea communications. Up until December, 1941 (even after Pearl Harbor), the army had decisively refused to consider the building of a highway. Suddenly on February 2, 1942, a committee consisting of the secretary of war, the secretary of the navy, and the secretary of the interior (the three most vitally concerned with Alaska) met with the members of the War Department General Staff and decided that a highway should be built and that it should be routed along the line of the existing air fields from Edmonton to Fairbanks. The project was approved by the chief of staff of the army on February 6, 1942, and on February 11 by the President. The army was to undertake the construction of a pioneer road from Fort St. John to the Big Delta. Army engineers were to be followed by the Public Works Administration. Final authority was issued to the chief of engineers on February 14, 1942.

On February 16 the secretary of war approached Canada through the regular diplomatic channels with reference to the highway. The Canadian authorities recommended that the matter be referred to the Permanent Joint Board on Defense, which had been created by the United States and Canada to prepare plans for the defense of both countries. This august body gave its blessing, and on March 6 the approval of the Canadian government was forthcoming. A series of notes exchanged between the two governments constituted the formal agreement by which the United States government undertook to have the road surveyed and constructed by army engineers as a pioneer road over this route, to have it completed by the Public Works Administration, and to maintain the road for the duration of the war and six months thereafter, unless the Canadian government wished to take the Canadian section over earlier. The Canadian government undertook, on receiving its section, to maintain it as an integral part of the Canadian highway system and to allow United States civilians to travel over it without imposing discriminatory conditions.

The work was begun almost simultaneously at three separate points; at the southern end at Dawson Creek (reached via the Northern Alberta Railway from Edmonton); at Whitehorse (accessible from the sea at Skagway); and at Big Delta (reached over the Richardson highway from Fairbanks or Valdez). The army moved in seven engineering battalions, a vast amount of road equipment, and mountains of miscellaneous material. Throughout the whole length of the road, save at a very few points, the country traversed was a howling wilderness, and the army had to bring with them everything they needed. All were ready to start by the early spring months of 1942. One unit had to rush supplies to Fort Nelson over the winter road since this intermediate point would be isolated by the spring thaw until construction again linked it with the outside world. Most of the other outfits worked from bases more readily accessible.

Despite setbacks work progressed rapidly during 1942. The figures for personnel, equipment, and earth and other construction material moved are prodigious and mean little to the layman. The parties working ceaselessly day and night eventually joined the separate sections. One hundred miles northwest of Whitehorse bulldozers from Fairbanks and Whitehorse respectively, crashing through the forest, suddenly met in the late fall, thus closing the last gap. Within a few weeks the pioneer road over which supplies could move (at least in winter) was complete, and this was duly recognized by a commemorative international ceremony.

Meanwhile the Public Works Administration had been organizing their part of the task. They engaged four management contractors to supervise the work and through them forty-seven civilian contractors (American and Canadian) on a cost-plus-fixed-fee basis. Men and equipment arrived early in 1942 and assisted the army in completing certain badly needed sections of the pioneer road. During the winter building operations were carried on and bridges begun over the Kiskatinaw, Peace, Sikanni Chief, Liard, Coal, Hyland, and Muskwa rivers, the work sometimes pushed in darkness and in sub-zero temperatures. A good many of the permanent bridges were completed before the spring thaw (there were eighty-six in all). The rest were in place before the spring of 1944. Work was in its final stages in the southern part in September, 1943, and buses were running from Dawson Creek to Whitehorse. The northern part of the road from Whitehorse to Big Delta gave some trouble because of flooding and icing conditions, and this section was completed much later than the other portions, and work continued to be subject to prolonged interruptions. The standard laid down for the road was a twenty-six foot roadbed with twenty to twenty-two feet of gravel surfacing; grades were kept below 10 per cent, and the speed provided for was forty miles per hour. The southern end attained a slightly higher standard.

The road builders had been called on to meet certain unique problems. In northern British Columbia, and indeed even in Alaska and the Yukon, there are encountered vast areas of muskeg. A muskeg, a seemingly bottomless morass, consists of partly decayed vegetation and water and is covered with sphagnum moss, a condition that had so far baffled engineers. The other difficulty to be overcome in Alaska and the Yukon is the accumulation of ice —known in the North as "glaciers." These occur in severe winter weather in ever increasing layers where the water from springs or seepages, when its ordinary exit is blocked, is likely to find a new outlet to the surface and form layers of ice, constantly growing in extent and thickness. Such ice may appear anywhere and can effectively put a road completely out of commission for the winter, until the spring thaw brings relief.

Muskeg was attacked by the engineers with the bulldozer. The vegetable matter was removed down to the subsoil. Gravel or other material was then dumped on and a solid roadbed built. The claim is made that this old enemy has thus been finally vanquished. "Glaciers" cannot apparently be more than partially eliminated and will probably continue to hamper maintenance of the road. Special difficulties of terrain and spring floods had also plagued the road building. Some of the glacier-fed rivers northwest of Whitehorse presented almost insuperable difficulties. The glacial silt spread over great areas is practically impassable when soaked. The average sourdough is inclined to be skeptical of the feasibility of maintaining an all-weather road under northern conditions without incurring prohibitive costs.

To complete the transportation facilities various feeders and branch lines had to be constructed. Such were the cut-off from Gulkana on the Richardson Highway to Tok Junction on the Alaska Highway (near the international boundary) and the road projected north from Haines Mission on Lynn Canal to Haines Junction on the Alaska Highway near Kluane Lake, both to be integral parts of the system.

The problem of fuel for vehicles using the highway was met by building two systems of pipe lines. One for the petroleum products was built from Skagway to Whitehorse and thence along the highway in one direction to Fairbanks and in the other to Watson Lake. Tankers come in to Skagway and discharge their cargoes, which are then piped to the various points on the highway for the use of motor vehicles.

The second pipe line was a more ambitious project, the laying of a four-inch line for pumping crude oil from Norman Wells in the Mackenzie Valley to Whitehorse, a distance of 550 miles across the uncharted wilderness of the Mackenzie Mountains. It involved building a road and the freighting of lengths of pipes hundreds of miles down the Mackenzie on river boats and thence overland along the selected route. At Whitehorse, a refinery was built to handle the four thousand barrels of crude oil which it was estimated would be moved every day from Norman Wells. These various oil projects, involving an immense outlay of labor and money, were finally brought to completion late in 1943.

These enormous undertakings were justified as emergency undertakings for war, but may of course serve some postwar purposes. This possibility led to the investigation of the prospects of future developments in the Far North. The two governments organized the North Pacific Project to undertake jointly to make a careful survey of the natural resources of these regions and to suggest joint plans for the utilization of the above-mentioned and other facilities. The tone of the reports prepared under this direction were moderate and sober and gave scant grounds for some of the over-optimistic forecasts which had been put out to exploit public interest in the North. On the other hand, it is the belief of these men that the long-range interests of Alaska and the Canadian Northwest can best be served and colonization best promoted by a careful study of actual conditions on which a policy of settlement can be based.

The fact is that Alaska has at present two basic industries in actual existence: these are mining and fishing.[1] A third potential industry, so far undeveloped, is lumbering and pulp manufacture. Mining tends to be transitory, placer mining particularly so. Lode mining, where extensive deposits are found, is perhaps capable of maintaining production over a longer period. Such was the Kennecott copper mine and such are the Alaska-Juneau properties, and there are perhaps others. The fishing industry is economically important and likely to be permanent. It now makes the most significant contribution to Alaska's territorial revenue. Unfortunately the fishing industry is controlled by absentee owners and hardly makes a contribution to the life of the community proportionate to the profits it derives.

The forests of southeastern Alaska probably are capable of considerable development, especially for the production of pulp for export; however little has yet been done, and the existence of sources nearer to the market militates against their expansion.

Coal exists in great quantities and a considerable coal mining industry is on the cards for some time in the future. But while this coal can be used for all needs in Alaska, it can scarcely compete in wider markets because of problems, and costs, of transportation.

Agriculture must of necessity live off other industries; that is, farmers can grow products to sell to the miners and the fishermen and to meet local needs, but they cannot export. Moreover, areas

[1] Total production of Alaska fisheries for 1941 (last year of peace) was 431,125,520 pounds, valued at $63,477,295. On this the territory collected in territorial license tax the sum of $843,189. *Alaska Fishery and Fur Seal Industries 1941 Statistical Digest,* No. 5, 9.

suitable for farming are not numerous nor extensive; there are only three such—the Kenai Peninsula, the Matanuska Valley, and the Tanana Valley. Certain other areas such as Kodiak and the Alaska Peninsula are suitable for stock raising. In each of these places peculiar conditions exist, and many obstacles must be overcome before farming can be regarded as successful.

On the basis of the present economic development of the territory an immediate and rapid increase in the permanent population is hardly to be expected. Industry must first be expanded and put on a year-round basis, and immigration adjusted to Alaska's need for workers.[2] Nor does it appear that undue encouragement should be given to a farming class to move to Alaska. The demand for farm products will, of course, continue to exceed the local supply within the immediate foreseeable future. But it would be folly to embark with undue haste on any schemes for extensive colonization. Progress will have to be made slowly, and each step made good before the next one is undertaken. We have, of course, the example of the Soviet Union in the successful exploitation of northern regions. Unfortunately our knowledge of this is largely hearsay since few foreigners have seen at first hand what the Russians have accomplished. However, there can be no doubt that they have worked wonders in harnessing modern science to man's needs and in particular in learning to live and prosper in regions formerly considered inhospitable.

What of the future, then? The governor of Alaska, Dr. Ernest Gruening, had this to say in 1941:

> The long-range problem which Alaska presents today is that of a raw materials country whose natural resources are being stripped from it with wholly inadequate return for the great riches extracted. Alaska is today the outstanding example of uncontrolled absenteeism under the American flag. The salmon and gold industries are almost wholly

[2] During the late months of 1944, the people of Alaska were greatly concerned over the influx into the coastal towns of workers and their families from continental United States. This was apparently caused by the over-optimistic reports of prospects in the North that had been appearing in the press. Since employment in Alaska is almost entirely seasonal, such a movement if unchecked might lead to disappointment and disillusionment among the workers and eventually cause distress for their families. See *The Alaska Weekly* (Seattle, Washington), Friday, December 15, 1944.

absentee-owned. This absentee capital pays negligible amounts to the Territory in return for the benefits received. . . .

The absenteeism from which Alaska suffers is by no means confined to capital. It is fully as detrimental in the field of labor. Every spring thousands of workers move northward from the States to work on the gold placers, in the canneries, and on the fishing grounds. Absentee labor unions discriminate against Alaskans and compel preferential treatment for their members, thus further handicapping and discouraging permanent residence. In many cases these invading cannery and mine hands receive, in addition to high wages, their board and lodging; they spend virtually nothing in Alaska. After a few weeks or months they leave the Territory taking with them earnings, which now average above four figures, and spend them outside the Territory. In some cases they actually receive their payment for the summer's work upon returning to the States. This seasonal migration perpetuates a condition which makes Alaska not a territory of permanent residence but a collection of mining and cannery camps. The social consequences of this are deplorable, since concern about the welfare of the Territory is naturally not found among those whose interest—whether in the realm of capital or of labor—is purely exploitative and transient.[3]

We cannot look for miracles, but there are certain hopeful signs. One is the resolve of the United States and Canada to co-operate in the opening up of the north country. Narrow nationalism is out of place there. The Arctic Brotherhood had for its motto, "There is no frontier here." Time has softened antagonisms and enabled Canadians and Americans to live together in harmony. We feel that somehow, in time, there will develop a race of native Northerners—true sourdoughs (there are many such already) who will live in the country because they prefer it and will develop, rather than merely exploit, its resources. It does not seem unreasonable to suppose that in good time it will be possessed by a people such as the Scandinavians or the Finns, and that in this way, and by such a people, its true destiny will be worked out. Robert Service expressed something of this thought in "The Law of the Yukon."

[3] *Annual Report* of the Governor of Alaska to the Secretary of the Interior, fiscal year ending June 30, 1941, 3–5.

ALASKA

Dreaming alone of a people, dreaming alone of a day,
When men shall not rape my riches and curse me and go away;
Making a bawd of my bounty, fouling the hand that gave . . .

Dreaming of men who will bless me, of women esteeming me good,
Of children born in my borders, of radiant motherhood;
Of cities leaping to stature, of fame like a flag unfurled,
As I pour the tide of my riches in the eager lap of the world.[4]

[4] *The Complete Poems of Robert Service,* (Dodd, Mead & Company, New York, 1944), 13. Reprinted by permission.

Bibliography

HISTORICAL LITERATURE on Alaska was already prodigious in amount in Bancroft's time and it has not decreased with the passing years. There are, however, substantial gaps in our knowledge of events connected with northwestern America since it was first discovered, and it is doubtful whether these ever will be filled.

Up until the time of Bering, the prevailing conceptions of the North Pacific and the adjacent coasts of Asia and America remained based largely on conjecture. With the Danish navigator began the correction and the clarification of these views—a process that slackened, though it did not quite cease, with Bering's death. The scientific and geographical results then attained were rather fully reported by the historians and scientists who accompanied the expeditions; and, since many of them were foreigners, they released some of this information through the connections they had outside of Russia. But despite the publicity thus given to the discoveries, the actual official documents were treated as state *arcana* and reserved for governmental use. Information continued, however, to find its way to Western Europe, either through indirect channels or through anonymous publications. Berg states that all the original journals of the Second Kamchatka Expedition, 1733–43, were in 1759 forwarded to Siberia to be made available for consultation by subsequent expeditions. They were destroyed in a fire at Tobolsk in 1788. Copies still remained in the archives of the Central Hydrographic Director in St. Petersburg, but during World War I, in 1915, they were transferred to Yaroslavl on the Volga. These, too, were lost in a fire. Thus some very valuable sources disappeared without ever having been published.

At the beginning of the nineteenth century Bering was rescued from oblivion by Vasilii Nikolayevich Berkh, who published one short study on Bering. His interest was afterwards diverted to the private traders who followed in Bering's tracks. About a generation later Lieutenant A. P. Sokolov wrote some articles on the Kamchatka expeditions which provoked a controversy with Karl E. von Baer and induced the latter to write his study, *Peters des Grossen Verdienste um die Ertweiterung der geogr. Kenntnisse,* later published by the Imperial

Academy of Sciences on the occasion of the two hundredth anniversary of the birth of Peter (1672). The ground was thus broken for systematic research in this field. Advantage was taken of this by Peter Lauridsen, a Dane, who wrote a life of Bering (based on these researches) which was published in English in the United States in 1889; but it remained for an American scholar to recover in the St. Petersburg archives and to publish the logs of the vessels *St. Paul* and *St. Peter* on the eventful voyage of 1741. Russian scholars now began to show new interest in this period. L. S. Berg has published a number of epoch-making books on the subject and has done what he could to assemble the somewhat scanty and disordered records of this earlier day.

If this alternation of periods of downright neglect with others of at least a mild interest has proved disastrous to the Bering records, it has made it all but impossible to rescue from oblivion the period that followed. The *promyshlenniki* (fur traders) who consigned their crude craft to the mercies of the North Pacific were unlettered and at best could keep very indifferent records of their experiences. Their voyages were undertaken solely for private gain, with no motive of extending geographical knowledge. Hence it was through chance alone or the fact that some information was incidental to the hearing of some suit or petition that shreds of information on these voyages found their way into the archives and give us a dim picture of these stirring days. The greater part of the exploits of these adventurers are still veiled in almost impenetrable darkness.

The case is little better when we reach the period of the dominance of the Russian American Company. In 1867, when Russia ceded her American possessions to the United States, it was stipulated in the treaty that the records of the company's office at Sitka should be turned over to the United States. This was done. Unfortunately there is one tragic gap. The records for the years 1802–17 are missing. It would seem that when Baranov sailed away to St. Petersburg on the *Kutuzov* in 1818, he took the records with him and that, after he died at sea, no one was concerned when the ship docked to take them into official custody. The story of the St. Petersburg office of the company is equally mournful. On the dissolution of the company the archives probably became the property of the state. If they were still in existence, Golder apparently did not locate them in 1914 when he visited the archives. In 1918, when the Germans were threatening Petrograd, the capital was removed to Moscow; and there was a hurried and disordered evacuation of government records from the city. There have been rumors that the missing files later turned up in Vologda or some other town to the east. But Okun' had not been able to locate them when he wrote his *Rossiisko-Amerikanskaya Kompaniya* in 1939 and admits that he was forced to rely on rather scattered material gleaned from archives of various government departments. The gap from 1802 to

1817 has in part been bridged by the accounts of Russian and other shipmasters who visited the colonies in this period—in particular the "round-the-world" expeditions which sailed from Kronstadt either to supply the Russian posts or to carry out exploratory work. American ship captains have also contributed their quota. In this way a story of these years has been pieced together, though it is still far from complete.

From 1774 the ships of other nations frequented the northwest coast—those of Spain, France, Great Britain, and, after the Revolutionary War, those of the United States. Spain's plan of colonial exclusiveness induced a policy of complete secrecy with regard to her explorations, and the records of them lay wholly buried in the archives for a generation or more to the prejudice of the interests of that country. Not until the end of the century did the Spanish government open these records to a Spanish scholar—Navarette—who was commissioned to tell the world something of Spain's achievements. But this beginning was not followed up, and we must still rely largely on unpublished manuscripts or the translations of such accounts as were smuggled abroad and published.

Great Britain gave full publicity to the exploits of her sailors and explorers. Apart altogether from the merits of these achievements—which were outstanding—the British profited not a little from being first on the street with their story. Accounts of the voyages of both Cook and Vancouver appeared in excellent editions within a few years of the deaths of the explorers. Meares, Portlock, and Dixon had hardly docked in the Thames before rushing into print readable and reliable accounts of their voyages.

The United States started in the race late. Moreover, though Gray and Kendrick had the blessing of Congress when they left Boston in 1788, their voyages could hardly be called official. Indeed, the exploits of many of the "Boston men" constitute a story still largely unwritten. Diligent search must be made in the business files of early shipowners, port authorities, and other local records of east-coast ports. Professor S. E. Morison in his *Maritime History of Massachusetts* has made a beginning. Judge F. W. Howay undertook the prodigious task of examining the shipping records of the New England and other cities along the Atlantic seaboard, with the result that he has identified most of the vessels frequenting these shores from 1785 to 1825. His list of such ships is within a reasonable distance of being complete.

After 1825, with the stagnation of the fur trade, the story of the northwest coast concerns whalers and walrus hunters. The cession of Alaska did not materially alter this condition, which prevailed until the discovery of gold brought Alaska once more on the world's stage. For the period of United States occupation we now have access to material—sometimes too abundant—in government publications, supplemented by files of old and sometimes defunct newspapers and periodicals. With the gold rush the jam was finally broken, and we had a spate of contemporary and other accounts full of impressions and of color not too critical. This abundance, of course, can scarcely throw much light on the earlier period still partly shrouded in darkness.

In the following bibliography considerations of space have imposed the task of making a careful selection from the original list of over eleven hundred titles. In view of the vast range of material, it seemed preferable, rather than to follow the conventional system, to arrange the titles under topics of restricted scope. Histories, bibliographies, and material of a geographical and ethnological nature are listed at the beginning, followed by titles arranged by periods or under some special phase. Comments are confined to cases where the uniqueness of the material requires them.

BIBLIOGRAPHIES AND GUIDES

Bolton, Herbert E. *Guide to Materials for the History of the United States in the Principal Archives of Mexico.* Washington, 1913.

Chapman, Charles E. *Catalogue of Materials in Archive of General de Indias* (for the history of the Pacific coast and the American southwest). Berkeley, 1919.

Fuller, Grace Hadley (compiler). *Alaska: A List of Selected References.* Washington, 1943.

———. *Aleutian Islands: A List of References.* Washington, 1943.

Golder, Frank A. *Guide to Materials for American History in Russian Archives.* 2 vols. Washington, Vol. 1, 1917; Vol. II, 1937.

Judson, Katharine Berry. *Subject Index to the History of the Pacific Northwest and of Alaska as Found in the United States Government Documents, Congressional Series, in the American State Papers, and in Other Documents 1798–1881;* prepared for the Seattle Public Library. Olympia, Wash., 1913.

Kerner, Robert J. *Russian Expansion to America: Its Bibliographical Foundations.* Bibliographical Society of America Papers, Vol. 25.

———. *Northeastern Asia: A Selected Bibliography.* 2 vols. Berkeley, 1939.

Mezhov, V. I. *Bibliographia Sibirica.* St. Petersburg, 1891–92.

Robertson, J. A. *List of Documents in Spanish Archives Relating to the United States.* Washington, 1910.

Shepherd, W. R. *Guide to the Materials for the History of the United States in Spanish Archives.* Washington, 1907.

Smith, Charles W. *Pacific Northwest Americana.* New York, 1921.

———. *Checklist of Books and Pamphlets Relating to the History of the Pacific Northwest.* Olympia, Wash., 1909.

Wagner, H. R. *Bibliography of Printed Works in Spanish Relating to Those Portions of the United States Belonging to Mexico.* Santiago de Chile, 1917.

Wickersham, James. *A Bibliography of Alaskan Literature, 1724–1924.* Cordova, Alaska, 1927. (Prepared in Library of Congress. Absolutely indispensable for students of Alaskan history.)

HISTORIES

Andrews, Clarence Leroy. *Story of Alaska.* Caldwell, Idaho, 1938. (Formerly published by Lowman and Hanford Co., Seattle, 1931.)
Bancroft, H. H. *The History of Alaska.* San Francisco, 1890.
———. *History of the Northwest Coast.* San Francisco, 1884.
———.*History of California.* 4 vols. San Francisco, 1885 ff.
———. *History of British Columbia, 1792–1887.* Vol. XXXII in *Bancroft's Works.* San Francisco, 1887.
Caughey, John Walton. *History of the Pacific Coast of North America.* New York, 1938.
Clark, Henry W. *Alaska: The Last Frontier.* New York, 1939. Published in 1930 under the title *History of Alaska.*
Cleland, Robert Glass. *A History of California, the American Period.* New York, 1922.
Fuller, G. W. *A History of the Pacific Northwest.* New York, 1931.
Morton, Arthur S. *A History of the Canadian West to 1870–71.* London, Paris, Toronto, Edinburgh, Melbourne, New York, no date.
Nichols, Jeanette P. *Alaska: A History of Its Administration, Exploitation, and Industrial Development During Its First Half Century Under the Rule of the United States.* Cleveland, 1924. (Indispensable for the development of self-government.)

GEOGRAPHY

Baker, Marcus. "Geographic Dictionary of Alaska," *United States Geological Survey Bulletin No. 299.* Washington, 1906. Second edition.
Baer, K. E. von, and Helmersen, Count von. *Beiträge zur Kenntniss des russischen Reiches u. der angränzenden Länder Asiens* (Pt. 1: Statistische u. ethnogr. Nachrichten über die russ. Besitzungen an der Nordwestküste von Amerika . . .). 44 vols. St. Peterburg, 1839–1900.
Bellin, Jacques N. *Remarques sur la carte de l'Amérique Septentrionale, comprise entre le 28e et le 72e degré de latitude, avec une description géographique de ces parties.* Paris, 1755.
Brooks, Alfred Hulse. *The Geography and Geology of Alaska. A Summary of Existing Knowledge.* Washington, 1906. (Extremely useful summary.)
Colby, Merle. *A Guide to Alaska.* New York, 1940.
Dall, William Healey. *Alaska and Its Resources.* Boston, 1897.
Delisle, J. N. *Nouvelles Cartes des Découvertes de l'Amiral de Fonte et autres Navigateurs. L'Histoire des Voyages, tant par Terre que*

par Mer, les Routes, Extraits des Journaux, Description des Pays, l'Histoire et les Moeurs des Habitans, et le Commerce que l'on y peut faire. Paris, 1753.

———. *Explication de la Carte des Nouvelles Découvertes au Nord de la Mer du Sud*. Paris, 1752.

Géographie Universelle. Publiée sous la direction de P. Vidal de La Blache et L. Gallois. Tome XIII, *Amérique Septentrionale Première Partie—Généralités—Canada*. Paris, 1935.

Grewingk, Constantin Caspar Andreas. *Beitrag zur Kenntniss der orographischen und geognostischen Beschaffenheit der Nord-West-Küste Amerikas, mit den anliegenden Inseln* . . . . St. Petersburg, 1850.

Phillips, P. Lee. *Alaska and the North West part of North America, 1588–1898:* Maps in the Library of Congress. Washington, 1898.

Stefansson, Vilhjalmur. "The Colonization of Northern Lands," *Climate and Man, Year Book of United States Department of Agriculture,* 1941.

United States Coast Pilot: Alaska. Part II, *Yakutat Bay to Arctic Ocean*. Washington, 1938. Fourth edition.

———. Part I, *Dixon Entrance to Yakutat Bay*. Washington, 1932. Eighth edition.

United States Department of State. *Geographical Notes Upon Russian America, 1868*. 40 Cong., 2 sess., *House Ex. Doc. 177,* part 2.

Supplement to United States Coast Pilot: Alaska. Part I, 1932. Eighth edition. *Dixon Entrance to Yakutat Bay*. March 25, 1938, and February 1, 1941. Washington, 1938 and 1941.

Supplement to the United States Coast Pilot: Alaska. Part II, 1931. Third edition. *Yakutat Bay to Arctic Ocean*. March 28, 1938. Washington, 1938.

ETHNOLOGY

Goddard, Pliny Earle. *Indians of the Northwest Coast*. American Museum of Natural History Handbook, Series No. 10. New York, 1924.

Hrdlička, Aleš. *Alaska Diary 1926–31*. Lancaster, Penn., 1943.

———. "The Coming of Man from Asia in the Light of Recent Discoveries," *Annual Report* of the Board of Regents of the Smithsonian Institution for 1935, 463–70.

———. *Remains in Eastern Asia of the Race That Peopled America*. Smithsonian Misc. Coll., Vol. 60, No. 16. Washington, 1912.

———. "Anthropological Survey in Alaska," *Forty-sixth Annual Report of the Bureau of American Ethnology, 1928–29*. Washington, 1930.

Jochelson, Waldemar (Vladimir Ilich). *Archeological Investigations in the Aleutian Islands*. Washington, 1925.

Jochelson, Vladimir Ilich. *Peoples of Asiatic Russia.* New York, 1928.
———. *History, Ethnology, and Anthropology of the Aleut.* Washington, 1933.

Jones, Livingston French. *A Study of the Thlingets of Alaska.* New York and Chicago, 1914.

Krause, Aurel and Arthur. *Die Tlinkit-Indianer. Ergebnisse einer Reise nach der Nordwestküste von Amerika und der Beringstrasse, ausgeführt in Auftrage der Bremer geographischen Gesellschaft in den Jahren 1880–1881.* Jena, 1885.

Swanton, J. R. "Social Conditions, Beliefs, and Linguistic Relationships of the Tlingit Indians," *Twenty-sixth Annual Report of the Bureau of American Ethnology, 1904–1905.* Washington, 1906.

SIBERIAN BACKGROUND

Andrievich, Vladimir Kalistratovich. *Kratkii ocherk istorii zabaikalya ot drevnikh vremen do 1762 goda.* St. Petersburg, 1887.
———. *Istorii Sibirii.* St. Petersburg, 1889.

Bakhrushin, S. V. *Ocherki po istorii i kolonizatsii Sibiri v XVI i XVII vv.* Moscow. Izdanie M. i S. Sabachinkovich, 1927.

Berkh, V. N. *Khronologicheskaya Istoriya Vsyekh Puteshestvii v sieverniya poliarniya Strany.* St. Petersburg, 1821–23.

Butsinskii, P. *Zaselenie Sibiri.* Kharkov, 1889.

Fisher, Raymond H. *The Russian Fur Trade 1550–1700.* Berkeley and Los Angeles, 1943.

Golder, F. A. *Russian Expansion on the Pacific, 1641–1850: an Account of the Earliest and Later Expeditions Made by the Russians along the Pacific Coast of Asia and North America; including Some Related Expeditions to the Arctic Regions.* Cleveland, 1914.

Kittlitz, H. von, Freiherr. *Denkwürdigkeiten einer Reise nach dem Russischen Amerika, nach Mikronesien und durch Kamtschatka.* Gotha, 1858.

Lantzeff, George V. *Siberia in the Seventeenth Century. A Study of the Colonial Administration.* Berkeley and Los Angeles, 1943.

Müller, Gerhard Friedrich. *Opisanie Sibirskago Tsarstva i vsyekh proizshedshikh v nem dyel ot nachala i osoblivo ot pokoreniya ego Rossiiskoi Derzhavye po sii vremena.* St. Petersburg, 1750.
———. *Nachrichten und Seereisen die von Russland aus Längst den Küsten des Eismeeres und Amerika geschehen sind.* St. Petersburg, 1759.
———. *Istoriya Sibiri.* In-t etnografii. Nauchnoissled. Assotsiatsiya. In-ta naroda Severa im. P. G. Smidovich. Vol. I, 1937; Vol. II, 1941. Izd-vo Akademii Nauk, SSSR.
———, and Pallas, P. S. *Conquest of Siberia and the History of the Transactions, Wars, Commerce, &c. Carried on Between Russia and China, from the Earliest Period.* London, 1842.

Nordenskiold, A. E. *The Voyage of the Vega round Asia and Europe.* 2 vols. London, 1881.

Pamyatniki Sibirskoi Istorii XVII Vyeka. 2 vols. St. Petersburg, 1882–85.

Ravenstein, Ernest George. *The Russians on the Amur: Its Discovery, Conquest, and Colonization.* London, 1861.

Sachot, O. L. M. *La Sibérie orientale et l'Amérique russe, le pôle nord et ses habitants, récits et voyages* .... Paris, 1875.

Sliunin, N. V. *Okhotsko-Kamchatskii Krai: (Skartoe) Estestvennoe-istoricheskoe opisanie Sostavyl.* 2 vols. St. Petersburg, 1900.

Slovtsov, Petr Andreyevich. *Istoricheskoe Obozryenie Sibiri.* 2 vols. Tobolsk, 1838–44.

Struve, B. V. *Vospominaniya o Sibiri.* St. Petersburg, 1889.

BERING

Adelung, Johann Christoph. *Geschichte der Schiffahrten und Versuche welche zur Entdeckung des Nordöstlichen Weges nach Japan und China von verschiedenen Nationen unternommen worden* .... Halle, 1768.

Algarotti, Francesco. *Lettres du Comte Algarotti sur la Russie* .... Traduites de l'Italien. A Londres, et se trouve à Paris. Chez Merlin, Libraire rue de la Harpe à St. Joseph, 1769. English edition, London, 1769.

Andreyev, V. "Svedeniya ob eksponatakh otpravlennykh glavnym gidrograficheskim upravleniem na Kolumbiiskuyu Vystavku v Chikago: dokumenty po ekspeditsii Kapitan Komandora Beringa v Ameriku v 1741 g.," *Morskoi Sbornik,* Vol. XXV, No. 5. (May, 1893), Neof. Otd., 1–16, parts 1–2.

Baer, K. E. von. *Zaslugi Petra Velikago po chasti rasprostranenii geograficheskikh poznanii o Russii i pogranichnikh s neiu zemlyakh Azii.* Zapiski Imperatorsko-Russkogo Geograficheskogo Obshchestvo, III, 1849, 217–53; IV, 1850, 260–83.

———. "Peters des Grossen Verdienste um die Erweiterung der geographischen Kenntnisse," *Beit. Kenntn. Russ. Reiches.* St. Petersburg, 1872. Vol. 16, i–xv, 1–290.

Berg, L. S. *Izvestiya o Beringom Prolive i ego beregakh do Beringa i Kuka.* Zapiski Gidrografii, II, 1919.

———. *Otkrytie Kamchatki i Kamchatskie Ekspeditsii Beringa.* Moscow and St. Petersburg, 1924.

———. *The Pacific Russian Scientific Investigations.* Leningrad, 1926.

Berkh, V. N. "Biograficheskoe Svedenie ob Kapitanom Komandirom, Vitusye Beringye," *Syevernyi Arkhiv,* Vol. VI, No. 8 (1828).

———. *Pervoe Morskoe Puteshestvie Rossian predprinyatoe dlya resheniya geogr. zadachi* .... St. Petersburg, 1823.

Dall, William Healey. "A Critical Review of Bering's First Expedition,

1725–30 Together with a Translation of His Original Report upon It," *National Geographic Magazine,* Vol. II, No. 2 (May, 1890).

Davidson, George. "The Tracks and Landfalls of Bering and Chirikof on the Northwest Coast of America. From the Point of their Separation . . . ," *Transactions and Proceedings* of the Geographical Society of the Pacific, Vol. I, Series II (October 31, 1901).

Gmelin, Johann Georg. *Reise durch Siberien von dem Jahr 1733 bis 1743.* In Sammlung Neuer u. Merkwürdiger Reisen zu Wasser u zu Lande, parts 4–7. 2 vols. Göttingen, 1751–52.

Golder, Frank A. *Bering's Voyages: An Account of the Efforts of the Russians to Determine the Relation of Asia and America.* 2 vols. New York, 1922–25.

Harris, John. *Navigantium atque Itinerantium Bibliotheca, or a Complete Collection of Voyages and Travels, Consisting of above 600 of the Most Authentic Writers.* 2 vols. London, 1744–48.

Histoire du Kamtchatka. Vol. XIX in *Histoire Générale des Voyages.* Paris, 1770.

Jefferys, Thomas, *Voyages from Asia to America for Completing the Discoveries of the North-West Coast of America* . . . . London, 1761.

———. *The Great Probability of a North West Passage Deduced from Observations on the Letter of Admiral De Fonte, Who Sailed from the Callao of Lima on the Discovery of a Communication Between the South Sea and the Atlantic Ocean* . . . . London, 1768.

Krasheninnikov, S. P. *The History of Kamtschatka and the Kurilski Islands with the Countries Adjacent.* Translated into English by James Grieve. London, 1764.

———. *An Account of the Part of America Which is Nearest to the Land of Kamtschatka; Extracted from the Description of Kamtschatka.* 2 vols. St. Petersburg, 1759.

———.*Opisanie zemli Kamchatki sochinennoe Stepanom Krasheninnikovom.* St. Petersburg, 1755. French edition, 1759.

Lauridsen, Peter. *Russian Explorations 1725–43; Vitus Bering the Discoverer of Bering Strait.* Chicago, 1889.

Materialy dlya istorii ekspeditsii Akademii Nauk v XVIII i XIX vekakh. Moscow, 1940.

Müller, G. F. *Extrait des voyages et des découvertes le long des côtes de la mer glaciale et sur l'océan oriental, tant vers Japon, que vers l'Amérique.* Vol. XIX of *Histoire générale des Voyages.* Paris, 1770.

———.*Voyages from Asia to America for Completing the Discoveries of the North West Coast of America.* London, 1761.

———. *A Letter from a Russian Sea Officer Containing his Remarks upon Mr. deLisle's Chart and Memoir Relative to the New Dis-*

coveries Northward and Eastward from Kamchatka. London, 1754.

Müller, Gerhard Friedrich (ed.) *Sammlung russischer Geschichte.* 9 vols. St. Petersburg, 1760.

Pallas, Peter Simon. "Erläuterungen über die im östlichen Ocean zwischen Sibirien und Amerika gesehenen Entdeckungen," *Neue Nordische Beiträge,* No. I (1781), 273–313.

———. "O Rossiiskikh otkrytiyakh na moryakh mezhdu Azieyu i Amerikoyu," *Mesyatsoslov istorii i geografii* (1781), 1–150.

Pekarskii, Petr. *Istoriya Imperatorskoi Akademii Nauk v Peterburg.* 2 vols. St. Petersburg, 1873.

Polevoi, N. A. *Otkrytie Ameriki.* St. Petersburg, 1839.

Polonskii, A. "Pervaya Kamchatskaya Ekspeditsiya Beringa 1725–29 goda," *Zapiski Gidrograficheskago Departmenta,* Morskago Ministerstva VIII (1850), 535–56.

Récueil de Voyages au Nord. Amsterdam, 1732.

Sokolov, A. P. *Syevernaia Ekspeditsiya 1733–43.* St. Petersburg, 1851.

Staehlin von Storcksburg, Jakob. *An Account of the New Northern Archipelago Lately Discovered by the Russians in the Seas of Kamtschatka and Anadir.* London, 1774.

———.*Das von den Russen in den Jahren 1765–67 entdekte nördliche Inselmeer zwischen Kamtschatka u. Nordamerika.* Stuttgart, 1774.

———. *A Short Information on the Newly Acquired Northern Archipelago.* Reprinted in the Collection of Writings selected from Calendar III. St. Petersburg, 1789.

———. *Neue Nachrichten von den neuentdeckten Inseln in der See zwischen Asien und Amerika aus mitgeteilten urkunden und Auszügen verfasset.* Hamburg and Leipzig, 1776. English edition, London, 1774.

Stejneger, Leonhard Hess. *Georg Wilhelm Steller, the Pioneer of Alaskan Natural History.* Cambridge, Mass., 1936.

———. "An early account of Bering's Voyages," *Geographical Review,* Vol. XXIV, part 4 (October, 1934), 638–42.

Steller, Georg Wilhelm. "Tagebuch seiner Seereise aus dem Petrepauls Hafen in Kamtschatka bis an den westlichen Küsten von Amerika," *Neue Nordische Beyträge,* No. V (1793), 129–236; No. VI (1793), 1–26.

———. *Steller's Journal of the Sea Voyage from Kamtchatka to America and Return on the Second Expedition 1741–42.* Translated and edited by Leonhard Stejneger. Vol. II in Golder's *Bering's Voyages.* New York, 1925.

———. *Reise von Kamtschatka nach Amerika mit dem Capt. Comm. Bering; ein Pendant zu dessen Beschreibung von Kamtschatka.* St. Petersburg, 1793.

Stralenberg, P. J. von. *An Historico-geographical Description of the North and Eastern Parts of Europe and Asia but More Particularly of Russia, Siberia, and Great Tartary* .... London, 1738.

Torrubia, José (F. Giuseppe). *I Moscoviti nella California o sia dimostrazione della verità del Passo all' America settentrionale* .... Rome, 1759.

Vakhtin, V. *Russkie Truzheniki Morya; Pervaya Morskaya Ekspeditsiya Beringa.* St. Petersburg, 1890.

Vaugondy, Robert. *Mémoire sur les pays de l'Asie,* .... Paris, 1774.

Witsen, Nicolaes. *Noord en Oost Tartarye ofte Bondig* .... Amsterdam, 1705.

EXPLORATION OF THE ALEUTIANS

Berkh, Vasilii Nikolayevich. *Khronologicheskaya Istoriya Otkrytiya Aleutskikh Ostrovov ili podvigi Rossiiskago kupechestva. S. Prisovokupleniiem istoricheskago izviestiya o myekhovoi torgovlye.* St. Petersburg, 1823.

———. *Pervoe morskoe puteshestvie Rossiian predpriniatoe dlya ryesheniya geogr. zadachi: Soediniaetsia li Azia s Amerikoyu? i Sovershennoe v 1727–29 godakh pod nachal'stvom Flota Kapitan 1–go ranga Vitusa Beringa.* St. Petersburg, 1823.

Bogoras, Waldemar. "Folklore of Northeastern Asia," *American Anthropologist,* Vol. IV, No. 4 (October-December, 1902), 577–683.

Campbell, Archibald. *Voyage Round the World in Which Japan, Kamschatka, the Aleutian Islands, etc., Were Visited.* Edinburgh, 1816.

Coxe, William. *Nouvelles Découvertes des Russes entre l'Asie et l'Amérique avec l'Histoire de la Sibérie et du Commerce des Russes et des Chinois.* Neuchatel and Paris, 1781.

———. *Account of the Russian Discoveries between Asia and America to Which Are Added the Conquest of Siberia and the History of the Transactions and Commerce between Russia and China.* London, 1780. Fourth edition, London, 1803.

Hutchinson, Isobel Wylie. *Stepping Stones from Alaska to Asia.* London, 1937.

"Istoricheskie svyedyeniya ob otkrytiyakh i ekspeditsiakh otnosyaschikhsya do Kamchatki, Aleutskikh i Kuril'skikh ostrovov i dr," *Morsk. Sbornik.* C. I, No. 4 (1869), 65–142; C. III, No. 5 (1869), 53–84, No. 6, 37–89; C. III, No. 8, 33–110 str.

Jochelson, Waldemar (Vladimir Ilich). *Archeological Investigations in the Aleutian Islands.* Washington, 1925.

———. *History, Ethnology, and Anthropology of the Aleut.* Washington, 1933.

Veniaminov, I. *Zapiski ob ostrovakh Unalashkinskago Otdyela.* 3 vols. in 2. St. Petersburg, 1840.

———. *Charakterzüge der Aleuten von den Fuchs-Inseln.* Beiträge, Tom I (1839), 177–225.

INTERNATIONAL RIVALRIES

1775–1800

Billings, Commodore. *Voyage par ordre de l'impératrice de Russie, Catherine II dans le nord de la Russie Asiatique, dans la mer glaciale, dans la mer d'Anadyr et sur le côtes de l'Amérique depuis 1785 jusqu'en 1794.* 2 vols. Paris, 1802.

Boit, John. "Log of the Columbia, 1790–1793," *Oregon Historical Quarterly,* Vol. XXII, No. 1 (January, 1921), 257–351.

Bolton, Herbert Eugene. *Fray Juan Crespi.* Berkeley, Cal., 1927.

Broughton, William R. *Voyage of Discovery to the North Pacific Ocean. Performed in His Majesty's Sloop "Providence" and Her Tender, 1795–8.* 2 vols. London, 1804.

Brown, R. (ed.). *The Adventures of John Jewitt.* London, 1896.

Buache, Ph. *Considérations géographiques et physiques sur les nouvelles découvertes au nord de la grande mer appelée vulgairment la mer du Sud, avec des cartes qui y sont relatives.* Paris, 1753.

Buache, Jean Nicolas. *Mémoire sur les pays de l'Asie et de l'Amérique situés au nord de la mer du Sud. Accompagné d'une carte de comparaison des plans de MM. Engel et De Vaugondy, avec le plan des cartes modernes.* Paris, 1775.

Burney, James A. *A Chronological History of the North-eastern Voyages of Discovery, and of the Early Eastern Navigations of the Russians.* London, 1819.

———. *A Chronological History of the Discoveries in the South Sea or Pacific Ocean.* 5 vols. London, 1803–17.

Caamano, Lieut. Don Jacinto. For an account of his voyage in 1792 *see* Salva (Miguel) y Baranda (Pedro Sainz de), *Colección de documentos inéditos.* 8–0 Vol. XV, 323–63. Madrid, 1849.

Chapman, Charles Edward. *The Founding of Spanish California.* New York, 1916.

Cleveland, Richard J. *A Narrative of Voyages and Commercial Enterprises.* 2 vols. London, 1840. Second edition, Cambridge, Mass., 1842. Third edition, Boston, 1850.

Colnett, James. *The Journal of Captain James Colnett Aboard the "Argonaut" from April 26th, 1789, to Nov. 3, 1791.* Edited by F. W. Howay. Toronto, 1940.

Cook, Captain James. *A Voyage to the Pacific Ocean. Undertaken by the Command of His Majesty for making discoveries in the Northern hemisphere. To determine the position and extent of the West Side of North America; its Distance from Asia; and the Prac-*

ticability of a Northern Passage to Europe. Performed under the Direction of Captains Cook, Clerk, and Gore in His Majesty's Ships "Resolution" and "Discovery." In the years 1776, 1777, 1778, 1779, and 1780. 3 vols. Vols. I and II written by Captain James Cook; Vol. III, by Captain James King, L.L.D. and F.R.S. London, 1784. Also Dublin, 1784. Second edition, London, 1785. (The most important editions of this work.)

Delano, Amasa. *A Narrative of Voyages and Travels.* Boston, 1817.

Dennett, Tyler. *Americans in Eastern Asia.* New York, 1941.

Dixon, George. *Remarks on the Voyages of John Meares, Esq., in a Letter to That Gentleman.* London, 1790.

———. *A Voyage Round the World but More Particularly to the North West Coast of America Performed in 1785–1788 in the "King George" and "Queen Charlotte."* London, 1789.

Espinosa, José de and Navarette, M. F. de. *Relación del Viage Hecho por los Goletas "Sutil" y "Mexicana" en el Año de 1792, para Reconocer el Estrecho de Fuca; con una Noticia de las Expediciones Executadas por los Españoles.* Madrid, 1802.

Etches, John. *An Authentic Statement of All the Facts Relative to Nootka Sound, Its Discovery, Trade and the Probable Advantages to Be Derived from It in an Address to the King.* London, 1790.

Fleurieu, Charles Pierre Claret, Comte de. *Voyage Round the World Performed during the years 1790, 1791, and 1792 by Etienne Marchand, Preceded by a Historical Introduction.* 2 vols. London, 1801.

Howay, F. W. "A List of Trading Vessels in Maritime Fur Trade, 1785–1794," *Proceedings and Transactions* of the Royal Society of Canada, Section 2, Third Series, Vol. XXIV (1930), 111–34.

———. "A List of Trading Vessels in the Maritime Fur Trade, 1795–1804," *Proceedings and Transactions* of the Royal Society of Canada, Section 2, Third Series, Vol. XXV (1931), 117–49.

———. "A List of Trading Vessels in the Maritime Fur Trade, 1805–1814," *Proceedings and Transactions* of the Royal Society of Canada, Section 2, Third Series, Vol. XXVI (1932), 43–86.

———. "A List of Trading Vessels in the Maritime Fur Trade, 1815–1819," *Proceedings and Transactions* of the Royal Society of Canada, Section 2, Third Series, Vol. XXVII (1933), 119–47.

———. "A List of Trading Vessels in the Maritime Fur Trade, 1820–1825," *Proceedings and Transactions* of the Royal Society of Canada, Section 2, Third Series, Vol. XXVIII (1934), 11–49.

———. *Voyages of the "Columbia" to the Northwest Coast, 1787–1790 and 1790 to 1793.* Boston, 1941.

———. "Letters Relating to the Second Voyage of the 'Columbia,'" *Oregon Historical Quarterly,* Vol. XXIV, No. 2 (June, 1923), 132–52.

———. "A Yankee Trader on the Northwest Coast, 1791–1795," *Washington Historical Quarterly,* Vol. XXI, No. 2 (April, 1930), 83–94.

——— (ed.). *The Dixon-Meares Controversy.* Toronto, 1929; New York, 1929.

Humboldt, Alexander de. *Political Essay on the Kingdom of New Spain.* 2 vols. New York, 1811.

———. *Essai politique sur le Royaume de la Nouvelle Espagne.* 5 vols. and Atlas. Paris, 1808–11.

Jane, Cecil (tran.). *A Spanish Voyage to Vancouver and the Northwest Coast of America, being the Narrative of the Voyage made in the year 1792 by the Schooners "Sutil" and "Mexicana" to explore the Strait of Fuca.* London, 1930.

Jewitt, John. *A Narrative of the Adventures and Sufferings of John R. Jewitt, Survivor of the Ship "Boston" During a Captivity of Nearly Three Years Among the Savages of Nootka Sound; with an Account of the Natives.* Middletown, 1815; New York, 1816; Wakefield, 1816; Edinburgh, 1824.

Krenitzin, Capt. Lieut. Peter Kuzmich (and Mikhail Levashev). "Expedition to the Aleutian Islands 1764–1769," *Journal of the Russian Hydrographic Department,* Vol. X (1852), 70–103.

LaPérouse, J. F. G. *A Voyage Round the World in the Years 1785–88.* 3 vols. London, 1798; Boston, 1801.

———. *Le Voyage de LaPérouse sur les côtes d'Alaska et de la Californie* (1786). Introduction et des Notes par Gilbert Chinard. Baltimore, 1937; London, 1937.

———. *Atlas du Voyage de le Pérouse.* 71 maps and 4 plates. Paris, n. d.

Ledyard, John. *Manuscript Journal of His Journey towards Eastern Siberia.* Photostat copy at Dartmouth College.

Lesseps, Jean B. B. M. de. *Travels in Kamtschatka* in 1787–88. London, 1790.

MacNair, H. F. (ed.) "The Log of the 'Caroline' (1799)," *Pacific Northwest Quarterly.* Vol. XXIX, No. 1 (January, 1938), 61–84 and 167–200.

Malaspina, D. Alejandro. *La Vuelta al Mundo por las Corbetas "Descubierta" y "Atrevida," desde 1789 a 1794.* Madrid, 1885.

———. *Viaje Político-Científico alrededor Mundo por las Corbetas "Descubierta" y "Atrevida" al mando de los Capitanes de Navío D. Alejandro Malaspina y José de Bustemente Guerra desde 1789–1794.* Madrid, 1885.

Manning, W. R. "The Nootka Sound Controversy," *American Historical Association Annual Report,* 1904.

Marchand, Etienne. *Voyage Autour du Monde pendant les Années 1790–92. Précédé d'une Introduction Historique; auquel on a joint recherches sur les terres australes de Drake et un examen critique du voyage de Roggeween;* par C. P. Claret Fleurieu. 3 vols. and Atlas. Paris, 1798–1800.

Martínez, Estevan José. Journal (February 17 to September 30, 1789). Contemporary copy of original MS in the Henry E. Huntingdon Library, San Marino, California. Translation made from microfilm copy of the above by Elizabeth Lees, University of Oklahoma. (Gives Martínez' version of the incidents in Nootka Sound.)

Maurelle (Mourelle), Francisco Antonio. *Journal of a Voyage in 1775.* Pages 469–534 in Daines Barrington's *Miscellanies,* London, 1781.

Meares, John. *Voyages Made in the Years 1788 and 1789 from China to the Northwest Coast of America to Which Is Prefixed an Introductory Narrative of a Voyage Performed in 1786 from Bengal in the Ship "Nootka."* London, 1790.

Memoirs for the Curious. From January, 1707, to December, 1708. "Containing an Abstract of the most Valuable Things that have been Published at Home and Abroad." 2 vols. in 1. London, 1710.

Menzies, Archibald. *Journal of Vancouver's Voyage, April–October, 1792.* Edited by C. F. Newcombe and John Forsyth. Archives of British Columbia, *Memoir* No. V. Victoria, 1923.

Morison, Samuel Eliot. *The Maritime History of Massachusetts, 1783–1860.* Boston and New York, 1931.

Müller, Gerhard Friedrich. *Nachrichten und Seereisen die von Russland aus Längst den Küsten des Eismeeres und Amerika Geschehen Sind.* St. Petrsburg, 1759.

———. *Voyages et découvertes faites par les Russes le long des côtes de la mer Glaciale et sur l'océan Oriental, tant vers le Japon que vers l'Amérique. On y a joint l'Histoire du fleuve Amur et des pays adjacens, depuis la conquête des Russes ....* Amsterdam, 1766.

———. *Extrait des voyages et des découvertes le long des côtes de la mer glaciale et sur l'Océan oriental, tant vers Japon, que vers l'Amérique.* Paris, 1770.

———. *Voyages from Asia to America for Completing the Discoveries of the North West Coast of America.* London, 1761. Second edition, 1764. (Title page of first edition has "S. Müller.")

Navarrete, D. Martín Fernández de. *Examen Historico-critico de los Viajes y Descubrimentos Apocrifos del Capitan Lorenzo Ferrer Maldonaldo, de Juan de Fuca y del Almirante Bartolome de Fonte. Memoria* (y arreglada y concluida por D. Eustaquio de Navarrete). Colección de Documentos para la Historia de Espana, Tom. XV. Madrid, 1849.

Palou, R. P. Fr. F. *Noticias de la Nueva California.* Documentos de la Historia de México. Quarta Serie, Toms. VI and VII. Mexico, 1857.

———. *Noticias de la Nueva California.* 4 vols. San Francisco, 1874.

Polonsky, A. *List of Journeys of Russian Hunters in the Pacific Ocean from 1743 to 1800.* MS of 99 sheets in the archives of the Geographical Society (Mark B.V.3). (In Russian.)

Portlock and Dixon. *An Abridgement of Portlock and Dixon's Voyage Round The World Performed in the Years 1785–88.* London, 1789.

Portlock, Captain Nathaniel. *A Voyage Round the World; but more particularly to the north-west coast of America ....* London, 1789.

Priestly, Herbert Ingram. "The Log of the *Princesa* by Estevan Josef Martínez," Oregon Historical Quarterly, Vol. XXI, No. 1 (January, 1920), 21–31.

Ross, Frank E. "American Adventures in the Early Marine Fur Trade with China," *Chinese Social and Political Science Review,* Vol. XXI (1937), 221–67.

Russia: Archives Department. *Papers Relating to the Russians in Alaska, 1732–1796.* 21 vols. Photostat copies of originals in Russian Archives in the University of Washington Library, Seattle.

Sarychev, Gavrilo. *Puteshestvie Flota Kapitana Sarycheva po syeverovostochnoi Sibiri, Ledovitomu Moryu i Vostochnomu Okeanu v prodolzhenie os'mi lyet, pri Geograficheskoi i Astronomicheskoi Morskoi Ekspeditsii, byvshei pod nachalstvom Flota Kapitana Billingsa s 1785 po 1793, god* (Journey of Fleet-Captain Sarychev in northeastern Siberia, in the Arctic Ocean and the Pacific for eight years on the geographical and astronomical maritime expedition under the command of Fleet-Captain Billings from 1785–1793). 2 vols. in 1 and Atlas. St. Petersburg, 1802.

———. *Puteshestvie Kapitana Billingsa cherez Chukotskye zemli ot Beringova Proliva do Nizhnekolymskago Ostroga i Plavanie Kapitana Galla na Sudnye Chernom Orlye po Syeverovostochnomy Okeanu v 1791 g.* (Journey of Captain Billings across the Chukchi Peninsula from Bering Strait to Nizhnokolymsk Ostrog and the voyage of Captain Hall in the *Black Eagle* in the North Pacific in 1791). St. Petersburg, 1811.

———. *Account of a Voyage of Discovery to the North East of Siberia, the Frozen Ocean and Northeast Sea.* In 2 parts, 2 vols. in 1. London, 1806–1807.

Sauer, Martin. *Reise nach den Nördlichen Gegenden von Russischen Asien, und Amerika unter dem Commodor J. Billings, 1785–94.* Weimar, 1803.

———. *An Account of a Geographical and Astronomical Expedition to the Northern parts of Russia, for ascertaining the degrees of Latitude and Longitude of the mouth of the river Kolima; of the coast of Tshutski, to East Cape; and of the Islands in the Northern Ocean, stretching to the American Coast. Performed by Commodore Joseph Billings in the years 1784–1794.* London, 1802.

Shelekhov, Grigorii Ioanovich. *Rossiiskago Kuptsa imenitago ryl'skogo*

Grazhdanina Grigor'ya Shelekhova Stranstvovanie s 1783 po 1787 god iz Okhotska po vostochnomu okeanu k amerikanskim Beregam (The wanderings of the celebrated Russian merchant, a citizen of Rylsk, from 1783 to 1787 in the Eastern Ocean to the shores of America). St. Petersburg, 1791.

———. *Rossiiskogo Kuptsa Grigor'ya Shelikova Prodolzhenie Stranstvovaniya po Vostochnomu Okeanu k Amerikanskim Beregam v 1788 godu* (A continuation of the Wanderings of the Russian merchant Grigorii Shelekhov in the Eastern Ocean to the shores of America). St. Petersburg, 1792. (These two publications are subject to some controversy as to the exact date and form of publication. It appears that they were reissued in 1793 and bound together, in which form they are usually found.)

———. Second edition contains both the above. St. Petersburg, J. Z. Logan, 1793.

———. (Shelekhof, Gregory). *Journal of the Voyages of Gregory Shelekhof, a Russian merchant from Okhotsk on the Eastern Ocean, to the Coast of America in 1783–87. With a description of the way of life, manners, habitations and dress of the people of the two new islands (Kuktah and Aphagnakh)*. 2 vols. London, 1795.

Sokolov, A. *Expedition of Captains Krenitsyn and Levashev to the Aleutian Islands, 1764–69. Memoires Hydrog. Dept.* Vol. X (1852). (In Russian.)

Sparks, Jared. *Life of John Ledyard the American Traveller*. Boston, 1847.

Stewart, Charles Lockwood. *Martínez and López de Haro on the Northwest Coast, 1788–1789*. MS dissertation for degree of Doctor of Philosophy, University of California at Berkeley, 1936.

Strange, James. *Records of Fort St. George. James Strange's Journal and Narrative of the Commercial Expedition from Bombay to the Northwest Coast of America, together with a Chart Showing the tract of the Expedition. With an introduction by A. V. Venkatarama Ayyar, Curator Madras Record Office*. Madras, 1929.

Vancouver, Captain George. *A Voyage of Discovery to the North Pacific Ocean and Round the World in Which the Coast of Northwest America Has Been carefully Examined and Accurately Surveyed in the Years 1790–1795*. 3 vols. London, 1798.

———. *Voyage de découvertes*. Paris, 1799.

Wagner, Henry R. *Spanish Voyages to the Northwest Coast in the Sixteenth Century*. San Francisco, 1929.

———. *The Cartography of the Northwest Coast of America*. 2 vols. Berkeley, Cal., 1937.

Yarmolinsky, Avrahm. "Shelekhov's Voyage to Alaska," a bibliographical note in *Bulletin* of the New York Public Library, Vol. XXXVI, No. 3 (March, 1932), 141–48.

———. "A Rambling note on the 'Russian Columbus,'" *Bulletin* of the New York Public Library, Vol. XXXI, No. 9 (September, 1927), 707–13.

Zimmerman, H. *Reise um die Welt mit Capitain Cook*. Mannheim, 1781.

INTERNATIONAL RIVALRIES
after 1800

Beechey, Captain Frederick William. *Narrative of a Voyage to the Pacific and Bering's Strait to Co-operate with the Polar Expeditions Performed in His Majesty's Ship Blossom . . . in the Years 1825, 1826, 1827, and 1828.* 2 vols. London, 1831. German edition, Weimar, 1832.

Chamisso, Adelbert von. *Reise um die Welt mit der Romanzoffischen Entdeckungs-Expedition in den Jahren 1815–18 auf der Brig "Rurik."* 2 vols. Leipzig, 1836.

Choris, Ludovik. *Voyage pittoresque autour du monde, avec des portraits de sauvages d'Amérique . . . .* Paris, 1822.

Corney, Peter. *Voyages in the North Pacific. The Narrative of Several Trading Voyages from 1813–18, between the Northwest Coast, the Hawaiian Islands and China, with a Description of the Russian Settlements and California.* Honolulu, 1896.

Davydov, G. I. *Dvukratnoe puteshestvie v Ameriku morskikh ofitserov Khvostova i Davydova, pisannoe sim poslyednom.* 2 vols. St. Petersburg, 1810–12.

———. *Dawydov's Nachrichten von der Insel Kadjak und den Russischen Niederlassungen daselbst.* Dorpat, 1816. (A translation of his Russian account of two voyages to America 1802–1804.)

Duflot de Mofras, Eugene. *Exploration du territoire de l'Orégon, des Californies et de la mer Vermeille, exécutée pendant les années 1840–42.* 2 vols. Paris, 1844.

———. *Travels on the Pacific Coast.* Translated and edited and annotated by Marguerite Eyer Wilbur. 2 vols. Santa Anna, Cal., 1937.

Golovnin, Vasilii Mikhailovich. *Sokrashchenniya Zapiski flota Kap. Lieut. Golovnina na shlyupye "Dianye" dlya opisi Kuriliiskikh ostrovov v 1811 goda.* St. Petersburg, 1819.

———. *Original Works and Translations.* 5 vols. St. Petersburg, 1864. (In Russian.)

———. *Memoirs of a Captivity in Japan during the years 1811, 1812, and 1813 . . . .* 3 vols. London, 1824. First edition, London, 1818, 2 vols. (No record of a Russian edition.)

———. *Voyage Round the World.* St. Petersburg, 1822.

———. *Puteshestvie vokrug svyeta. Po poveleniyu Gosudarya Imp. Sovershennoe no voennom shlyupye "Kamchatkye." v 1817–19 flota Kap. Golovnina* (Journey round the world. Carried out by command of His Imperial Majesty in the war sloop *Kamchatka* in the years 1817–1819). 2 vols. St. Petersburg, 1822.

———. *Puteshestvie Ross. Imp. Shlyupa "Diany" iz Kronshtata v Kamchatku sovershennoe pod nachalstvom flota Leit. Golovnina v 1807–8 godakh* (Journey of the Imperial sloop *Diana* from Kronstadt to Kamchatka, carried out under the command of Fleet Lieutenant Golovnin in the years 1807–1808). 2 vols. St. Petersburg, 1819.

Ivanshinstov, N. *Obozryenie Russkikh Krugosvyentnykh Puteshestvii.* St. Petersburg, 1872.

Kotzebue, Otto von. *Entdeckungsreise in die Südsee und nach der Beringstrasse zur Erforschung einer nordöstlichen Durchfahrt.* 3 vols. Wien, 1825.

———. *Puteshestvie v Yuzhnyi Okean i Beringov proliv dlya otyskaniya syeverovostochnogo morskago prokhoda, predprinyatoe v 1815–18 godakh na korablye "Rurikye"* (Voyage to the Pacific Ocean and Bering Strait for the discovery of the northeast passage, undertaken in 1815–18 in the ship *Rurik*). 2 vols. St. Petersburg, 1821–23.

———. *Puteshestvie vokrug svyeta sovershennoe po poveleniyu Gosudarya Imp. Aleksandra 1-ago na voennom Shlyupye "Predpriyatii" v 1823–1826 godakh pod nachalstvom flota Kap Lieut. Kotsebu* (Journey around the world, undertaken by command of his Imperial Majesty Alexander I in the war sloop *Predpriyatiya* in the years 1823–26 under command of Fleet Capt. Lieut. Kotzebue). St. Petersburg, 1828.

———. *Neue Reise um die Welt in den Jahren 1823–26.* 2 vols. in 1. Weimar, 1830.

———. *A Voyage of Discovery into the South Sea and Bering Straits for the Purpose of Exploring a North-East Passage Undertaken in the Years 1815–1818 at the Command of His Highness, the Chancellor of the Empire, Count Romanzoff in the Ship "Rurik."* 3 vols. London, 1821.

———. *A New Voyage round the World in the years 1823, 1824, 1825, and 1826.* 2 vols. London, 1830.

Krusenstern, I. F. (Adam Johann) von. *Puteshestvie Vokrug Svyeta v 1803–6 g. po povelyeniyu Ego. Imp. Vel. Aleksandra I-ago na korablyakh "Nadezhdye" i "Nevye," pod nachalstvom flota Kap. Leit. Kruzhensterna.* 3 vols. St. Petersburg, 1809–12.

———. *Reise um die Welt in den Jahren 1803, 1804, 1805, 1806 auf Befehl seiner Kaiserl. Majestät Alexander des Ersten auf den Schiffen "Nadesha" and "Newa."* Berlin, 1812. St. Petersburg, 1810. Atlas, St. Petersburg, 1814.

———. *Beyträge zur Hydrographie der Grossen Oceane als erläuter-*

ungen zu einer Charte des ganzen Erdkreises nach Mercator's Projection von J. von Krusenstern. Leipzig, 1819.

———. *Voyage autour du monde de 1803 à 1806 sur la "Nadiejeda" et la "Neva."* 2 vols. Paris, 1821.

———. *Voyage round the World in the Years 1803, 1804, 1805, 1806 by Order of His Imperial Majesty Alexander the First on Board the Ships "Nadeshda" and "Neva" under the Command of Captain A. J. von Krusenstern of the Imperial Navy.* 2 vols. in 1. London, 1813.

———. *Memoirs Hydrographic of Services and Analysis and Explanation of Krusenstern's Atlas of the Pacific Ocean.* 3 vols. St. Petersburg, 1823 and 1826.

———. *Memoir of the Celebrated Admiral Adam John de Krusenstern the First Russian Circumnavigator.* London, 1856.

Langsdorff, Georg Heinrich von. *Voyages and Travels in Various Parts of the World during the Years 1803–06.* 2 vols. London, 1813–14. Carlisle, Penn., 1817.

———. *Bemerkungen auf einer Reise um die Welt in den Jahren 1803–1807.* 2 vols. Frankfurt am Main, 1812–13.

———. *Langsdorff's Narrative of the Rezanov Voyage to Nueva California in 1806, Being that division of Dr. Georg H. von Langsdorff's "Bemerkungen auf einer reise um die welt," When as Personal Physician . . . .* San Francisco, 1927.

Lisianskii, I. F. *A Voyage round the World in the Years 1803–04–05–06 Performed by Order of His Imperial Majesty Alexander I Emperor of Russia in the Ship "Neva."* London, 1814.

———. *Puteshestvie vokrug svyeta v 1803–1806 godakh.* St. Petersburg, 1812. (The Russian original of the preceding item.)

Lütke, Fedor Petrovich. *Chetyrekatnoe puteshestvie v syevernyi Ledovityi Okean sovershennoe po poveleniyu Imp. Aleksandra I-ago no voennom brigye "Novaya Zemlya v 1821–24, godakh, flota Kap-Leit. L. Litke.* 2 vols. St. Petersburg, 1828.

———. *Puteshestvie vokrug svyeta, sovershennoe po poveleniya Imp. Nikolaya na voennom shlyupye "Senavinye" v 1826–9 godakh, flota Kap. Fedorom Litke (Otdyelenie Istoricheskoe).* St. Petersburg, 1834–36.

———. *Voyage autour du monde exécuté par ordre de Sa Majesté l'empereur Nicolas I sur la corvette "Seniavine" en 1826–9.* Paris, 1835–36.

Mahr, August C. *The Visit of the "Rurik" to San Francisco in 1816* (Stanford University *Publications,* University Series, *History, Economics, and Political Science,* Vol. II, No. 2). Stanford University, Cal., 1932.

Porter, Kenneth Wiggins. *John Jacob Astor, Business Man.* 2 vols. Cambridge, Mass., 1931.

Records of the Russian American Company (MS), 1802–67 (with a gap from 1802–17). 92 vols. National Archives, Washington, D. C.

Roquefeuil, Camille de. *Journal d'un Voyage Autour du Monde, pendant les années 1816–19.* 2 vols. Paris, 1823.

———. *A Voyage Round the World, 1816–19 in the Ship "Bordelais."* London, 1823.

Ross, Alexander. *Adventures of the First Settlers on the Columbia River; Being a Narrative of the Expedition fitted out by John Jacob Astor to Establish the "Pacific Fur Company."* London, 1849. Chicago, 1923.

Shemelin, Feodor. *Zhurnal Pervago Puteshestviia Rossian vokrug Zemnago Shara.* 2 vols. in 1. St. Petersburg, 1816–18.

Sokolov, A. P. "Khvostov i Davydov," *Journal of the Russian Hydrographic Department,* Vol. X (1852), 391–433.

Wrangell, Ferdinand von. *Narrative of the Expedition to the Polar Sea in the Years 1820–23 Commanded by Lieut. Now Admiral Ferdinand von Wrangell of the Russian Imperial Navy.* Edited by Lieut. Col. Edward Sabine, R. A. London, 1844.

Zagoskin, Lieut. L. A. *Peshekhodnaya opis chasti russkikh vladyenii v Amerikye v 1842, 1843, 1844 godakh.* 2 vols. St. Petersburg, 1847.

———. *Auszug aus dem Tagebuche des Herrn Lieutenant Sagoskin über seine Expedition auf dem Festen Land des Nordwestlichen Amerikas.* In *Denktschriften der Russischen Gesellschaft.* Weimar, 1849.

THE RUSSIAN MONOPOLY

Adams, James Truslow. *The Adams Family.* Boston, 1930.

Alaska Boundary Tribunal. Proceedings of the Alaska Boundary Tribunal convened at London under the treaty between the United States of America and Great Britain concluded at Washington, January 24, 1903, for the settlement of questions . . . with respect to the boundary line between the territory of Alaska and the British possessions in North America. 58 Cong., 2 sess., *Senate Doc. 162.* Washington, 1904.

American State Papers. Class I, Foreign Relations, Vols. IV and V. Washington, 1858.

Atherton, Gertrude. "Essay on Rezanov," *North American Review,* May, 1909.

Bagot, Josceline. *George Canning and his Friends, Containing Some Hitherto Unpublished Letters.* 2 vols. London and New York, 1909.

Bagot, Sir Charles. *Bagot Papers—Russian Correspondence.* Transcripts of original private letters from Sir Charles Bagot in St. Petersburg to George Canning and others, with a few miscellaneous ones, covering the years 1822–25. Ottawa, Canada Archives.

Brooks, Philip Coolidge. *Diplomacy and the Borderlands—The Adams-Onis Treaty of 1819* (University of California *Publications in History,* Vol. XXIV). Berkeley, Cal., 1939.

Chevigny, Hector. *Lord of Alaska: Baranov and the Russian Adventure.* New York, 1942.

———. *Lost Empire: The Life and Adventures of Nikolai Petrovich Rezanov.* New York, 1937.

"Correspondence of the Russian Ministers in Washington, 1818–1825," *American Historical Review,* Vol. XVIII, No. 2 (January, 1913), 309–45 and 537–62.

Erman, A. von. "Einige Bemerkungen über die Russischen und Spanischen Colonien in Californien," *Archiv für Wissenschaftliche Kunde von Russland,* Vol. VI, 426–32. Berlin, 1848.

———. "Aus dem Bericht der Russisch-Amerikanischen Handels Compagnie fur das Jahr 1850–51," *Archiv für Wissenschaftliche Kunde von Russland,* Vol. XI (1852), 621–27. Berlin, 1852.

Franchère, Gabriel. *Relation d'un Voyage à la Côte du Nord-Ouest de l'Amérique Septentrionale, dans les Années 1810–1814.* Montreal, 1820.

———. *Narrative of a Voyage to the Northwest Coast or the First American Settlement on the Pacific.* New York, 1854.

Golovin, P. N. "Die Russischen Colonien an der Nordwestküste von Amerika (zum Theil)," *Archiv für Wissenschaftliche Kunde von Russland,* Vol. XX (1863), 47–70. Berlin, 1863.

———. "Obzor Russkikh Kolonii v Syevernoi Amerikye," *Morskoi Sbornik,* No. 7 (1862), 19–192.

Greenhow's *Memoir* on the Northwest Coast of America. 26 Cong., 1 sess., *Senate Doc. 174.*

Greenhow, Robert. *The History of Oregon and California.* Boston, 1845. First edition published in London, 1844.

Hildt, J. C. *Early Diplomatic Negotiations of the United States with Russia* (Johns Hopkins University *Studies in Historical and Political Science,* Series XXIV, Nos. 5–6). Baltimore, 1906.

Hodgins, Thomas. *The Alaska-Canada Boundary Dispute under the Anglo-Russian Treaty of 1825; the Russian-America Alaska Treaty of 1867; and the Anglo-American Conventions of 1892, 1894, and 1897.* Toronto, 1903.

Irving, Washington. *Astoria, or Anecdotes of an Enterprise Beyond the Rocky Mountains.* 2 vols. New York, 1895. Holly edition.

Khlebnikov, Kiril Timofeyvich. *Zhiznopisanie A. A. Baranova, glavnogo pravitelya rossiiskikh kolonii v Amerikye* (Biography of A. A. Baranov, the Governor of Russian Colonies in America). St. Petersburg, 1835.

———. *Pervonachalynoe poselenye Russkikh v Amerikye* (First Settlement of Russians in America. Reval, 1833. Reprinted in Supplement to *Morskoi Sbornik,* No. 4 (1861), 40–56.

Lane-Poole, Stanley. *Life of the Right Honourable Stratford Canning, Viscount Stratford de Redcliffe . . . from His Memoirs and Private and Public Papers.* 2 vols. London and New York, 1888.

Markov, Alexander. *Russkie na Vostochnom Okeanye . . . .* Moscow, 1849.

Materialy dlya istorii russkikh zaselenii po beregam vostochnago okeana. 4 parts in 1 vol. St. Petersburg, 1861. Supplement to *Morskoi Sbornik,* Nos. 1–4 (1861).

Mazour, Anatole, G. "Doctor Yegor Scheffer; Dreamer of a Russian Empire in the Pacific," *The Pacific Historical Review,* Vol. VI, No. 1 (March, 1937), 15–20.

———. "The Russian-American Company; Private or Government Enterprise?" *The Pacific Historical Review,* Vol. XIII, No. 2 (June, 1944), 168–73.

———. "The Prelude to Russia's Departure from America," *The Pacific Historical Review,* Vol. X, No. 3 (September, 1941), 311–19.

———. "Dimitry Zavalashin, Dreamer of a Russian-American Empire," *The Pacific Historical Review,* Vol. V, No. 1 (March, 1936), 26–37.

McNeilly, Mildred Masterson. *Heaven is Too High.* New York, 1944.

Okun', S. B. "Polozhenie promyshlovykh rabochikh v Russkikh poseleniyakh v *Amerikye,*" *Ucheniye Zapiski,* Seriya istoricheskikh Nauk, No. 48, issue 5 (1939), 157–70.

———. *Rossiisko-Amerikanskaya Kompaniya.* (pod redaktsei i so predisloviem Akademika B. A. Grekova) Leningradskii Gosudarstvennyi Universitet-Istoricheskii Fakultet. Sotsekiz, 1939.

Otchety Rossiikso-Amerikanskaya Kompanii (organized in 1798 as Soedinennaia Amerikanskaia Kompaniia). No place, 1844–62.

Perkins, Dexter. *The Monroe Doctrine, 1823–1826.* Cambridge, Mass., 1927.

Pilder, Hans. *Die russisch-amerikanische Handels Kompanie bis 1825.* Berlin and Leipzic, 1914.

Politovskii, V. G. *Kratkoe istoricheskoe obozryenie obrazovanii i deistvii R. A. K-a.* St. Petersburg, 1861.

Polnoe Sobranie Zakonov Rossiiskoi Imperii. 44 vols. St. Petersburg, 1830.

Records of the Russian American Company (MS), 1802–67 (with a gap from 1802–17). 92 vols. National Archives, Washington, D. C.

Reddaway, W. F. *The Monroe Doctrine.* New York, 1902.

Rezanov, Nikolai Petrovich. *The Rezanov Voyage to Nueva California in 1806, the report of Nikolai Petrovich Rezanov of his voyage to that provincia of Nueva España from New Archangel.* An English translation revised and corrected with notes, etc., by Thomas C. Russell. San Francisco, 1926.

———. "Pervoe Puteshestvie Rossiian vokrug Svyeta Opisannye Rezanovim," *Otechestvie Zapiski,* Nos. X–XII (1822); No. XX (1824); Nos. XXIII–XXIV (1825).

Rodionov, N. R. "Shelekov," *Dictionary of American Biography.* New York, 1922.

Rush, Richard. *Memoranda of a Residence at the Court of London ....* Philadelphia, 1845.

Russia. Archives Department. *Papers Relating to the Russians in Alaska, 1732–1796.* 21 vols. Photostat copies of original papers in University of Washington Library, Seattle.

"Russian America," *Message from the President of the United States in Answer to a Resolution of the House of the 19th of Dec. Last Transmitting Correspondence in Relation to Russian-America.* February 19, 1868. 40 Cong., 2 sess., *House Ex. Doc. 177,* part 2.

Russian-American Company. "Der Jahresbericht der Russisch Amerikanischen Kompanie für 1856–57," *Archiv für Wissenschaftliche Kunde von Russland,* Vol. XVII (1858), 471–78. Berlin, 1858.

Shashkov, S. S. *Rossiisko-Amerikanskaya Kompaniya.* Soch. Tom. II. St. Petersburg, 1898.

Slavinskii, Nikolai. *Letters about America and Russian Colonies.* St. Petersburg, 1873. (In Russian.)

Stapleton, Augustus G. *Political Life of the Right Honourable George Canning, 1822–1827.* 3 vols. London, 1831. Second revised edition.

Stapleton, Edward J. (ed.). *Some Official Correspondence of George Canning, 1821–1827.* 2 vols. London, 1887.

Stuart, Robert. *The Discovery of the Oregon Trail. Robert Stuart's Narratives of his Overland Trip Eastward from Astoria in 1812–13. From the Original Manuscripts in the Collection of William Robertson Coe, Esq., and an Account of the "Tonquin's" Voyage.* Edited by Philip Ashton Rollins. New York and London, 1935.

Svod Zakonov Rossiiskoi Imperii. St. Petersburg, 1832.

Tikhmenev, P. *Istoricheskoe obozryenie obrazovaniya Rossiisko-Amerikanskoi Kompanii.* 2 vols. St. Petersburg, 1861–63. (The most important single source on Baranov and the Russian American Company. Appendices contain copies of many documents now lost.)

"Tsarskaia Rossiia i Gavaiskie Ostrova," *Krasnyi Arkhiv,* Vol. LXX, 161–86.

Twiss, Travers. *The Oregon Territory, its History and Discovery including an Account of the Convention of the Escurial, also Treaties & Negotiations between the United States and Great Britain.* New York, 1846.

Webster, C. K. *Britain and the Independence of Latin America,*

1812–30. 2 vols. London and New York, 1938. Published by the Ibero-American Institution of Great Britain.

White, James. "Boundary Disputes and Treaties." In *The Dominion Political Development,* Vol. VIII of *Canada and Its Provinces.* Edinburgh, 1913.

Wrangell, Ferdinand Petrovich. *Statistische und ethnographische Nachrichten über die Russischen Besitzungen an der Nordwest-küste von Amerika.* St. Petersburg, 1839.

Yarmolinsky, Avrahm. "Nikolai Petrovich Rezanov," *Dictionary of American Biography.* New York, 1922.

Zavalishin, D. I. *Rossiisko-amerikanskaya Kompaniya.* Moscow, 1865.

THE HUDSON'S BAY COMPANY *and* THE RUSSIAN AMERICAN COMPANY

Barsukov, Ivan. *Graf N. N. Murav'ev-Amurskii.* 2 vols. Moscow, 1891.

Campbell, Robert. *The Discovery and Exploration of the Pelly River.* In *The Royal Readers.* Toronto, 1883.

Davidson, Donald C. "The War Scare of 1854," *The British Columbia Historical Quarterly,* Vol. V, No. 3 (October, 1941), 243–53.

———. "Relations of the Hudson's Bay Company with the Russian American Company on the Northwest Coast, 1829–1867," *The British Columbia Historical Quarterly,* Vol. V, No. 1 (January, 1941), 33–38.

Doroshin, Peter P. "The Prince William Sound and Copper River," *Russian Mining Journal* for 1866. No. 1, part 4, 136; No. 2, part 6, 277–82; No. 3, part 3, 365–401. (In Russian.)

———. "Einige Beobachtungen u. Bemerkungen über das Gold-vorkommen in den Besitzungen der Russisch-Amerikanische Co.," *Archiv für Wissenschaftliche Kunde von Russland,* Vol. XXV (1867), 229–37. Berlin, 1867.

Erman, A. von. "L. Sagoskin's Reise und Entdeckungen im Russischen Amerika," *Archiv für Wissenschaftliche Kunde von Russland,* Vol. VI (1848), 499–552 and 613–72; Vol. VII (1848), 429–512. Berlin, 1848.

Essig, E. O., Ogden, Adele, and DuFour, Clarence John. *The Russians in California.* San Francisco, 1933.

Golder, Frank A. "Mining in Alaska before 1867," *Washington Historical Quarterly,* Vol. VII, No. ? (July, 1916), 233–38.

Hargrave, James. *The Hargrave Correspondence, 1821–1843.* Edited by G. P. de T. Glazebrook. Toronto, 1938.

Hudson's Bay Company. *Certain Correspondence of the Foreign Office and of the Hudson's Bay Company Copied from the Original Documents, London, 1898, by Otto C. Klotz.* Ottawa, 1899.

Ireland, Willard E. "James Douglas and the Russian American Company, 1840," *The British Columbia Historical Quarterly,* Vol. V., No. 1 (January, 1941), 53–66.

Khlebnikov, K. T. "Memoirs of California" (translated from the Russian by A. G. Mazour), *The Pacific Historical Review,* Vol. IX, No. 3 (September, 1940), 307–36.

Mackay, Douglas. *The Honourable Company, A History of the Hudson's Bay Company.* Indianapolis and New York, 1936.

McLoughlin's Fort Vancouver Letters. First Series, 1825–38. London, 1941.

Merk, Frederick (ed.). *Fur Trade and Empire—George Simpson's Journal* (Harvard *Historical Studies).* Cambridge, Mass., 1931.

Murray, Alexander Hunter. *Journal of the Yukon, 1847–48.* Edited by L. J. Burpee. (*Publications* of the Canadian Archives, No. 4.) Ottawa, 1910.

Ogden, Adele. *The California Sea Otter Trade,* 1784–1848 (University of California *Publications in History,* Vol. 26). Berkeley and Los Angeles, 1941.

Oliver, E. H. *The Canadian North-West; its Early Development and Legislative Records.* 2 vols. (*Publications* of the Canadian Archives, No. 9.) Ottawa, 1914.

Potiekhin, V. *Zaselenie Rossa, Kaliforniia.* St. Petersburg, 1859.

Ravenstein, E. G. "Sitka and the Russian Territories in America," pages 584–94 in Vol. XXXVIII of Bentley's *Miscellanies,* London, 1855.

Roche, A. R. *A View of Russian America in Connection with the Present War.* Montreal, 1855.

Simpson, Sir George. *Narrative of a Journey Round the World during the Years 1841 and 1842.* 2 vols. London, 1847.

Stow, Nellie. *The Russians in California.* San Francisco, 1939.

Teb'enkov, Capt. M. D. *Atlas Syevyerzapadnykh Beregov Ameriki* (Atlas of the Northwest Coast of America). Moscow, 1852.

Thompson, Robert A. *The Russian Settlement in California Known as Fort Ross. Founded 1812, Abandoned 1841. Why the Russians Came and Why They Left.* Santa Rosa, Cal., 1896.

Veniaminov, I. *Pis'ma Innokentiya Metropolita Moskovskago i Kolomenskago, 1828–1878, Sobrannye Ivanom Barsukovym.* St. Petersburg, 1897–1901.

Whymper, Frederick. *Travel and Adventure in the Territory of Alaska Formerly Russian America—Now Ceded to the United States—and in Various Other Parts of the North Pacific.* London, 1868. New York, 1869.

Zollinger, James Peter. *Sutter, The Man and His Empire.* New York, 1939.

Bibliography

THE ALASKA PURCHASE

Adams, Ephraim Douglass. *Great Britain and the American Civil War.* 2 vols. New York and London, 1925.

Bailey, Thomas A. "Why the United States Purchased Alaska," *The Pacific Historical Review,* Vol. III, No. 1 (March, 1943), 39–49.

Callahan, James Morton. *The Alaska Purchase and Americo-Canadian Relations* (West Virginia University *Studies in American History,* Series 1, Nos. 2 and 3). Morgantown, W. Va., 1908.

Collins, P. McD. *A Voyage down the Amoor; with a Land Journey through Siberia and Incidental Notice of Manchooria, Kamchatka, and Japan.* New York, 1860.

———. *Overland Explorations in Siberia, Northern Asia and the Great Amoor River Country.* New York, 1864.

Depperman, W. H. "Two Cents an Acre," *North American Review,* Vol. 245 (1938), 127–33.

Doklad Komiteta ob Ustroistvye Russkikh Amerikanskikh Kolonii. St. Petersburg, 1863. (Report of Committee on Organization of the Russian American Colonies.)

Dunning, William A. "Paying for Alaska, Some Unfamiliar Incidents in the Process," *Political Science Quarterly,* Vol. XXVII, No. 3 (September, 1912), 385–98.

Farrar, Victor J. "The Background of the Purchase of Alaska," *Washington Historical Quarterly,* Vol. XIII, No. 2 (April, 1922), 93–104.

———. *The Purchase of Alaska.* Washington, 1934.

———. *The Purchase of Alaska.* Washington, 1935.

———. *The Annexation of Russian America to the United States.* Washington, 1937.

Golder, F. A. "The Purchase of Alaska," *American Historical Review,* Vol. XXV, No. 3 (April, 1920), 411–25.

———. "Russian-American Relations during the Crimean War," *American Historical Review,* Vol. XXXI, No. 3 (April, 1926), 462–76.

James, James Alton. *The First Scientific Exploration of Russian America and the Purchase of Alaska* (Northwestern University *Studies in the Social Sciences,* No. 4). Evanston and Chicago, 1942.

Kennan, George F. "Russia and the Alaska Purchase," *American Foreign Service Journal,* Vol. XV, No. 2 (February, 1938), 78–80.

Kirby, W. W. "A Journey to the Youcan, Russian America," *Annual Report* of the Board of Regents of the Smithsonian Institution for 1864, 416–20.

"K Istorii russko-amerikanskikh otnoshenii vo vremya grazhdanskoi voiny v Soedinennykh Shtatakh Ameriki," *Krasnyi Arkhiv.* Vol. III (94) (1939), 97–153.

Loubat, Joseph Florimond. *Narrative of the Mission to Russia in 1866 of the Hon. Gustavus Vasa Fox, Assistant Secretary to the Navy.* Edited by John D. Champlin. New York, 1873.

Luthin, R. "The Sale of Alaska," *Slavonic and East European Review,* Vol. XVII, No. 3 (July, 1937), 168–82.

Malkin, M. M. *Grazhdanskaya Voina v S. Sh. A. i Tsarskaya Rossiya.* Ogiz, Leningradskii Gosudarstvennyi Universitet, Istoricheskii Fakultet, 1939.

McPherson, Hallie M. "The Projected Purchase of Alaska, 1859–60" (Documents edited and translated into English). *The Pacific Historical Review,* Vol. III, No. 1 (March, 1934), 80–87.

———. "The Interest of William McKendree Gwin in the Purchase of Alaska, 1854–1861," *The Pacific Historical Review,* Vol. III, No. 1 (March, 1934), 28–38.

Okun', S. B. *Russkie Poseleniya v Severnoi Amerikye.* Moscow, 1930.

———. "K. Istorii Prodazhi Russkikh Kolonii v Amerikye," *Istoricheskie Zapiski,* Vol. II (1938), 209–39.

Parry, Albert. "Cassius Clay's Glimpse into the Future," *The Russian Review,* Vol. II, No. 2 (Spring, 1943), pp. 52–67.

Robertson, James R. *A Kentuckian at the Court of the Tsars: the Ministry of Cassius Marcellus Clay to Russia, 1861–1862 and 1863–1869.* Berea College, Kentucky, 1935.

Russia. Ministry of Ways of Communications. . . . *Copies of Grants by the Governments of Russia and Great Britain of the Right of Way of Perry McD. Collins for the Purpose of Establishing a Telegraph Connecting Europe with U. S.,* June 18, 1864. 38 Cong., 1 sess., *Senate Misc. Doc. 126.*

"Russian Opinion on the Cession of Alaska," *American Historical Review,* Vol. XLVIII, No. 3 (April, 1943), 521–31.

Thomas, B. P. *Russo-American Relations,* 1815–1867 (Johns Hopkins University *Studies in Historical and Political Science,* Series XLVIII, No. 2). Baltimore, 1930.

Tompkins, Stuart R. "Drawing the Alaska Boundary," *The Canadian Historical Review,* Vol. XXVI, No. 1 (March, 1945), 1–24.

Underwood, John J. *Alaska: an Empire in the Making.* New York, 1913.

United States Adjutant General's Office. Military Information Division. *Explorations in Alaska 1899 for an All-American Overland Route from Cook Inlet, Pacific Ocean, to the Yukon.* Washington, 1901.

———. *Reports of Explorations in the Territory of Alaska in 1898 Made under the Direction of the Secretary of War by Captain F. Glenn and Captain W. R. Abercrombie.* Washington, 1899.

United States Congress. " . . . History of the Discovery of Gold at Cape Nome . . . . Paper entitled the 'History of the Discovery of Gold at Cape Nome,' by H. L. Blake, June 5, 1900." 56 Cong., 1 sess., *Senate Doc. 441.*

United States Department of the Interior, Office of the Secretary. *General Information Regarding the Territory of Alaska.* Washington, 1930.

United States Department of State. *Papers Relating to Foreign Affairs (1866–67).* 3 parts. 39 Cong., 2 sess., *House Ex. Doc. 1.* Washington, 1867.

———. "... Emperor of Russia ... Message from the President of the United States Transmitting Correspondence upon the Presentation of Resolutions of Congress in Reference to the Attempted Assassination of the Emperor of Russia," March 2, 1867. 39 Cong., 2 sess., *House Ex. Doc. 112.* Washington, 1867.

———. *Papers Relating to Foreign Affairs (1866–67).* 3 parts. 40 Cong., 2 sess., *House Ex. Doc. 1.* Washington, 1868.

———. " ... Letter from the Secretary of State (January 15, 1859) in relation to the Memorial of P. McD. Collins asking compensation and reimbursement of expenses incurred while exploring the Amoor River; January 18, 1859." 35 Cong., 2 sess., *House Ex. Doc. 53.*

———. "Geographical Notes upon Russian America, 1868." 40 Cong., 2 sess., *House Ex. Doc. 177,* part 2.

United States Embassy, Russia. "Papers relating to the cession of Alaska (enclosures Nos. 2 and 3 to Dispatch No. 2115 of December, 1936, from the United States Embassy at Moscow), 1856–57 [*sic!* 1867]." Photostatic reproductions of copies (on file in the Archives of the Department of State, Washington, D. C.) secured by the U. S. Embassy, Moscow, from the Soviet Archives of forty-five documents relating to the sale of Alaska. MS, 248 pages.

United States Senate. " ... Report on Introduction of Domestic Reindeer into Alaska with Illustrations by Sheldon Jackson, D. D., General Agent of Education in Alaska, 1896 (January 6, 1897)." 54 Cong., 2 sess., *Senate Doc. 49.*

STAGNATION
1867–1898

Arctander, John W. *The Apostle of Alaska: the Story of William Duncan of Metlakatla.* New York, 1909.

Bering Sea Tribunal of Arbitration. Fur Seal Arbitration. Proceedings of the Tribunal of Arbitration, convened at Paris under the treaty between the United States . . . and Great Britain, concluded at Washington, February 29, 1892, for the determination of questions between the two governments concerning the jurisdictional rights of the U. S. in the waters of the Bering Sea. 16 vols. Washington, 1895. (Vol. 16 contains facsimiles of documents.)

Hawden, Seymour, and Palmer, Lawrence J. "Reindeer in Alaska."

United States Department of Agriculture Bulletin No. 1089. Washington, 1922.

Jackson, Sheldon. *Alaska.* New York, no date.

Moore, John Bassett. *History and Digest of the International Arbitrations to which the United States has been a party together with appendices containing the treaties relating to such arbitrations and historical and legal notes on other international arbitrations ancient and modern and of the domestic commissions of the United States for the adjustment of international claims.* 6 vols. Washington, 1898. (Vol. I, Chap. XVII, deals with fur-seal arbitration.)

Muir, John. *Travels in Alaska.* Boston and New York, 1915.

Petroff, Ivan. *Report on Population, Industry and Resources of Alaska.* In Vol. VIII of *Tenth Census of the United States, 1880.* Washington, 1884.

Quaife, Milo Milton (ed.). *The Fur Hunters of the Far West. See* Alexander Ross. Chicago, 1924.

"Russian America." In Vol. XIII, House Committee on Foreign Affairs, 40 Cong., 2 sess., *Ex. Doc. 177,* Part 1. Washington, 1868.

Schwatka, Frederick. *A Summer in Alaska.* St. Louis, 1893.

Tansill, C. C. *Canadian-American Relations,* 1875–1911. New Haven, 1943.

United States Congress. "House . . . *Memorial* of Louis Goldstone relative to the Alaska Seal Fishery, March 13, 1871." 42 Cong., 1 sess., *House Misc. Doc. 5.*

United States Senate. . . . *Revenue from Rental of Seal Islands of Alaska,* January 23, 1897. 54 Cong., 2 sess., *Senate Doc. 81.*

United States Congress. Senate Committee on Military Affairs. *Compilation of Narratives of Explorations in Alaska.* Washington, 1900.

United States Treasury Department. . . . *Alaska Seal Fishery Lease . . . ,* February 7, 1871. 41 Cong., 3 sess., *House Ex. Doc. 108.*

THE GOLD RUSH

Adney, Tappan. *The Klondike Stampede.* New York and London, 1900.

Auzias-Turenne, Raymond. *Voyage au Pays des Mines d'or de Klondike.* Paris, 1899.

Bankson, R. A. *The Klondike Nugget.* Caldwell, Idaho, 1935.

Becker, George F. "Reconnaissance of the Gold Fields of Southern Alaska," *18th Annual Report of the United States Geological Survey, 1896–97,* Part III, 7–86. Washington, 1898.

Brown, J. N. E. *The Evolution of Law and Government in the Yukon Territory* (University of Toronto *Studies, History and Economics,* Vol. II). Toronto, 1907.

Bruce, Miner. *Alaska.* New York and London, 1899.

Cadell, H. M. "The Klondike and Yukon Goldfields in 1913," *Scottish Geographical Magazine,* Vol. XXX, 337–56.

Canada. Department of the Interior. *Annual Report.* (Years 1897–. Contains the report of the Commissioner of Yukon Territory as well as that of the Gold Commissioner.)

Canada. *Report* of the Commissioner of the Northwest Mounted Police. (Years 1896–. Contains reports of the senior Mounted Police officer in Yukon Territory.)

Case, R. O. *The Yukon Drive.* Garden City, N. Y., 1930.

Cockfield, W. E. "Silver-Lead Deposits of the Keno Hill Area, Mayo District, Yukon," *Summary Report, Part A, Canada Geological Survey,* 1920.

———. "Silver-lead Deposits of the Davidson Mountains, Mayo District, Yukon," *Summary Report, Part A, Canada Geological Survey,* 1921.

Cody, H. A. *An Apostle of the North.* London, Toronto, 1908.

Collier, William Ross, and Westrate, Edwin Victor. *The Reign of Soapy Smith.* Garden City, N. Y., 1935.

Dafoe, J. W. *Clifford Sifton in Relation to his Times.* Toronto, 1931.

Dawson, George M. *Report on an Exploration in the Yukon District and Adjacent Northern Portion of British Columbia, 1887.* Ottawa, 1898.

———. "Historical Notes on Events in the Yukon District," *Review of Historical Publications,* Vol. II, 173–89.

Goodrich, H. B. "History and Condition of the Yukon Gold District to 1897," *18th Annual Report of the United States Geological Survey,* Part III, 103–33.

Harris, A. C. *Alaska and the Klondike Gold Fields.* Philadelphia, 1897.

Haskell, W. B. *Two Years in the Klondike and Alaskan Goldfields.* Hartford, Conn., 1898.

Hayne, M. H. E., and Taylor, H. West. *Pioneers of the Klondike.* London, 1897.

Heilprin, Angelo. *Alaska and the Klondike.* New York, 1899.

Hitchcock, Mary E. *Two Women in the Klondike.* New York and London, 1899.

Ingersoll, Ernest. *Gold Fields of the Klondike.* Chicago, 1897.

———. *Golden Alaska, a Complete Account to Date of the Yukon Valley.* Chicago and New York, 1897.

Innis, Harold A. *Settlement and the Mining Frontier.* Part II of Vol. IX in *Canadian Frontiers of Settlement,* edited by W. A. Mackintosh and W. L. G. Goerg. Toronto, 1936.

Keeler, N. E. *A Trip to Alaska and the Klondike in the Summer of 1905.* Cincinnati, 1906.

Kirk, R. C. *Twelve Months in the Klondike.* London, 1899.

Kitto, F. H. *Yukon; Land of the Klondike.* Ottawa, 1930.

Klondike; the Chicago Record's *Book for Gold Seekers.* Chicago, 1897.
Ladue, Joseph. *Klondyke Facts.* New York, 1897.
———. *Klondyke Nuggets.* New York, 1897.
Lynch, Jeremiah. *Three Years in the Klondike.* London, 1904.
McConnell, R. G., *Report on Gold Values in the Klondike High Level Gravels.* Ottawa, 1907.
———. *Report on the Klondike Gold Fields.* Ottawa, 1907.
McElwaine, Eugene. *The Truth about Alaska* (Title on cover of book is *Alaska: The Land of Gold*). Chicago, 1901.
McLain, James Scudder. *Alaska and the Klondike.* New York, 1905.
Mertie, J. B., Jr. "Gold Placers of the Fortymile, Eagle, and Circle Districts, Alaska," *United States Geological Survey Bulletin No. 897.* Washington, 1938.
Morrell, W. P. *The Gold Rushes.* New York, 1941.
Nachod, O. *Ein Unentdecktes Goldland.* Tokyo, 1900.
Ogilvie, William. *Early Days on the Yukon; the Story of its Gold Finds.* Ottawa, 1913.
Prindle, L. M. "The Fairbanks and Rampart Quadrangles, Yukon-Tanana Region, Alaska," *United States Geological Survey Bulletin No. 337.* Washington, 1908.
Rand, McNally Guide to Alaska and the Yukon. New York, 1922.
Reports of the Commissioner of the Yukon Territory. *Annual Reports,* Department of the Interior. Ottawa, 1898–1910.
Secretan, J. H. E. *To Klondyke and Back, a Journey down the Yukon from its Source to its Mouth.* London, 1898.
Service, Robert W. *The Complete Poems of Robert Service.* New York, 1944.
Sola, A. E. I. *Klondyke: Truth and Facts of the New Eldorado.* London, 1897.
Spurr, J. E. *Through the Klondike Gold Diggings.* Boston, 1900.
Steele, S. B. *Forty Years in Canada.* London, 1915.
Thompson, A. R. *Gold Seeking on the Dalton Trail.* Boston, 1900.
Tollemache, Stratford. *Reminiscences of the Yukon.* London, 1912.
Treadgold, A. N. C. *Report on the Goldfields of the Klondike.* Toronto, 1899.
Tyrrell, J. B. "The Gold of the Klondike," *Transactions* of the Royal Society of Canada, Section IV, 1912.
United States Congress. " . . . History of the Discovery of Gold at Cape Nome . . . Paper entitled 'The History of the Discovery of Gold at Cape Nome,' by H. L. Blake, June 5, 1900." 56 Cong., 1 sess., *Senate Doc. 441.*
Wickersham, Hon. James. *Old Yukon; Tales—Trails—and Trials.* Washington, 1938.
Young, S. Hall. *Alaska Days with John Muir.* New York and Chicago, 1915.

The Yukon Territory; its History and Resources. Issued by direction of the Hon. W. J. Roche, minister of the interior. Ottawa, 1916.

The Yukon Territory 1926. Northwest Territories and Yukon Branch, Department of the Interior. Ottawa, 1926.

The Yukon Territory; a Brief Description of its Administration, Resources, Development. Bureau of Northwest Territories and Yukon Affairs, Lands, Parks and Forests Branch. Ottawa, Department of Mines and Resources. Ottawa, 1943.

POST-KLONDIKE ERA

Annual Report of the Governor of Alaska to the Secretary of the Interior. Washington, 1941.

Bailey, Thomas A. "Theodore Roosevelt and the Alaska Boundary Settlement," *The Canadian Historical Review* (New Series of the Review of Historical Publications Relating to Canada), Vol. XVIII, No. 2 (June, 1937), 123–30.

Brooks, Alfred H., and others. "The Gold Placers of Parts of Seward Peninsula, Alaska," *United States Geological Survey Bulletin No. 328.* Washington, 1908.

Conrad, Sherman, "The Matanuska Valley Colonization Project," *Monthly Report of Federal Emergency Relief Administration,* 30–37. Washington, 1936.

Doherty, Beka, and Hepner, Arthur. "Alaska; Last American Frontier," *Foreign Policy Reports,* December 1, 1942.

Edelstein, Julius C. *Alaska Comes of Age. Far Eastern Pamphlets No. 8,* American Council, Institute of Pacific Relations. New York, San Francisco, and Honolulu, 1942.

Elliott, Henry Wood. *Our Arctic Province, Alaska and the Seal Islands.* New York, 1887.

———. *A Monograph of the Seal Islands of the Alaska.* Washington, 1882.

———. *The Seal Islands of Alaska.* Department of the Interior Census Office. Washington, 1884.

"Exchange of Notes between the Secretary of State for External Affairs of Canada and the American Minister Concerning a Military Highway to Alaska, March, 1942," *American Journal of International Law Supplement,* Vol. XXXVI, No. 3 (July, 1942), 153–55.

Ford, Corey. *Short Cut to Tokyo; the Battle for the Aleutians.* New York, 1943.

Griffin, Harold. *Alaska and the Canadian Northwest.* New York, 1944.

Harriman Alaska Expedition 1899, with the co-operation of Washington Academy of Sciences. Edited by C. Hart Merriam. 14 vols. in 16. New York, 1901.

Lanks, Herbert C. *Highway to Alaska.* New York and London, 1944.

McKee, Lanier. *The Land of Nome.* New York, 1902.

National Resources Committee. *Regional Planning; Part VII, Alaska—Its Resources and Development.* Prepared in accordance with Concurrent Resolution No. 24, 75 Cong., 1 sess. Washington, 1938.

Potter, Jean. *Alaska Under Arms.* New York, 1942.

Rickard, T. A. *Through the Yukon and Alaska.* San Francisco, 1909.

Smith, Philip S. "Past Placer-Gold Production from Alaska," in "Mineral Resources of Alaska," *United States Geological Survey Bulletin No. 857.* Washington, 1934.

———. "Past Lode-Production from Alaska," in "Mineral Resources of Alaska; Report on Progress of Investigations in 1938," *United States Geological Survey Bulletin No. 917C.* Washington, 1942.

Spicer, George Washington. *The Constitutional Status and Government of Alaska* (Johns Hopkins University *Studies in Historical and Political Science,* Vol. XLV, No. 4). Baltimore, 1927.

Stuck, Hudson. *A Winter Circuit of our Arctic Coast.* New York, 1920.

———. *Ten Thousand Miles with a Dog Sled.* New York, 1916.

United States Department of the Interior, Office of the Secretary. *General Information Regarding the Territory of Alaska.* Washington, 1930.

Walker, Ernest P. *Alaska; America's Continental Frontier Outpost* (Smithsonian Institution *War Background Studies,* No. 13). Washington, 1943.

Williamson, Thames. *Far North Country.* New York, 1944.

Index

ALASKA

Index

Index

Index

Index

A L A S K A

PROMYSHLENNIK

AND SOURDOUGH

has been set on the Linotype

in the eleven-point size of Granjon

with one point of leading

and printed upon

antique wove

paper

UNIVERSITY OF OKLAHOMA PRESS

NORMAN

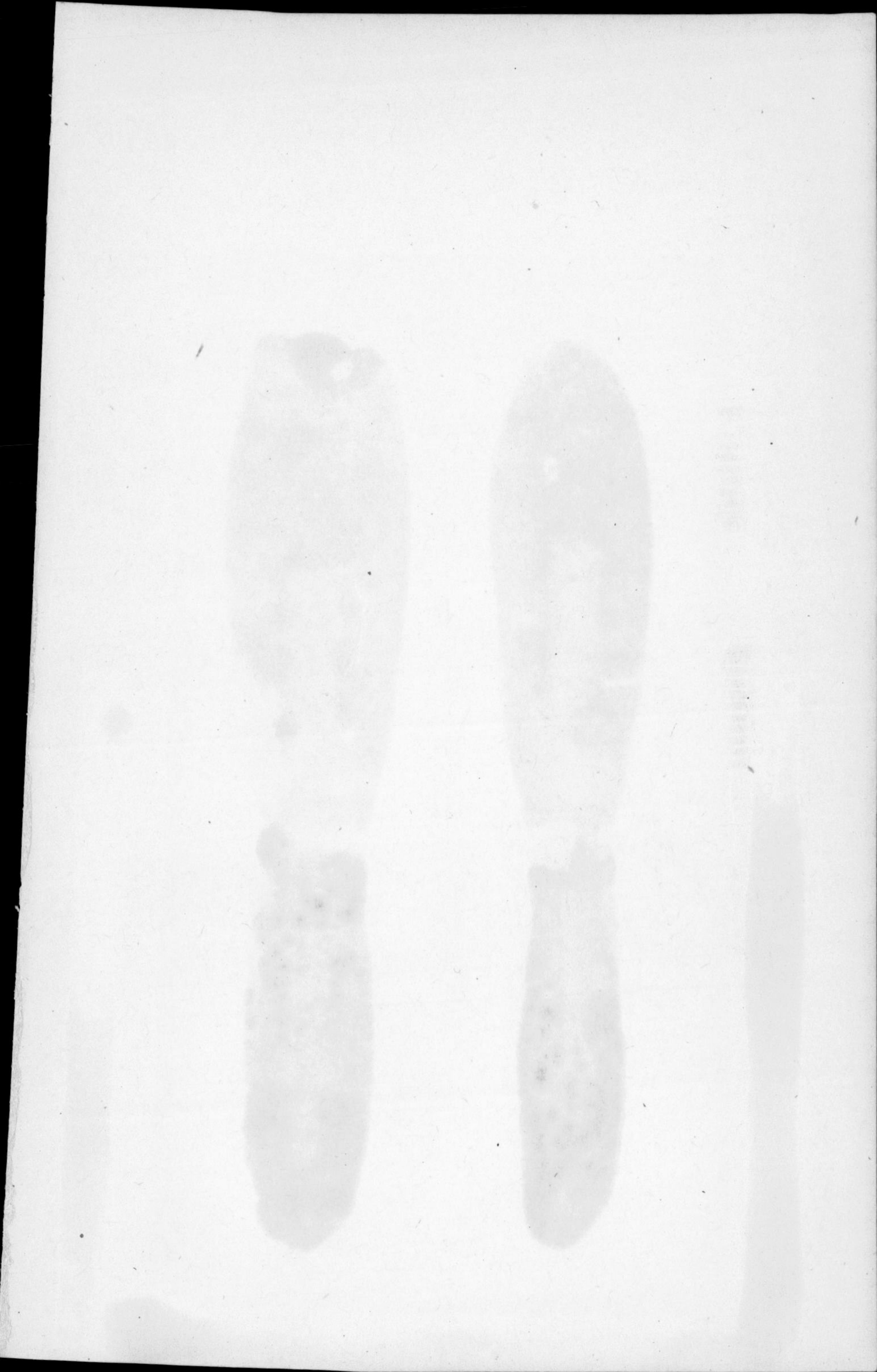